Cities for Children

Cities for Children
Children's Rights, Poverty and Urban Management

Sheridan Bartlett,
Roger Hart, David Satterthwaite,
Ximena de la Barra and
Alfredo Missair

unicef
United Nations Childrens Fund

EARTHSCAN

Earthscan Publications Ltd, London

First published in the UK in 1999 by
Earthscan Publications Ltd

A catalogue record for this book is available from the British Library

ISBN: 1 85383 470 X paperback
1 85383 471 8 hardback

Typesetting by PCS Mapping & DTP, Newcastle upon Tyne
Printed and bound by Thanet Press Limited, Margate, Kent
Cover design by Declan Buckley

For a full list of publications please contact:
Earthscan Publications Ltd
120 Pentonville Road
London, N1 9JN, UK
Tel: +44 (0)171 278 0433
Fax: +44 (0)171 278 1142
Email: earthinfo@earthscan.co.uk
http://www.earthscan.co.uk

Earthscan is an editorially independent subsidiary of Kogan Page Ltd and publishes in association with WWF-UK and the International Institute for Environment and Development

This book is printed on elemental chlorine free paper

Contents

Part Three
Governance for Children's Rights

Acknowledgements

There are many whose contributions should be acknowledged here. First of all, the UNICEF members of the team: Ximena de la Barra conceived and commissioned this book, and critiqued each draft from the perspective of her long experience tackling urban poverty within various contexts. Alfredo Missair contributed not only his broad practical knowledge and love of ideas, but a high level of care and patience in his mindful editing, and a willingness to discuss every alternative in spite of heavy demands on his time. Along with Selim Iltus of the Children's Environments Research Group, Alfredo also worked on the graphic design of the book.

Many other people within UNICEF also contributed their time to reading and commenting on various chapters. We would like to thank Oscar Castillo-Velasquez MD, Joanne Csete, France Donnay, Elaine Furniss, Alec Fyfe, Sree Gururaja, Gulbadan Habibi, James R Himes, Alfhild Petren, Mary Racelis and Marta Santos Pais. Readers from outside of UNICEF were also invaluable, and we are grateful for their generosity; their names and affiliations are listed below.

Special thanks go to Ladislau Dowbor, who reviewed the entire manuscript, and who brought a great deal of kindness, patience and good humour to this demanding task.

Thanks also to UNICEF staff members who managed various aspects of this effort – to Bradley Winneshiek, who coordinated the task of communicating with reviewers; to Michael Kovach, who hunted down details on the availability of resources, and to Theresa Kilbane, who took charge of this project when her colleagues moved to other postings, and who graciously managed it to its conclusion. Lisa Adelson, Nicole Toutounji and Ellen Tolmie in the New York UNICEF photo library, and Caroline Coomber, in the London branch, were all generous with their time and resources. Vicky Haeri coordinated UNICEF relations with our publisher, and we thank her too.

In London, we have an entire institute to thank. The International Institute for Environment and Development (IIED), where David Satterthwaite is based, provided desk space and support for Roger Hart and myself over a period of several months, to make it possible for us to draw on London resources and to collaborate closely with David in writing the book. And finally, thanks to Jonathan Sinclair Wilson, Ruth Coleman and other staff at Earthscan for their work in publishing the book.

Sheridan Bartlett
1999

Names and affiliations of non-UNICEF readers:

Eileen Adams is a Research Fellow at University College, Bretton Hall, a Visiting Academic at Middlesex University and a Tutor on the MSc course in Environmental Education and Development Education at South Bank University.

Caroline Arnold is the regional child development adviser for Asia with Save the Children (US) and Radda Barna.

Rachel Baker is currently lecturing in social anthropology on childhood, South Asia and research methods, as well as consultant for international agencies on child rights issues.

Jeff Bishop, an architect, focuses on community participation in environmental change, with an emphasis on children.

Louise Chawla, a developmental and environmental psychologist, coordinates UNESCO's Growing Up in Cities Project.

Nilda Cosco, educational psychologist, is co-director of the Argentine component of the Growing Up in Cities Project.

Leonard Duhl has been Professor of Public Health and Urban Planning, and Professor of Psychiatry at the University of California in Berkeley and San Francisco and has worked as a consultant with UNICEF, HABITAT, PAHO, WHO (Healthy Cities Programme), and US-based organisations.

Lalitha Iyer is Manager of Habitat Domain Development for PLAN International and has authored several publications on child centred habitat programming.

Pratibha Mehta, LIFE Global Coordinator at the UNDP, Past-Director of LA21 Model Communities Programme at ICLEI, Toronto, Canada and National Research and Training Coordinator, Urban Basic Services for the Poor (UBSP) at the National Institute of Urban Affairs, New Delhi, India.

Robin C Moore, architect and city planner, teaches landscape architecture at NC State University, USA, and is president of the International Association for the Child's Right to Play.

Chongcharoen Sornkaew, Coordinator, child labour programmes in Thailand with IPEC/ILO and others since 1988.

Franz Vanderschueren, Ph.D. Sociology, is presently working in UNCHS (Habitat) within the Urban Management Programme, Safer Cities Programme.

Erik Vittrup C is the Regional Programme Coordinator for CDP/UNCHS (Habitat).

Heidi Watts, formerly Chair of the Education Department at Antioch New England, is now Professor Emerita, and a trainer of teachers in Tamil Nadu.

Hundreds of millions of children in the world's cities live in conditions that threaten their health, wellbeing and long term prospects. The responsibility for these endangered children is increasingly being delegated to local governments. Here a girl stands with her brother outside their home in a squatter settlement near Kamlapur Railway Station in Dhaka, Bangaldesh. UNICEF 1997, Shehzad Noorani

Introduction

This book is intended as a source of information for local authorities and their partners as they work to make their cities better places for children and adolescents. It looks at the responsibilities that authorities face in this regard, and discusses practical measures for meeting these challenges in the context of limited resources and multiple demands.

Children throughout the world have much in common. They want to live among family and friends and to feel safe in their homes and communities. They want clean water to drink and enough to eat. Around the world they tell us that they want space for play, and places where they can escape from noise and smells and garbage. They would like to be respected by adults and to have a real part in the lives of their communities. And they want the kind of education that will give them a future. These are not unreasonable requests, but for more than one third of the world's children they are only a dream.

Twelve million children under the age of five still die every year, most of them from preventible causes.[1] Hundreds of millions live in appalling conditions, have too little to eat and little chance of effective treatment when they are ill or injured. Over a million children each year are forced into prostitution, and many millions more work in hazardous and exhausting conditions.[2] Vast numbers of children roam city streets and live by their wits, poignant reminders of the failure of their families and societies. This global scandal is a function not only of resources, but

[1] WHO (1995) *The World Health Report 1995: Bridging the Gaps*, Geneva: World Health Organization
[2] UNICEF (ed) (1997) *The Progress of Nations 1997*, New York: UNICEF

[3] Children's Defense Fund (1997) *The State of America's Children Yearbook 1997*, Washington DC: Children's Defense Fund
[4] Anand, S and Ravallion M (1993) 'Human Development in Poor Countries: On the Role of Private Incomes and Public Services', *Journal of Economic Perspectives*, 7 (1 Winter): 133–150
[5] UNDP (1996) *Human Development Report 1996*, New York: Oxford University Press
[6] UNDP (1992) *Human Development Report 1992*, New York: Oxford University Press
[7] UNDP (1997) *Human Development Report 1997*, New York: Oxford University Press
[8] UNCHS (1996) *An Urbanizing World: Global Report on Human Settlements 1996*, New York: Oxford University Press

of priorities. In the United States of America, the world's largest economy, a quarter of the children live in poverty.[3] But experience has shown that where political will is strong, high levels of social development are possible even in the absence of wealth, and with little or no economic growth.[4]

In the world at large, however, social development has *not* been a priority. The world economy has expanded dramatically over the last thirty years, but during that same period, disparities in per capita income between rich and poor countries have tripled.[5] By 1990, the income of the richest 20 per cent of the world's people was 150 times that of the poorest 20 per cent.[6] Far from eradicating poverty, the prevailing global economic model is exacerbating the political, economic and social exclusion of the majority of the world's population. In many countries, debt repayment has essentially taken the place of investment in human development. In this age of unprecedented wealth one third of the people in the world live on less than a dollar a day.[7] Almost half of them are children, and their numbers continue to climb.

These children cannot wait for some distant economic prosperity. It is an elementary moral responsibility to ensure that no child goes hungry, or sleeps in the street, or is submitted to violence, or excluded from school. This moral obligation also makes good economic sense. The cost of ensuring a child's basic rights are minimal compared to the lifetime costs of a failure to respond. And the necessary measures are quite feasible. Most of the requirements of children can be met by improved or reoriented management of the resources we already have. It is a question of rescuing some basic values of human dignity, of fighting for the right priorities.

This book deals with just a part of children's global predicament it focuses on the everyday situation of the growing number of children who live in poverty in the cities of Asia, Africa and Latin America. It does not attempt to address the brutalities of war which affect the lives of so many children and families, but is limited to more silent emergencies that can easily be forgotten. Close to half of the world's population now lives in urban areas. Not all cities continue to grow, but the trend is still for rapidly increasing numbers of people to live and work in urban areas, especially in Africa and Asia.[8]

the underestimation of urban poverty

It has long been assumed that absolute poverty is concentrated in rural areas, and that urban populations earn more and are better provided with infrastructure and basic services. But official figures often distort and oversimplify reality. Many of the urban poor living in shanty towns around cities are excluded when city populations are counted. Those who are counted are lumped together with the city's wealthy, resulting in averages that fail to reveal the plight of poorer inhabitants. Nor do most national statistics take into account the higher costs of urban living. More sophisticated analysis indicates that the scale and depth of urban poverty has been underestimated in many nations, and that the worst disparities and deprivations exist in cities and towns.

Children in urban poverty are unquestionably at high risk. Many of them live on land unfit for habitation and under constant threat of eviction. They lack easy access to clean water, and their toilets, if they have them, are dark, foul, pit latrines or dirty communal facilities. In crowded areas where infectious disease can spread rapidly, the threats to health are acute. If these children attend school, they find it overcrowded, understaffed, poorly equipped and of little relevance to their culture, interests or chances of future employment. Opportunities for play are almost always inadequate – outdoor space is contaminated with garbage and excreta, and indoor space may be insufficient for even the most basic family needs.

high-risks for children

Cities are also places of social turmoil for children. When people are crowded together under conditions of deprivation and uncertainty, their dealings with one another can become marked by suspicion and hostility. Neighbourhoods are often torn by violence. Large-scale migration, rapid urban growth and high rates of urban poverty have contributed to the erosion of family and community structure. Old safety nets have disappeared, often leaving little to replace them. The capacity of adults to function adequately as caregivers can be stretched to the limit by the many burdens of poverty. Adrift in a confusing and uncaring world, many children are pulled into the streets, into prostitution, drug addiction and gangs.

social turmoil

The responsibility for these endangered children is increasingly being delegated to local governments. Far from being simply the custodians of parks and drains, under worldwide processes of decentralization, local authorities are routinely becoming the primary guardians of human wellbeing. In many cases this is an overwhelming challenge. Many of the factors underlying urban poverty are a function of macroeconomic trends and sectoral priorities far beyond the control of local authorities. Even those factors that *can* theoretically be controlled at the local level are often beyond their practical capability to respond to comprehensively. Local authorities are frequently not allotted sufficient funds to discharge their responsibilities adequately. Nor do they always have the authority to raise revenues locally, or to make significant policy decisions.

local responses

Action at national and international levels is clearly critical in tackling the roots of poverty and exclusion. But this book focuses on what can reasonably and effectively be undertaken at the most local level. Even when urban authorities are seriously constrained by lack of funds, skills and power, they can still make a significant difference to the quality of children's lives. Every day at the local level, decisions are taken that have substantial implications for children, not only in critical areas such as education, health and social welfare, but also in areas not so commonly associated with children, such as land use planning and management, water and sanitation, policing and job creation. If cities are to be friendlier, safer, more supportive places for children and adolescents, people in all areas of urban planning, management and politics must consider the far-reaching impact that their decisions and activities have on children's everyday lives and on their long term welfare. Only when cities are managed from this perspective can they truly become places where children matter.

Creating cities that are supportive of children calls in many cases for new attitudes, new skills and new tools. For the last decade we have had available a powerful legal tool for supporting those engaged in this task, and for ensuring that the plight of children is no longer taken for granted. In 1989, the General Assembly of the United Nations formally adopted the Convention on the Rights of the Child, and as of 1997, 191 countries had taken the initiative of accepting these legal provisions that address the concerns of children on every level. Taken seriously as a set of guidelines, the Convention becomes a document that can inform and drive public policy and action at every level. It is in this spirit that the Convention is used in this book – as a framework for defining obligations, goals, and strategies for meeting children's needs in urban areas.

The issue of rights may seem unnecessary in this discussion. Why not approach municipal action simply from the perspective of children's needs, rather than complicating the issue by introducing this added dimension? There is an important difference between a rights-based and a needs-based approach, and the key lies in the concept of citizenship, with its implications of both active involvement and entitlement. A rights-based approach promotes the opportunity for those who are excluded to negotiate from a position of strength and dignity. It means that poor children and their families are active participants in the processes that involve them, and not the passive and dependent objects of social policy. An emphasis on children's rights also ensures that the definition of basic minimum needs is broad enough not only to cover immediate survival, but to guarantee long term welfare.

rights vs needs

Responding to children's rights is not a superficial or trivial activity. It means nothing less than tackling poverty and exclusion on every front, and mobilizing the whole of society to create a city-wide culture that is friendly and supportive for every child. This is a considerable undertaking, but it does not call for unusual strategies. An agenda that supports the Convention will also comply with the goals and standards of sustainable development, social justice and eradication of poverty. Implementing children's rights is not merely an extra task for overstretched officials. On the contrary, it makes good practical sense to put the collective needs of all our children at the forefront of our concerns. The well-being of children is a significant indicator of a healthy society. When the requirements of our youngest citizens are attended to, this enhances the quality of life for everyone.

urban challenges and urban opportunities

Urban authorities unquestionably face great challenges. The concentrations of people and economic activity in urban areas make enormous demands on the environment and on local inhabitants, and cities can be sites of intense degradation and squalor. But these same concentrations create opportunities for improving the quality of life for everyone. Higher densities mean lower costs per household for water supply, the collection and disposal of waste, and most forms of health care and education. Specialized services become more feasible when larger numbers require them. Environmental standards can be monitored more easily and cheaply. Most urban residents are within media reach, and this presents a rich and constructive opportunity for raising awareness and promoting change. When citizens can gather easily, they can also mobilize more effectively on their own behalf. The concentrations in urban areas can give rise to levels of vitality and diversity that are hard to find elsewhere, and that enrich life. There is great potential for creative partnerships and innovative solutions.

Using the Convention on the Rights of the Child as a framework for defining the world that children deserve to occupy, this book offers a general understanding of the stresses of urban life for children in poverty, as well as a set of guidelines for practical action. The nature of children's lives, the opportunities available to them and the stresses they are subject to can vary significantly between countries and even within cities. The understanding of children's best interests and the resources available for responding to them also differ from place to place.

This book cannot be a blueprint for action, and no single formula can possibly respond to the range of complex realities.in different cities and communities. But within the framework provided by the Convention, certain basic principles emerge and provide a perspective through which complexity and variation can be viewed. We hope that these principles, in combination with the rich diversity of examples from around the world, will inspire and support local actors as they work to find solutions for local problems and to create cities that sustain the rights of children and youth.

Part One

Understanding Children's Rights and Development

Part One

Some local governments have already been recognized for their committed championship of children and adolescents. But for many local authorities, becoming the guardian and promoter of children's rights is a new, challenging and perhaps bewildering role. In many cases some basic orientation is needed for this role to take on real meaning. These preliminary chapters provide the background information and perspective necessary for this undertaking.

Chapter 1 introduces the concept and the history of children's rights, and discusses some questions that are raised by a rights-based approach to children. A synopsis of the provisions of the Convention is followed by an account of the obligations they create, and the formal mechanisms for implementing children's rights.

Chapter 2 provides a brief introduction to the development of children and adolescents, and discusses the contribution of both social and physical environments to this process. While acknowledging the cultural, social and economic differences in children's lives and in the construction of their development, this chapter discusses some basic guidelines for meeting their requirements at different ages.

The Convention stresses that children's rights are best met within the context of stable, loving families. But family stability is seriously undermined by the pressures of urban poverty. Chapter 3 discusses the kinds of support local authorities can provide to make it possible for families to fulfill their responsibilities towards their children.

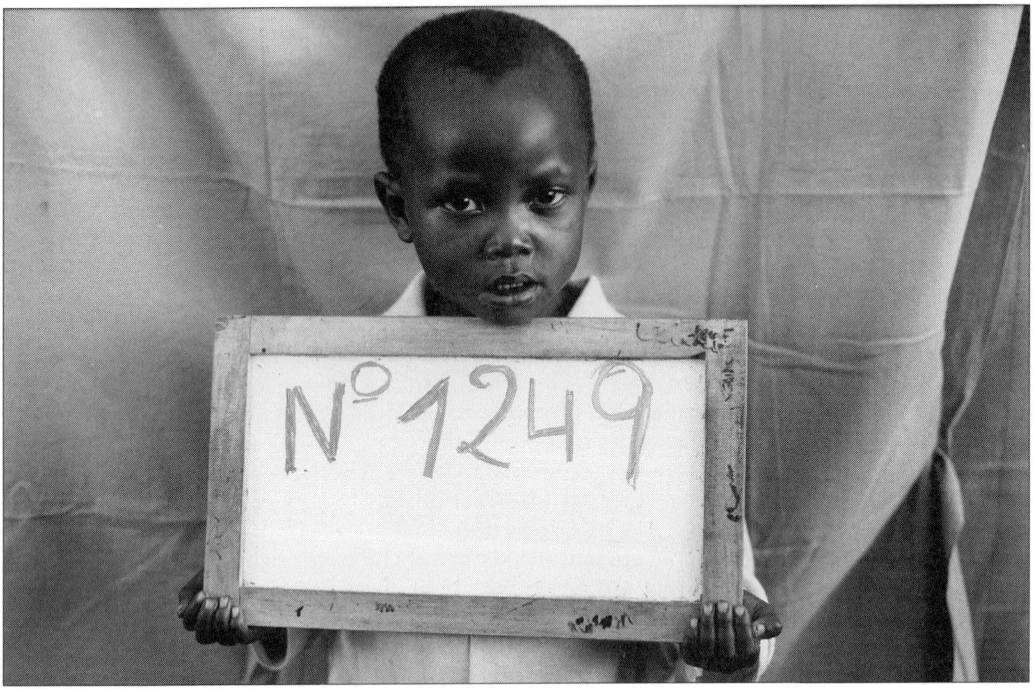

Children's right to family and to an identity are recognized as fundamental by the Convention on the Rights of the Child. This Rwandan child is photographed as part of a family tracing programme. UNICEF 1994, Giacomo Pirozzi

1 The Convention on the Rights of the Child

The Convention on the Rights of the Child, the most widely accepted international treaty in the world, defines how children should be treated in the various areas of their lives. It recognizes their rights to survival, development and protection, and to an active role in matters that concern them. The breadth of the Convention's provisions confers considerable responsibility on local governments – along with other sectors of society, other levels of government and the international community – but it also provides a framework for action that has the potential for creating inclusive and vital cities, not only for children but for everyone.

The development of human rights during the last century has been fuelled by a growing discomfort with the notion that any one group of people can legitimately be considered the property of another, or be excluded from rights extended to others. Slavery is no longer legally tolerated, caste systems are being dismantled, and women are realizing their right to self-determination in growing numbers. Children and youth are the most recent group to become the focus of debates on rights, and the history of children's rights reflects more generally the changing public awareness of the meaning of childhood.[1]

The situation of children is complicated by their biological lifestage and the inherent complexities of the growing process. Young children in

[1] Therborn, G (1996) 'Child Politics: Dimensions and Perspectives', *Childhood*, 3(1): 29–44

particular are dependent on their parents and others for protection and care. It is still difficult for many people to accept that children can be regarded as people with rights of their own, rather than as the property of their parents. For the most part, children are seen as lacking the status of full human beings and as being in training for adulthood.

But there is increasing recognition that our image of childhood is largely a social and cultural construction.[2] Children at different times in history, and in different parts of the world, have been the focus of very different expectations. Their capabilities and requirements are determined at least to some degree by the needs and assumptions of those around them. Both economic realities and cultural patterns shape the experience of childhood in a given time and place.

Because this understanding varies between and even within cultures, there has been considerable disagreement on the issue of children's rights. At one extreme it is argued that children, as human beings, should have the same rights as adults. At the other extreme are those who believe that children lack the competence to exercise rights, and that, protected as they are by their parents, they have no need for rights. Most of those involved in the child rights debate support an approach that recognizes both children's need for protection and their developing potential to act on their own behalf. The broad trend in the child rights movement has been from a primarily protective stance towards a growing acceptance of children's capacity to be active, contributing citizens, who deserve the rights to exercise that capacity.[3]

A BRIEF HISTORY OF THE CONVENTION ON THE RIGHTS OF THE CHILD

The Convention on the Rights of the Child (referred to in this book simply as the Convention or the CRC) was not the first international instrument to recognize the rights of children. The 1924 Geneva Declaration and the 1959 Declaration of the Rights of the Child, both broadly accepted within the international community, had considerable moral weight in promoting the rights of children to protection and care. But neither of these documents had the force of law, and a need was felt for a single legally binding convention.[4]

In response to a 1978 initiative by Poland, the Commission on Human Rights began developing such a legal treaty. After ten years of debate and preparation by an open working group, a final text was unanimously adopted by the General Assembly in 1989. This document went beyond the 1959 Declaration in a number of ways. Its provisions were more specific; it extended dramatically the civil and political rights offered to children, and it stressed the capacity of children to be not simply the passive recipients of protection, but active and involved bearers of rights.[5] Acceptance of the Convention was rapid and widespread. By September 1997 the Convention was in force in 191 countries, and only two had failed to become parties to it. One is Somalia, which is currently without government, and the other the United States of America. No human rights convention in existence has achieved such broad or rapid acceptance.

[2] James, A and Prout, A (eds) (1990) *Constructing and Reconstructing Childhood: Contemporary Issues in the Sociological Study of Childhood*, London: Falmer Press

[3] LeBlanc, L J (1995) *The Convention on the Rights of the Child: United Nations Lawmaking on Human Rights*, Lincoln, Nebraska:University of Nebraska Press

[4] Hammarberg, T (1992) 'Making Reality of the Rights of the Child' in Verhellen, E (ed) *Rights of the Child Lectures, Part 2*, Ghent: Children's Rights Centre

[5] Verhellen, E (1994) *Convention on the Rights of the Child: Background, Motivation, Strategies, Main Themes*, Leuven Kessel-Lo, Belgium: Garant

The Convention is a significant document largely because of this remarkable level of support. It has established in a highly visible and definitive way the fact that the world's children have a legal claim on the attention and resources of their governments and every sector of their societies. Not only has it clarified goals for children's well-being; it has also set in place a system for monitoring implementation, without which progress would be less likely. The Convention has been embraced not only as a set of legal guidelines, but also as an educational tool and a frame of reference for all serious discussion pertaining to children and youth. It has become a platform for action for international agencies focused on children, and for many kinds of organizations within civil society.

THE PROVISIONS OF THE CONVENTION

indivisibility of rights

Traditionally in the field of human rights there have been political pressures to distinguish between civil and political rights on the one hand, and social, economic and cultural rights on the other. In international law, these rights are enshrined within different covenants.[6] Rather than distinguishing between these classes of rights, the drafters of the Convention insisted on an integrated approach and emphasized the indivisibility of rights as a significant principle. Protection, provision, and respect for a child's capabilities are viewed from this perspective as complementary and mutually reinforcing supports for full well-being.[7] The fulfilment of social, economic and cultural rights creates the conditions for full compliance with civil and political rights, and vice versa.

The definition of the child

The Convention defines as a child every human being below 18, except in countries where majority is attained earlier (Article 1). This bill of rights is intended not only for young children, but also for adolescents who may already be functioning in many ways as adults. Adolescent mothers and working youth, for instance, deserve the level of support and consideration legally extended to children.

In a few areas the Convention sets specific age limits: it bars capital punishment and life imprisonment for children under 18, and it requires States to refrain from conscripting into armed services anyone below the age of 15.[8] But it permits individual States to determine the age of majority and, in most cases, the minimum ages at which children may legally become involved in various activities. The ages at which children may legally marry, leave school, begin work, consume alcohol and obtain medical treatment without parental consent may vary from one country to another. It is expected, however, that States will review their legislation regarding such age limits in the light of the Convention's general principles; nor may individual States absolve themselves from obligations to children under 18 even if they have reached the age of majority under domestic law.[9]

[6] The International Covenant on Civil and Political Rights, and the International Covenant on Economic, Social and Cultural Rights, were both adopted by the General Assembly of the United Nations in 1966
[7] Le Blanc, 1995, op cit Note 3
[8] There is currently an initiative to encourage the adoption of an Optional Protocol to the Convention on the Rights of the Child to raise the minimum age for military recruitment from 15 to 18
[9] Hodgkin, R and Newell, P (1998) *Implementation Handbook for the Convention on the Rights of the Child*, New York: UNICEF

General principles

The Convention contains some fundamental principles which lay the groundwork for the document as a whole, and together define a particular attitude towards children and their rights.[10] All other provisions of the Convention must be considered in the light of these principles.

- The first is the principle of non-discrimination. Article 2 establishes that every child is covered by the Convention's provisions. Girls, children with disabilities, children on the street, and children of minority groups, for example, are all entitled by law to enjoy equal rights and opportunities.

non-discrimination

- The principle of the best interests of the child, presented in Article 3(1), asserts that when decisions are made or actions taken that affect children, the interests of the child should be a primary consideration rather than being placed after the concerns of either the parents, the wider community, or the State. This principle should particularly be applied when the Convention does not set a precise standard. It cannot be used to override other rights guaranteed to the child.[11]

best interests

- A related principle concerns the views of the child, in Article 12. When a child's interests are being considered, the Convention supports the right of that child to have his or her views taken into consideration, with due regard being given to age and maturity.

the child's view

- The final general principle concerns the child's right to survival and development. Article 6 is the foundation for all other social, economic and cultural rights provided by the Convention. Aside from asserting the child's inherent right to life, it makes explicit the fact that without adequate means for survival and development, the right to life is meaningless.

survival and development

Rights to care and provision

Children's right to the fulfilment of basic human needs is elaborated on in a number of other Articles which emphasize the full development of the child, and establish the ways in which this development must be supported. The Convention stresses that children should be raised in a loving and understanding family environment (Preamble; Article 9); and have the right to be protected from interference with family (Article 16). If children have been separated from family because of such factors as conflict, displacement or illegal adoption, the State must, where possible, promote reunification or contact with parents (Articles 9, 10, 11). If children are victims of family abuse, the State is responsible for ensuring alternative care that resembles a family home as far as possible, and that ensures respect for the child's cultural, ethnic, linguistic and religious background (Article 20.)

family

The Convention recognizes children's right to a standard of living adequate for their physical, mental, spiritual, moral, and social development (Article 27). This implies not simply enough food to prevent

[10] Hammarberg, 1992, op cit Note 4
[11] Hodgkin and Newell, 1998, op cit Note 9

standard of living

starvation, but adequate nourishment for healthy bodies and alert minds; not only shelter from the elements, but housing that can support health, emotional security, family stability and a sense of belonging. Parents are recognized as having primary responsibility for providing such a standard of living, but the State is obliged to ensure that this responsibility is met, and to provide material assistance and support programmes to children and parents where necessary (Articles 18, 26).

health

Children are guaranteed the right to the highest attainable level of health (Article 24). This means not only access to health care, but a living environment that promotes health. Disabled children are recognized as having the right to special care which, as far as possible, supports their potential for self-reliance and guarantees them a full and decent life as part of their community (Article 23).

education

The State is responsible for ensuring that primary education is free and compulsory, and that further education is available on the basis of equal opportunity (Article 28). This education should be directed to the child's fullest development, to respect for cultural values and identity, and to preparation for active adult life in a free society (Article 29). The Convention also recognizes children's right to play and leisure activities (Article 31), implying not only sufficient time for leisure, but also the provision of safe and appropriate space within their communities for play and recreation. Access to cultural life and the arts is also recognized as a right (Article 31).

play

The Convention acknowledges that these levels of provision may be beyond the immediate capacity of both families and the State, but it stresses that they should be addressed as fully as possible, and to the maximum extent of the State's available resources (Article 4). Children's well-being must be a primary consideration in any decisions regarding allocation of resources, and where necessary the international community is expected to assist (Articles 3, 4).

Rights of protection

maltreatment

Children have the right to protection in a number of difficult situations, and from a range of abuses. The State is required to protect children from all forms of maltreatment from parents and others responsible for their care, and to offer them appropriate support and treatment when they have suffered from abuse or neglect (Articles 19, 39). Although the laws of most nations continue to sanction physical punishment for children, the Convention expressly bars the use of physical or mental violence.[12]

exploitation

The Convention takes a strong stand against sexual and economic exploitation. It recognizes children's right to protection from prostitution and pornography, abduction and trafficking, and involvement in the production, sale and use of narcotics, calling for both national and multilateral measures on these fronts (Articles 33,34, 35). The Convention also asserts the right of children to be protected from any work that interferes with their safety, health, education or development, and it calls on individual States to set minimum ages for employment, and to regulate working hours and conditions (Article 32).

The Convention ensures children accused of crimes the same legal guarantees that are extended to adults, but in addition, calls for adapta-

[12] Newell, P (1995) 'Respecting children's right to physical integrity' in Franklin, B (ed) *The Handbook of Children's Rights: Comparative Policy and Practice*, London/New York: Routledge, 215–226

tion of legal procedures and punishment appropriate to the age of the child. Capital punishment and life imprisonment are not permitted. Wherever possible, judicial proceedings are to be avoided entirely. While ensuring respect for human rights and legal safeguards, imprisonment is to be a measure of last resort, and for the shortest time possible. Conditions must be humane, and rehabilitation and social reintegration must be promoted (Article 40).

justice

The Convention grants special protection to refugee children and asylum seekers, and those who are displaced or exposed to armed conflict (Articles 22, 37). Proper humanitarian care is to be offered, and help in reuniting children with parents when necessary, and wherever possible. When children have suffered physical or psychological harm, they have the right to rehabilitative treatment aimed at their recovery and social reintegration (Article 39).

refugees

Rights of participation

The Convention does not extend to children the full range of political rights accorded to adults, such as the right to vote, but it grants them certain of the freedoms and protections that are considered to be more general human rights. Children have the right to a name, an identity and a nationality, and must be registered at birth (Articles 7, 8). They are protected by the Convention from invasion of their privacy and their family life (Article 16). The Convention grants children the right to express their opinions in matters that concern them, and to have these opinions weighed when decisions are made, in accordance with their age, maturity and understanding of the situation (Article 12). Children are also guaranteed the right to freedom of thought and conscience, subject to the guidance of parents or other guardians. They have the right to enjoy their own culture, religion and language without interference or discrimination (Articles 13, 14).

civil and political rights

Children have the right to seek, obtain and impart information, and to have access to informational material that is not deemed harmful to their well-being (Article 17). They have the right to associate with others and to assemble freely (Article 15). These civil and political rights unquestionably define children as active agents capable of exercising rights, and not simply as the recipients of protective care. This lays the groundwork for children's right to active citizenship, in spite of the fact that they are not yet granted the right to vote.

Implementation and monitoring

It is not enough simply to recognize rights. They must also be implemented. Article 4 of the Convention requires States to do all they can in this regard through legislative and administrative reforms, and the maximum possible allocation of resources. The Convention defines specific procedures for supporting and monitoring progress (Articles 42–54). It calls for the establishment of an international committee of experts, presented by member nations for election by the United Nations General Assembly. Each State Party is required to submit to this commit-

country reports

tee regular reports which are intended to be comprehensive and self-critical, and to discuss difficulties as well as progress in implementing the Convention. Pertinent information from non-governmental organizations and specialized agencies of the United Nations, such as UNICEF, is also accepted. As a result of the Committee's consideration of the material submitted, and their discussion with representatives of the country in question, concluding observations are drawn up which are intended to be widely disseminated within the country and to serve as the basis for further discussion and action. The Committee's function is not to respond in a punitive way to national shortcomings and failures, but to provide a constructive and collaborative opportunity to identify successes and difficulties, and to set goals.[13]

SOME QUESTIONS RAISED BY THE CONVENTION

Why we need a separate bill of rights for children

When work began on drafting the Convention, there was by no means general consensus on the need for such a document. Critics argued that a separate treaty would call into question the status of children as human beings by suggesting that they do not qualify for the protection routinely offered to all people through existing human rights instruments.[14] Those who supported a separate convention argued that the protection offered to children by general human rights provisions is inadequate. A number of instruments refer to the status of children, but both terminology and intent vary. Before the acceptance of the Convention, for instance, there was no universal age limit for children's legitimate involvement in armed combat. The inevitable inconsistencies pointed to a need for a single set of standards.

conditions faced by children

Conditions faced by children around the world served as the strongest argument for a separate convention.[15] Infant mortality, malnutrition, life on the street, child prostitution, intolerable working and living conditions, involvement in armed conflict, and the incarceration of children all called for an aggressive response by the international community.

The realities of children's developmental and social status also pointed to the need for a special treaty. Adult-oriented safety and health standards and provisions for health and emergency care often fail to offer children the protection they need.[16] Children are more vulnerable to disease, especially when young or malnourished, their rapidly growing bodies are more at risk from pollutants, and they are less able to guard against physical hazards. They are disproportionately affected by poor housing and the many other disadvantages that accompany poverty.

The dependence of children on adults makes them especially vulnerable to mistreatment and exploitation. Whether at home, at school, in the community or in the workplace, children need protections that take into account their disadvantage in relation to those who are older, stronger and more powerful. Early in their lives when their cognitive skills are less developed, children are considered to be more vulnerable to emotional harm. When faced with traumatic situations, they are more likely than

13 Verhellen, 1994, op cit Note 5
14 Le Blanc, 1995, op cit Note 3
15 Hammarberg, 1992, op cit Note 4
16 Satterthwaite, D, Hart, R, Levy, C, Mitlin, D, Ross, D, Smit, J, Stephens, C (1996) *The Environment for Children*, London: Earthscan
17 Garbarino, J and Bedard, C (1996) 'Spiritual Challenges to Children facing Violent Trauma', *Childhood*, 3(4): 467–479

adults to suffer serious and debilitating stress with long term implications.[17] A special bill of rights creates the opportunity to recognize and respond to the developmentally specific requirements of children.

children's tenuous status

Children's status as human beings is also significant. To regard their rights as implicit within human rights fails to take account of the fact that children are not commonly respected as bearers of rights, nor considered capable of exercising them. Children do not have the vote and can exercise no direct political power. Although adults may try to ensure that children are well cared for, this often expresses the perception of them as adult property rather than as citizens with rights of their own. A separate instrument, which leaves no doubt that children have rights, is necessary in order to combat such assumptions.

broad social support

For those who see no need for rights, but would leave the protection of children to their parents, it must be pointed out that parents cannot control every sphere of life. Even with the best of intentions, they cannot dictate the quality of the air they breathe, the availability of housing, or access to resources for children with special needs. They require broad social support to ensure that their children have the environments they need to prosper. For children without parents, the issue is even clearer. And there are, regrettably, those situations in which their parents are the very people from whom children most sorely need protection.

Parents' rights and children's rights: balancing protection and participation

The tension between the protection of children and their competence to act on their own behalf is sometimes polarized by opponents of the Convention into a conflict between parents' rights and children's rights. A certain amount of protection is necessary for children, and must form a significant part of any recognition of their rights. But protection as an end in itself may deny children the right to take part in decisions that involve them, in keeping with their evolving capabilities. Some critics are reluctant to allow children an active voice in their own affairs, and feel that the rights of minors should always be exercised on their behalf by concerned adults.[18] There are two issues at stake here: the question of children's competence, and the implicit challenge to parental and adult authority.

children's competence

The matter of competence is to some degree a question of expectations and experience. Very young children require adults to act for them. But the capacity to exercise responsibility and make important decisions is not suddenly acquired as children reach their majority. It is a gradual process, affected not only by the child's biological development, but by the actual experience of making decisions and taking responsibility. In their day-to-day lives, many children shoulder responsibilities that call on their skills as seasoned decision makers long before they are adults. There is little difference between older children and adults in this regard, except for the skills that are acquired in exercising this capacity. Children's right to have a voice in matters that concern them must be recognized for this very reason – in order to encourage and support the development of their growing competence.[19]

Especially in societies where respect and obedience are the expected behaviour, the child's right to have a voice is likely to be contentious.

[18] Verhellen, 1994, op cit Note 5
[19] Hart, R (1997) *Children's Participation: The Theory and Practice of Involving Young Citizens in Community Development and Environmental Care*, London: Earthscan/UNICEF

the challenge to adult authority

This is true especially if adults have little chance to experience themselves as rights-bearing individuals. Promoting children's rights in this area is unlikely to be successful if it meets the angry resistance of parents and community members. Measures must be taken to ensure that parental rights are also understood and respected, and that parents have the opportunity to discuss and consider the implications of the Convention. Children are more likely to realize their right to participation if they are taught to express their views in ways that do not violate the expectation of respect for adults, and if there is a recognition that responsibilities complement rights. There are important implications for educational systems, which must give children opportunities for participatory and interactive learning (see p172).

Decisions about human rights almost always imply striking a balance between conflicting interests. Tension between protection and participation is not only part of the child rights debate; it is integral to the process of growing up, and to the relationship between parents and their children, adults and minors. Children's claims to independence are a matter of on-going negotiation within families and within societies. They cannot be simply resolved within a bill of rights. But by being presented within a single document, these often conflicting claims can best be put into productive relationship with one another in the attempt to find an appropriate balance in a given situation.

The issue of culture and children's rights

Human rights are based on the assumption that certain principles should apply universally regardless of differences in race, religion, culture, economic status, or gender. This assumption can be difficult to reconcile with the reality of a world in which beliefs, practices, social relations and economic realities vary widely between and even within different societies. This difficulty is particularly evident in the understanding and acceptance of children's rights.[20]

the threat of cultural imperialism

The issue is complicated by the perceived threat of cultural imperialism. The Convention, like other human rights documents, has philosophical roots in the European tradition of liberal individualism. It also approaches childhood through the lens of child development, which many critics have seen as biased by Northern theory and research (see p18). Despite the goal of universality, the children's rights project starts from a perspective on the individual which is more congenial to some groups than to others. The privileged position accorded to children by the Convention may be distinctly at odds with the values of societies where the rights of the extended family are given precedence over those of the individual, or where age is the basis for respect and rights.[21]

It is oversimplistic, however, to reduce this tension to a struggle between Northern values and the conservation of otherwise intact traditional systems. Few systems of belief are coherent and untroubled by conflict, be they 'traditional' or not. Culture is not rigid, but adapts, of necessity, to changing circumstances and lifestyles. Even within families, it is common to find disagreement on beliefs and goals, whether on the rearing of children or the spending of money. Relations between groups are equally complicated by conflicting sets of values. Nor are the values

[20] Alston, P (ed) (1994) *The Best Interests of the Child: Reconciling Culture and Human Rights*, Florence, Italy: International Child Development Centre, UNICEF and Oxford: Clarendon Press

[21] Burman, E (1996) 'Local, Gobal or Globalized? Child Development and International Child Rights Legislation', Childhood, 3(1): 45–67

espoused by the Convention universally endorsed in the North, where there may be widely divergent views on the role of parents and the capabilities of children.

conflicts in values

Conflicts in values, then, are as much a phenomenon within, as between, societies, and are frequently expressed in societal ambivalence or disagreement on issues affecting children. Standards regarding the education of girls, for instance, or the appropriate relationship of children to labour, are hotly contested in many places. Throughout the world, long-accepted responses to childhood and children are being challenged for a number of reasons.

The decline in infant and child mortality during the 20th century, for instance, has had an impact on family structure and priorities. As child survival has become more of a certainty, there has been a growing preference in many countries for smaller families, which has permitted increased parental investment in individual children. The effects have been dramatically evident in China, where the one-child policy led to radical changes in the status of children.[22]

Changes have also occurred as a result of the spread of the global market economy and of impoverished urbanization. In many places the traditional fabric of society has disintegrated, and with it the validity of many traditional expectations for children. The fate of children is generally more visible, and has become increasingly a topic for concern. There is a widespread reconsideration of how best to respond both to children's present situations and to their preparation for the future.

a minimum basis for decision making

For those intent on protecting local ways of life, the Convention may appear to be yet another frontal attack. A more realistic assessment will acknowledge that it offers an opportunity to address precisely the confusions and contradictions created by contemporary life in both the North and the South by defining a minimum basis for decision making where interests clash. All societies, including the wealthiest, need to make internal adjustments in order to come to terms with the high standards of this treaty.

allowing for local interpretation

The Convention does not promote a universal, rigid set of solutions to the problems confronting children. It contains certain core principles that demand a clear response – we are required to acknowledge and respect children, to ensure their survival, to protect them from harm, to equip them adequately for life, and to listen to them. In situations where accepted practices permit the oppression of children, these principles may be found unacceptable. But within the parameters of the Convention there is a great deal of latitude. Detailed implementation of these principles is never specified. On the contrary, the Convention is a flexible instrument designed to accommodate complexity and difference.[23] On most issues the Convention's stand is formulated in sufficiently general terms to leave considerable scope for accomodation to local standards, where these are not harmful to the well-being of children.

The best interests principle provides the basis through which the provisions of the Convention can be interpreted and applied to local conditions.[24] The Convention, for instance, may mandate an education that prepares a child adequately for life, but it does not specify the curriculum. Only local debate can determine the education that will best serve the interests of local children. This principle serves at the same time as a means for evaluating the merits of conflicting claims, whether within the family or the broader society. In a given context, it may well

22 Tobin, J J, Wu, Y H, Davidson, D H (1989) *Preschool in Three Cultures: Japan, China, and the United States*, New Haven: Yale University Press
23 Alston, 1994, op cit Note 20
24 Ibid

be determined that a traditional or culturally specific response will best answer a particular child's interests.

negotiating the best solutions

Since a determination of children's best interests must necessarily be local and contingent, this provision runs the risk of being inadequately prescriptive and allowing convenient solutions to be justified. This is an unavoidable risk. A less elastic principle could not be genuinely responsive to the complexities of the world. The appropriate application of the best interests principle, and of children's rights in general, implies the involvement of a broad range of independent social actors in order to negotiate the best solution for local children. A free press, active NGOs, and independent advocacy organizations are critical supports for the interpretation of the Convention at a local level. Perhaps most important, families, who have the primary responsibility for managing children's rights, must be involved in dialogue in order to develop an understanding of the Convention within the context of local child rearing practices.

Children's rights and women's rights

Women's rights were formally adopted by the international community in 1979, and in many ways this recognition laid the groundwork for subsequent attention to the rights of children.[25] But the introduction of children's rights has generated concern among some advocates for women. The attainment of equity and justice for women has involved, among other things, ensuring that their reproductive and caregiving roles do not interfere with their self-determination and their full and equal access to resources and opportunities. Children's right to protection and care is seen by some as a potential threat to the gradual gains being made by women. As Savitri Goonesekere has demonstrated, however, the two Conventions are quite compatible and contain no provisions which set the interests of the two groups in conflict with each other. On the contrary, they can be seen as complementary and mutually reinforcing.[26]

comple-mentary rights

The implementation of children's rights has the effect of reducing the actual burden for most women and enhancing their quality of life. If the child's right to a healthy environment and to adequate health care is realized, it can only ease the responsibilities of mothers. The child's right to decent child care services, again supports the woman's right to work outside the family and to take part in community life. Far from increasing the load for mothers, the Convention requires that supports be in place to make their complex responsibilities more manageable.

The Convention to End All Forms of Discrimination Against Women (CEDAW) supports the protection of children in specific ways through the rights that it guarantees for their mothers. For instance, women have the right to prenatal and postnatal care, when necessary without cost (Article 12). Working women have the right to special protection during pregnancy, to maternity leave, and to social services (both for themselves and for fathers) that enable them to combine family obligations with work responsibilities (Article 11.2). Women also have the right to participate fully in political life (Article 7) – in many cases a guarantee that children's interests will be more fully addressed in the political arena.

A potential area of conflict concerns reproductive rights. The Convention preamble states that children have the right to legal protec-

25 Therborn, 1996, op cit Note 1

26 Goonesekere, S (1992) *Women's Rights and Children's Rights: the United Nations Conventions as Compatible and Complementary International Treaties*, Florence, Italy: UNICEF International Child Development Centre

tion before as well as after birth. This has been seen by some as a measure to limit woman's reproductive freedom. The history of this statement, however, and the consensus of legal commentary on it, make it clear that it is intended as a deliberate compromise, leaving the issue of abortion to the discretion of individual countries.[27] Nor does CEDAW confer a legal right to abortion.[28]

Most fundamentally, the children's Convention addresses the issue of gender discrimination at its roots by holding as a basic principle that children's rights apply equally to all children. By taking into account the developmental realities of childhood, the Convention is able to specify for girls as well as boys, the measures that must be taken to ensure the basis for equality in adulthood.

THE OBLIGATIONS CREATED BY THE CONVENTION FOR LOCAL URBAN GOVERNMENT

The legally binding obligations of the Convention are most frequently associated with formal agencies of the State at the national level, but in reality, obligation extends to the whole governing structure of a country, from national to community level. Local governments are as fully obligated by this treaty as their national counterparts (except in terms of the responsibility to submit reports, as provided in Article 44).

local authorities on the front line

In some ways, obligations are even more pressing at the local level. Local authorities are on the front line: because of the trend towards both urbanization and government decentralization, they have in many cases become the primary actors in the provision of basic services which affect children's lives, in spite of the fact that their capacity has seldom kept pace with the growing needs. The Convention acknowledges that heavily resource-related obligations may be difficult to realize and may call for progressive implementation. But a lack of capacity does not mean that any provisions can be ignored. The Convention requires that obligations be implemented to the maximum extent of available resources (Article 4). Himes points out that this implies not only financial and material resources, but also human skills, knowledge, creativity, and time, as well as the wisdom to use natural resources efficiently and appropriately.[29] The pivotal role of urban authorities involves direct provision or support for other service providers, as well as adequate assessment, regulation, enforcement and monitoring.

resources

social mobilization

No one group of actors can possibly bring about the fundamental changes in attitude and practice that are required to achieve the Convention's goals. This is a challenge that must involve everybody. The capacity of local government to raise awareness, coordinate action, support collaboration, and to enlist broad involvement is most significant for child well-being, especially for weaker and less well-funded authorities. A critical aspect of social mobilization is the effective use of mass communications, which reach the vast majority of people in urban areas and can have a profound effect in shaping public attitudes.

Changes in understanding must be accompanied by practical measures. Social and economic disparities which undermine the realization of rights for so many children must be addressed, and this cannot

27 Hammarberg, 1992, op cit Note 4
28 Goonesekere, 1992, op cit Note 26
29 Himes, J R (1995) *Implementing the Convention on the Rights of the Child: Resource Mobilization in Low-income Countries*, The Hague: Martinus Nijhoff/UNICEF

happen effectively without a well developed framework of support from municipal government. Although non-governmental organizations and community groups are more frequently associated with poverty reduction, they do not have the capacity of municipal authorities to address systemic inadequacies. Only these authorities can develop the regulatory frameworks to promote health and safety, to establish building codes and planning norms, to assign responsibilities to other groups, and to be responsible for monitoring the cost and quality of private or community provision. Through collaboration and partnerships, local authorities can make the fullest use of all available resources.

redistribution

Although every society has at its disposal rich human resources, there are limits to reducing poverty in poor communities without funding from outside. Local government must find ways of investing in infrastructure and services for its poorest residents. Measures must be taken towards equality in provision, whether through taxation, cross-subsidization or other redistributive means. When local authorities lack the resources to provide the necessary services and infrastructure – whether directly or in support of other providers – they have the responsibility to turn not only to community members, but to higher levels of government and other partners. The Convention can be a powerful tool in supporting local authorities to fight for decision making authority, including the right to participate at national level in decisions regarding the allocation of aid. Strong advocacy and coalition building are critical in such efforts, and will be discussed in greater detail on p269.

Children's rights in the context of sustainable urban development

In theory, economic development should not conflict with human rights; but in practice there are often serious conflicts – for instance, over ownership of resources or access to them, over wages and working conditions and over social provision. Many governments have justified their contravention rights as necessary for rapid economic development. A concern with social justice and equity is not compatible with a single-minded reliance on market forces. Within this context, children's rights are no exception. Any reallocation of public funds towards the well being of children may increase taxes for citizens or businesses, or draw public resources away from funding the forms of infrastructure that primarily benefit businesses. Respecting children's rights also means limiting the rights of enterprises and users to pollute and destroy human environments, precipitate social and community disintegration, or exploit child labour.

sustainable development: resolving divergent interests

The principles of sustainable development promote a resolution between these apparently incompatible goals and divergent interests, for they demand the simultaneous achievement of economic, social and ecological goals by requiring that we meet the needs of the present generation without compromising the ability of future generations to meet their own needs, as described by the Brundtland Commission.[30] There is natural convergence between the principles of sustainable development and children's rights. Children are especially vulnerable to many environmental hazards, both in terms of their threshold for damage and the constraints that such hazards place on their freedom within their

[30] World Commission on Environment and Development (1987) *Our Common Future*, Oxford: Oxford University Press

surroundings. The goals of sustainable development support social equity, and hence the integrity of the social fabric, in ways that affect children more profoundly than anyone else. The connection between children's rights and sustainable development was formally articulated both in the Plan of Action that resulted from the 1990 World Summit for Children, and in Agenda 21, the action plan endorsed by the Earth Summit in Rio de Janeiro in 1992. In both documents special chapters are devoted to the interactions between child-centered development and environmental care, and children are acknowledged as having both the greatest stake in environmental stability, and the capacity to act as protagonists in achieving that stability. At the local level, the goals of sustainable development are best expressed through Local Agenda 21, in ways that are responsive to local conditions.[31]

Local Agenda 21

Any local authority committed to realizing children's rights will have to acknowledge that such a commitment cannot be expressed through the adoption of goals that only superficially enhance the lives of children. The achievement of children's rights means viewing the world from a different perspective, and radically altering some basic assumptions. Part of the change involves foregoing a commitment to economic growth as a virtually exclusive goal, adopting a commitment to greater social and economic equity and limiting social and environmental degradation within development. Only when systemic inequities are acknowledged and addressed, can children's rights be genuinely achieved.

changing basic assumptions

A call to action

In spite of broad acceptance of the Convention over the last decade, overall conditions for children have not improved dramatically, and in some countries have actually deteriorated. Many of the countries that were quickest to ratify the Convention at national level are failing to find ways to fulfill it through concrete local measures. For too many children around the world the Convention is only an empty promise. Basic health care has improved in most parts of the world, and children are more likely than ever to survive their early years, but they are surviving in a world that appears to be increasingly violent, hostile, and uncaring. Although we have proven our ability to achieve some focused goals, we still lack the political will to address successfully the overwhelming totality of the situation.

But it is also true that there are many instances of effective and inspiring progress. This book contains numerous examples of efforts that have been successful in radically changing the quality of children's lives. We can and must learn from these examples. The fact that children's rights continue to be violated must be a call to action, not a cause for despair. With the Convention in hand, we have a set of guidelines and goals which enable us to set our moral compass as we struggle to find acceptable ways of living together wherever we are, and working with our children for a future based on values of inclusiveness and solidarity.

[31] ICLEI (1996) *Local Agenda 21 Planning Guide: An Introduction to Sustainable Development Planning*, The International Council for Local Environmental Initiatives

Play is an integral, productive part of children's development, a source of pleasure, competence and identity. Through their engagement with the world around them children acquire a range of skills which they will draw on throughout their lives. Here children play outside their homes in Davao, Philippines. UNICEF 1996, Shehzad Noorani

2 Children's Development

The Convention establishes the right of all children to support for their survival and full development, and to a concern for their best interests (Articles 3, 6). In order to respond to these principles we need to understand how children develop and to determine what their best interests might involve at different times in their lives. This is no simple task. All children undergo dramatic changes between conception and adulthood. But to generalize about these changes is a risky undertaking, for the process has deep roots in social and economic realities and in cultural beliefs. The norms and goals that children respond to, and the opportunities made available to them, vary widely. It is increasingly acknowledged that there is no such universal as 'childhood', but that the meaning and experience of childhood are constructed differently by different cultures.[1]

The field of developmental psychology has been justifiably accused of neglecting this reality, and of promoting an understanding of children's development shaped mostly by studies of middle-class Northern children.[2] It is clearly short-sighted to accept this perspective as relevant to all children. But in responding overzealously to this neglect, there is a danger that we may dismiss the concept of develop-

[1] See, for example, Frones, I (1993) 'Changing Childhood', *Childhood*, 1(1)

[2] Burman, E (1994) *Deconstructing Developmental Psychology*, London: Routledge

ment itself as an irrelevance. Cross-cultural and contextual efforts in this field have made significant contributions to our theoretical understanding of children, and can help us come to a practical understanding of children's 'best interests'.[3]

social construction of childhood

Childhood as a social construction is not a universal. But children do share certain realities related to their biological lifestage and their humanity. Across different cultures there is a core of experience and developmental change that is more or less common to all children, and associated with their neurological and physiological maturation.[4] An understanding of this makes it easier to look objectively at social, environmental or nutritional variations, and to recognize when a child is receiving adequate developmental support and when intervention might be helpful. We must respect the different ways that the experience of childhood is understood and responded to – but cultural relativism should not become a justification for a lack of practical attention to children's rights and their requirements for health and general welfare.[5] This chapter will describe the process of development in children and adolescents as a function of both biological and cultural realities, and discuss basic prerequisites for health, care and well-being that can be interpreted in the light of local realities.

THE SIGNIFICANCE OF SUPPORTIVE ENVIRONMENTS FOR CHILDREN'S DEVELOPMENT

Children's development is not the same as growth, although these words are used interchangeably at times. Growth means becoming larger. Development implies that growth and change take place in an organized and integrated way. An organism becomes more complex and differentiated as it develops. A seedling with its first two leaves does not simply become larger; it grows into a complicated plant with branches, flowers and fruits. Development must also be distinguished from learning. Many of the skills that children acquire are learned, but the capacity to acquire these skills depends on the process of maturation. Regardless of the level of effort, a one year-old child cannot learn to read the way a seven year-old can. The necessary mental capacities have not yet fully developed.

There are differences of opinion about what drives development. Does an infant respond to some pattern within herself, or is she more affected by her interaction with everything she experiences in her life? The consensus is that these factors cannot be separated. Every child is a unique expression of the interplay between innate biological qualities and her response to the particular environment that surrounds her. Genetic endowment determines potential, but that potential unfolds in the world of experience. If a child's social and material environment do not supply the necessary support for survival and development, the genetic potential goes unrealized. Even when children have serious biological complications at birth, supportive social and physical environments make a difference over time in their capacity to overcome difficulties and to live rewarding lives.[6]

Although the ecology of children's lives can vary dramatically, research from around the world has pointed to some common environ-

3 An overview of cross-cultural efforts can be found in Dasen, P R and Jahoda, G (1986) 'Cross-cultural Human Development', *International Journal of Behavioral Development*, 9: 413–416. A fine recent example of such cross-cultural work is Kagitçibasi, C (1996) *Family and Human Development Across Cultures*, Mahwah, New Jersey: Lawrence Erlbaum. A frequently referred to text stressing the contextual nature of development is Bronfenbrenner, U (1979) *The Ecology of Human Development: Experiments by Nature and Design*, Cambridge, MA: Harvard University Press

4 Kagitçibasi, 1996, op cit Note 3

5 Goonesekere, S (1994) 'National Policies on Children's Rights and International Norms' in Asquith, S and Hill, M (eds) *Justice for Children*, Dordrecht: Martinus Nijhoff Publishers

6 Brown, W, Thurman, S K, L F Pearl, S (1993) *Family-centered Early Intervention with Infants and Toddlers: Innovative Cross Disciplinary Approaches*, Baltimore: Paul H Brookes

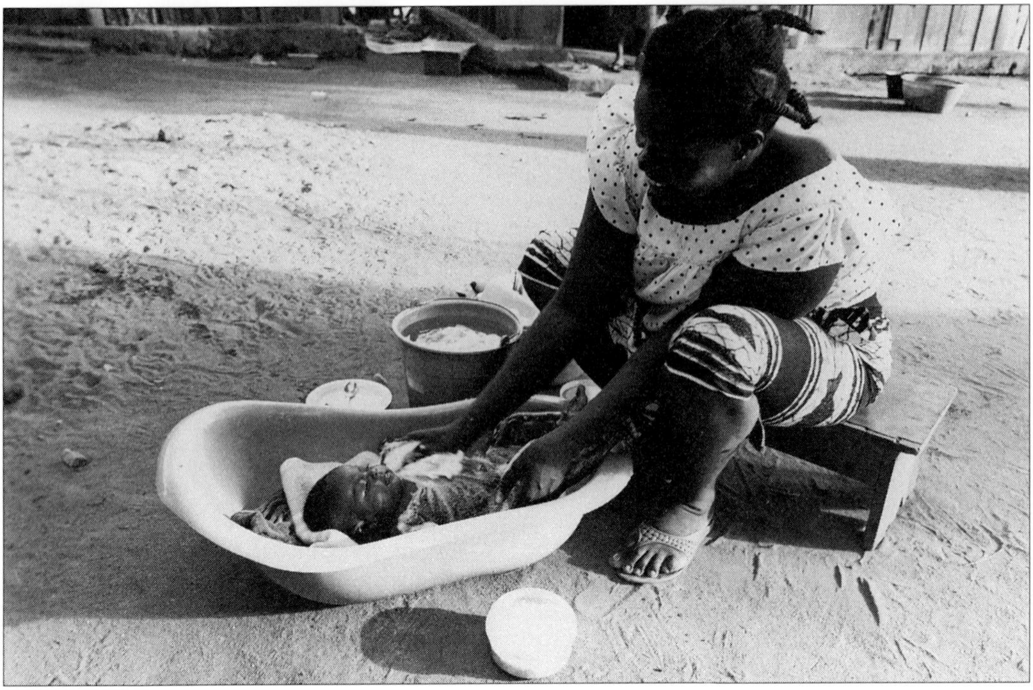

Children want to be nourished emotionally as well as physically. Their innate potential as curious, alert, responsive learners is activated through caring and stimulating relationships. A mother and her child in a settlement near Abidjan, Cote d'Ivoire. UNICEF, Maggie Murray-Lee

mental factors that cut across culture and class, and are fundamental in supporting the resilience of children and their capacity to thrive as confident, capable human beings.

Health and nutrition

Children must have access to the highest possible standards of health and nutrition, not only for physical growth and well-being, but in order to develop in every other way as well. Sickly, malnourished infants and children lack the energy to become actively engaged in the processes that stimulate their development. Even mild malnutrition in young children can cause stunting. Children may be better nourished when they are older, but the effects will still be seen in the growth and capacities of both their bodies and brains.[7] Older children and adolescents continue to need healthy and well-fueled bodies in order to realize their capacity for active learning and involvement. But nutrition and good health are not enough to ensure optimal physical and psychological development.

Reliable love and attention

Children want to be nourished emotionally as well as physically. Their potential as curious, alert, responsive learners is activated largely through interaction with a stimulating, caring social environment.[8] From the beginning of life they appear to crave relationships with people who love them and whom they can love in return. This relationship is usually with the mother, but it can be with any caregiver who is committed to being

[7] See the excellent account of malnutrition in UNICEF (1998) *The State of the World's Children 1998*, New York: Oxford University Press

[8] Bronfenbrenner, U and Ceci S J (1994) 'Nature-Nurture Reconceptualized in Developmental Perspective: a Bioecological Model', *Psychological Review*, 101(4): 568–586

attentive, sensitive and responsive to a child over time. Nor does it have to be a single person – this kind of relationship can flourish with more than one caregiver. The key is that it be continuous and reliable, which implicitly limits the number of people with whom it can take place.

The responsive relationship between child and caregiver becomes more complex as it unfolds, fostering not only emotional bonds but also social and intellectual development.[9] When this relationship is missing, especially during the early years, it has been argued that development on every front can be affected; there can be effects even for physical health and growth. The intimate, reciprocal bond between child and caregivers is the first expression of our capacity to be involved in social relationships based on collaboration and trust; children who are deprived of this experience may find it difficult to form strong, secure and trusting ties with others.

emotional bonds foster development

The realities of poverty and frequent early mortality can discourage in mothers and other caregivers, a willingness to commit themselves emotionally to some infants. Nancy Scheper-Hughes, who worked for many years among the wretchedly poor people of northeastern Brazil has described with compassion the resignation of mothers faced with weak, ailing infants who appear to lack the will for life. These mothers keep an emotional distance from such children, permitting the deaths that seem inevitable, and curtailing lives that appear to be compromised from the start. Neither the financial nor the emotional economy of their situation permits the kind of intense involvement that is so frequently considered to be a 'natural' component of motherhood.[10] It is important to recognize that the quality of emotional care can hinge significantly on a family's life circumstances and on the potential for hope.

security fosters resilience

Emotional support is not only a stimulus for early development. It can also be of untold value throughout childhood and adolescence in supporting the strength of spirit to overcome the damaging effects of poverty and marginalization. The security that grows out of trusting relationships has been found to be one of the most significant protective factors in the life of a child or adolescent who faces adversity and disadvantage.[11] As far as possible, government policies and practices must promote the conditions that support responsive, loving and consistent care for children. These will be discussed in more detail later, especially in Chapters 3, 5 and 8.

Social support for children and caregivers

Providing the involved, sustained care and support that allows a child to thrive calls for time, energy and commitment. The capacity of parents or other caregivers to be available to children at this level is seriously challenged by stressful life circumstances, especially in the absence of support from other adults.[12]

The evidence that children from poor, single parent households are at higher risk for a range of behavioural and educational problems reflects the difficulties of providing for children on one's own.[13] This does not mean that children must come from well-to-do two parent or extended family households in order to develop successfully. Single parent families can function extremely well when there is strong support from other

9 Bronfenbrenner, U (1989) 'Who Cares for Children', UNESCO, Paris

10 Scheper-Hughes, N (1992) *Death without Weeping: The Violence of Everyday Life in Brazil*, Berkeley: University of California Press

11 See Werner, E E and Smith, R S (1992) *Overcoming the Odds: High Risk Children from Birth to Adulthood*, Ithaca NY: Cornell University Press, a longitudinal study of 500 children on the island of Kaiuai from birth to age 30

12 Bronfenbrenner, 1989, op cit Note 9

13 Bronfenbrenner and Ceci, 1994, op cit Note 8

people, be they grandparents, childcare workers or supportive neighbours, either in the home or in the community.[14] But the capacity of any one adult to provide high quality care alone under unfavourable conditions requires disproportionate effort. Through material assistance, sharing of work, and simply listening or giving advice, family, friends and community members can offer critical support that can lessen the negative effects of stress in the life of a child and her caregivers. Local authorities can take a number of measures to promote strong social support systems, and these will be discussed throughout the book (see pp54, 72, 124, 160)

The child's engagement with the world through play

play – a passionate engagement with the world

Development does not just 'happen' to children. Through their involvement in the world around them they are active participants in this reciprocal process. Children have a deep urge for competence and understanding that drives them to watch, touch, imitate, experiment and explore. 'Play' is the term we use to describe this quality of passionate engagement that is driven by the thirst for experience. Healthy, adequately nourished and emotionally secure young children, if they have the opportunity, will spend most of their waking hours actively involved in play, and this is an essential component of their development.[15] Play covers a wide range of behaviour – from noisy physical activity with other children, to quiet and solitary exploration; from spontaneous and unstructured sequences of pretense and imagination, to complex and highly structured games of skill. Play is a highly productive part of growing up; it has been referred to as the child's work, and this is intended most seriously. It is no accident that the most intelligent mammals are also the most playful. Erikson proposed that children's play is the early expression of the human capacity to deal with experience and control reality through experiment and planning.[16] Through this intense interaction with their world, children learn rapidly and acquire the physical, social and mental skills that they need for life. Here are a few examples:

- In active play children learn to use their bodies and to understand their physical relationship with the world. Especially with adequate space and other children to play with, their motor skills and grasp of physical laws and spatial relationships develops rapidly.
- Through their manipulation of objects children begin to understand a number of complex concepts – the properties of different substances, quantity, number and size, the principle of cause and effect, and their own ability to affect and transform their environment. Their mastery of a range of skills gives children a growing sense of competence, and supports the self-assurance necessary for tackling new challenges.
- Play with other children promotes an understanding of social roles and relationships, and provides practice in resolving conflict, agreeing on rules and learning from others. Imaginative play, alone or with other children, is an opportunity to practice the activities that children see around them in daily life, and to experiment with different social roles and ideas.

[14] See, for instance, Garbarino, J (1992) *Children and Families in the Social Environment*, New York: Aldine de Gruyter
[15] Wohlwill, J and Heft, H (1987) 'The Physical Environment and the Development of the Child' in Stokols and Altman, I (eds) *Handbook of Environmental Psychology*, New York: Wiley
[16] Erikson, E H (1950/ 1963) *Childhood and Society*, New York: W W Norton and Company

The way children play and what they play with are determined quite directly by the environment.[17] They should have access to diverse, stimulating, safe environments that give them the chance to explore, pretend, experiment and learn from the results of their own actions. Children also require time for play, and for this they need understanding family members, teachers and even employers. The importance of play is not always understood. Especially in the context of poverty and its demands, play may be seen as a frivolity that interferes with more pressing needs. Parents and others who deal with children should be encouraged to support play as a right for children, and a basic component in the growth of competence and identity. The satisfaction of mastering new skills will drive a child to draw the maximum stimulation from the opportunities around her – the responsibility of parents, communities, and authorities is to ensure that the opportunities are there. We will look at how local authorities can support this vital component of development at different ages and within the different environments that children occupy (see pp84, 134, 157, 180).

play is basic to the growth of competence

diverse, safe stimulating environments

The contribution of parental and cultural beliefs and child rearing practices

From the earliest days of life and even during pregnancy, the ways that parents and other caregivers structure their children's experience is influenced by different beliefs and goals, some determined by the culture, others by the individual family context. Assumptions about feeding, sleeping, schooling, responsibility and discipline are often geared towards adapting a child to particular conditions, and developing the skills that parents believe necessary for successful adult life.[18] The opportunities and constraints that parents and the culture introduce into children's experience help to shape the direction their development takes.

The customs of a particular group may not always be optimal for a child's full development. The decision to restrict a young girl to domestic work at home, for instance, may be a matter of traditional expectations as well as household economy. Parents should be encouraged to consider the long term requirements of their children in the context of contemporary urban life. Solutions can often be found which compromise neither cultural identity nor the child's potential. Culture is dynamic, and the establishment of new norms and values is inevitable as conditions change. It is important for parents to have the opportunity to reflect on these changes, ideally with other parents, as they adapt their child rearing patterns and expectations to new realities (see p161 on parent workshops).

A significant aspect of child rearing has to do with approaches to structure and discipline. These can vary dramatically, and may have implications for the quality of a child's long term relationship to society. A useful framework is Baumrind's classic typology of child rearing styles.[19] She describes three basic patterns of parenting: authoritarian, authoritative and permissive. (These patterns hold true not only for parents and other caregivers, but for all who deal with children across the range of social institutions.)

[17] Valsiner, J (1989) *Human Development and Culture; The Social Nature of Personality and its Study*, Lexington, Massachusetts: Lexington Books

[18] See for example LeVine, R A (1988) 'Human Parental Care: Universal Goals, Cultural Strategies, Individual Behavior' in LeVine, R, Miller, P M, and West, M M (eds) *New Directions for Child Development, 40: Parental Behavior in Diverse Societies*, San Francisco: Jossey Bass;also Ogbu, J (1981) 'Origins of Human Competence: a Cultural-Ecological Perspective', Child Development, 52: 413–429

[19] Baumrind, D (1971) 'Current Patterns of Parental Authority', *Developmental Psychology*, 4, Monograph 1, 1–103; and Baumrind, D (1989) 'Rearing Competent Children' in Damon, W (ed) *Child Development Today and Tomorrow*, San Francisco: Jossey Bass, 349–378

- Authoritarian parents believe that children must be firmly controlled in order to acquire the habits necessary for life. Their word is law, disobedience is punished, and they may offer little praise or affection.
- Permissive parents go to the other extreme and give control over to their children. Discipline is minimal and there is little sense of structure.
- Authoritative parents stress guidance rather than control. They believe that children require clear direction and support; they set limits and enforce rules, but tend to be flexible and responsive to the situation and the individual child. For them, child rearing is a reciprocal process, involving the use of reason and discussion with children.

This framework was developed in North America but is still a useful point of reference. Variation within the categories is to be expected, not only from one society to another, but even between households in the same community. There is no one 'correct' method for raising children, but child rearing styles at the extremes of this continuum can undermine children's capacity to become responsible, thoughtful people. Children raised too permissively are often not accustomed to accepting limits, respecting the rights of others and taking on the responsibilities expected of contributing adults. Also of concern are children raised in strictly authoritarian ways. Stella Ogbuagu, discussing African children, points out that when obedience in a child is the highest value, and opportunities for open discussion or negotiation are few, this may encourage timidity and a lack of inquisitiveness.[20] Children are less likely to be capable of making thoughtful and informed decisions, and will be inclined to follow the lead of any authoritarian figure. In some cases they may come to rebel with anger against authority. Either way, these are not the experiences that build constructive participation in civic life. On the other hand, authoritative parenting, involving give and take, has been found in a number of cultural settings to promote psychosocial competence and academic success.[21]

In many households and communities physical punishment is regarded as an effective means of discipline and a routine, acceptable way of responding to inappropriate behaviour. But it can sometimes be hard to draw the line between firm, loving discipline and excessive violence. Adults who are themselves overwhelmed by stress may be most prone to cross this line.[22] This is more likely to be the case when physical punishment is accepted within a community. In such cases, the frustrations of adults are given precedence over the well-being of children. There is increasing evidence that violence used against children tends to breed violence in children, and that being subjected to the humiliation of either physical abuse or mental cruelty may shape children's development to the long term detriment of all.[23]

The experience of violence, especially for very young children, whether directed at themselves or others, can be seriously traumatizing. A research group looking at the effects of violence for children under three years of age points out that children this young have fewer ways to communicate their fears, and less capacity to understand violence or accept reassurance. Exposure to serious or repeated violence may under-

[20] Ogbuagu, S C (1994) 'Facilitating the Empowerment of African Children for the Defence of their Rights' in Pearce, T O and Falola, T (eds) *Child Health in Nigeria: The Impact of Depressed Economy*, Aldershot, United Kingdom: Avebury

[21] Kagitçibasi, C (1996) *Family and Human Development Across Cultures*, Mahwah, New Jersey: Lawrence Erlbaum reviews some of these studies. Also a study among the Yoruba of Lagos, Nigeria, found that children who received less harsh treatment from caregivers, and experienced more affection and intimacy, tested higher in measures of cognitive and social competence (Zeitlin, M F and Babatunde, E D (1995) 'The Yoruba Family: Kinship, Socialization and Child Development' in Zeitlin, M F, Megawangi, R, Krameret, E M (eds) *Strengthening the Family: Implications for International Development*, Tokyo, New York, Paris: United Nations University Press)

[22] An excellent review of literature related to this topic is McLoyd, V C (1990) 'The Impact of Economic Hardship on Black Families and Children: Psychological Distress, Parenting, and Socioemotional Development', *Child Development*, 61: 311–346

[23] Newell, P (1997) 'Children and Violence', *Innocenti Digest #2*, Florence, UNICEF International Child Development Centre

mine their basic sense of trust and cause them to respond to the world with fear and confusion. Instead of eagerly exploring their surroundings, they are likely to become withdrawn and apathetic, or in some cases to become increasingly aggressive. The significance for their overall development can be profound.[24]

the impact of violence for small children

Local authorities must recognize that the ways children are treated can ripple out to affect the whole society. Parents and other caregivers, as well as those dealing with children in an official capacity, must be encouraged to reject violence as a means of solving problems, and to respond to children in ways that encourage their development as healthy, effective, responsible people (See also pp82, 128, 174).

Children as active agents in their own development

Children are not passively shaped by external forces. They respond to the world and take an active role in constructing their own lives.[25] From the young infant who decides when to accept eye contact and when to reject it, to the adolescent who makes strategic and responsible decisions about her life, children are part of a reciprocal process.

This capacity and desire on the part of children to participate in creating their world and themselves is not only a developmental reality, but also a clearly articulated right within the Convention (Article 12). It is a mistake to assume that the right to express views and have them taken seriously is relevant only for those children who are mature and confident enough to make formal verbal claims on the adult world. Whenever children make choices on their own behalf, they are expressing their views and preferences. The small child's desire to climb a flight of stairs is as valid as an older child's request for relevant education. Taking a child's views seriously does not mean allowing a one year-old to climb to unprotected heights; it means acknowledging the drive for exploration and competence, and helping that child find safe ways to act on her self-expressed needs. Providing children and adolescents with environments that make choices possible, and respecting the impulses underlying these choices, can help them to draw the greatest benefit from their urge to be active in their own development. Within any cultural setting, it is important to learn how children understand their own lives, and to build on this, as well as on adult understandings of their 'best interests', in developing adequate local supports.

responding to children's drive for competence

The broader ecology of children's development

The factors that best support children's development are profoundly affected by larger realities. Employment opportunities, housing possibilities, levels of discrimination and exclusion, the availability of schooling, health care and other services all contribute to determining the opportunities available to a child or adolescent. Families in poverty or social upheaval have comparatively little control over the complex ecology of their children's lives. Because of the constraints under which they operate, the decisions they make on a day-to-day basis are likely to be responses to immediate needs rather than long term goals. Their

24 Osofsky, J D and Fenichel, E (eds) (1994) *Caring for Infants and Toddlers in Violent Environments: Hurt, Healing, and Hope*, Arlington, Virginia: Zero to Three/ National Center for Clinical Infant Programs

25 See Hutchby, I and Ellis, J M (1998) *Children and Social Competence: Arenas of Action*, London: Falmer Press; also Valsiner, J (ed) (1988) *Child Development Within Culturally Structured Environments*, Norwood, New Jersey: Ablex

children's longer term interests may be repeatedly required to take second place to the pressing concerns of the moment.

The Convention requires that parents and other family members be assisted where necessary in providing for their children's needs. Part of this unquestionably lies in providing the level of control in life that is essential both to respond to immediate needs and to make informed, long term decisions. Whether their official role is that of direct provision, or simply that of coordination and indirect support, local governments can influence substantially the capacity of caregivers and communities to care for their children, and to provide the opportunities they need. They can also, as we suggested above, support the desire of children and adolescents to contribute to their own development. We will discuss the developmental agenda of children at different ages, and consider how local authorities can best provide support throughout children's lives.

THE DEVELOPMENTAL EXPERIENCE AND REQUIREMENTS OF CHILDREN AT DIFFERENT AGES

The CRC refers to children's physical, mental, social, moral and spiritual development. These categories are not separate domains, but a way of simplifying our understanding of a complex whole. The various dimensions of a child's development are closely connected and interdependent – emotional suffering, for instance, can interfere with the absorption of nutrients and normal physical growth; and a hungry body undermines a child's capacity to learn.

'stages' of development – an artificial construct

It is also artificial to look at children's lives in terms of neatly defined 'stages' of development. This has been commonly accepted in developmental psychology, but experience shows that children's capacities and need for support at different ages are affected by the realities of their lives and the expectations imposed on them. But it is also true that the supports required by most two year-olds will not be useful to most adolescents. Some broad age-related categories are useful in defining the responsibilities of local agencies. The following discussion is not an attempt to impose a rigid time frame on children's lives, but to provide some practical guidance which should be interpreted and applied in terms of local realities.

Infants and toddlers

The first two or three years of life, along with the months before birth, are widely considered to be the most significant for a child's long term development. Interventions during this period can be particularly powerful in their effect. Infants born without complications and then adequately nourished grow rapidly in the first year. Inadequate nutrition is a critical insult during this period, affecting not only growth, but development on every front.[26] In the second and third years, although the rate of growth slows down, adequate nutrition continues to be essential.

[26] UNICEF (1998) *The State of the World's Children 1998*, New York: Oxford University Press

Young children are drawn to imitate the actions they see around them every day, and to make sense of the world and their own place in it. Two small girls play at washing clothes in Llallagua, Bolivia. UNICEF 1997 Alejandro Balaguer

Assuming a reasonable level of health, infant motor development follows a similar pattern worldwide. From the time infants are first able to move around they increasingly explore their surroundings, and this activity tends to reach a peak at about two or three years of age. The activity and curiosity of young children who are learning about their world is an important part of healthy development, but it can be trying for caregivers, especially in environments that do not lend themselves easily to a child's desire for exploration. It is important for children this age to learn to deal with restrictions, but it is also important to their confidence and mental growth that they not be overly restricted. An environment that is both safe and stimulating is a high priority. There should be support for families in creating household environments that allow for safe exploration and play (see p84).

From their earliest days, infants are equipped to be communicative social partners, and within the first few months their smiles, gestures and vocalizations allow for increasingly complex interactions. Not all societies respond to these behaviours in the same way. In some cases touch is a more common means of communicating with infants than eye-to-eye contact or vocalization. Whatever form it takes, communication itself is a vital stimulus to an infant's social and mental development. Malnourished infants are less able to elicit responses from their caregivers, who may themselves be overstressed and debilitated. Even from these early days, the effects of poverty shape a child's opportunities for development.

During the first year of life, infants across cultures tend to become especially attached to their primary caregivers, and to protest or become disturbed when they are separated from the people they love and trust. This attachment continues through the early years, and provides a secure

[27] Bowlby, J (1969) *Attachment and Loss: Vol 1 Attachment*, New York: Basic Books; Valsiner, J (ed) (1988) *Child Development Within Culturally Structured Environments*, Norwood, New Jersey: Ablex

base for the child's exploration of the world. The child who has experienced the security of healthy attachment early in life is well equipped to develop into a trusting and confident individual.[27] This depends not only on the reliable presence of familiar caregivers, but on being kept for the most part well-fed, warm and dry in a fairly predictable and kindly way. There are important implications for the continuity of care that is made available to children in their earliest months and years. This does not mean that care outside the home should not be considered – in many cases it is unavoidable if mothers or other primary caregivers are to be wage earners. But such care should be consistent and of high quality.

identifying disabilities

Early identification of disabilities in infants and young children is important so that appropriate support and stimulation can be provided from the earliest months (see also pp86, 161). Traditionally, these early years are thought of as the domain of parents, but there is a good deal that local authorities can do to foster positive development even at this age. All these measures will be discussed in greater detail in following chapters.

- *Provide prenatal care for mothers, support for breastfeeding (pp62, 65), primary health care for mother and child, and feeding programmes where appropriate (pp103, 113).*
- *Establish simple birth registration procedures to ensure that services will not be denied for lack of identification (p66).*
- *Provide assessment and appropriate interventions for children with disabilities (pp86, 109, 161).*
- *Ensure adequate supplies of clean water close by, safe sanitation and sustainable waste management, and support clean, safe household environments for play and exploration (pp74, 84, 96).*
- *Establish household-level monitoring procedures on the health, growth and development of young children (p104).*
- *Provide education on nutritional awareness, household hygiene, injury prevention and the developmental needs of infants and toddlers (pp78, 115, 160).*
- *Promote the provision of suitable work opportunities for mothers and high quality child care (pp50, 152).*

Early childhood

language

The period from roughly two and-a-half to six years of age is still a time of rapid learning, growth and development. The most notable achievement is the continued acquisition of language; a young child's growing skill in this area allows for ever more complex human interactions. Language also supports the development of symbolic thought, and mental growth moves rapidly forward during this period.

imaginative play

Young children's desire to understand the world continues to be expressed through avid interaction with their social and physical surroundings. Children become gradually more cooperative, inclusive and hungry for group play. Through imaginative play, both alone and with others, they strive to imitate the actions they see around them, and to make sense of the world and their own place in it. This dramatic play is also a chance to express the fears and anxieties that can beset them. Although children may thrive in response to the opportunities offered to them at a creche, child care centre or nursery school, they tend to remain emotionally dependent on their primary caregivers.

traffic

Contact with other children stimulates social development, but it is also important that children have clean, safe space for play that is both familiar, diverse and ideally within sight of home.

It is critical that young children be protected from traffic. Although they may appear competent to handle themselves safely from an early age, traffic remains a considerable hazard. Even cautious and carefully trained children are ill-equipped to deal with traffic. Research in the North has shown that the capacity to localize the sound of an approaching car or to predict the speed at which it is moving is still quite limited before the age of six or seven.[28]

imitating behaviour

As part of their interest in imitating the behaviour of those around them, young children are increasingly able to use toilets, wash their hands and dispose of garbage. This is the ideal time for instilling a consciousness of hygienic behaviour. If appropriate facilities are available, such learning can happen more easily. It becomes increasingly important during this period to find ways to build on the strengths of children with disabilities, to encourage the development of skills that will permit self-sufficiency and a sense of confidence, and to allow for interaction with other children.

- *Continue providing the environmental supports necessary for healthy development.*
- *Support the provision of non-threatening toilets, easy to reach water sources, and waste disposal containers appropriate for the use of young children (p75).*
- *Using outreach workers, continue to monitor neighbourhoods to determine which households are in need of assistance with their children*
- *Support neighbourhood residents in creating safe, contained play spaces close to home, and responsive to the physical and social needs of young children (p85).*
- *Ensure adequate protection from traffic (p132).*
- *Provide support for early child development centers, as well as for parents at home (p157).*
- *Support provision of community and family-based rehabilitation for children with disabilities (p109).*

growing competence

Middle childhood

The years from approximately 6 to 12 are a time of growing competence and independence for children, both physically and psychologically. They grow more slowly during this period, and this allows for improved physical control. They delight in practising and refining their physical skills, and need environments that allow for challenge and a range of activity. As they grow older, children want not simply to imitate but actually to master the skills that are valued within a culture. Growing physical competence, together with important developments in understanding

[28] Ward, C (1978) *The Child and the City*, London: Architectural Press

excessive demands

and social abilities at the age of six or seven, lead almost every culture to begin assigning greater responsibility to children at this period.[29] They can follow complex instructions, and are more frequently given tasks that do not involve direct adult supervision.

It is important that their competence be exercised in ways that support continued development and growth. Parents, especially if they are poor and overburdened, may be pressed to make excessive demands on their children, sending them out to work long hours, or expecting them to assume a heavy load of responsibility at home. Children may be capable of handling these demands, but will pay a price over the long term if their opportunities to play, rest and learn are threatened. Formal schooling generally begins at this age. The same intellectual development that allows children to appreciate rules and to take a larger perspective, also enables them to understand and enjoy complex systems and logical principles, and gives them a readiness for formal learning.

independence

School-age children for the most part enjoy spending time with peers. Increasingly, they have the ability to form and maintain close friendships, and to understand the perspective of others. Ideally, their surroundings should support their growing sociability and independence, allowing them to move out into the community and become competent in navigating a larger world. If facilities are too distant and neighbourhoods unsafe, children's ability to take charge of their lives will be compromised. This is particularly so for girls. Too often, just when independence becomes increasingly possible, the freedom of girls is more severely constrained because of fears for their safety and the expectation that they will take on a range of domestic chores.

participation

The growing capacity of children, both intellectually and socially, to make responsible decisions needs to be respected and supported, not only in the home but in the community. Offering children opportunities to participate in community action and decision making will support their development as responsible citizens. This may present a challenge for officials in communities where the opinions and involvement of children are not valued.

- *Locate schools, recreational facilities, cultural opportunities and other community resources for children, including children with disabilities, within easy access of their dwellings (pp136, 177).*
- *Promote measures to guarantee physically and socially secure neighborhoods (pp124, 132).*
- *Provide support for cultural diversity and for the open celebration of differences within the community (p142).*
- *Provide education to support healthy lifestyles and responsible decision making (pp116, 119, 176).*
- *Determine which children are unable to attend school, and for what reasons, and provide household assistance where possible (p168).*
- *Provide childcare services to ensure that older siblings are free to attend school (p152).*
- *Raise general awareness of the need to foster citizenship skills in children; create opportunities for the meaningful participation of children in community development projects and care of the local environment (pp149, 172, 181, 259).*

[29] Whiting, B B and Edwards, C P1988) *Children of Different Worlds: The Formation of Social Behavior*, Cambridge MA: Harvard University Press

Adolescence

Adolescence, generally thought of as the years from about 12 onwards, is a period of rapid growth and development. In the few short years of puberty, earlier for girls than for boys, children go through the dramatic transition of becoming adults This is also a time of intense psychological activity, some of it related to the hormonal changes of puberty and the child's emerging sexuality, and some connected to the pressures that accompany the transition to the social role of adulthood.

the transition to adulthood

These pressures vary from one society to another, and can be different for boys and girls. Among more traditional groups, the physical changes of adolescence are often accompanied by clear social expectations and equally clear changes in status. Rituals frequently formalize the transition from childhood to adulthood and provide guidelines for young people stepping into new social roles. But where young people face rapid social change, especially in complex urban areas, the transitions of adolescence are seldom so clearly defined. Many adolescents may find themselves anxiously in search of an identity. They yearn to build a meaningful place for themselves in the world and may find few constructive ways of doing this. Young people of this age are often in a kind of limbo. They have the bodies and mental capacities of adults, but are not accorded the respect and autonomy that accompanies adulthood. They are increasingly ready for serious commitment, but may find they have limited options in life and little opportunity to develop their skills and their ability to contribute.

challenging behaviour

Adolescence is a time of acute self-awareness. This can be the source of positive reflection and growth, but also cause retreat and painful isolation. A common response for many young people is to take refuge in the security of peer group allegiance. Tensions and uncertainty can underlie many of the behaviours that are challenging, even threatening, for family and others, and for the personal health and well-being of young people themselves. Sexual experimentation, drug use, gang membership and illegal activity are frequently expressions of loneliness, confusion and the yearning to belong. The willingness to take risks can express the desire of adolescents to find acceptance and to prove themselves, but also their lack of hope for the future.

allowing for continued growth

Not all adolescents challenge the values and expectations of adult society. Many have already assumed the full range of adult responsibility, working long hours, supporting themselves and often their families. In some countries early marriage is the norm, and many teenage girls are already mothers. But because an adolescent is able to perform adult functions does not mean this is ideal. Assuming responsibility is an important part of development. But it can also expose young people to unnecessary risk and close off the potential for further growth and learning. For many girls, adolescence may mean a new isolation. Activities that were enjoyed by an eight or ten year-old, including schooling and play, may no longer be acceptable once a girl reaches puberty. Instead, she will be required to stay close to home, out of the public eye, and her opportunities in life may be constrained more than ever.

a time of potential

Adolescence is a time of great potential, not only for young people themselves but for those around them who can benefit from their energy, intensity and strong ideals. With supportive opportunities, places and role models, adolescents are likely to be among the more creative, productive members of society. As they mature, they have a growing capacity both for complex and abstract thought, and for deep commitment. When these capacities are nurtured through appropriate schooling or other supportive experiences, adolescents become increasingly skilled at applying critical and logical thinking in constructive ways, and at taking a moral and committed stance on issues that affect themselves and their communities. Those who deal with adolescents should recognize and respect their potential, and provide them with the opportunities not only to discover this potential but to prove it to others in productive ways as they move into adulthood. Because of their capacity for coming to harm, adolescents need protection as well as opportunity. It is essential that through education, health services, legal protection, and appropriate juvenile justice, they receive the support and guidance they need to negotiate their way through this vulnerable period.

the need for opportunities

- *Support education, both formal and non-formal, to ensure that young peoples' options for the future remain as broad as possible (pp184, 186).*
- *Provide health care appropriate to the needs of adolescents, including reproductive health care, and education on substance abuse, sexually transmitted disease and other health issues (p117).*
- *For adolescents who are working, ensure that working conditions are appropriate, and that there is the possibility for education, rest and recreation (p206).*
- *Support appropriate, accessible opportunities for sport and recreation (p137).*
- *Encourage young people to be centrally involved in planning and managing their own programmes and organizations (pp128, 137).*
- *Allow for opportunities to participate in local decision making, especially in areas that specifically affect adolescents (pp149, 259).*
- *Work to eliminate gender barriers in opportunities for education, recreation, meaningful work and participation in community (pp138, 168).*
- *Provide access to assistive technologies, education, recreation and sports, vocational training and preparation for gainful employment for adolescents with disabilities (pp169, 211).*
- *Establish access to legal protections for those in conflict with the law, and responses appropriate to the age of offenders (p225).*

CHILDREN WHO FACE SPECIAL DEVELOPMENTAL CHALLENGES

Some groups of children are at particular risk of missing the opportunities they need, and are most likely to be victims of discrimination that is systemic, entrenched and sometimes even unconscious. Local authorities must make particular efforts to be aware of these children, to act as advocates for them, and to support their equal rights.

Children in severe poverty

Poverty is the single most formidable obstacle to children's well-being. Infants born into poverty are more likely to have malnourished and debilitated mothers, and to be born underweight and undernourished themselves, a significant risk to their subsequent health and well-being (see Chapter 4). Mortality rates for young children in deprived urban areas can be many times higher than in wealthier neighbourhoods.[30] Supportive environments can counteract many of the effects of low birth weight and ill health, but these supports are unlikely to be present for children in severe poverty. Instead, inadequate food, poor sanitation, unclean water and polluted air may result in malnutrition, frequent illness and apathy. These mental and physical insults, combined with a lack of stimulation and opportunity, and the level of stress experienced by their overburdened caregivers, mean that these children will be seriously handicapped in reaching their full potential. It is disturbing to contemplate the talents, vision and productive energy that may be forever lost to a community through its failure to protect its youngest members from the burdens of poverty and disadvantage.

the absence of critical supports

Many children in poverty become workers early in their lives, and this creates particular challenges for development. Work can be a source of learning and socialization, but for too many children in poverty it means long hours spent in repetitive or arduous labor. Working conditions can be seriously damaging to health, and children may carry the effects throughout their lives. Time devoted to work is time taken away from the rest, play and education necessary for optimal development.

child work

- *Identify families most in need of support through community-based assessment.*
- *Promote job training and support for microenterprise (p50).*
- *Ensure accessible, affordable primary health care for these households (p100).*
- *Support high quality child care services, so that adults can work (p152).*
- *See Chapter 10 for recommendations for working children.*

Girls

early discrimination

The challenges for children in poverty are frequently compounded for girls. In many societies, and especially among people for whom resources are limited, it is not unusual to find that boys are given preferential treatment. Discrimination can begin even before birth, when parents who have the option may decide to abort female fetuses.[31] Although figures are hard to come by, it is generally accepted that far more girls than boys are victims of infanticide. During the early weeks and months, girl infants, despite their greater biological resilience, die at higher rates than boys because of shorter breastfeeding and less attention to health care. During early childhood, girls are more frequently ill and undernourished. A study in India reported that among pre-school children 71 per cent of girls were severely malnourished, as compared to only 28 per cent of

30 Stephens, C (1996) 'Healthy Cities or Unhealthy Islands? The Health and Social Implications of Urban Inequality', *Environment and Urbanization*, 8(2): 9–30

31 Narasimhan, S (1993) 'The Unwanted Sex', *The New Internationalist*, (240)

boys.[32] In Bangladesh, girls between the ages of one and four are almost twice as likely to die as boys.[33]

lack of opportunity

Of the world's children who are not in school, two-thirds are girls.[34] Their education is more likely to be considered unimportant or to be interrupted by domestic duties, which are often burdensome enough to deny them time for rest or play. Although official figures show that more boys work than girls, many girls are involved in undocumented hidden occupations such as domestic service, working long arduous hours for little or no pay. The daily work burden of girls is commonly far greater than that of boys. Lacking skills and education, girls are often married off at an early age, sometimes for the financial gain of their families. Babies born to adolescent girls, aside from being at risk themselves, cause extra health risks for their mothers. Girls under 19 are twice as to likely to die from complications in childbirth as women in their twenties; and girls under 15 are at still greater risk.[35] The net result of nutritional deprivation, a lack of education, overwork, and a general dearth of opportunity is that millions of girls never reach their full potential. This is a personal tragedy, a threat to the next generation, and a loss for the world.

overwork

early marriage

- *Raise general awareness of the equal rights of girls, and the particular needs of girls.*
- *Pay special attention to the health and nutrition of girls, especially in the earliest years.*
- *Make high quality schooling more accessible for girls and more acceptable to parents (p168).*
- *Provide high quality reproductive health care for girls and women (p60).*
- *Promote equal opportunities for participation for girls and young women.*

Children with disabilities

Poor children with disabilities can face overwhelming developmental challenges. With appropriate training, and through the thoughtful modification of their environments, many children with disabilities can be supported to achieve a wider range of skills, and helped to live independent, fulfilling lives. But for children in poverty, there may be few opportunities for training and skilled support, and the capacity of their caregivers to modify physical environments may be extremely limited. Children with disabilities may become increasingly handicapped as a consequence of inattention and local constraints.[36]

Attitudes towards disabilities vary between cultures. A condition that meets with acceptance and respect in one society may inspire hostility and ostracism in another. Children may face greater difficulty in situations where achievement is highly prized. They may also be disproportionately singled out for abuse and harsh treatment.[37] But even where they are treated with warmth and compassion, there may be an assumption that their condition is the will of God and should not call for active intervention. An attitude of acceptance is not to be lightly dismissed. But adherence to the provisions of the Convention, and respect for the

32 Boyden, J and Holden, P (1991) *Children of the Cities*, London: Zed Books
33 Cameron, S, Kandula, N, Leng, J, Arnold, C (1998) *Urban Childcare in Bangladesh*, Save the Children (USA)
34 Friedman, S A (1998) *Girls at Work*, New York: UNICEF
35 United Nations (1991) *The World's Women: Trends and Statistics 1970–1990*, New York: United Nations
36 Werner, D (1987) *Disabled Village Children: A Guide for Community Health Workers, Rehabilitation Workers, and Families*, Palo Alto CA: The Hesperian Foundation
37 Boyden and Holden 1991, op cit Note 31

child's identity and for his or her capacity to have the greatest degree possible of control over life, dictates that every effort be made to build this capacity and support the acquisition of skills.

- *Support programmes that prevent disabilities, such as salt iodisation, folate supplements in pregnancy, and vitamin A to prevent blindness (p61).*
- *Raise general awareness of the rights of children with disabilities, and work to discourage discrimination.*
- *Offer education and assistance to parents in providing appropriate care for their children (pp86, 109, 161).*
- *Support community-based rehabilitation services (p109).*
- *Ensure that appropriate and non-discriminatory education is available to children with disabilities (p169).*
- *Ensure access to training and opportunities for meaningful work for young people with disabilities (p211).*
- *Eliminate physical barriers in the community that reduce access for those with disabilities (p139).*

necessary investment minimal relative to the return

The basic supports for children's development are relatively simple. Responsive, loving care and attention to their physical requirements can ensure that they have the opportunity to become bright, capable and productive human beings with the ability to lead fulfilling lives. The investment required is minimal relative to the return. The failure to make this investment is shockingly expensive, both in practical and moral terms. Unfortunately it is also all too common – priorities for children are routinely dismissed as insignificant in the context of a city's 'larger' problems. A fundamental change in attitude at all levels is essential if cities are to take the enlightened course of supporting the development and the rights of all their youngest citizens. Constructive responses to children's rights occur best within an understanding of their development, but must be understood and elaborated in the light of local realities.

Strong families, regardless of their size and composition, provide a stable, nurturing environment that can buffer children from inappropriate stress during their years of growth and dependence. The best way to realize the rights of most children is to ensure that their families have access to the conditions that will allow them to establish and sustain stability. A Haitian woman and her daughter. UNICEF, Nicole Toutounji

3 Stable Families

Most children grow up within a family, where close connections can provide warmth and security, and where relationships and daily activities echo the values and realities of the larger world. A strong family can be a stable, nurturing environment that is flexible enough to adapt to changing circumstances and to buffer children from inappropriate stress during their years of growth and dependence. The Convention places repeated emphasis on the importance of family as an environment for the development and well-being of children. Only in the most extreme cases, when children are abused, neglected or seriously exploited, does it consider that alternatives to family life are appropriate (Article 19).

Some critics have argued that the Convention pays insufficient attention to extended family and to the informal fostering arrangements that are commonplace in many countries and especially in the South.[1] The document does refer repeatedly to 'parents', but Article 5 makes it clear that the rights and responsibilities of parents are understood to extend to relatives and even to community members 'as provided for by local custom'. Responsibility for a child's care depends on local traditions, patterns of residence, relationships with kin and community members, as well as economic pressures and realities. A child may have a number

[1] Burman, E (1996) 'Local, Global or Globalized? Child Development and International Child Rights Legislation', *Childhood*, 3(1): 45–67

of adults who take an active role in her life, or she may be raised alone by a working grandmother. The Convention acknowledges the variations imposed by culture and circumstance, and recognizes the profound importance of even the most vulnerable families to the children who depend on them.

CHANGING SOCIAL REALITIES

Around the world observers have pointed to the erosion of traditional extended family over the last century. Migration to cities has been accompanied everywhere by fundamental changes in the social fabric and in household organization.[2] This has been in large part an adaptation to physical and economic conditions. Smaller family groups are more mobile and can more easily follow opportunities for work. In cities, where accomodations are tight and overcrowded, a smaller group may be more likely to find a place to live. In global terms, this process has been reported as a significant shift towards the nuclear family, away from extended kinship support.

This generalization oversimplifies a complex phenomenon. Although there has been a trend towards smaller family units, extended family continues to serve as a survival strategy in many urban areas. Nuclear families, once established, may expand into extended households as they take in relatives in an attempt to provide a safety net or to pool resources more effectively. Even where families live in smaller groups, relatives may live in close proximity and continue to function as extended family in terms of mutual support. Many urban households also continue to have close and mutually supportive connections with rural family members.[3]

These complexities notwithstanding, it is clear that urban realities, particularly for those in poverty, have contributed to changes in household organization, and that these changes have in general, decreased the availability of nurturant adults for children. Not only are there fewer concerned adults in their lives, but those who are there are less likely to be working in the immediate vicinity. Overall there has been a dramatic increase not only in smaller households, but in the number of single parents raising children, and particularly in the incidence of households where a single mother is the sole source of support either temporarily or longer term.[4]

Children can thrive within a wide range of family forms. No one kind of family can be considered 'best' for their needs, and it is a mistake to view single parent households as deviant family forms. But throughout the world women earn less than men, and female headed households are disproportionately poor.[5] No matter how dedicated and determined a caregiver a solo mother may be balancing the conflicting claims of child rearing, household management, and financial support often means making compromises, especially in the absence of strong support systems, and children can be short-changed in the process.

At the same time, it is true that in many cases children may do better in households maintained by women.[6] Although women earn less than men, they have long been observed to be more responsible and cautious fiscal managers with an eye on children's survival, well-being and long

[2] See for example Zeitlin, M F, Megawangi,R, Kramer,E, Colletta, N. Babatunde, E D and Garman, D (1995) *Strengthening the Family: Implications for International Development*, Tokyo, New York, Paris: United Nations University Press

[3] Tacoli, C (1998) 'Beyond the Rural Urban Divide', *Environment and Urbanization*, 10(1): 3–4

[4] Lloyd, C B and Duffy, N (1995) 'Families in Transition' in J Bruce, Lloyd, C B and Leonard, A (eds) *Families in Focus: New Perspectives on Mothers, Fathers, and Children*, New York: The Population Council

[5] UNDP (1994) *Human Development Report 1994*, New York, Oxford: Oxford University Press

[6] O'Connell, H (1994) *Women and the Family*, London and New Jersey: Zed Books

term success.[7] Some studies have shown that children in such households are less likely to be withdrawn from school and have better diets than children in households headed by men with similar incomes.[8] Regardless of family make-up, a strong social support system is invaluable in raising children, decreasing vulnerability and serving as a buffer in times of stress (see p21).

The larger economic picture

urban poverty

The large migration flows to and between cities in recent decades have been a response to the search for livelihood and improved opportunities. But the number of urban families with inadequate incomes has also grown rapidly. The relative concentrations of wealth and services in cities create the impression that city dwellers are better off than those in rural areas. But such assessments are based on averages that ignore the huge disparities between affluent and poor in urban areas. More than a third of the urban dwellers in Africa, Asia and Latin America live in conditions of considerable hardship, and their numbers are growing all the time. Their dependence on a cash income limits their options for livelihood and survival. Nor is meeting basic needs a function of money alone. It is also a matter of access to the resources and services that are essential to an adequate standard of living. Vast numbers of urban residents are excluded from such access because of serious inequities in the allocation of social resources. City living can be harsh indeed for those who are condemned to overcrowding, a lack of water, poor sanitation, inadequate transport, pollution, disease and noise.

exclusion and inequality

Fundamental to the ecology of urban poverty is the pervasive influence of the global market economy on peoples' lives. In many countries, the supports available to the poor have been reduced – heavy debt burdens, poor economic performance and structural adjustment have resulted in cuts to public services and a lack of new investment. This has also helped to create a climate of competition which undermines collaboration and solidarity, leaving in their place hostility, suspicion and confrontation over scarce resources.[9] At the same time, the mass media reach further into the lives of the poor, and the culture of consumption creates desires and needs that can seldom be fulfilled. This is felt most dramatically in cities, where wealth and abundance exist alongside stark poverty. The sense of opportunity that cities can promote is overshadowed for many by deep frustration and dissatisfaction.

Routes to disintegration and failure

There are certainly urban families in poverty which remain strong and intact, and somehow manage to provide the physical and emotional support their children need. We can learn a good deal from their coping strategies. But too often the capacity of poor parents to provide for their children depends on factors beyond their control, and many families are truly at risk of failure. Raising children who are healthy, safe, confident and equipped to deal with the responsibilities of adult life is a challenge for every caregiver. But to manage this in the face of

[7] See for example Lee Smith, D and Schlyter, A (1991) 'Women, Environment and Urbanization: Editor's Introduction', *Environment and Urbanization*, 3(2): 3–6; and UNDP (1995) 'Living Arrangements of Women and their Children in Developing Countries', Department for Economic and Social Information and Policy Analysis, Population Division, United Nations

[8] United Nations (1991) *The World's Women: Trends and Statistics 1970–1990*, New York: United Nations

[9] Moser, C O N, Herbert, A J, Makonnen, R E (1993) 'Urban Poverty in the Context of Structural Adjustment: Recent Evidence and Policy Responses', Washington DC: Urban Development Division, World Bank, TWU Discussion paper 140

squalid living conditions, underemployment and inadequate social support is a daunting task. How does one care for a two-year-old when there is no clean water to drink, and no way to keep the flies off his food; when the nearest toilet is a dilapidated, filthy latrine at the end of the street, and the only place to play contains an open sewer and an unguarded cooking stove? How can an eight-year-old be ensured an education when her school uniform costs more than the family earns in a month, when the school is a dangerous mile away, and when she is needed at home to carry water and help with younger children? The pressures that cause families to fail their children often take the form of unforgiving choices. To invest in schooling means cutting back on food; to take a sick child to the health clinic means losing a day's wages; to pay for the treatment of a parent's chronic illness means sending a ten-year-old out to work.

unforgiving choices

The assets that a poor family can call on in the face of adversity are limited, and usually consist of little more than their own time and labour. The most common response is for women to take on extra work, often in demanding jobs with long hours and low pay. When mothers work, there are frequently no adults in the household during the day and children may be inadequately supervised, especially in the absence of extended family support. In Dhaka, Bangladesh it was found that 20 per cent of the children under five of women working in garment factories, lived away from their families because of the lack of child care in the city.[10] In some cases, because of inadequate supervision, children are locked in their homes while parents are away at work. Frequently older children, most often girls, are required to leave school to care for younger siblings. Even when this is not the case, the lack of adult supervision may interfere with school attendance, and children are more likely to be drawn to life on the street.

extra work for women

lack of child care

It is easier when mothers can create money-making opportunities at home. But even then they are likely to be torn by the conflicting demands of household management and income generation, and forced to turn to children for help. The more vulnerable a family is, the more inevitably it will rely on children's labour, either outside the home supplementing family income, or within the home freeing up others to work.[11] This too easily becomes a burden that affects health and interferes with play, rest and education. The vast majority of poor working children attend school only sporadically or not at all, and their long term chances of success are sacrificed to their families' immediate needs. In extreme cases, as when children are sold into grinding bonded labour or prostitution, the damage can be profound (p190).

relying on children's work

The very strategies families employ to decrease vulnerability can have the perverse effect of adding stress and contributing to failure over the long term. Single mothers, for instance, often remarry or take on companions to reduce their insecurity. But such liaisons frequently result in increased hardship for children, who may be resented, and either victimized or sent away to live with relatives. Some families, in an attempt to pool scarce resources, may take relatives into their household. But when employment is scarce, such an arrangement may mean a higher ratio of dependent household members to those producing an income, and effectively undermine the family's capacity to cope. Almost invariably it means additional crowding with its attendant stresses.

[10] Cameron, S, Kandula, N, Leng, J, Arnold, C (1998) *Urban Childcare in Bangladesh*, Save the Children (USA)
[11] Moser and Herbert, 1996, op cit Note 9

When adults are exhausted and overworked, when access to basic amenities is difficult, and when resources are too limited to fill the needs of all, it is inevitable that children will be neglected to a degree. In some cases neglect may be selective and even purposeful – some children may suffer in order to improve the chances of others. Girls are frequently less well-nourished than boys, for instance, and infants who seem ill-equipped for survival may be ignored or abandoned.[12] Such discriminatory treatment seems heartless and even shocking, but the real crime is the situation that imposes such choices.

neglect

The pressures and anxieties of marginal living can also contribute to conflict within the family, and may lead to abusiveness. Parents who are overwhelmed and undersupported are more likely to be harsh in their treatment of children.[13] Cross-cultural research points to higher rates of child abuse and neglect in cities, especially in areas undergoing rapid social or economic change.[14] Men may feel that they have no productive role when they fail to earn enough, and may take out their frustration on their wives and children. Studies report connections between declining male incomes and both increased alcohol use and domestic violence.[15] There is increased likelihood that adults will become abusive towards children when stress and anxiety are combined with high levels of violence within society, and with a cultural acceptance of physical discipline (see also p81). The most vulnerable children have been identified as those from families that are socially isolated and separated from traditional patterns of child rearing, or from households that include stepfathers or other unrelated males.[16] Abusiveness within the family becomes a significant factor in pushing children towards a life on the streets, the freedom of which may seem preferable to conditions at home. When the family system experiences more external pressure than it can flexibly bear, children, with their rapidly growing minds and bodies, can be the most sensitive and vulnerable point of distress. Instead of buffering children from stresses that might undermine their development and their rights, families become the arena within which these rights are most frequently violated. Through personal failure, and as victims of broader social failure, parents and other caregivers become the agents through which children are neglected, abused, abandoned and sold into servitude.

abuse

the precarious equilibrium of poor families

The most dramatic evidence of family failure is the presence of children living by their wits on the streets of the world's cities. These children, a painfully visible reminder of society's inadequacies, are the focus of worldwide attention, and are high on the list of municipal concerns. But they are only the tip of the iceberg. For every child scavenging for a living on the streets, many more have their rights more invisibly violated – children labouring long hours in sweatshops; hungry babies whose minds and bodies will always be stunted; four-year-olds playing in raw sewage; young girls trapped in the daily round of domestic chores.

There is no single route to child distress, and no one family problem that can be addressed in order to eliminate it. It can take very little to push a marginal family over the edge. Just one event – eviction, loss of a job, or illness – may be sufficient to destroy a precarious equilibrium. But it also may take relatively minimal support at the right moment to maintain viability. A loan when it is most needed, access to medication, or the availability of a neighbour for child care, may keep a family functioning adequately for the time being. But for success over the long

[12] Scheper-Hughes, N (1989) 'Culture, Scarcity and Maternal Thinking: Mother Love and Child Death in North-east Brazil' in Scheper-Hughes (ed) *Child Survival: Anthropological Perspectives on the Treatment and Maltreatment of Children*, Dordrecht: Reidel

[13] McLoyd, V C (1990) 'The Impact of Economic Hardship on Black Families and Children: Psychological Distress, Parenting, and Socioemotional Development', *Child Development*, 61: 311–346

[14] Boyden, J and Holden, P (1991) *Children of the Cities*, London: Zed Books

[15] Moser and Herbert, 1996, op cit Note 9

[16] Boyden and Holden, 1991, op cit Note 14

term, it is critical that families be guaranteed ongoing access to the conditions that allow them to establish and sustain stability.

Basic requirements for family stability and integrity

families need supportive communities

The most sensible, efficient way to realize the rights of most children is to help their families remain functional. Such stability does not happen reliably at the level of the individual household. Just as children need stable families, so do families need healthy and supportive communities. Communities have greater leverage than individual families, and progress is more likely when people can pool their skills and work cooperatively. But research has shown that when things become chronically difficult, people tend to pull away, to be suspicious of others, and to focus on their own survival.[17]

measures to support the coping strategies of families

Constructive cooperation can and does happen as a result of community initiatives. But it is also possible for local government to support and contribute to the process of community building, knowing that a strong community will be an invaluable ally in stretching scarce resources and in building a base for healthy and stable families (see p261). In order for communities to fulfil this role, certain requirements must be in place. It is not necessarily a matter of outright provision. Poverty does not mean simply a lack of economic resources, but is also a function of exclusion or lack of access. By preventing systemic inequities and injustices, removing unnecessary barriers and supporting redistributive strategies, local authorities can do a great deal to combat urban poverty, to support communities, and through them to support the effective coping strategies of urban families.

In subsequent chapters we will discuss measures that local authorities can take to improve the various environments in which children and families spend their lives. In the remainder of this chapter we will focus specifically on measures that affect the capacity of families to function as supportive environments for children.

ADEQUATE AND SECURE HOUSING

housing as a base for stability

Housing adequate for family life must provide more than shelter. It must offer secure tenure, permit access to other necessities, support membership in a community, and allow the family to function as a secure base both physically and emotionally. And yet, simply keeping a roof over their heads is an insoluble problem for millions. Lack of financial resources is not the only reason. Even when the poor can pay a reasonable amount, or can construct their own housing, they are frequently constrained by discrimination, barred from access to land, materials, and credit, and burdened by unreasonable regulations. Commercial developments and high-income housing may generate more income for municipal authorities in the short run, but adequate housing, by providing a secure base for families, will mobilize the city's human capital and do more to enhance its stability and productivity in the long term. In Chapter 5, we will discuss the features that make housing appropriate for children's needs. Here we will consider issues of access and security.

[17] Moser and Herbert, 1996, op cit Note 9

Even when the poor can pay a reasonable amount, or are willing and able to construct their own housing, they are frequently constrained by discrimination in the housing market, barred from access to land, materials and credit, and burdened by unreasonable regulations. A young Romany woman in a settlement outside Tirana, Albania. UNICEF 1997, Roger LeMoyne

Access to land

In most urban areas in the South, access to housing means access to land, the price and availability of which is determined by market forces. Public intervention is frequently biased in favour of commercial interests and wealthier groups, and official permission to develop land for housing can be costly and complex to obtain. The result is a high proportion of the urban poor concentrated in the few areas where they can find land or cheap rental accommodation. The land they occupy is often the least suitable, concentrated on dangerous sites such as flood plains, or steep hillsides at risk from landslides, around waste dumps or on polluted sites close to industry. Many illegal or informal settlements develop on the outskirts of cities, distant from basic infrastructure and services or opportunities for work. As cities grow and such sites become more valuable, their inhabitants are often evicted without compensation to make way for higher income housing developments, or commercial and industrial concerns. Even when land is set aside for low-income groups, the costs and the criteria used to select beneficiaries often primarily benefit middle-income groups, and few plots go to those with the greatest need. Authorities can take a number of measures.

- *Identify and maintain an inventory of suitable unused and underused public land, and allocate it where possible for low-income households.*
- *Penalize landowners who leave land sites undeveloped.*
- *Simplify the legal and regulatory processes through which land can be acquired for development.*
- *Increase the area of land with access to services and employment through the extension of roads and improvement of public transport.*

Regulatory constraints and building materials

responding to local conditions

The capacity of low-income people to build acceptable housing is often thwarted by regulations which barr the use of affordable local materials such as mud or bamboo for construction, and which often have little relevance for safety or for the requirements and realities of the urban poor. Many of the building approaches of the poor may in fact be creative, time-tested solutions that respond effectively to local conditions and natural hazards.[18] Although materials considered to be substandard are used regardless of regulatory constraints, this becomes one more factor excluding the poor from formal support. The cost of building materials may be the single largest cost faced by a low-income household when building or upgrading their home. There are various ways to increase the supply and reduce the cost of materials, fixtures and fittings needed for house construction or upgrading.

- *Establish zoning and building codes that do not discriminate against the poor, and that allow for progressive improvement.*
- *Support the establishment of building material depots within low-income settlements that can offer advice and assistance to self-builders, pass on savings from bulk purchases, and offer credit to low-income households.*

Housing finance

Lack of access to credit is another obstacle that prevents the poor from both entering the housing market and improving existing housing. Low-income families are generally considered to be uncreditworthy, but in fact there are dozens of loan programmes serving low-income households that work with little or no subsidy and very high levels of loan repayments.[19] (See p53 for more details).

- *Support loan programmes that serve low-income households.*

Rental problems

It is common for one third or more of a city's inhabitants, including a higher proportion of its low-income inhabitants, to rent accommodation. But in recent years, little has been done to improve conditions for tenants. Rent control programmes fell out of favour because they discouraged maintenance by landlords and new rental construction. Public housing rental programmes fell out of favour because of their high costs, the limited capacity of public authorities to build and maintain them and the fact that it was usually the more prosperous and well-connected households who received them, not those most in need. Authorities can take a number of steps.

- *Encourage and support clear legal rights for tenants (this may include the promotion of model contracts between tenants and landlords).*

[18] Missair, A (1994) 'Construction Technology in Developing Countries' in J W Wescott and Henak, R M (eds) *Construction in Technology Education*, Columbus, Ohio: Macmillan/McGraw Hill

[19] Examples of successful housing finance programmes include the credit programme of the Thai Fund for Community Initiatives (Boonyabancha, S (1996) *The Urban Community Development Office*, London: IIED); and the work of FONHAPO, the Mexican Government's National Fund for Low Cost Housing during the 1980s (Ortiz, E (1998) *The Experience of the National Fund for Low-Income Housing in Mexico*, London: IIED)

- *Support the extension or modification of housing in existing settlements, so that owners who wish to can rent out space within their homes.*
- *Support the availability of loans to long term tenants who wish to negotiate a collective purchase of their dwellings.*
- *Where appropriate, support the development of non-profit housing institutions that build rental accomodation.*

Discrimination

constraints for women

Housing access issues are often even more complicated for women, because of outright discrimination or traditions governing inheritance and ownership. In some countries, women cannot own or inherit property and cannot sign for loans. Poor women are doubly disadvantaged, and when they are single parents their children suffer the consequences by being among those most frequently without homes. Discrimination in both rentals and home ownership may also affect minority groups.

- *Ensure that women and other excluded groups are not discriminated against in processes to promote housing access.*

Security of tenure

legal tenure a foothold for tackling poverty

When housing and land are secure, they can be significant assets in reducing the overall vulnerability of the poor. Families are more likely to improve their holdings, thereby increasing their own asset base, and contributing to the stability of the community. Housing can become a base for informal economic enterprises, and space can be rented out or sold in times of serious need. When people know their housing is secure, they are more likely to become constructively involved in the community. Legal tenure provides a secure foothold from which other problems of poverty can be more successfully tackled.

But the poor lack bargaining power, and are more likely than other groups to fall victim to arbitrary evictions. It is not uncommon for squatters to be displaced in favour of more lucrative enterprises or the creation of infrastructure that primarily benefits the well-to-do, since municipalities are better able to collect taxes from wealthy citizens. Sometimes evictions are an attempt to discourage the development of illegal settlements. A fruitless effort, since those evicted will be forced to find a new place to squat, or will further increase overcrowding in rental accomodations.

the costs of eviction

The loss of familiar surroundings and social networks, the time-consuming burden of finding new housing, the impact on work and income – especially for those with home-based occupations – and the effects on mental health can be considerable, and can have the long term effect of undermining a family's capacity to cope. Even a minimal shack represents an investment in time and labour, and the economic loss should not be underestimated. Evictions are directly linked to subsequent homelessness, and are a violation not only of children's right to family and survival, but of the international human right to housing.

Cities with rapidly growing economies and populations need land for new or expanded infrastructure. The question is how and where this development should take place. Authorities are urged to weigh the immediate and long term implications for the families affected by eviction. Consultation with residents can result in land-sharing solutions that will minimize the number of households to be moved and ensure that they do not have to relocate away from their neighbourhood. Relocation should be a last resort, but if it is found to benefit the greatest number, it must not be handled in a dehumanizing manner or in ways that undermine family stability.

responses

- *Wherever possible, ensure that low-income families living in illegal or informal settlements obtain legal title to their land and homes.*
- *Require consultation between developers and those faced with eviction, with clear guidelines for procedures that support the reaching of acceptable solutions.*
- *Include child and family impact assessments prior to urban planning decisions.*
- *Ensure that no evictions take place before families have secured suitable alternative housing, schooling and other services.*
- *In budgeting for redevelopment, include sufficient funding to adequately reimburse those who are relocated for all their lost investments.*

Security of tenure is also an important factor for children's social and emotional stability and this will be discussed p70.

Disaster relief and rehousing

the vulnerable housing of the poor

Much of the housing of the urban poor is vulnerable to serious damage from natural disasters. Housing on steep hillsides and in flood plains may be destroyed by heavy storms; and the flimsy materials available to the poor are unlikely to withstand earthquakes, high winds or fire. The destruction of even marginal housing can be calamitous for families with few resources.

This poses a regulatory problem. On the one hand, authorities are urged to relax building and zoning regulations which push legal housing out of the reach of the poor. On the other hand, when standards are not sufficiently high, large numbers of people may be killed, injured or left homeless in the wake of natural disasters. Careful distinction must be made between regulations which set unnecessarily high standards, and those which improve safety.

Reducing vulnerability for households is related to the capacity to anticipate and avoid the disaster, to limit the impact if it occurs, and to cope with the consequences.[20] The city of Santos, Brazil established an ongoing programme in an unplanned settlement prone to devastating landslides. With the collaboration of local residents and a team of experts, a civil defense group was organized, made up of volunteers trained to identify problems in advance and find solutions. This was combined with efforts to discourage building in vulnerable areas.[21]

[20] International Federation of Red Cross and Red Crescent Societies (1998) *World Disasters Report 1998*, Oxford: Oxford University Press

[21] City of Santos (1996) 'Santos na Habitat II: Integrated Children's and Family Program', The City of Santos, SP, Brazil

- *Ensure that regulatory codes for buildings and land development balance the need for safety with the recognition of limitations imposed by inadequate incomes.*
- *Allow for, and support, progressive improvements with safety and durability as a goal.*
- *Develop disaster prevention and emergency preparedness plans with all relevant public agencies in coordination with community governance organizations.*
- *Test out emergency preparedness strategies with the participation of local residents.*
- *Enforce regulations on industrial plant safety and waste disposal to limit the fires and chemical spills that often accompany natural disasters.*
- *Coordinate with other local authorities – for instance, in watershed management outside the city's jurisdiction.*
- *Seek technical assistance from academic institutions and international organizations.*
- *Learn from other municipalities with experience in emergency preparedness, relief and management, and establish regional solidarity networks (see p269).*

The participatory planning, design, management and upgrading of family housing

Over the last 10 or 15 years, most governments have reduced public housing programmes or scrapped them altogether. More common now are serviced site schemes which place responsibility for building on the beneficiary family. Because intended users are rarely involved in the planning process, these schemes frequently fail to meet the priorities of low-income households. They are often located far from shops, services and sources of employment; site designs usually follow standard grid patterns, with no attempt to incorporate the common spaces so important for children's play and for community life; and many schemes provide poor quality infrastructure which local authorities fail to maintain. These schemes also assume that low-income households have the time and income to develop their own housing, but it is often difficult for adults, and especially for single parents, to take sufficient time off from work or domestic responsibilities to do so.

Resident participation can result in radically different outcomes. In South Africa, when low-income families were given control of housing subsidies that were usually managed by building firms, they organized the construction of larger houses of higher quality for the same cost. Cooperative savings and loans groups have demonstrated that they can build high quality three bedroom houses with the same amount of money that the government gives to contractors to build just a serviced site.[22] There are numerous examples of innovative self-build housing programmes.[23]

Women repeatedly demonstrate their capacity to design housing best suited to family needs, and to use limited funds economically. In the

[22] Bolnick, J (1996) 'uTshani Buyakhuluma (the grass speaks); Peoples' Dialogue and the South African Homeless Peoples' Federation, 1993–1996', *Environment and Urbanization*, 8(2): 153–170

[23] For other examples of innovative, community-directed self-build housing programmes, see case studies on the work of FEGIP in Goiania in Brazil (Barbosa, R, Cabannes, Y et al (1997) 'Tenant Today, Posseiro Tomorrow', *Environment and Urbanization*, 9(2): 17–41); FUPROVI in Costa Rica and PRODEL in Nicaragua (Sida (1997) 'Seeking more Effective and Sustainable Support to Improving Housing and Living Conditions for Low Income Households in Urban Areas: Sida's Initiatives in Costa Rica, Chile and Nicaragua', Environment and Urbanization, 9(2): 213–231); Serviced site programme in Hyderabad, Pakistan (van der Linden, J (1997) 'On Popular Participation in a Culture of Patronage: Patrons and Grassroots Organizations in a Sites and Services Project', *Environment and Urbanization*, 9(1): 81–90)

[24] Dennis, F and Castleton, D (1991) 'Women's Mobilization in Human Settlements Case Study: The Guarari Housing Project, Costa Rica' in Sontheimer, S (ed) *Women and the Environment: A Reader*, London: Earthscan, 147–162

Guarari housing project in Costa Rica, women objected to the housing designs of government programmes and negotiated with engineers and financing agencies for units better adapted to their needs – for instance, allowing proper supervision of children at play and more ventilation in kitchens and other workplaces.[24] In both India and South Africa, women in savings groups have developed their own house designs, first as drawings, then as cardboard models, then as life-size models, so that they can determine appropriate size and design, and make informed decisions about how to reduce costs.[25]

The upgrading of illegal or informal settlements should also be undertaken in partnership with inhabitants. In too many cases, public works departments provide improved facilities without establishing what inhabitants want or are prepared to pay for, and with no maintenance provision. Areas may be improved to the point where low-income groups are forced to move out and higher income groups move in. More comprehensive, long-lasting improvements could be achieved with a formal process of consultation to establish priorities and reach agreement on the role of individual households and their own organizations. The needs and priorities of children and their families should be closely attended to. No upgrading programme we know has ever explicitly sought to consider the broad range of environmental priorities that are important for child health and development, (although many programmes have improved conditions for children). There are examples of community-directed and financed upgrading schemes whose design, implementation and capacity to reduce costs have important lessons for city authorities and international agencies.[26]

- *Involve low-income groups and their organizations in the design and implementation of serviced site schemes or other schemes to develop new affordable housing.*
- *Develop more participatory methods for designing, implementing and managing upgrading schemes.*
- *Support community efforts for developing or upgrading settlements by providing technical advice and, where appropriate, financial support.*
- *See p263 for recommendations on supporting community planning and management.*
- *Always work closely with residents in any plans for upgrading a settlement.*
- *Consider the particular requirements of children in making plans for upgrading.*

BASIC MUNICIPAL SERVICES

Urban areas occupied by the poor are seldom provided with basic infrastructure and services, for several reasons. Piped water, sewers, electricity, street lighting, drainage and road access and maintenance all involve heavy capital investment. Standards set for the provision and maintenance of infrastructure often push capital costs to levels unaffordable for cities, and inhibit the automatic expansion of service networks

[25] Patel, S (1996) *SPARC and its Work with the National Slum Dwellers Federation and Mahila Milan, India*, IIED Paper Series on Poverty Reduction in Urban Areas, London: IIED

[26] For case studies of community-directed upgrading programmes, see the upgrading of Orangi in Karachi (OPP (1995) 'Orangi Pilot Project', *Environment and Urbanization*, 7(2): 227–236); the upgrading of El Mesquital in Guatemala City (Espinosa, L and Lopez Rivera, O A (1994) 'UNICEF's Urban Basic Services Programme in Illegal Settlements in Guatamala City', *Environment and Urbanization*, 6(2): 9–31); the upgrading of Rufisque in Senegal (Gaye, M and Diallo, F (1997) 'Community Participation in the Management of the Urban Environment in Rufisque (Senegal)', *Environment and Urbanization*, 7(2): 91–119); and the upgrading of Barrio San Jorge in Buenos Aires (Schusterman, R and Hardoy, A (1997) 'Reconstructing Social Capital in a Poor Urban Settlement: the Integrated Improvement Programme, Barrio San Jorge', *Environment and Urbanization*, Programme, 9 (1): 91–119); Stein, A (1996) *Decentralization and Urban Poverty Reduction in Nicaragua: The Experience of the Local Development Programme* (PRODEL), London: IIED

when cities grow. There is also a concern that initial costs are less likely to be recovered from poor communities. And cost issues aside, municipalities are frequently unwilling to encourage and legitimate the development of informal settlements by providing them with services.

the costs of being poor and undeserved

The long term costs of such exclusion, both in human and financial terms, are almost certainly higher than the cost of provision. When there is not adequate access to high quality piped water, for instance, the poor often turn to private vendors and end up paying 5 or 10 times more per litre than the rates charged by public utilities for piped water. The differences can be greater.[27] Low-income groups also pay more for other services.

higher rates

In Accra, a progressive rate for electricity use appears to favour the poor by charging more for higher use, but the reverse is actually the case. In low-income neighbourhoods one electric meter is often provided for a whole street. Use per meter is high, and so poor families end up paying far more for their electricity than is true in better serviced neighbourhoods.[28] The greatest disparities are generally found in the provision of sanitation and solid waste management. Well-off sections of cities commonly have sewage systems which charge households a nominal rate. In poor areas, solutions are more likely to involve low capital investment but higher maintenance costs, such as the hiring of sweepers for the removal of household waste, or payment for the use of communal facilities. In many cities, it simply costs more to be poor than to be rich. Limited public expenditures provide benefits to middle and upper income groups, and penalize low-income groups.

loss of time

The lack of adequate infrastructure also results in disproportionate expenditure of time. When people must line up for long periods to use a shared toilets or to collect water from shared taps, the time spent is in effect time taken away from income generation, child care or rest. When children are sent repeatedly to fetch water, or to dump refuse at a distant site, it is one more factor interfering with their chances for schooling. The sheer drudgery resulting from a lack of capital investment in the poor takes its toll on the ability of families to function optimally, and the burden usually falls disproportionately on women and girls.

health

Costs to health are also considerable, and have been long under-estimated. Insufficient or contaminated water, poor drainage and inadequate sanitation result in disease, general debilitation and added medical costs. The impact for community health and morale is significant. (See p96 for more on environmental health measures through infrastructure provision.)

A number of examples have shown how much can be achieved for low-income households even when municipalities have relatively little power, and when there is little external funding. The capacity and willingness of many low-income households to pay towards costs are often under-estimated. So too are the savings that arise from efficient provision or innovations. When these are combined, the gap between costs of provision and possible cost recovery are much reduced or even removed.[29] Where resources are scarce or incomes very low, incremental solutions may be necessary.

Recovering costs from those with very little capital may be possible through the use of credit or through user charges that spread repayment over a number of years. Water supply systems have achieved full cost recovery by charging users who end up paying less per month than they previously paid to water vendors.[30] In retrofitting efforts, inhabitants of

[27] World Bank (1988) *World Development Report*, New York: Oxford University Press

[28] S Bartlett and Hart,R, field trip

[29] Anzorena, J, Bolnick, J et al (1998) 'Reducing Urban Poverty: Some Lessons from Experience', *Environment and Urbanization*, 10(1): 167–186

[30] Espinosa, L and Lopez Rivera, O A (1994) 'UNICEF's Urban Basic Services Programme in Illegal Settlements in Guatamala City', *Environment and Urbanization*. 6(2): 9–31

informal settlements may be prepared to contribute labour and management which can greatly lower costs – for instance in preparing the ditches for installing water pipes and sewers. The El Mesquital programme, for instance, included a shallow sewage system managed by a water cooperative.[31] Another well-known example is the classic Orangi project in Karachi, Pakistan.[32] Households should always be included in planning discussions to allow an analysis of household capacity and willingness to pay, and where necessary, to support the build-up of income capability.

retaining control

A focus on seeking full cost recovery may seem inappropriate and unfair in addressing the problems of low-income households, when middle and upper income households are so often the beneficiaries of public services or loan finance. But when there is less reliance on external funding, there is more chance for low-income groups and their organizations to retain control, and to sustain or expand initiatives when external funds are no longer available.[33]

tenants

Improving provision is often more difficult for tenants. It may be difficult to induce landlords to invest in this, and tenants may be unwilling to do so because they will not benefit over the long term.[34] In low-income settlements with a high level of renting, good quality public provision of piped water, toilets and facilities for washing and perhaps laundry may be the most appropriate response, as has been tried in various settlements in Nairobi.[35] Such provision needs careful management if costs are to be recovered and facilities well-maintained.

- *Approach the problems of infrastructure provision systemically, taking into account regional relationships and needs, and the need to reduce intra-urban health disparities.*
- *Review and modify standards for the design and provision of infrastructure, in the interests of increasing potential coverage and keeping costs low. Design regulations should not inhibit informal solutions, but ensure that pricing is fair, that reasonable health standards are maintained, and that coverage is universal – that is, that rights are protected.*
- *Assess demand for services and the capacity to pay, in order to facilitate planning, correct any mistaken assumptions about the ability of poor communities to support infrastructure provision, and e tablish the need for subsidization.*
- *Allow for progressive upgrading.*
- *Use loans to allow low-income households to spread costs over a longer period.*
- *Wherever possible, combine the provision of infrastructure with improved livelihood possibilities for community members; for instance, promoting better waste management and increased recycling by working with the urban poor groups involved in waste collection and processing.*[36]
- *When water, sanitation and waste removal are provided by entities legally separate from the municipality, ensure that there is public control over pricing structures and quality in order to promote equitable treatment.*

[31] Ibid; and UNICEF (1991) 'Guatemala Urban Basic Services', Guatamala, UNICEF
[32] Hasan, A (1997) *Working with Government: The Story of the Orangi Pilot Project's Collaboration with State Agencies for Replicating its Low Cost Sanitation Programme*, Karachi: City Press
[33] Anzorena et al, 1998, op cit Note 29
[34] Cairncross, S (1992) 'Sanitation and Watersupply: Practical Lessons from the Decade', *Water and Sanitation Discussion Paper Series #9*, Washington DC, World Bank
[35] Wegelin-Schuringa, M and Kodo, T (1997) 'Tenancy and Sanitation Provision in Informal Settlements in Nairobi: Revisiting the Public Latrine Option', *Environment and Urbanization*, 9(2): 181–190
[36] Pacheco, M (1992) 'Recycling in Bogota: Developing a Culture for Urban Sustainability', *Environment and Urbanization*, 4(2): 74–79

- *Consider municipal-community partnerships, where efforts within communities are supported, and coordinated with formal systems (for instance, roads, water and sewer mains, electricity supplies, drains).*
- *Consider cross-subsidies as a solution for cost recovery.*
- *Draw on the experience of other municipalities that have developed successful innovations in increasing coverage, improving quality and reducing costs.*

Access to employment or livelihood

A scarcity of jobs in the formal sector, lack of capital, regulatory constraints, inadequate markets, poor skills, ill health and a lack of child care can all play a role in undermining livelihood.

the formal sector

Municipalities can enhance job opportunities for the poor by promoting locally based economic development. In San Nicolas, Argentina, for instance, with the technical assistance of the International Labour Office, the mayor signed an agreement with the local workers union, the Chamber of Commerce and Industry and his administration to encourage cooperation for the creation of productive forms of income generation for. the poor and unemployed of the city.[37] In Santos, Brazil, the municipality, as part of the search for employment solutions, reconsidered the municipal budget to determine how future city investments could be structured to contribute to the generation of jobs, even if temporary.[38]

the informal sector

Between 30 and 80 per cent of the urban poor depend on informal activities for their livelihood.[39] But informal entrepreneurs can be constrained by a number of factors. Regulations may cause many informal workers to operate outside the law and run the risk of fines or confiscation of property. Those involved in microenterprise often have difficulty in accessing formal credit for start-up costs or expansion. Small entrepreneurs may also lack the skills to take advantage of opportunities, and are unlikely to have the necessary knowledge of management or marketing.

Informal initiatives should be encouraged and recognized for their important contribution to the economy of the city, and the energies and skills of informal workers drawn on to supplement the activity of the formal sector. In the area of recycling, for instance, the poor should be recognized as the experts they are, and their activities should be coordinated with formal contractors. In Dakar, Senegal, the municipality launched a decentralized city-wide project supporting the formation of Groups of Economic Interest (CGI) to create income generating activities. The project resulted in 5000 new jobs for young unemployed people building or maintaining the city's infrastructure.[40]

The means of livelihood should not undermine family life. Employment may provide the necessary financial resources for survival; but if it requires adults to travel for long hours and leaves them little time at home, if it means leaving young children untended, or means setting up hazardous enterprises within the home, then it cannot be considered adequate for a family's needs. High quality child care frees women for income earning, makes it possible for older siblings to attend school, and increases the time available for routine daily tasks. A strong

37 UNDP (1994) 'Report of the International Colloquium of Mayors on Social Development', New York, UNDP
38 City of Santos (1996) 'Santos na Habitat II: Integrated Children's and Family Program', The City of Santos, SP, Brazil
39 Vanderschueren, F, Wegelin, E, Wekwete, K (1996) *Policy Programme Options for Urban Poverty Reduction*, Washington DC: The World Bank/Urban Management Programme
40 UNDP 1994, op cit Note 37

child care programme will also support the physical and mental development of the children who attend it.

- *Protect existing jobs, and encourage the creation of new jobs in the vicinity of poor communities.*
- *Wherever possible, legitimize and support the activities of the informal sector; adopt regulations which will permit the development of employment opportunities.*
- *Provide appropriate training to increase employment options, especially for jobs available through municipal contracts.*
- *Coordinate the activities of the informal sector with municipal provision and with the private sector (At the same time ensure that informal workers are not exploited in order to subsidize the formal sector, for instance in hazardous work that the formal sector chooses not to undertake).*
- *Encourage and support commercial lenders to extend credit to micro-entrepreneurs (p53).*
- *Create a center to provide administrative and regulatory advice, information and assistance on obtaining credit, training programmes, technical assistance and other supports for micro-entrepreneurs.*
- *Increase the availability of affordable high quality child care (see p152).*

Support for urban agriculture

examples from Kenya and Colombia

Livelihood can be directly enhanced through food and fuel production. Even in urban areas, significant quantities of food can be grown or raised on small patches of land, on rooftops, flood plains, utility rights-of-way, roadsides or in public parks. Urban agriculture may simply be a way to supplement the family diet, or it can become a profit-making enterprise. Either way it is an important survival strategy for hundreds of millions of urban dwellers worldwide. A survey of six urban centres in Kenya, for instance, found that almost two-thirds of respondents grew food or fuel, and half kept livestock either for subsistence or for sale; 40 per cent of these urban farmers depended on their produce for survival.[41] In Jerusalem, a settlement near Bogota, Colombia, poor inhabitants were assisted by the NGO, Las Gaviotas, in growing crops on their rooftops using hydroponic techniques which produce 20 times more per square metre than traditional methods. Many of these Bogota families were able to grow food at one third of its market cost; they improved their diets and increased their incomes through the sale of surplus food.[42]

Urban agriculture also has significant environmental benefits. Both solid and liquid wastes can effectively be recycled as fertilizer, with proper safety controls, and areas that might otherwise be barren and waste-strewn can become inviting, well-managed plots. In Bangkok, 320,000 papaya trees were planted around homes, temples and schools by young people on World Environment Day in 1988. Papaya was chosen for its high nutritional value and the capacity of the trees to reduce soil erosion and offer shade and beauty.[43]

41 cited in Satterthwaite, D, Hart, R, Levy, C, Mitlin, D, Ross, D, Smit, J, Stephens, C (1996) *The Environment for Children*, London: Earthscan

42 Robson, B (1989) 'Premature Obituaries: Change and Adaptation in Great Cities' in Lawton, R (ed) *The Rise and Fall of Great Cities*, London and New York: Belhaven Press, 45–54

43 UNEP (1988) *Young Action for the Future*, Nairobi: UNEP

Although the potential for intensive food production has been actively recognized and supported in some parts of the world, most municipalities have not given it attention, and urban farmers may be constrained by zoning regulations, land ownership problems, and lack of access to uncontaminated water.

- *Promote an understanding of the benefits of urban agriculture, both economic and environmental.*
- *Facilitate land use for urban agriculture, both through the review of zoning regulations, by making public lands available and encouraging institutional cooperation.*
- *Support innovative and efficient technologies in partnership with agricultural institutions and research centres.*
- *Provide technical assistance for urban farmers, both to support and increase production, and to ensure sound agricultural practices.*
- *Prevent the spread of livestock-related diseases through appropriate regulatory controls.*

OTHER CRITICAL SUPPORTS

Health and education

Adequate health care and education are basic for family stability. Poor health threatens the quality of care available to children, absorbs funds that might otherwise be used for housing, food and education, and interferes with the capacity to earn. Basic education can be critical to promoting important life skills related to livelihoods, health, environmental management and family life. These two critical supports for family stability will be discussed in detail in Chapters 6 and 9.

- *See Chapters 6 and 9.*

Public transportation

increasing the range of options

Many of the urban poor are forced to live on the outskirts of cities, distant from jobs, markets and social services. Without cheap, efficient transportation their opportunities are seriously restricted. If they go any distance for work, they must either walk prohibitive distances, pay more than they can afford, or remain away from home. In all cities there are family members, often children, who are unable to return home at night. This becomes yet another route to family disintegration. Inexpensive, rapid transport can dramatically simplify the lives of the urban poor and increase the range of options open to them, including the possibility of cheaper housing, and the ability to make use of schools and other services. Affordable transportation between cities and rural areas can also help extended families to retain their mutually supportive connections.

Attention to transport is by no means a substitute for attention to systemic social injustice, but may in the short term lend itself more easily to intervention than more complex issues such as land reform. Massive investment in mass transport is not the only viable approach. Less formal solutions can supplement or partially replace more expensive systems, and provide links to larger networks.[44] Subsidies for low income groups may improve access to existing transport, but subsidized prices may also undermine the quality and extent of public transport.

- *Consult with the inhabitants of each residential area about needs and priorities in regard to public transport and, where appropriate, seek better integration of formal and informal services to ensure adequate coverage of all areas.*
- *Support informal alternatives such as minibus services and rickshaws that can provide links to larger networks; seek ways to improve safety and affordability.*
- *Where heavy traffic is an issue, invest in walkways and bicycle lanes to broaden options, enhance the mobility and safety of children, and encourage school attendance.*
- *Consider the practicality of subsidized public transport within the local context.*

Access to credit

Many of the problems faced by the urban poor are complicated by their difficulty in getting credit. The capacity to enter the housing market, to start a small business or to respond to family crises are all limited by lack of capital. Formal banking systems are usually not a solution because of high collateral requirements and social barriers. Nor do formal lenders see the relatively small loan requirements of the poor as an attractive business proposition. Administrative costs are high for the amounts involved, and a high risk of default is assumed. (Experience has in fact indicated that the poor, and women in particular, are reliable credit risks.[45]) Since formal systems are closed to them, low-income households are forced to turn to informal moneylenders who charge high interest rates that can quickly cripple a family financially.

community-based savings groups

Informal community-based savings groups have been a successful approach in many countries. But because their accumulated capital is a function of the capacity of their poor members to save, they face definite limits. Generally such groups are unable to respond to larger credit requirements. There are exceptions, however. The Praja Sahayaka Sevaya group in Colombo, Sri Lanka, for example, makes credit available for housing, micro-enterprise and emergencies, using money raised entirely from the savings of its own female membership. As is typical of such groups, members deposit regular amounts, and only after a period of time become eligible to borrow money.

Connections for low-income groups to the formal banking system have been successfully developed through community-based schemes, substantially expanding access to credit for the poor. Commercial lenders are more willing to work with groups than with poor individuals, since the groups function as a mutual credit guarantee, ensuring repayment through mutual trust and peer pressure.[46] This approach also opens the door to

[44] Vanderschueren, Wegelin, Wekwete 1996, op cit Note 39
[45] Anzorena, J (1994) 'Grameen Bank – November 1993', SELAVIP Newsletter, *Journal of Low-Income Housing in Asia and the World*, April 1994
[46] Iyer, L and Goldenberg, D A (1996) *We live here too! Moving toward Child-centred Habitat Programmes*, PLAN International: South Asia Regional Office

new skills for those who participate, and supports group solidarity. An interesting example is the Baroda Citizens Council in Gujarat, India, where Community Loans and Savings Systems, a committee of community leaders, municipal staff and NGOs, has been effective in linking a network of 15 slum communities to formal resources within the city.[47]

- *Make information and technical support available to encourage the creation of community-based credit societies.*
- *Facilitate links between such groups and the formal banking system, and with international, national and local NGOs.*

Justice and protection

Of all urban dwellers, the poor are most in need of justice, law enforcement and legal protection, and least likely to have access to it. They lack the resources for formal legal representation, they tend to have fewer personal contacts with those in powerful positions and, owing to a lack of formal education, they may be unaware of their legal rights and lack the skills to negotiate with complex bureaucracies. There will be discussion of these issues and recommendations in other chapters.

- *See p81 for a discussion of domestic violence and recommendations.*
- *See p124 for a discussion of community responses to violence, insecurity and lack of protection.*
- *See p225 for a discussion of juvenile justice.*

Support in times of difficulty or crisis

links with extended family

community supports

When families are under stress, children feel the effects and may suffer from serious neglect, often unavoidably. A study in Bangladesh indicated that 40 per cent of all severely undernourished children came from households where the primary earners were ill.[48] The traditional structure of rural society offered families a margin of safety during times of difficulty. Through shared responsibility for child care and household tasks, pooled resources and mutual support in the face of changing circumstances, the impact of challenging events such as illness, death or reduced income could be more easily absorbed. One of the difficulties of urban living has been the loss of this safety net. It is important that ways be found to reproduce some of the strengths of traditional society within the often very different context of urban poverty. An important means of increasing social support is to facilitate links with extended family. Even when they do not occupy the same household, family members can be an active force in children's lives and a strong stabilizing factor for parents, as long as they are accessible. Cheap efficient transportation can help to make a difference, as can housing policies that take into account the importance of extended family networks. But in the absence of family members, support from the community, both formal and informal, becomes critical to families in times of difficulty. Within most communities, and especially those where there is a sense of community,

[47] Information from UNICEF's Urban Section, New York
[48] Pryer, J (1993) 'The Impact of Adult Ill-Health on Household Income and Nutrition in Khulna, Bangladesh', *Environment and Urbanisation*, 5(2)

there tend to be natural helpers – people whose inclination it is to offer support and assistance in times of distress. They may include women who are willing to take in extra children during times of need, for instance, or storekeepers who will extend credit to needy families. Often community organizations are able to lend a helping hand. The community kitchens of Peru, for example, (see p113), made low-cost or free meals available during a time of particular economic hardship. These kitchens were operated and managed for no pay by women from the community who were able to spare time from their own families.[49] This kind of human capital should be identified and acknowledged as a precious resource, and whenever possible such community volunteers and helpers should be provided with the support and back-up they need.

formal responses

Sometimes more formal responses to crises are also necessary. Generally these will come from social welfare agencies, whose interventions have traditionally included both family support and child protection. The functions of such agencies have often been associated with surveillance and social control, but they have the potential to be a resource for increasing the control that families have over their situations. When poverty is widespread, welfare resources rarely allow for the levels of cash assistance that can assure family stability. But even when financial resources are meagre, welfare agencies can help to coordinate existing resources, both formal and informal, and promote preventive and integrated approaches to issues that are commonly responded to in sectoral and reactive ways. When strong ties exist among formal agencies such as health and education, as well as local voluntary resources, it is less likely that any family will fall between the cracks.

links between services

Links between services make it easier to identify families at risk of collapse, and to offer timely support. A health worker who makes routine home visits, for instance, may know when the chief breadwinner is ill and be able to rally temporary support. If a child drops out of school because of family difficulties, a teacher may be the source of information. When a social welfare agency acts as a clearing house for existing resources, it helps to ensure that families are making use of the full range of supports available within the community. Existing services and supports that already work well should be used as entry points for building more effective support systems. A child care centre, for instance, may be an ideal place to set up healthcare and parenting classes and provide information about job training (see Chapter 8). In later chapters we will discuss a range of responses, including supplemental feeding (p113), child care programmes that address the child's full developmental needs, home-based support for parents – especially for parents of disabled children (p86) – and parent education on nutrition, hygiene and children's developmental needs (pp115, 160).

community 'befrienders'

community centres for family support

Where existing community supports are inadequate, welfare agencies, with the support of community members and voluntary agencies, can work to develop the resources regarded as most critical. They can also increase the availability of informal support within the community by offering training for volunteers who are willing to act as 'befrienders' and advocates for families or children in difficulty. This coordinating role need not be reserved for social workers. It could also be taken up by community development organizations, community liaison officers, or through a city-wide initiative to coordinate service provision (see pp257, 261).

49 UNICEF (1994) *The Urban Poor and Household Food Security: Urban Examples #19*, New York: UNICEF

A goal in any community could be to establish a centre for family development and support, which could serve a number of functions. Besides housing relevant agency offices or community organizations, and offering space for local meetings, it could serve as a base for parent education, literacy classes, children's playgroups, and a toy library or resource centre. It could also offer quiet and well-lit study space for older children, space for health provision or supplemental feeding, and act as a clearing house for information on legal issues, access to credit, employment opportunities and training. Support and funding for such a centre could do much to promote the kind of integrated, participatory, community-based services that are a wellspring for vital community development and an essential basis for fulfilling children's rights.

- *Assess local welfare needs (p254).*
- *Establish links between all resources for family assistance within the community, both formal and informal (p257).*
- *Work with communities and voluntary organizations to provide missing services.*
- *Provide training for community volunteers and support.*
- *Establish family development centers offering a range of integrated supportive services (pp104, 167).*
- *Contribute to the establishment and activity of coordinating councils for children's rights (p260).*
- *See p81 for a discussion of domestic violence and child abuse.*

Part Two

Working for Urban Children's Rights

Part Two

Achieving children's rights requires attention to the most practical details in the varied environments that children and adolescents occupy – from the most public to the most private; from the institutional to the informal. Children have rights whether they are in school or at home, at work or at play, in prison or living on the streets.

In some cases families can ensure that these rights are met, with the support and assistance of local authorities when necessary. In others, authorities assume basic responsibility, with the cooperation of a range of partners. Either way, it is essential that authorities understand how children's rights can best be supported within various situations. The following chapters consider the range of environments that children and adolescents occupy, and present guidelines, recommendations and examples for ensuring that each of these environments is as supportive as possible. As in the earlier part of the book, we will make cross-references to pertinent information in other chapters in order to stress the connections and coordination that are the basis for an integrated response.

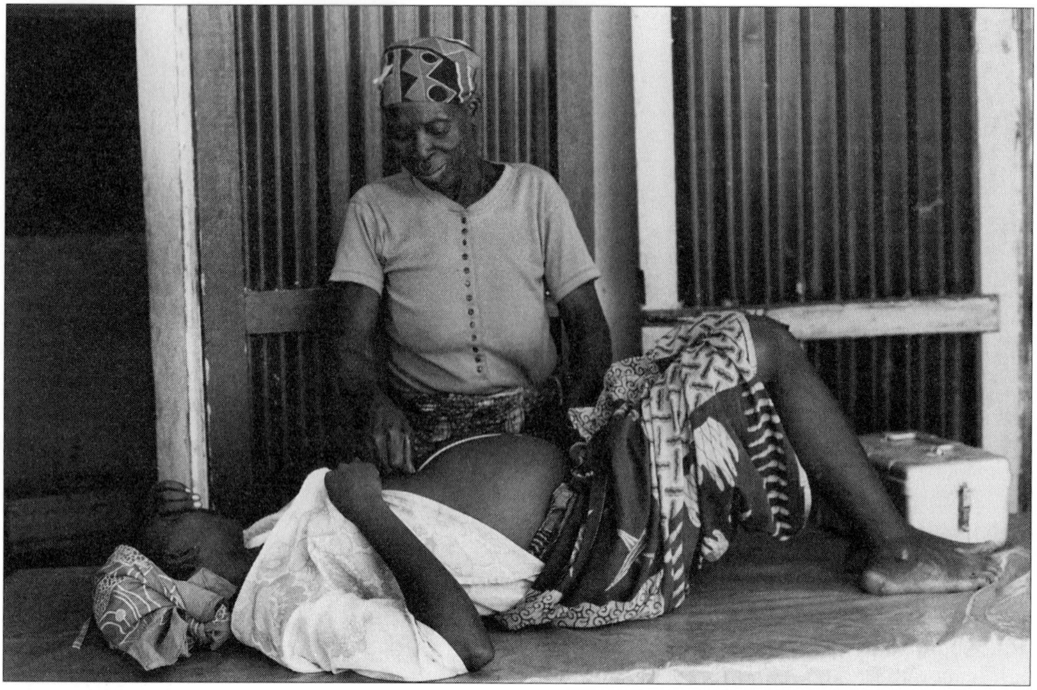

Prenatal care, properly assisted births and follow-up after birth are essential for the well-being of both mothers and their infants. A woman and her trained birth assistant in Chad. UNICEF 1995, Giacomo Pirozzi

4 Prenatal and Birth Environments

The Convention recognizes the right of all children to the highest attainable standard of health (Article 24). But some children begin life already disadvantaged because of inadequate care before and during birth. The well-being of infants is critically linked to the prenatal health of their mothers, and to the care their mothers receive during childbirth. Major strides have been made worldwide in providing for maternal health, but too many poor women and girls are still overlooked. Complications in childbirth and pregnancy are the leading cause of death and disability for women of childbearing age in developing countries. The surviving children of women who die are themselves three to ten times more likely to die in the following two years than they would be otherwise.[1] For every woman who dies, 30 more suffer from pregnancy-related injuries and infections which may be permanently disabling.[2] More than one quarter of all women in the developing world suffer from disabilities related to pregnancy.[3] The risks are particularly high for adolescent girls.[4] Pregnant girls aged 15 to 19 are twice as likely as older women to die in childbirth, and for those under 15 the risk is sharply higher.[5]

Half of all infant deaths occur in the weeks after birth, and many of the infants who survive are ill-equipped to meet the ongoing challenges of

[1] Safe Motherhood Initiative (1998) 'Safe Motherhood Fact Sheets', New York: Family Care International
[2] UNICEF (ed) (1996) *The Progress of Nations 1996*, New York: UNICEF
[3] Safe Motherhood Initiative 1998, op cit Note 1
[4] UNICEF (1997) *Youth Health – – For a Change: A UNICEF Notebook on Programming for Young People's Health and Development*, Working draft
[5] United Nations (1991) *The World's Women: Trends and Statistics 1970–1990*, New York: United Nations

poverty.[6] Poor children grow up to be poor, debilitated adults who in their turn give birth to children who are disadvantaged before they even enter the world. This is part of the larger cycle of chronic poverty that is becoming further entrenched as a result of global economic realities which have the most devastating effects for those who are already poor. Both children's and women's rights require that adequate services be available for pregnancy, birth and post-natal care to ensure the health and well-being of mothers and infants. Improved care for women directly affects their children, their families and communities.

THE INTRAUTERINE ENVIRONMENT OF THE CHILD

Even in the sheltered environment of the mother's womb, a foetus is vulnerable to the effects of poverty, inequity and environmental risk. The mother's diet, the air she breathes, her general health, and even her emotional state have a profound impact on the developing fetus. A malnourished and debilitated mother, burdened by stress and anxiety, cannot provide the nurturing environment that her unborn child requires.

stress

The exposure of pregnant women to various environmental agents can result in miscarriage or stillbirth of the growing fetus, lead to low birth weight, neurological damage, birth defects, and a range of developmental problems after birth. Emissions from inadequately vented heat sources, unclean drinking water and a lack of sanitation, for instance, may present challenges to fetal health. Exposure to high concentrations of lead, various pesticides, or methyl mercury from contaminated fish can have a critical influence, depending on the the stage of pregnancy and the intensity of the exposure. Diseases, such as rubella, toxoplasmosis, AIDS, syphilis, measles, chickenpox, polio and some kinds of influenza can all damage the developing fetus.[7]

environmental hazards

A mother's caloric intake and the quality of her diet have a direct effect on an infant's size, birth weight, and vulnerability to stress after birth. Low birth weight infants (those weighing less than 2500 grams) can be more difficult to care for, are more likely to have developmental problems, and are at higher risk for illness and death in their early months. Birth weight is the most significant predictor of survival and healthy development. Eighteen per cent of infants worldwide are below an ideal weight at birth, and this figure climbs as high as 50 per cent in Bangladesh, where many mothers are poorly nourished.[8] Low birth weight matters little when a child is born into a healthy, supportive environment, but it becomes signficant under conditions of poverty and stress. A mother's adequate prenatal diet gives her infant an important head start in the ability to survive and thrive under difficult conditions. Sufficient and appropriate food for the mother is not the only criterion; it is also a matter of awareness. It is frequently not understood that women need extra food during pregnancy, and there is a belief in some places that eating less will mean an easier labour.

maternal diet

low birth weight

Many pregnant women are exposed to hazards and still have healthy babies. The healthier the mother is, the more resilient the child is likely to be before and after birth. It is critically important that all pregnant women have adequate prenatal care not only to ensure general good

6 UNICEF 1996, op cit Note 2
7 UNICEF (1990) *The State of the Environment 1990: Children and the Environment*, UNICEF/UNEP
8 UNICEF (1997) *The State of the World's Children 1997*, New York: Oxford University Press

pre-natal care

health, but to detect early signs of danger. Most of the significant problems of pregnancy, such as iron deficiency, can be cheaply and easily prevented. In an area of Nepal where vitamin A deficiency is common, for instance, deaths among pregnant women were found by one study to drop by 44 per cent when supplements were made available.[9] Good prenatal attention can also help determine the likelihood of some birth complications, and make it possible to plan ahead. A healthy, informed and well-nourished mother is far more likely to cope well with childbirth, be energetic and responsive to her infant's needs after birth, and able to care for any other children in the home. Prenatal care is also a most effective means of saving the lives of infants and improving their health status.

The more cynical members of society might argue that high infant mortality is a 'natural' way to control population in overcrowded cities. But ensuring the health of pregnant mothers and unborn children, besides being humane and a requirement of international law, is also extremely practical. High rates of infant mortality are associated with higher birth rates. Experience around the world has shown that when parents are confident that their children will survive and do well birth rates tend to go down.[10] And for every child that dies as a result of inadequate prenatal and delivery care, others survive unfairly handicapped in general health and capacities.

In spite of major gains, too many women still go without adequate prenatal care and education. Efforts must continue to make care available in ways that women will respond to. Among many pregnant women a preference has been noted for informal care within the community from people they know and trust, over that from trained professionals in facilities that may feel intimidating.[11] Prenatal care should be locally available, affordable, and women should be able to develop a personal relationship with providers.

- *Make family planning and reproductive health care easily available and affordable for all women and adolescent girls, in ways that they will find comfortable and acceptable (pp105, 118).*
- *Educate women and girls on basic hygiene, nutrition and reproductive information (pp115, 119).*
- *Raise awareness of pregnancy as a time of risk for both mother and child.*
- *Provide accessible, affordable prenatal care, nutritional supplements, and information for pregnant women (p103).*

ENVIRONMENTS OF CHILDBIRTH

Prenatal care is vital, but should never be considered a substitute for attention during birth. Ninety-nine percent of all deaths related to pregnancy and childbirth occur in the developing world, and the great majority are linked to deliveries.[12] Home births can be a fine solution when risks are low. But too many urban women in poverty, because of poor health and inadequate, unsanitary home environments, are at high risk for infection and other complications.

[9] UNICEF (1998) *The State of the World's Children 1998*, New York: Oxford University Press

[10] In Niger, for instance, where the under-five mortality rate has remained at 320 since 1960, the birth rate has dropped only from 54 to 53 per 1000 over that period of time. In Costa Rica, by contrast, where there is an unusual national focus on health care, under-five mortality rate has dropped from 112 to 16 over those years, and the birth rate is 25, or half of what it was in 1960. (UNICEF 1997, op cit Note 8)

[11] Ebrahim, G J (1985) *Social and Community Paediatrics in Developing Countries: Caring for the Rural and Urban Poor*, Houndmills, Basingstoke, Hampshire: Macmillan

[12] Safe Motherhood Initiative 1998, op cit Note 1

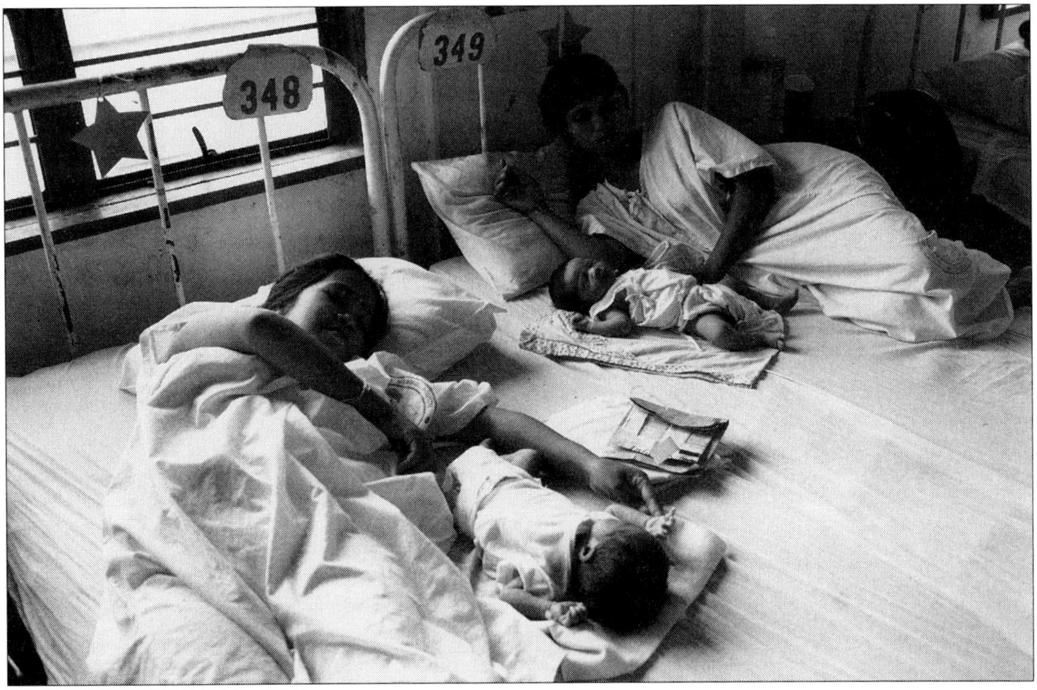

Hospitals frequently keep infants in separate nurseries after birth in the interests of efficient management. But when mothers and infants are kept together, breastfeeding rates go up and infant mortality drops. Here two new mothers enjoy the rooming-in policy at a 'baby friendly' hospital in Manila, Philippines.
UNICEF 1996, Shehzad Noorani

In spite of the recognized importance of trained assistance, nearly half the women in the world still give birth without the help of a skilled professional, using instead family members or untrained traditional birth attendants. In some countries the percentage is far higher.[13] Often women prefer the comfort of familiar attendants who share common beliefs and values. But harmful practices, such as the use of rusty, soiled razor blades for cutting the umbilical cord, can result in tragedy.

The lack of training for responding to obstetrical emergencies is also a danger, especially when neither emergency transport nor skilled back-up are reliably available. All these factors together contribute to extremely high levels of maternal and infant death, and to injuries and handicaps which are a lifelong drain on financial and emotional resources. Birth within high quality health care facilities, or at very least with a professional birth attendant (doctor or midwife), should be a priority. But the availability of adequate facilities and trained personnel is woefully lacking, and is unlikely to be a solution in most cities over the short term. In the meantime, measures must be taken to ensure that home births are as risk-free as possible.

Measures to improve the safety of home births

Routine prenatal care can determine whether a woman is a good candidate for home birth. If potential complications are identified, she should be referred for professional obstetrical care. For those whose births will take place at home, adequate preparations must be made, trained birth attendants should be present, and suitable back-up be in place in case of complications. Until more comprehensive services are made available, it

[13] Giri, K (1995) 'Safe Motherhood Strategies in the Developing Countries' in H M Wallace, Giri, K and Serrano, C V (eds) *Health Care of Women and Children in Developing Countries*, Oakland CA: Third Party Publishing Company

trained birth attendants

is critical that the role of traditional birth attendants be recognized, and that they be given training, supervision and support by the formal health system. A trained birth attendant can be a vital link with the formal system. Although she can do little in the event of serious obstetric emergencies, she can provide basic reproductive care, ensure good hygiene, refer mothers at high risk for complications, and call for back-up when necessary.[14]

birth kits

A safe birth can be difficult to ensure in the absence of sterile equipment or the means for keeping hands and surroundings clean. A number of programmes have made 'birth kits' available to trained birth attendants or to expectant mothers. At a bare minimum these kits contain a clean razor blade and sterile cord ties, but can also include disinfectant, soap, a clean sheet of plastic to cover the delivery surface, and sterile gauze pads and swabs for cord care. When supplied to trained birth attendants, they can also include items requiring some training for proper use, such as a thermometer, stethoscope or relevant drugs. The contents of such kits are best determined in the light of local conditions and local training programmes.[15]

emergency referral

Every woman, regardless of the quality of prenatal care, can develop life-threatening complications during childbirth. Delays or inaction can cost women their lives. A smoothly operating emergency referral system must be in place, and more specialized services must be readily available. There must be some means of rapid communication with the appropriate health facilities, or easily available emergency transportation. In Lusaka, Zambia, an agreement with a cab company allows any pregnant women with a problem to get a free ride to the hospital.

Birth in healthcare facilities

Many health facilities may themselves be inadequately equipped or maintained to provide appropriate care, especially in emergencies. Even minimal upgrading can make a significant difference. But even when hospitals offer a safe setting, they may be less than ideal in other ways.

hospital practices

Hospitals and other medical facilities have traditionally been organized to function efficiently for the busy professionals that staff them, and routine practices surrounding childbirth and post-partum care reflect this priority. Regulations frequently prevent family and friends from attending a woman while she is in labour, and her fears and uncertainties may not be met with the emotional support she needs. Births may be unnecessarily medicalized to save time for doctors and nursing staff; this can be challenging for infants, who remain vulnerable to drugs entering the mother's bloodstream up to the moment of birth.

A common practice, influenced by western models of care, is to separate mother and infant after delivery. Infants are routinely kept in hospital nurseries, where all their needs can be efficiently dealt with in one place. This may be effective for hospital management, but it violates the need for mother and infant to remain close after birth. The immature systems of the human infant are most effectively regulated by close physical contact. The warmth provided by skin contact ensures that the infant's temperature is evenly maintained. Touching, stroking and rocking activate breathing and digestion, and, together with the

14 Levitt, M J and Minden, M (1995) 'The Role of Traditional Birth Attendants in Safe Motherhood' in *Health care of Women and Children in Developing Countries*, Oakland CA: Third Party Publishing Company

15 Smith, J B and Fortney, J A (1996) *Birth Kits: an Assessment*, New York, UNICEF

familiar sound of the mother's heartbeat, serve to calm and reassure the child. Infants in constant contact with the mother are found to cry less and to sleep more peacefully. Research evidence indicates that early contact helps to get this vital relationship off to a good start, and may contribute to creating a close bond which becomes an emotional buffer in the face of later difficulties.[16]

bottle feeding

An important feature of hospital care is its relationship to bottle feeding. Beginning in the 1960s, there was a dramatic decline in breast-feeding in the South, in part owing to the pressure on urban women to go out to work. But the promotional efforts of infant formula companies also helped persuade mothers to abandon the healthy and economical tradition of breastfeeding. Practices in many hospitals, including the separation of infants from their mothers, supported bottle feeding. Formula companies often made free samples available to mothers while they were in hospital, and the overall pressure to take the 'modern' route was more than most mothers could resist!

Bottle feeding continues to be a troublesome issue. Especially in poor urban areas, conditions do not permit the sanitary precautions necessary for bottle feeding, and a practice promoted as being in the infant's best interest was in fact a threat both to infant health and the household economy. In addition, breastfeeding inhibits ovulation and functions as a natural form of birth control. In areas where breastfeeding generally continues until a child is three years old, the common spacing between children is more than three years. This safeguard disappears when bottle feeding becomes the norm. For more information on the benefits of breastfeeding, and on the issues raised by breastfeeding for mothers with HIV/AIDS, see p112.

baby-friendly hospitals

Since the early 1980s there has been a worldwide campaign to re-establish breastfeeding. Part of it has focused on creating an environment in hospital maternity units that is supportive of breastfeeding. Within these 'baby-friendly' hospitals, infants room in with their mothers, formula companies are kept out, and breastfeeding is encouraged by all means possible, so that it is comfortably established before mothers return home. These basic changes can have dramatic effects. At Baguio General Hospital in the Philippines, where many 'baby friendly' initiatives were pioneered, the infant mortality rate dropped by 95 per cent in two years.[17] The most difficult challenge has been to persuade hospital staff how important these changes are. It is vital that municipalities put their weight behind efforts to support breastfeeding, with the knowledge that it can contribute significantly both to child health and the family economy.

Many women return home after childbirth to trying conditions and quick resumption of a heavy workload. The time spent in the hospital or maternity clinic should be as far as possible one of rest and restoration. At Dulukal Hospital in Kathmandu, for instance, there is an outdoor 'birthing park' for mothers who have just given birth, a place of quiet, privacy and sunshine for rest and casual interaction with other mothers.[18]

- *Provide high quality training for birth assistants, including training in recognizing the need for referral and emergency care.*
- *Ensure the availability of hygienic supplies for home births.*

16 Trevathan, W R and McKenna, J J (1994) 'Evolutionary Environments of Birth and Infancy: Insights to Apply to Contemporary Life', *Children's Environments*, 11(2): 88–105

17 Black, M (1996) *Children First: The Story of UNICEF, Past and Present*, Oxford: Oxford University Press

18 Roger Hart, field trip, Nepal 1997

- *Make professional obstetrical care available for women with high risk pregnancies.*
- *Ensure the rapid availability of emergency care, including transportation to the hospital, in case of birth complications.*
- *Support hospitals and maternity centres to become 'baby-friendly'.*

FOLLOW-UP AFTER BIRTH

support for mothers

The days and weeks after birth can be a challenging time, especially for mothers in poor health and those with other children. Reliable support can help ensure both the mother's recovery and a good start for the infant. Maternal and infant health should be monitored by birth attendants or health outreach workers, and where there is a lack of support from fathers or household members, efforts must be made to ensure that adequate back-up is available within the community. Infants at risk must be identified, and should be given special medical attention. Support for breastfeeding is a high priority.

child spacing

It is generally agreed that in order to recover fully after pregnancy, a mother needs at least 24 months on an adequate diet. If pregnancies are spaced too closely, the risk of child mortality is greatly increased. When mothers have only a subsistence diet, recovery takes longer, and ready access to information about child spacing is even more important. Family planning should be easily available.[19]

birth registration

Another important concern is registration of the new child. This may seem unimportant relative to health and survival concerns, but it can affect a child seriously over the long term. When children lack official identification they may be prevented from being legally vaccinated, having access to health services or starting school. In later years they may be unable to vote, get married or enter formal employment. Children without birth certificates are also more vulnerable to such hazards as sexual trafficking, dangerous work and illegal recruitment into armies. In a number of countries, registration in hospital right after birth is a routine procedure. But the many children born outside of hospital must also be reached. Birth attendants can remind parents of this important procedure, and might even be given the authority to see that it is accomplished at the child's home in the days following birth. This is now happening in Ghana.[20]

- *Raise public awareness of the values of breastfeeding.*
- *Educate men on ways to support women during pregnancy, delivery and after birth.*
- *Make counseling about child spacing available.*
- *Facilitate birth registration.*

THE LARGER CONTEXT

The provision of prenatal care, properly assisted births and follow-up after childbirth are critical. But authorities must also recognize the wide

[19] Ebrahim, 1985, op cit Note 11
[20] Dow, U (1998) 'Birth Registration: the "First" Right' in UNICEF (ed) *Progress of Nations 1998*, New York: UNICEF

range of social, cultural and economic factors that underpin high fertility rates, high mortality, and maternal ill health. The risks associated with childbearing during teenage years have long been recognized. Yet early marriage and early pregnancy continue to be the norm in many countries. Not all pregnancies are desired, but ignorance, the unavailability of contraception, and the low status of women as decision makers prevent proper planning. As a result, women often take extreme measures to avoid pregnancy – 25 per cent of all maternal deaths in poor countries occur as a result of complications from unsafe abortions.[21] The low status of women contributes to their illiteracy and malnourishment, both of which are known to play a role in the outcomes of pregnancy. Education for girls, and efforts to raise awareness of women as human beings with rights, are essential starting points for tackling issues of fertility, childbirth, maternal and infant health.

women's status

[21] Giri, 1995, op cit Note 13

In unsafe, overcrowded and underserved housing, child care becomes an overwhelming task that can seldom be satisfactorily handled. Measures that result in improved living conditions affect children not only through the direct impact on health and development, but by easing parental burdens and anxieties. A woman and her children in the settlement of Sao Francisco do Palafitas, in San Luis, Brazil. UNICEF 1992, Sean Sprague

5 Housing for Children

Decent, affordable, secure housing is fundamental to the realization of a number of rights recognized by the Convention. Children have the right to a standard of living that supports their full development, and adequate housing is essential to this. Their right to grow up in a family environment has implications for the location and size of housing. The right to a cultural identity is supported by the living patterns that are possible within a dwelling. The right to non-discrimination applies in housing as elsewhere. Children are also protected by the Convention from arbitrary interference with family and home, which has implications for policy regarding eviction and forced removal.[1]

Standards for adequate housing, while established in general terms within discussions of broader human rights,[2] must be reconsidered in the light of children's particular requirements. Conditions that may be adequate for adults are not necessarily optimal for children's physical, emotional and intellectual development. The physical environment of the home should support parents and other caregivers in their efforts to provide reponsive, loving, nurturant care for children, and to create, within the framework of their culture, a setting that ensures safety and health and promotes children's full development. This chapter outlines

[1] See CRC preamble, and Articles 2, 9, 16, 27, 30

some specific measures that local authorities can take towards these ends.

In many cities and communities, activities associated with everyday household life take place in shared courtyards, on pavements or even in the street. Discussion of 'the dwelling' in this chapter refers not only to the enclosed space occupied by a household, but to these shared outdoor spaces.

THE SIGNIFICANCE OF THE DWELLING FOR CHILDREN'S DEVELOPMENT

Environmental policy in urban areas tends to stress large-scale environmental issues that affect the population as a whole. But problems within housing and its immediate surroundings exert the most significant influence on health and well-being, particularly for young children who spend the greater part of their time at home or close by. Children are disproportionately affected by many environmental stressors. Their capacity to tolerate pollution and toxins is lower, they are more vulnerable to disease, and their propensity for injury is higher. Water quality and quantity, sanitation, drainage and waste removal, location in regard to traffic, air quality in the home, facilities for food preparation and storage, and safety awareness can all profoundly affect both children's current health and their long term development.[3]

Reliable housing supports not only physical health, but also emotional security, stability, and the comfort of daily routines. Children can become deeply attached to familiar surroundings, and this, like their human attachments, is a wellspring for their trust in the world.[4] This security is challenged when housing is vulnerable to flooding, mudslides and other disasters; or when tenure is insecure. The home may also be the site of violence and abusive behaviour, and far from being a refuge and a source of security in a child's life, may become instead a domain of terror.

Home is the primary environment for children's early social and intellectual development. If they are well cared-for and have had adequate loving human contact, most of their energy in early years will be focused on interaction with features of the physical environment – with objects and settings that invite exploration, manipulation and imaginative experimentation, both together and with others.[5] But the living conditions of many poor urban children deny them access to safe, stimulating, varied play environments, and can deprive them of the opportunities they need to develop as socially competent and intellectually curious beings.

The dwelling is also a means of socialization. The culture of any group is anchored in patterns of household life and shaped by the material environment. The way that food is prepared and eaten, the way that family members deal with one another and with neighbours, understandings about territory and privacy, are all affected by physical space and the kinds of organization and interaction it allows. The level of crowding, access to outdoor space, opportunities for withdrawal, space to play with other children, all contribute to a child's social identity and understanding. Through these daily interactions, children acquire the values and norms of family and culture.[6] But especially under conditions of poverty there

2 The following seven criteria have been recognized as the functional parameters for adequate housing under Article 11(1) of the International Covenant on Economic, Social and Cultural Rights: legal security of tenure; availability of services, materials, facilities and infrastructure; affordability; habitability; accessibility; location; cultural adequacy. From General Comment No 4 (1991) of the Committee on Economic, Social and Cultural Rights on the right to adequate housing.

3 Satterthwaite, D, Hart, R, Levy, C, Mitlin, D, Ross, D, Smit, J, Stephens, C (1996) *The Environment for Children*, London: Earthscan

4 Chawla, L (1992) 'Childhood Place Attachments' in Altman, I and Low, S (eds) *Place Attachment*, New York: Plenum

5 Valsiner, J (1987) *Culture and the Development of Children's Action*, New York: Wiley; Wohlwill, J and Heft, H (1987) 'The Physical Environment and the Development of the Child' in Stokols, D and Altman, I (eds) *Handbook of Environmental Psychology*, New York: Wiley

6 Valsiner, J (ed) (1988) *Child Development Within Culturally Structured Environments*, Norwood, New Jersey: Ablex; Whiting, B B and Edwards, C P (1988) Children of Different Worlds: *The Formation of Social Behavior*, Cambridge MA: Harvard University Press

may be many aspects of their environment over which residents have little control, and patterns of interaction will be affected. In the case of minority or refugee families, the dwelling becomes particularly critical as a medium for acquiring cultural identity, since community life is less likely to reinforce the values of the family.

the impact of housing for the quality of care

Poor housing also affects parents. In unsafe dwellings with insufficient space and poor facilities, child care becomes an overwhelming task. Many difficult choices must be made, and the inevitable compromises cannot help but affect children's well-being. Is it better to let children go hungry, or to give them food that may be contaminated because of inadequate storage? Should toddlers play next to an open sewer, or be kept indoors where air quality is poor because of unventilated cooking? Anxiety may accompany even minor decisions, and the burdens of child and household management can result in parental fatigue and debilitation. This is bound to affect their capacity to be the warm, responsive and proactive caregivers that children need. Any improvements to living environments will affect children positively, not only through the direct impact on health and development, but by easing parental anxieties and responsibilities.[7]

WORKING TOWARDS HOMES THAT SUPPORT CHILDREN'S RIGHTS

Better living conditions for children can be achieved by a range of measures. Some, but not all, call for significant investment. Primarily they call for a willingness on the part of local authorities to consider the interests of children and their families, and to involve residents in local planning and management decisions.

Security of tenure

A high proportion of families in urban areas of the South live in constant fear of eviction or forced removal. We have discussed the implications of insecure tenure for family stability earlier (see p44). Here we will focus on the implications for children.

The costs of eviction for children are enormous, and can affect both immediate welfare and long term development. Evictions often precipitate homelessness. Even when families are relocated or find new housing, there is major economic upheaval. Home and possessions are often destroyed, and the family's means of livelihood may be threatened. Evictions can lead to family separation if breadwinners are forced to look for new work further away. The loss of social networks can undermine the family's capacity to cope. Schooling is frequently interrupted, and financial difficulties related to eviction may make it difficult for children to resume schooling in a new location. Not infrequently, children are pushed into the labour market.

Children faced with violent evictions may experience real trauma, with significant long term effects for their psychological health. In metro Manila, where housing demolitions affect on average more than 1,800 children each month, Urban Poor Associates have recorded the experi-

7 Bartlett, S N (1997) 'Housing as a Factor in the Socialization of Children: A Critical Review of the Literature', *Merrill-Palmer Quarterly*, 43(2): 169–198

ence of some young victims of forced removal. Children as young as four years of age describe the violence and confusion of the proceedings, the presence of heavily armed police, the bulldozers destroying homes and valued possessions, the teargas fumes, the family members and friends wounded or even killed. They speak of sleeping rough after the evictions, of becoming separated from family, of being hungry and sick. They mourn the loss of friends and playmates and familiar surroundings, and they describe the subsequent disruption in their families. Many of these children exhibit symptoms of trauma long after the event. Some refuse to remember that eviction ever happened. Others, on recalling it, re-experience the panic of the day, and the dizziness and headaches from the teargas. Some children have recurring nightmares, others become apathetic and withdrawn. Many are fearful when they see people in uniform.[8] The impact tends to be greatest for the youngest victims. Research has indicated that children under the age of ten, when faced with traumatic experiences, are three times more likely than adults to respond with long term psychological disturbances.[9]

While millions around the world are forcibly evicted each year, hundreds of millions more have insecure tenure, and must cope with the resulting anxiety and the stress of frequent relocation. Relocation to cheaper neighbourhoods is also a frequent survival strategy, and the realities of the labour market make transience unavoidable for many families. Young children who move frequently may have difficulty establishing the sense of belonging that is a source of emotional strength, especially when relocation takes place in an atmosphere of adult anxiety and distress.

the psychological impacts of forced eviction

Whenever possible, municipal assistance should be available to help prevent unwanted moves. If relocation is unavoidable, the emotional disruption for children can be kept to a minimum when parents are able to plan the move, when the new home is adequate and secure, when provision has been made for the family's needs, and when serious loss of income is not a factor.

- *See Chapter 3 for a full discussion of measures local authorities can take to improve security of tenure and housing stability.*

Location

The location of housing is critical to children's well-being, not only because it directly affects their activities, but because of its impact on overall family functioning and survival. The following factors should be considered in locating housing that is adequate for children:

- *Proximity to open sewers, contaminated water, standing water, toxins, environmental waste, heavy traffic, hazards such as flooding and mudslides, and other factors that affect children's health and safety (see pp45, 96, 132).*
- *Proximity to health services, schools, child care and social welfare services.*
- *Access to opportunities for livelihood (p50).*
- *Proximity to extended family, friends and other social support systems (p54).*

8 Dizon, A M and Quijano, S (1997) 'Impact of Eviction on Children', Urban Poor Associates/Asian Coalition for Housing Rights (ACHR)/United Nations Economic and Social Commission for Asia and the Pacific (UN-ESCA)

9 Garbarino, J and Bedard, C (1996) 'Spiritual Challenges to Children facing Violent Trauma', *Childhood*, 3(4): 467–479

- *Proximity to safe opportunities for recreation and play (see p134).*
- *Affordable public transportation (p52).*
- *Educate families about the dangers for their children of settling in high-risk areas.*
- *Use all available means to provide access to safe and supportive locations for housing (see p42).*

Relationships with neighbours and with the street

social relations and space

Social relations, community functioning and the use of outdoor space can all be affected by the layout and management of the area surrounding housing. Small changes may affect the incidence of vandalism and crime, promote children's play, and encourage interaction between neighbours (see Chapter 7).[10] Here we will review some ways to help families provide appropriate environments for child rearing and mutual support. Where housing is formally provided by municipalities or community associations, these issues should be kept in mind from the beginning of the planning process, and residents should be involved in the discussion But even in existing settlements, modifications and improvements can continue to be made. The subtleties of altering and managing the space around housing are best handled by neighbours themselves, with the support of municipal agencies.

Traffic calming

Especially for families who live along heavily trafficked roads and whose living space extends of necessity out into the street, dangers to young children can be severe. Various measures have been employed around the world to help residents lay claim to the space around their homes, and to improve their children's safety, and these will be discussed in Chapter 7.

- *See p132 for a discussion of traffic calming approaches.*

Common space, territory and control

courtyards

For many families in cities of the South, a range of daily functions is performed outside their overcrowded dwellings. People may cook, hang laundry, wash, and even sleep in public space. Measures can be taken to increase the level of control that people are able to exercise over this space. The arrangement of dwelling units around a central shared space, for instance, can support children's safe play and the cooperative interaction of neighbours. Even with existing dwellings, areas can be clearly demarcated from the street and the public domain, whether by fencing, trees or shrubs. Residents can then more easily lay claim to space for their common use. The effects for children can be dramatic. Observers from both North and South report the heavy use of such communal areas for play, with reduced use of dangerous streets and other unsafe areas. Municipalities can support such efforts by providing appropriate materials, funds and technical support.

[10] Kaplan, S and Kaplan, R (eds) (1982) *Humanscape: Environments for People,* Ann Arbor: Ulrich's Books

Harmony between close neighbours improves the quality of life for small children, promoting shared responsibility for child care and greater opportunities for play. A number of measures can be taken to foster positive relations and the cooperative use of shared space. Neighbourhood women and their children on a porch in Thailand. UNICEF, Marcus Halevi

It is widely recognized that the presence of vegetation surrounding housing has positive social effects. In a low-income inner-city area of Chicago, for instance, trees and vegetation were found to attract residents outdoors and to foster neighbourhood ties. Compared to those living next to more barren areas, residents had increased social activity, knew more of their neighbours, had stronger feelings of belonging, and reported that their neighbours were more concerned with helping one another.[11] Municipalities can support residents by making plants and trees available for planting.

- *Involve residents in any efforts to improve space near their dwellings.*
- *When possible make communal space available to near neighbours, and support them in using it effectively.*
- *Support efforts to plant vegetation in residential areas.*

Hostilities among neighbours

It is important to children that relations with close neighbours be positive. Their enjoyment of common space for play and their access to other children may be affected by tension and hostility. Child care is also more difficult to share when relations deteriorate. Disputes between neighbours occur around use of common space or facilities. If garbage is deposited for pick-up outside a particular family's door, for instance, there can be resentment when it is not promptly collected. If shared toilets are poorly maintained, feelings can run high. When water or electricity are paid for jointly, there are many opportunities for disagreement. Simple measures can often improve the situation. Schedules for

[11] Kuo, F E, Sullivan, W C, Coley, R L, Brunson, L (1998) 'Fertile Ground for Community: Inner City Neighborhood Common Space', *American Journal of Community Psychology*, in press

garbage collection, for instance, can be clearly communicated and adhered to. Electricity rates can be based on the number of appliances used by a household. Neighbours need to come together to discuss issues with one another and with agency representatives, so that locally acceptable standards can be established.

- *Encourage the participation of community members in establishing acceptable standards for group provision.*

Cultural issues

housing, culture and identity

Although different groups have different ways of achieving a sense of privacy or territory, there is no question that people from all cultures have strong feelings about the control of the space they occupy.[12] Culture is dynamic, and changes in response to changing physical and economic conditions. But when change is too rapid to be assimilated, as is the case for many urban residents, it can result in a loss of group identity and in confusion about social roles. When families can find ways to hold on to routines and rituals that are important to them, this can strengthen family and group cohesion and enhance security for children.

To strengthen cultural identity at household level, municipalities should ensure maximum resident participation. Especially in the planning of new settlements and in relocation, residents, and particularly women, should be involved in decisions about the distribution and arrangement of housing. When such decisions are based on kinship and existing social relationships, they are more likely to foster harmony and solidarity among neighbours, and understandings about territory are more likely to be respected.

- *Ensure maximum resident participation in the planning and management of housing and service provision (see p46).*

Water and sanitation

The personal and environmental health benefits of adequate sanitation, drainage, and water provision are well known, and will be discussed on p96. Here we will briefly summarize some implications of such provision, or its absence, for children, and for those who care for them in the home.

Water provision

The easy availability of safe and sufficient water supplies is important not only for children's health, but for easing the burden of daily life in conditions of poverty. The quantity of water is as important, or even more important, to health than water quality. Contaminated water contributes to outbreaks of disease, but too little water makes it impossible to maintain sanitary conditions, and contributes to levels of endemic disease that are a major cause of child mortality.[13] The amount of water needed daily in households with young children is considerable. Simply keeping the hands, faces and bottoms of young children clean requires a

12 Altman, I (1975) *The Environment and Social Behavior: Privacy, Personal Space, Territory and Crowding*, Monterey, California: Brooks/Cole

13 Cairncross, S (1990) 'Water Supply and the Urban Poor' in Hardoy, J Cairncross, S, Satterthwaite, D (eds) *The Poor Die Young: Housing and Health in Third World Cities*, London: Earthscan

steady supply. Cooking, drinking, washing, toileting and laundry together can take easily 30 to 40 litres per person every day. It is not unusual for 400 to 500 litres per person to be used daily by the rich or those with private supplies.[14] If water must be purchased from vendors, expense is likely to get in the way of sufficient supplies to run a household and meet the needs of young children. If water must be carried from public standpipes, then the greater the distance and the longer the lines, the less likely it is that sufficient water will be fetched, even when supplies are adequate. Children are often responsible for carrying water, and this, too, must be taken into consideration. A distance acceptable for an adult can be punishing for a small child. Wherever possible, water should be piped to individual dwellings or yards, and be made available on a regular basis. When public standpipes are unavoidable, they must be shared with as few households as possible. Even when piped water is available, supplies may be irregular and water pressure low. Irregular supplies encourage households to store water, which increases risk of contamination. When water must be stored, tanks or containers must be covered to prevent breeding insects such as the Aedes group of mosquitoes, that transmit diseases such as dengue and yellow fever.[15] The possibility of children drowning must also be considered.

implications of water supply for children and caregivers

- *Consider the daily needs of households with young children when determining adequate water supplies.*
- *Consider the implications for children and overtaxed caregivers of carrying water long distances.*
- *Whenever possible pipe water to individual dwellings and ensure regular availability.*

Sanitation

Many low-income settlements are served, at best, by communal latrines that may be filthy, foul smelling, crowded, and distant from many of the dwellings they serve. Such arrangements are particularly challenging for young children and their caregivers. Taking a young child any distance for toileting is impractical, especially when there is more than one child to be tended, and when a line at the latrine is likely. It is difficult for young children to wait when they need to eliminate, and this problem intensifies when frequent bouts of diarrhoea are common. The darkness and stench of many latrines can make their use an unpleasant and frightening prospect for a young child. In many cases they are fearful of falling through an over-large pit opening. Where there are long lines children may also be elbowed out of the way. Under such conditions they are likely to squat in lanes or gutters, which will quickly become fouled. Because of the frequently unsanitary habits of young children and their proximity to the ground, their excreta tend to be a particularly potent source of infection. Studies in Sri Lanka showed that 70 per cent of children from disadvantaged communities were afflicted with worms as a result of poor sanitation.[16] Shared facilities can also present a safety hazard for older children, and for girls in particular, who may be victims of harassment.

In order to promote safety and health, encoura' e hygienic habits in children, and simplify the demands of child care, it ' critical that latrines

[14] Godin, L (1987) 'Preparation des projets urbains d'amenagement', Washington DC: World Bank
[15] Rossi-Espagnet, A, Goldstein, G B, Tabibzadeh, I (1991) 'Urbanization and Health in Developing Countries: A Challenge for the Health of All', *World Health Statistical Quarterly*, 44(4): 186–244
[16] Boyden, J and Holden, P (1991) *Children of the Cities*, London: Zed Books

latrines that meet children's needs

be close by, and designed to accomodate young children. Wherever possible, easily maintained in-house toilets or latrines are the ideal. It is essential that these be maintained properly or they, too, will present health hazards. Water sources are needed close by for hand washing. Because of difficulties in ensuring access and cleanliness, shared latrines are the least desirable solution and should be used only when all else fails, or when the use of in-house latrines is not acceptable. There are some excellent examples in India of shared latrines designed especially for children, usually adjacent to the latrines used by adults. They are generally basic open air constructions, with smaller seats and drains, and often with bars for children to hold on to. They tend to be technically simple pour-flush designs, easy to maintain, and inexpensive to construct. A recent example is the ten-seat children's latrine in the crowded Viyamshala settlement of Bangalore, constructed by the Mahila Milan women's federation with funds contributed by local families. Mothers can keep a look-out nearby, while they wash clothes at the tap or talk to friends. The latrine's low boundary walls have been decorated with patterns of pebbles, so that children can practice counting as they sit.1In the absence of household facilities, municipalities can also encourage the use of simple, easy-to-clean commodes for the youngest children.

- *Provision for sanitation must take into account the health, safety and comfort of children, as well as the convenience of overworked caregivers.*
- *Wherever possible, support the provision of easily maintained in-house toilets.*
- *See p96, for more detail on provision of community sanitation.*
- *Develop educational programms and media campaigns to persuade parents of the importance of sanitation to their children's health.*

Drainage and garbage removal

the effects for health and play

The efficient removal of garbage and drainage of waste water is important not only to prevent the breeding of certain disease vectors, but to ensure that the surroundings of the dwelling are safe and inviting for children's play. Especially when sanitation is inadequate, excreta may be dumped in garbage piles or in drainage channels. When clogging or flooding occurs, waste and excreta can be widely spread.

- *See p98 for recommendations.*

Food storage and preparation

cooking facilities and nutrition

Child health and the quality of child care are affected by the ease and safety with which food can be prepared and stored. Malnutrition is not simply a function of the amount of food a household can purchase, but is affected by the difficulty of preparation. Young children need a number of small meals in a day, particularly when their primary sources of nourishment are bulky foods that quickly fill small stomachs without providing concentrated nutrition. The ability to cook or warm food easily can be essential to ensuring that young children get the nutrition they need. This is difficult when fires must be built, when fuel supplies are inadequate, or when there are heavy demands on a caregiver's time. The tendency will then be to produce one or two larger meals each day, and young children may be seriously shortchanged (see p111).

Cooking facilities can also have a significant effect on air quality. Open fires and inadequately ventilated stoves can help to cause respiratory ailments, especially for women and small children who are likely to spend more time inside.[17] Open fires and unstable burners also risk burns to small children, especially under crowded conditions. Local authorities can help by investigating the most appropriate, safe and fuel-efficient cooking methods for local conditions, and by supporting efforts to make the right equipment cheaply available to poor households, along with the training for using it. Subsidization of appropriate fuel can serve as an incentive.

cooking facilities and respiratory ailments

Adequate storage for food is also important. In hot climates, cooked food left standing even for short periods may contain high levels of pathogens; to eat it is to risk diarrhoeal disease. Many fresh foods also require refrigeration. Even grains and legumes need appropriate storage to avoid infestation by insects and rodents. If food cannot be stored safely, it is necessary to purchase and cook it in smaller quantities, thereby sacrificing economy and convenience. The costs of making local solutions available are likely to be less than those experienced over time through the loss of spoiled food or the burdens of illness. Local community-managed 'fair price' shops that are able to buy in bulk and retail in small portions with minimal surcharge can be a big help (see p114).

food storage

Food also has cultural and emotional implications for children and their families. The way it is prepared and eaten can be a source of comfort and predictability in life, a way of connecting with tradition and celebration and strengthening the social fabric. In any effort to promote safety and efficiency, it is important to take into account the significance of cooking and eating as a medium for group identity.

food preparation and culture

- *Support the availability of affordable, safe, fuel-efficient cooking equipment, along with training for using it.*
- *Find appropriate local solutions for safe food storage, and make them easily available.*

The construction of housing

The physical construction of housing can affect child health in a number of ways:

- Rodents and insects which infest the walls and roofs of many dwellings are frequently vectors of disease. Construction materials which will not harbour pests can make a significant difference to children's health.
- Walls which stay damp may encourage molds, asthma attacks and respiratory infections. Housing materials should be moisture proof.
- Inadequate ventilation encourages the spread of airborne infections.

disease vectors

dampness

[17] Satterthwaite and others, 1996, op cit Note 3

ventilation

comfort

It also affects the body's capacity to regulate heat and can cause lethargy, discomfort and sleeping difficulties. Windows and other openings should be oriented to promote air flow. For reasons of security people often close windows and doors at night, just when ventilation may be most necessary. Fixed ventilation openings which are louvered or have security bars can ensure air flow at night.

- Roofing materials which are light in colour deflect heat and can promote greater indoor comfort.

air quality

- Proper exits for smoke from cooking fires can improve interior air quality and prevent respiratory and eye problems.

malaria

- Screening can protect children and their families from flies and malaria-carrying mosquitoes. Rats can be controlled by blocking entry ways.
- Floors which can be easily cleaned minimize the contact of small children with pathogens and disease vectors.[18]

The most efficient and economical construction measures for supporting children's health should be locally assessed, and where possible, both technical and material support should be made available to ensure the most healthful and appropriate local adaptations.

- *Determine the most efficient and economical building materials and construction methods for supporting children's health under local conditions.*
- *Make technical and material assistance available to ensure the construction of healthful housing.*

Preventing injury and poisoning in the home

Unintentional injuries are a major cause of death and disability for young children. In the United States 64 per cent of all such injuries for children under three occur at home, and are a leading cause of hospitalization.[19] Because of the higher prevalence of disease in the South, injuries may appear to be less significant. But some kinds of household injuries are far more common in cities of the South, owing to such factors as overcrowding, poor lighting, open cooking and the domestic work demands on children.

Once infants are mobile, safety becomes an increasing concern. They are driven by the desire to investigate and to extend their skills by crawling, climbing, exploring and putting objects in their mouths. In conditions of urban poverty, excreta, broken glass, crawling insects, plastic bags, rotted food and burning coals are common hazards. Children of this age have the highest incidence of intestinal disease, as they make intimate contact with the numerous pathogens in their environment.

As children learn to walk they experience a growing need for independence and experimentation, and are perhaps more prone to injury than at any other age – they have mobility and intense curiosity without an understanding of danger. Exposed cooking arrangements, dangerous equipment, open sewers, heavy traffic, unsafe construction

[18] Davey and Lightbody (1987, 5th edition, revised by David Stevenson) *The Control of Disease in the Tropics: A Handbook for Physicians and Other Workers in Tropical and International Community Health*, London: H K Lewis & Co

[19] US Department of Health and Human Services (1996) *Child and Adolescent Emergency Department Visit Handbook*, Washington DC: US Department of Health and Human Services

and debris all contribute to making their surroundings extremely hazardous. The demands on caregivers are at their most extreme during these earliest years, and there is a critical need for education and support on safety and hygiene by outreach workers. Injuries are also common for children as they grow older and begin to help with household tasks. They may trip and fall carrying heavy loads, or be seriously burned as they attempt to deal with heavy cooking equipment or work surfaces that are too high for them.

'accidents' are not inevitable; they are events that can be prevented

Too little attention is paid to the problem of household injury. There is a tendency to take a fatalistic attitude to it, and to see children's injuries as 'accidents' that are somehow inevitable instead of events that can be prevented. Improved public information and minor modifications to homes can make a significant difference, not only in preventing injury or even death, but also ensuring that play is not unnecessarily restricted.[20] It is unrealistic to argue that all environments occupied by children should be completely risk-free; children must learn to respond mindfully to risk. But unnecessary hazards have no place in a child's surroundings. An important beginning is a concerted public campaign to raise awareness of how injury can be avoided.

finding local solutions

Because of the wide range of housing types, a universal set of guidelines is not feasible. A more practical strategy is to establish a process for informing families so that they can adopt injury prevention strategies. It is not enough simply to raise awareness. Parents must also have access to practical measures for addressing the prevalent issues in a particular area, such as simple guards that can be set up around stoves, or lockable boxes for medicines, bleach and other dangerous chemicals.

A large number of children are injured when they are left unattended at home by working parents who have no access to child care. Infants tied to heavy objects to prevent them from coming to harm, for instance, may be strangled by the very cords that secure them. In such cases the availability of good child care is the only reasonable solution.

lead poisoning

In Chapter 6 (p98) we discuss the hazard that lead poisoning presents for children. Motor vehicle exhaust is the most significant source, but it is important to be aware that peeling paint in old buildings is also a common cause of lead poisoning, as well as utensils used in cooking and eating which have been soldered or glazed with substances containing lead. Health authorities should raise awareness of these dangers, and families with young children should be actively discouraged from living in buildings where there is old, peeling lead-based paint.

- *Raise awareness of the fact that 'accidents' are preventable.*
- *Assess common injury patterns within communities.*
- *Create locally relevant posters or pamphlets illustrating strategies for preventing common household injuries.*
- *Train outreach workers to assist parents in performing household safety checks.*
- *Make practical solutions available for particularly common problems.*
- *Support the availability of high quality child care.*
- *Use child care centres as models for safe design and organization.*

[20] Iltus, S (1994) *Parental Ideologies in the Home Safety Management of One to Four Year Old Children*, dissertation for the Environmental Psychology Program, New York, The Graduate School and University Center of the City University of New York

Problems with overcrowding

The experience of crowding is in part culturally mediated: conditions considered stressful by one group may be acceptable or even comforting for another.[21] But without question there is a point at which high densities begin to have a negative effect on the quality of life, resulting in both physical and psychological stress.[22] Overcrowding is a serious issue in many poor urban settlements. Many low-income families occupy dwellings that are too small to allow all household members to sleep at one time. It is not uncommon for families to live in a single room with as little as one square meter per person of floor space.[23]

Overcrowding exacerbates health problems. Infectious diseases are more easily transmitted, the need for ventilation is increased, more waste is generated, and there are added demands for water and sanitation. The frequency of household injury for children increases with insufficient space.[24] Crowding also affects psychological well-being. More household traffic, higher noise levels and more frequent interpersonal encounters can all contribute to stress and social tensions for both children and adults. Recent research with working class children in urban India links chronic residential crowding with behavioural difficulties at school, poor academic achievement, heightened vulnerability to learned helplessness for girls, elevated blood pressure for boys, and impaired parent-child relationships.[25]

When space is tight indoors and out, and especially when it is combined with unsafe conditions for play, children may feel restricted and the need for discipline will increase.[26] When neighbours live in close quarters and are likely to complain about noise, parents have additional reason to control and subdue their children. Under these conditions, developmental opportunities for children often take second place to expedient management.

Research from different cultures suggests that crowded conditions contribute to lower levels of responsiveness on the part of parents.[27] A number of researchers have related crowded household conditions to punitive parenting practices, and some have argued that household space may be a factor in child abuse.[28] For both parents and children, the ability to get away from a potentially explosive situation can be important to maintaining control. It is not possible on the basis of limited evidence to conclude that inadequate space is a cause for abusive behaviour across a range of settings, but it seems clear that a lack of space can contribute to the parental stress that is a factor in child abuse (see p81).

Overcrowding as a strategy for survival

Low-income families often have to cope with dangerously overcrowded conditions because these offer other essential advantages. Most frequently, because of location or affordability, they free up time or income for other basic needs. Married children may stay on with parents because of the high cost of finding their own accomodation; or families may rent out space to generate income. A more crowded central location may cut the time and expense of travel to work, make health services and education more accessible, and allow proximity to family members and social support. Low-income families may choose overcrowded condi-

21 See, for example, Altman, I and Chemers, M M (1983) *Culture and Environment*, New York: Cambridge University Press; Hall, E T (1966) *The Hidden Dimension*, New York: Doubleday

22 Evans, G W and Cohen, S (1987) 'Environmental Stress' in Stokols, D and Altman, I (eds) *Handbook of Environmental Psychology*, New York: Wiley; Evans, G W, Lepore, S J, Shejwal, B R, Palsane, M N (1998) 'Chronic Residential Crowding and Children's Wellbeing: an Ecological Perspective', *Child Development*, in press; Wohlwill, J and van Vliet, W (1985) *Habitats for Children: The Impacts of Density*, Hillsdale NJ: Lawrence Erlbaum

23 Aina, T A (1989) 'Health, Habitat and Underdevelopment – with Special Reference to a Low- Income Settlement in Metropolitan Lagos', London: IIED Technical Report

24 Satterthwaite and others, 1996, op cit Note 3

25 Evans and others, 1998, op cit Note 22

26 See for instance Newson, J and Newson, E (1970) *Four Years Old in an Urban Community (2nd edition)*, New York: Penguin Books

tions in areas with adequate provision of water and sanitation, against less crowded conditions where provision is poor or non-existent.

For all these reasons 'slum-clearance' programmes are no solution to overcrowding. They are often justified on the grounds of improving public health, but they may actually increase health problems, destroy social support systems and jeopardize livelihood. Even when displaced residents are provided with less crowded accommodation, their tenuous strategies for survival may be destroyed. Instead of undermining these strategies by displacing people, local authorities can take the more effective and economical route of lessening the negative impacts of overcrowding.

'slum clearance' is not the solution to overcrowding

Factors that alleviate the impact of crowding

The impact of crowding can be mitigated by the quality of the surroundings. It is not necessarily the high density that is the problem, but such factors as inadequate facilities for food storage and preparation; inadequate washing and laundry facilities; inadequate provision of toilets; poor ventilation (especially in kitchens); the type of fuel used for cooking or heating; the lack of a regular waste collection service; floor surfaces that are not easily cleaned; the lack of safe, well-maintained play space for children; lack of space for income generation.

Addressing these problems directly through improved provision is more likely to meet the priorities of more residents than any attempt to resettle people. A good example is a programme in Nicaragua, PRODEL, which makes loans available for families in poor squatter areas for small-scale upgrading and repairs. Municipal authorities provide technical assistance to households in developing upgrading plans and calculating how repayments can be made.[29]

- *Support the expansion of homes, if necessary by changing regulations (for instance, permitting the development of two- or three-storey structures where one-storey structures currently exist).*
- *Support home improvements that alleviate the stress of overcrowding.*
- *Promote solutions within the community that help alleviate the problems of crowding at home – for instance, through the provision of play space in the neighbourhood, a place where older children can study, or space for small-scale livelihoods.*

Violence in the home

Violence in the home cannot be seen as an outcome of housing conditions (although some links have been demonstrated). Nonetheless, it makes sense to discuss the issue in this chapter, since it is related to family life. The experience of violence at home is devastating for children, whether directed at themselves or others. It undermines trust in those who should be their protectors, and destroys any sense of home as a refuge from stress. The developmental implications are discussed in more detail in Chapter 2 (p24).

In most countries there has been little research on the prevalence of domestic violence and child abuse. When there are official figures, they

[27] Wachs, T D and O Camli (1991) 'Do Ecological or Individual Characteristics Mediate the Influence of the Physical Environment upon Maternal Behavior?', *Journal of Environmental Psychology*, 11: 249–264; Whiting, B B and J W M Whiting (1975) *Children of Six Cultures: A Psychocultural Analysis*, Cambridge, MA: Harvard University Press

[28] See for example Bartlett, S N (1998) 'Does Poor Housing Perpetuate Poverty?', Childhood, 5(4): 403–421; Peterman, P J (1981) 'Parenting and Environmental Considerations', *American Journal of Orthopsychiatry*, 5(2): 351–355

[29] Stein, A (1996) *Decentralization and Urban Poverty Reduction in Nicaragua: The Experience of the Local Development Programme (PRODEL)*, IIED Paper Series on Poverty Reduction in Urban Areas, London: IIED

may be misleading. Confidential interviews with children suggest that rates of violence and sexual abuse are far higher than statistics indicate.[30] It seems likely that a significant proportion of women and children fall victim to violence within the home. Some children appear to be more vulnerable to abuse than others. Stepchildren and foster children, girls, children with disabilities and children under two years of age are more often victims of harsh treatment.[31]

pressures of poverty can contribute to abuse

The mistreatment of children is closely associated with families' overall quality of life.[32] Pressures on parents in poverty can sometimes make it difficult to draw the line between abuse and neglect. There is some indication in the North that the higher reported rates of child abuse among poorer families may be simply a function of the scrutiny that poor families endure. But there seems to be no question that ill-health, overwork, fatigue and anxiety can contribute, along with substandard conditions, to undermine parental patience and feed frustration. Tensions are often released against those who are weakest and least able to defend themselves.[33] The relationship with poverty holds true for the abuse of women. Research on domestic violence among low-income urban households in Ecuador found that episodes of abuse were always identified by women as the direct consequence of insufficient cash; the frustration of men who were not earning enough was quickly translated into anger and violence.[34]

The prevalence of domestic violence is also a function of social attitudes. In many countries it is assumed that men have the right to settle domestic disputes without outside interference. In the same way it is considered the right of adults to 'manage' children as they see fit. When physical punishment is condoned in this way, it can easily spill over into violence. The use of force against children or those close to them encourages children to think of it as an acceptable way of solving problems, and this can stimulate their own aggression. Research (mostly from the United States) indicates that the best predictor of violence in adults is the experience of violent behaviour in childhood. One study found that abused and neglected children were 53 per cent more likely to be arrested as juveniles, and 38 per cent more likely to be involved in violent crime.[35] Another study found that boys who witness violence by their fathers are ten times more likely to become batterers themselves.[36] Violence in the home spills out into the larger world, and helps to shape a society that is tolerant of violence.

Measures to combat household violence must begin with recognizing the prevalence and seriousness of the issue, and the rights of both women and children to protection. Parents and other caregivers can be encouraged to recognize that violence can escalate out of control, and to consider other forms of discipline. Awareness can be raised through the media, parent education classes, community health and other outreach workers. Legal reforms should be undertaken to ban violence on any level against both women and children.

In every community there should be easily accessible and well-publicized resources for women and children who wish to seek confidential advice or assistance. Police, health workers, teachers, and others in contact with children should be trained to respond with alertness and sensitivity. The responsibility of local authorities, and specifically of child protection agencies, is a challenging one. Some of the most damaging situations for

30 Newell, P (1997) 'Children and Violence', *Innocenti Digest #2*, Florence: UNICEF International Child Development Centre
31 Boyden and Holden, 1991, op cit, Note 16
32 Ibid
33 McLoyd, V C (1990) 'The Impact of Economic Hardship on Black Families and Children: Psychological Distress, Parenting, and Socioemotional Development', *Child Development*, 61: 311–346
34 Moser, C O N (1993) 'Domestic Violence and its Economic Causes', *The Urban Age*, 1(4): 13
35 Cited by Newell 1997, op cit Note 30
36 Kenning, M, Merchant, A, Tomkins, A (1991) 'Research on the Effects of Witnessing Parental Battering: Clinical and Legal Policy Implications' in Steinman, M (ed) *Woman Battering: Policy responses*, Cincinnati OH: Anderson

children, such as repeated sexual abuse, may be hard to detect or to prove. It can also be difficult to draw the line between physical abuse and the disciplinary practices considered acceptable within a given community. If large numbers of children are regularly beaten, removing them all from their homes is clearly not feasible. In such cases, working towards community-wide awareness is the only appropriate response.

Acceptable alternatives for victimized children may be difficult to find. Residential care is not always available, and even when it is, is seldom an ideal solution (see p87). Responding to the situation of an individual child may fail to take into account the plight of others in the family: a child may be enduring harmful labour, for instance, in order to provide essential support for younger siblings. There are few simple solutions, and no formulas appropriate to all situations. Local authorities must accept, however, that they have the responsibility to protect children from harm, and must do all in their power to discharge it. Although abused children must be provided with relief, measures responding to this one symptom of family distress are not an alternative to addressing the larger context of inequity and poverty.

responses to domestic violence

To tackle the issue of violence against women, it is essential that local authorities encourage women's organizations and mutual support groups, and find ways to respond to their concerns. In Brazil, Argentina and Chile, special female police units have been established to provide an unthreatening presence for women.[37] The city of Cebu in the Philippines provides an excellent example of an integrated effort. Local women sought assistance from the city council and the mayor to force the police to deal with domestic violence. Police were required by municipal authorities to listen to women and to be responsive to their safety concerns. Local women trained the police in effective ways to respond to crimes against women by family members. In response to a careful collection of data on the incidence of domestic violence in Cebu, community watch groups, including local citizens, police representatives, lawyers and community leaders, were established in a number of neighbourhoods to monitor the situation of women in the area and to offer support. Through a local NGO, a women's Support and Crisis Centre was established to provide legal and medical assistance, counseling, temporary shelter and alternative livelihoods.[38]

- *Give children and women easy access to confidential advice and support.*
- *Establish well publicized procedures for reporting abuse.*
- *Create safe havens for children and women where they can receive temporary shelter, food, medical treatment and counseling.*
- *Establish a network of longer term care facilities for children, wherever possible within a family-like setting.*
- *Provide employment opportunities and support for families.*
- *Support the creation of good affordable child care facilities.*
- *Adopt measures to promote positive and non-violent forms of child care and discipline.*
- *Keep careful records on the incidence of abuse against children and women as an aid in developing and evaluating prevention programmes.*

[37] Vanderschueren, F (1996) 'From Violence to Justice and Security in Cities', *Environment and Urbanization,* 8(1): 93–112

[38] Banaynal-Fernandez, T (1994) 'Fighting Violence against Women: the Experience of the Lihok-Pilipina Foundation in Cebu', *Environment and Urbanization,* 6(2): 31–56

The measures suggested above must all be taken within the context of broad-based efforts to raise community awareness of children's and women's rights, educate parents and create a culture of non-violence. Some children respond to abuse at the hands of family members by leaving home and living on the street. Measures that can be taken to assist these children will be discussed on p212.

Play and exploration within the dwelling and its immediate vicinity

We have already discussed children's right to play, and its significance for their social, physical and mental development (see p22). Under conditions of urban poverty the home environment is often less than ideal for play. But the availability of varied and stimulating opportunities can generally be improved through simple and creative modifications and support for parental efforts. Measures to support play within the larger community will be discussed in Chapter 7 (see p134).

Parental awareness

Most children create absorbing activities for themselves with only minimal support. But even concerned parents and caregivers may unwittingly deny children opportunities if they do not accept the significance of play. If parents are made aware of the long term benefits, and assisted in giving their children opportunities, it can make a great difference.

domestic work

The issue of domestic work for children is a factor, especially for girls. As part of their evolving understanding of themselves and their role in the world, young children are drawn to mimic household routines, and to become involved in fetching water, sweeping, carrying wood and so on. Sometimes it is difficult to draw the line between work and play. Children want to be useful, and opportunities to be productive and responsible can be a source of pleasure and self-esteem. But this inclination can quickly lose its spontaneous quality when assistance is required too frequently by overworked caregivers. Although involvement in household work is an important part of learning and family membership, parents must be encouraged to allow their children time for unstructured play.

- *Raise parental awareness of the benefits of play for their children through parent education programmes and the media.*

Safe space

Children need safe space for play. Parents and officials should make every effort to ensure that children's activities are not unnecessarily restricted by hazards that can be managed or removed. See above, p78.

The availability of outdoor space

The more crowded housing is, the more essential outdoor space becomes for children's play. For too many children this means turning to the streets where a high level of danger may await them. Safe, contained outdoor space adjacent to the dwelling, where adults can supervise easily as they go about their chores, is perhaps the highest priority for younger children.[39] Families living around shared, contained outdoor space have the best situation. Such an arrangement allows children safe and easy access to playmates, and caregivers are able to share child care responsibilities. It also allows young children the chance to develop competence and confidence in familiar surroundings before heading out into the larger neighbourhood. When safe, satisfying play space cannot be created in the immediate vicinity, it is important that there be alternatives close by, especially for more active play. Local authorities, as described above (p73), can support residents and community organizations in creating controlled pockets of common space. Simple local play spaces can also be constructed to meet the needs of young children (p134).

safe, contained outdoor play space

- *Support local residents in creating small safe play spaces between dwellings.*

Toys and equipment

Expensive toys and equipment are unnecessary for children's play. Children are resourceful and creative in using what comes to hand. If caregivers are alert to their curiosity and changing interests, they can introduce everyday objects and opportunities appropriate to their capacities, fascinations and need for challenge. Well-intentioned programmes may be inclined to focus on the provision of costly manufactured objects for play. Municipalities should do all they can to redirect such initiatives and to ensure a more productive use of available resources – such as supporting safety measures and parent education.

being alert to children's curiosity and changing interests

When the quality of the living environment confines children to indoor play, possibilities should be as rich and varied as possible. Most children can play happily and productively in confined space when they have sufficient options available. In such cases, home support for child development, toy libraries and community playrooms can be especially valuable (see p162).

Working at home

The physical conditions of housing can make a significant difference to the burden that domestic work imposes for many children. Cooking arrangements, as discussed above, may threaten children's safety (p78); indoor pollution and heavy loads can damage their health and growth; distance from water sources or from parents' places of employment may dramatically affect the number of hours that they are required to spend working. This issue is discussed in more detail in Chapter 10 (see p208).

[39] Bartlett, S N (1997) 'No Place to Play: Implications for the Interaction of Parents and Children', *Journal for Children and Poverty,* 3(1)

The needs of older children

quiet space for study

As children grow older, the significance of the home for their well-being diminishes. Increasingly, the outside world becomes the focus of social life and the source of stimulation. But ideally the home continues to be a source of security and comfort, and a place to withdraw to. It can also be an important component of success at school, if it can provide a quiet well-lit space for work. This can be difficult, where limited space must suffice for cooking, sleeping, storage, playing, socializing, working. For many young students, progress in school suffers as a result.

Older children tend to demonstrate a growing need for independence as a natural part of their development. Wherever possible, attempts should be made to accomodate the need in adolescents for control over their own lives. In Chapters 7 and 9 there will be discussion of various ways within the community to respond to the needs of older children and adolescents.

- *Support the establishment of quiet places for study within the community when this is not being met within children's homes (see p128).*
- *Create within the community special meeting places and organizations for young people (see p145).*

Helping parents provide for children with special needs

The Convention recognizes the right of children with disabilities to live a full life in conditions that promote dignity and self-reliance. This is challenging in the context of urban poverty. Constraints in physical surroundings can make it difficult for children's potential to be realized. A child with limited mobility who might be able to tend to her own toileting needs, for instance, will still be dependent on others if there is only a physically inaccessible communal latrine available. When caregivers are burdened by multiple demands and few resources, they may accept the situation in a fatalistic way.

home assessment

aids for mobility and learning

Parents must be not only determined and resourceful, but also informed and supported, in order to create the conditions that a child with disabilities needs in order to live as fully as possible. They require, first of all, an understanding of their child's condition and potential, so that they can set realistic goals and use their energies to good effect. They need technical support to help them assess their home environment and determine how to expand their child's range of independent action and learning, and to lessen their own burden. Seating aids, toilet chairs, self-propelled trolleys, wayfinding devices for blind children, can all be helpful in contributing to independence while stimulating exploration and development. Because of the range of disabilities and the specificity of the aids needed, it is impossible to go into detail. There are a number of good resources, however, that can provide both parents and community rehabilitation workers with sustainable approaches and solutions (see resource list pp276, 278). Helping children in the home is just the beginning. From earliest years it is also important to find ways to make the community accessible and welcoming for them, and to integrate them into community life (see also pp109, 138, 169).

- *Ensure that caregivers have the information, technical support and material assistance they need to provide the conditions necessary to expand their children's range of independent action and learning.*

RESIDENTIAL CARE FOR CHILDREN

Not all children are able to live with their families. The majority of such children in the South are absorbed into extended family or other community networks, or move out into the public domain. But some children end up in institutional or residential care, in some cases with the purpose of rehabilitation, training or special care. Their numbers are not large, relatively speaking, because of the high costs involved. In India, for instance, it has been estimated that there are at most 200,000 to 300,000 institutionalized children in a country of many millions.[40] In the countries of central and eastern Europe institutionalization rates are higher.[41] But regardless of numbers, this is a significant issue for the children involved, since residential care poses particular challenges to their development and welfare. Although there are exceptions, most of these institutions are unlikely to provide children with the family-like care that the Convention calls for, or to prepare them adequately for community life. At worst, they may even be hostile and abusive environments. In this section we will discuss the concerns posed by institutional care, and some alternative models for children living outside of family. Recent research conducted by David Tolfree for Save the Children Fund (UK) in 20 countries, reveals many of the problems presented by institutional care for children, and we will draw heavily on his findings.[42]

The implications of institutional living for children

Although most institutions are theoretically required to meet standards for physical care, and may in some cases exceed what children in poverty are likely to receive at home, acceptable levels of care cannot be assumed. Poor conditions in many institutions have been well-documented. There are cases where malnutrition is common and facilities are sorely lacking. Some institutions, especially those for juvenile offenders, are at best grim holding pens for children (see p225).

The psychosocial implications for children may be serious even when physical conditions are acceptable. Because of the regimented nature of institutional life, children may not experience the close emotional ties that are so critical to their well-being. Research has indicated that the organizational structure of many institutions has an unfortunate effect on the relationships between adults and children. When authority is top heavy, and little responsibility is delegated to staff, their function becomes largely to maintain order, and communication with children may be perfunctory[43] This can be especially damaging to infants and very young children.

The depression, withdrawal and general failure to thrive of institutionalized infants who lack a close one-on-one relationship with a caregiver have long been recognized (see p21). But older children also

[40] Blanc, C S and contributors (1994) *Urban Children in Distress: Global Predicaments and Innovative Strategies*, Florence, Italy: UNICEF International Child Development Centre and London: Gordon and Breach
[41] Black, M and Smith, C (1997) 'Rights of Institutionalized Children', European Conference on the Rights of Institutionalized Children, Bucharest, Romania, UNICEF
[42] Tolfree, D (1995) 'Residential Care for Children and Alternative Approaches to Care in Developing Countries', Save the Children (UK) Working paper # 11
[43] Ibid

Staffing in residential care facilities should reflect children's need for continuity and affection – whenever possible a stable group of caregivers should have ongoing responsibility for a small group of children. These children play outside the Children's Home in Kyzl-Orda, Kazakstan . UNICEF, Maggie Murray-Lee.

need affection and the experience of being valued and wanted. Many young people within institutions have found vital emotional support from close friendships with other children. But particularly in highly structured institutional settings, rivalry, bullying and abuse may be more common. Institutional life can leave children without a sense of self-worth or belonging.

Institutional settings are often characterized by a high degree of control and minimal choice. The more children there are, the more likely it is that their lives will be shaped by the need for efficiency, uniformity and order. Rigid routines, fixed schedules and regimented activities leave little opportunity for self-determination. Under these conditions children may lose a sense of personal identity. They may also lack the stimulation necessary for the full development of cognitive skills, language and social growth. Tolfree's report suggests that the boredom and inactivity often observed in institutional settings leads to passivity and depression among young residents, especially in countries of the South. Hostility and aggression have been found to be more common responses in the North.

the hazards of institutional care

Treatment is harsh in many institutions. Control of children can take the form of corporal punishment, physical restraint, isolation and mental cruelty. In recent years there has been growing evidence of extensive sexual abuse.[44] Children may also be brutal with one another, and those who are least able to defend themselves or call on the support of others may suffer real abuse.

Children in long term residential care often grow up isolated from ordinary domestic or community experience. As a result, they lack the knowledge and skills necessary for life in other settings, and may have trouble becoming integrated into society. They tend to lack self-motivation and often find it difficult to function away from institutional life.

44 Newell, 1997, op cit Note 30

Few institutions, however, offer any kind of ongoing support to young people once they have left.

Tolfree's report reveals an alarming fact – that in the 20 countries investigated, the majority of children in institutions have parents or other family members who could care for them, given the appropriate resources. Institutional placement is almost always a response to poverty. It may be an attempt to find adequate care for a disabled child, or free education for a child who would not otherwise go to school. It may simply be a short term survival strategy on the part of an overstressed family. Children are frequently admitted to institutions without adequate assessment to determine their real needs. What may have been intended as a temporary solution too frequently becomes a long term arrangement. Little is done by most institutions to maintain family ties which may be seen as a hindrance to their smooth operation. In too many cases, entry into an institution means a permanent break with family, which may cause children considerable anguish and leave them without a long term social support system. This can be especially difficult in cultures where family connections are an essential context for community life, such as in arranging a marriage or finding work.

reasons for placement

Tolfree argues that the availability of residential care rather than the need for it lies behind most admissions. In order to ensure their own survival, institutions must maintain attendance and demonstrate a need for their services. Donors may be particularly responsive to appeals from homes for disadvantaged or disabled children. Care within their own families would in most cases serve children better, and would cost less than institutional solutions. Aside from the general disadvantages of residential care, the perpetuation of such institutions may inhibit the development of more appropriate solutions. The promotion of residential care as a solution for disabled children, for instance, makes funding for community-based rehabilitation and social integration less likely.

Alternative approaches to residential care

Various steps can be taken to ensure that children do not spend their formative years in institutional settings that are ill-equipped to address their needs or support their rights.

Adequate assessment and ongoing planning

When a child is a candidate for residential care, whether because of abandonment, disabilities, the need for rehabilitation, or the incapacity of family to provide, it is imperative that there be a careful assessment of that child's needs and of the range of solutions possible. This should include an open acknowledgement of the disadvantages of institutional care and a willingness to explore other options. For children who have become separated from parents and family, an attempt should be made to explore family reunification (see also p224).

assessment of needs and possible alternatives

Support for family or other caregivers

Preventive measures always make the most sense. When the primary reason for residential care is the economic incapacity of families to provide adequately for their children, a more humane and cost-effective solution is to work with families towards solutions for adequate livelihood. Literacy programmes, job training, availability of child care, and assistance with food security and parenting classes may all give families the edge they need to avoid unnecessary separations. In some cases it may make sense to provide a level of material assistance for the family. Responses should focus on the particular circumstances of individual families.

Family-based foster care

cultural barriers to family based care

A number of countries are recognizing the inherent shortcomings of large-scale institutional care for children, and looking for solutions within regular communities. In Hungary, for instance, where the great majority of children under state protection have been in institutional care, there is a move to eliminate this in favour of a family-based foster parent system.[45] But foster care is not always a simple solution. In many countries in the South, children have routinely been absorbed into the extended family when necessary as a matter of custom, and this should be supported. But taking in unrelated children can be a different matter, and willing families may be hard to find. Reports from Korea, for instance, suggest that this practice is still difficult for people to accept.[46] If children are taken in, they may be exploited or neglected.

a solution in India

These cultural barriers can be difficult, although not impossible, to surmount. A creative response is found in southern India. Reaching the Unreached, a community-based organization in Tamil Nadu, which has for many years run an exemplary foster care 'village' for children who have been orphaned or abandoned. Care is provided by women from both rural and urban areas who have themselves been widowed or cast off, and who consequently have no status in society. These women are carefully screened and are each given a small house where they take in up to five children. The household functions permanently as a family – children attend local schools, and the mother is given a living allowance by the organization to allow her to provide full-time care for her family. After three years she is given title to the house. A number of rooms within this 'village' have also been made available for destitute old people who often form close bonds with the children. Funding for the project comes from a number of sources, including the organization's successful small industries.[47] Although this is a rural solution, there is no reason why it could not be adapted to urban conditions.

- *Require an assessment of children's needs and an investigation of all possible solutions to prevent inappropriate placement in residential care facilities.*
- *Find sources of support for families as an alternative to investment in residential care.*
- *Support family-based foster care.*
- *Monitor foster care solutions, whether formal or informal, to ensure that they are meeting children's needs.*

45 Szilagyi, J (1997) 'Some Specialties of the Hungarian Child Law', paper presented at the Urban Childhood Conference, 9–12 June 1997, Trondheim, Norway

46 A Discussion of Institutionalization in Korea with Yeun Sook Lee at the IAPS (International Association for People-Environment Studies) conference, July 1996, Stockholm, Sweden

47 S Bartlett, field visit 1991

When institutional care is necessary

When institutional care is the best or only alternative, authorities must work with management to ensure that certain basic principles and practices are respected.

Ongoing assessment and long term planning

Children's needs must be carefully assessed, and institutional placement should be a positive, and ideally a temporary, response to those needs. Throughout a child's residential stay there must be regular assessment to determine the appropriateness of the placement and to work on a long term plan.

Family contact

Every effort must be made to establish and maintain regular contact with family, to place children as close as possible to family, to encourage visits, and to work with families towards returning children when this is appropriate. Space should be made available for parents and children to have private time together. Children should be allowed to keep photographs of family members and correspondence should be encouraged.

Family-like care

The physical environment and the daily regime at an institution must be as 'homelike'as possible, both addressing daily needs and reflecting local norms for family living. Even large institutions can successfully be broken down in a way that allows children to eat, sleep, and live within smaller groups and in smaller less institutional spaces. Staffing should reflect children's need for continuity and affection in their relationships with adults, and a stable group of caretakers should have ongoing responsibility for a small group of children. Staff must be carefully chosen with the recognition that they are the children's primary models for adult behaviour; and must be trained to respect children's rights and developmental needs. Where possible, siblings should be kept together, and contact between older and younger children, boys and girls should be encouraged.

Recognizing children's developmental needs

Children's developmental needs should not take second place to an institution's need for control and routine. There should be opportunities for spontaneous play in a warm and informal environment. Attempts must be made to respond to children's particular interests and needs. Children need the chance to make choices in their daily activities, so that they develop a sense of identity and effectiveness.

Protection from maltreatment

Clear policies must be in place for preventing any form of violence against children, either by staff members or other children. These policies must be known to all and firmly implemented. Staff members who abuse children should be dismissed. Children who bully others should be helped to learn more appropriate behaviour. A confidential system should be established allowing children to discuss problems they are having within the institution, without fear of reprisals. This could be a phone line or personal access to an independent advocate who has the capacity to advise the child, look into concerns and act on them appropriately (see p260).

Children's active participation

Children in residential care should be able to participate in management and decision making according to their capacities. At the very minimum, decisions that affect children should be openly discussed. Wherever possible, children should be personally involved in decisions regarding such matters as the scheduling of chores, the assignment of rooms, provision for play and so on. This may be inconvenient, but it is their right. Institutionalized children, living relatively regimented and controlled lives, need as many opportunities as possible to develop a positive sense of their own efficacy.

Monitoring

There should be ongoing monitoring of residential institutions by objective and independent groups who are equipped to assess the quality of care being offered, and able to respond to concerns and complaints. Monitoring groups should include young people who have themselves been in residential care. Within the institution there should be regular opportunities for self-evaluation with staff, and for ongoing training.

Integration into the community

Institutions must aim to equip children in every way for independent life in the community. This cannot happen if all they know is life within the walls of the institution. While they are resident, opportunities must be made available for regular contact with children, adults and activities outside the institution through schooling, religious services, community events and informal activity. But it is also important to ensure a framework of support for young people when they leave an institution. Employment opportunities, housing and social support must all be available to ease their transition back into the community as self-supporting individuals, especially when they lack family connections.

Community health means attention not only to health services, but to the broad range of factors that affect health, including the quality of the local environment. Here a child washes her hands in a garbage filled stream near Manila, Philippines. UNICEF 1997, Jeremy Horner

6 Community Health

The CRC recognizes children's right to survival and to the highest attainable standard of health (Articles 6, 24). But in spite of enormous gains worldwide over the last decade, 12 million children under the age of five in the South still die each year, largely from causes that could easily be prevented or cured. Ninety-seven per cent of these deaths would not occur if these children had acceptable living conditions, adequate nutrition and good health services.[1] For hundreds of millions of the children who survive, the capacity to live full and productive lives is challenged by disease and injury. Health problems also undermine family stability. When children are sick, the drain on family time and resources can be considerable. When adults are ill, the quality of care that children receive is rapidly affected.[2] Sick caregivers mean neglected children, and the incapacitation of breadwinners leads quickly to debt and deprivation. The poor are dependent for survival on their capacity to work, and health is critical to productivity. Poor health perpetuates poverty, and is in turn perpetuated by poverty.

The realization of children's rights requires comprehensive responses to the health issues of the poor. At issue are not only health services, but the broad range of environmental, social and economic factors that affect

[1] WHO (1995) *The World Health Report 1995: Bridging the Gaps*, Geneva: World Health Organization

[2] Pryer, J (1993) 'The Impact of Adult Ill-Health on Household Income and Nutrition in Khulna, Bangladesh', *Environment and Urbanization*, 5(2): 35–50

health. In most urban centres, municipal authorities face constraints on their capacity to respond. But even within these constraints, much more can be done to improve health and to prevent disease and injury for children and their families. This chapter outlines some basic approaches.

THE HEALTH PROBLEMS OF THE URBAN POOR

Statistics suggest that urban dwellers are healthier than those in rural areas in most countries of the South. But aggregate figures hide the realities in low-income urban neighbourhoodss, where the challenges to health are often greater than in rural areas. Between one fifth and one third of children in poor urban communities still die before the age of five, at least 5 to 10 times more than in wealthier parts of the same cities.[3] The frequency of disease and injury is subject to comparable disparities.

Inadequate sanitation, drainage and water provision, uncollected waste, overcrowding and daily exposure to infectious and parasitic diseases are standard components of urban poverty. Low-income settlements are more often in polluted areas or on land at risk from landslides, floods or other hazards. Attempts to practice good hygiene and to ensure safety under such difficult conditions are nigh impossible. The environmental stresses of urban poverty are often accompanied by increased social stress, which has an impact on health: alcohol and drug use, domestic and community violence, sexual exploitation, discrimination and exclusion, all occur at higher levels in urban areas.[4]

The living conditions of the poor are often a function of inequities: the rich are not only better endowed, but also benefit at the expense of the poor.[5] Many industries, for instance, support the wealthy with their profits, but provide hazardous working conditions for employees and contaminate the environments of nearby settlements. Many of the vehicles in the developing world are owned by the well-to-do, but the children of the poor are more likely to live close to busy, polluted roadways and to suffer the consequences of traffic accidents, lead poisoning and polluted air.

Inequities are also found in the provision of health services. Although so much illness, injury and premature death is related to poverty, a high percentage of health budgets worldwide is invested in capital-intensive central hospitals, high technology and acute care, which siphon scarce resources away from provision of good water, sanitation, and primary health care. National teaching hospitals have been estimated to absorb 20 to 60 per cent of national health budgets.[6] Health care is becoming a big business, and the health industry can generate higher levels of return this way. Politicians may also be more supportive of elaborate medical facilities, seen to be vote-winners, than of less impressive primary care centres.[7]

Although hospitals and other health facilities may be clustered in cities, many are only available to those who can pay. Even government subsidies and aid agencies often fund health services commonly used by middle and upper income groups.[8] Use of health facilities may also require documentation – a legal address, an identity card or birth certificate – which the poor are more likely to lack. Even when affordable care is avail-

[3] Stephens, C (1996) 'Healthy Cities or Unhealthy Islands? The Health and Social Implications of Urban Inequality', *Environment and Urbanization*, 8(2): 9–30

[4] Parry-Jones, W L and Queloz, N (eds) (1991) *Mental Health and Deviance in Inner Cities*, Geneva: WHO/ UNICRI/University of Naples; and WHO (1991) *Environmental Health in Urban Development*, Geneva: World Health Organization

[5] de la Barra, X (1998) 'Poverty: the Main Cause of Ill-health in Urban Children', *Health, Education and Behavior*, 25(1): 45–49

[6] Feuerstein, M-T (1997) *Poverty and Health: Reaping a Richer Harvest*, London: Macmillan

[7] Lorenz, N and Garner, P (1995) 'Organizing and Managing Urban Health Services' in Harpham, T and Tanner, M (eds) *Urban Health in Developing Countries: Progress and Prospects*, London: Earthscan, 48–63

[8] Hecht, R (1995) 'Urban Health: an Emerging Priority for the World Bank' in Harpham, T and Tanner, M (eds) *Urban Health in Developing Countries: Progress and Prospects*, London: Earthscan, 121–141

able, it is often of poor quality or so understaffed that long waits for treatment discourage its use. Health care centres may be open only for limited periods each week, and visits outside working hours may be difficult to arrange, especially for single parent households. Some studies show that low-income households use private sector clinics, which they can ill afford, because they get more rapid, effective treatment.[9]

inaccessible facilities

The quality of medical training compounds the problem. Most professionals prefer to work in settings that make use of their highly specialized skills, and are generally not equipped to cope with the mundane constellation of health problems that accompany poverty. Their salary structure also reflects an undervaluation of community-based, primary health care. In addition, the social background of many doctors and other personnel puts them out of touch with the needs and fears of the poor. This results in a system that can feel remote and insensitive, and does not encourage the confident use of health facilities.

out-of-touch doctors

The provision of medical services is at best a partial solution to the health problems of the urban poor. The larger context of poverty, illiteracy, hazardous environmental conditions and social injustice must also be addressed. An urban health plan must focus on the prevention of disease and injury through environmental actions, on improvements in the quality and availability of housing, on better nutrition, and on a broad understanding of the effects of a healthy lifestyle. The epidemic of violence which affects so many cities is also increasingly recognized as a public health problem. There is also the matter of livelihood. Health for most children hinges on the ability of their families to care for them. From this perspective even support for job training and micro-enterprise become health interventions. A comprehensive plan for community health is in effect a plan for community development.

Effective health care is not only a function of resources, but of the political will to address inequity. In Cuba, for instance, the under-five mortality rate is approximately the same as that of the United States, a country with a per capita income 23 times higher.[10] There are practical as well as moral reasons for wealthier groups to support interventions that meet the multiple health needs of the poor. The wretched environmental conditions of the poor ultimately affect the quality of life for all. Epidemics can have serious economic consequences – as was demonstrated by the cholera epidemic in Lima in 1991.[11]

providing effective health care means addressing inequalities

Urban areas clearly offer potential advantages for the health of their residents. The availability of more specialized services, the economies of scale that are possible, and the concentration of support organizations are all significant assets. Most municipal authorities face some real constraints; they are limited both by resources and by the relatively minor role they often play in health care provision compared to higher levels of government, private providers and voluntary organizations. But even so, they can help to develop a comprehensive approach to local health, and to ensure that the needs of the poorest are met through adequate assessment and analysis of local needs, through appropriate regulation, and by coordinating existing services – all with an emphasis on equity.

9 Misra, H (1990) 'Housing and Health Problems in Three Squatter Settlements in Allahabad, India' in Hardoy, J E, Cairncross, S and Satterthwaite, D (eds) *The Poor Die Young: Housing and Health in Third World Cities*, London: Earthscan

10 UNICEF (ed) (1997) *The Progress of Nations 1997*, New York: UNICEF

11 WHO (1996) *Creating Healthy Cities in the Twenty-First Century*, Geneva: WHO

ASSESSMENT AND ANALYSIS

A comprehensive and integrated response to the city's health issues requires an assessment of both local needs and the level of provision city-wide. An evaluation of the quality and extent of environmental health services, the contribution of all health service providers, including public, private, voluntary and community-based, as well as other factors that influence the health of the population, will allow the development of a municipal strategy that makes best use of existing resources and avoids unnecessary duplication.[12] GIS technology is a particularly useful tool for such complex analysis, (see p254).

collecting information at the local level

Assessment must include strategies for identifying those most in need and hardest to reach. Information must be collected at the most local level, drawing on the knowledge of community members and organizations familiar with local residents. Residents should also be involved in assessing their own health needs and priorities. Any such participatory effort should recognize the time constraints of the urban poor, and not demand uncompensated involvement. An excellent example of local health assessment is found in the El Mesquital settlement on the outskirts of Guatamala City, where women elected by small groups of about 50 families served as 'reproinsas' or local health workers. Each worker carried out a detailed house-to-house survey of her own small territory to discover the living conditions and specific health problems of each family. Their results were analyzed with technical teams in order to identify problems and develop a work plan, as part of a larger basic services programme supported by UNICEF.[13]

- *See p253, for a discussion of information systems, data collection and participatory methods.*

CREATING HEALTHY AND LIVABLE NEIGHBOURHOODS

The requirements for environmental health within residential areas are similar in all urban centres, although the best means to achieve them will vary greatly, and will depend on existing levels of provision, on the competence, funding and accountability of providers, and their willingness to work with other groups. Some basic guidelines and practical approaches for provision have been described in Chapter 3, p47. Here we will discuss the standards necessary for healthy urban environments.

Provision of water, sanitation, drainage and waste removal

Clean water is essential to health, but it is important to remember that many diseases are related not so much to water quality as to quantity. The amount necessary for washing, laundry and personal hygiene is frequently underestimated. Water supplies must be safe, sufficient,

[12] Lorenz and Garner 1995, op cit Note 7
[13] Espinosa, L and Lopez Rivera, O A (1994) 'UNICEF's Urban Basic Services Programme in Illegal Settlements in Guatamala City', *Environment and Urbanization*, 6(2): 9–31

regular and accessible to all households, ideally piped into individual homes or yards. We have already discussed the disadvantages of distant standpipes, irregular supplies and the need to store water (see p74).

water quantity

The sheer quantity of untreated human faeces that may be present in urban communities of the South poses a most significant public health risk. As discussed in the previous chapter, toilets should be accessible to all, minimize human contact with excreta and be easy to maintain and to keep clean. Where possible, this means toilets within each house or house plot (p75). In urban centres or districts where crowded and poorly maintained communal toilets are all that is available, many people defecate in the open; well-maintained, shared toilets remain the exception.

toilets

Water closets connected to sewers, the safest and most convenient option, are only possible where households have a reliable piped water supply, and are usually considered 'too expensive' for poor families. There are many examples, however, of sewer construction where costs have been kept affordable for low-income groups (see p49). Where water is scarce, there are also ways of reducing the volume that these systems need. Sewers also have the advantage of removing other domestic waste waters which can contain disease-causing agents, encourage their breeding, and facilitate the development of soil-based parasitic worms such as hookworm.[14]

sewers

Various non-sewered sanitation options can also provide safe, hygienic and easy to clean options.[15] But such systems need an efficient, hygienic, affordable service to empty or desludge them. For hundreds of millions of urban dwellers who are not connected to sewers, such services are lacking or inadequate. Where pit latrines are the most appropriate response to improved sanitation, it must be ensured that they can be easily and hygienically emptied.[16]

Neighbourhoods drainage systems should remove surface water efficiently and prevent flooding and pools of standing water that can serve as breeding grounds for mosquitoes. Especially where there are no sewers, well-functioning drains can help reduce human contact with excreta and excreta-laden water. Good drainage is particularly important in settlements prone to flooding. When pit latrines are relied on, flooding can bring extensive fecal contamination to the whole site. Adequate drainage, like sanitation, is generally considered to be too expensive for low-income settlements, but again, there are examples of successful, low cost schemes.[17] Costs can be kept down if drainage is integrated into the construction of roads, paths or sewers.

All residential areas need reliable and regular solid waste collection services. Without this, it is difficult or even impossible to prevent the accumulation of uncollected wastes, especially on open sites where children play. Uncollected waste attracts pests, including those that spread disease. Without regular waste collection it is also difficult to keep drainage channels clear, and this can encourage flooding when it rains.

There are important links between water supply, sanitation, drainage and the most common diseases. Behavioural change with regard to hygiene is irrelevant if not backed up by investment in infrastructure and service provision.

[14] Sinnatamby, G (1990) 'Low-cost Sanitation' in in Hardoy, J E, Cairncross, S and Satterthwaite, D (eds) *The Poor Die Young: Housing and Health in Third World Cities*, London: Earthscan

[15] Ibid; and Mara, D and S Cairncross (1990) *Guidelines for the Safe Use of Wastewater and Excreta in Agriculture and Aquiculture*, Geneva: WHO; and Sida (1997) 'Seeking More Effective and Sustainable Support to Improving Housing and Living Conditions for Low-income Households in Urban Areas: Sida's Initiatives in Costa Rica, Chile and Nicaragua', *Environment and Urbanization*, 9(2): 213–231

[16] Cairncross, S (1992) 'Sanitation and Water Supply: Practical Lessons from the Decade', Water and Sanitation Discussion Paper Series #9, Washington DC, World Bank

[17] Cairncross, S and Ouano, E A R (1990) *Surface Water Drainage in Low-income Communities*, Geneva: WHO

[18] WHO 1996, op cit Note 11
[19] Ibid and WHO (1996) 'Lead and Health', Copenhagen, WHO Regional Office for Europe, one of a special series of reports for local authorities
[20] Needleman, H L, Schell, A, Bellinger, O, Leviton, A, Allred, E N (1991) 'The Long-term Effects of Exposure to Low Doses of Lead in Childhood: An Eleven Year Follow-up Report', *New England Journal of Medicine*, 322(2): 83–88

- *Ensure that regulations for infrastructure facilitate provision and meet a high standard for health.*
- *Water supplies must be safe, sufficient, regular and accessible to all households, and wherever possible should be piped into each individual home or yard; when public standpipes are the only feasible solution, they should be shared between relatively few households. (See p74).*
- *Toilets should be accessible to all, ideally within each house or house plot, should minimize human contact with excreta and be easy to maintain and keep clean. Where water is scarce, look into proven methods for providing adequate sanitation without piped water. (See p75).*
- *Through education programmes and media campaigns, educate children and their families in the importance of good sanitation and hygienic practices (see p115).*
- *Integrate the provision of drainage into the construction of roads, paths or sewers.*
- *Provide regular and reliable waste collection.*

Controlling hazardous chemical emissions and wastes

household pollutants

air pollution

Although biological pathogens present a greater overall risk, children can also sustain significant damage to health from exposure to various chemical substances, which may be harmful to them at levels not considered damaging for adults. Impacts are likely to be greater for children in poverty, whose vulnerability may be increased by poor nutrition and by their parents' inability, through lack of knowledge or resources, to minimize risks. Some of the pollutants that most seriously affect children are present within their homes, where open fires or inadequately vented stoves can cause serious respiratory problems, or where they may ingest or handle dangerous household chemicals (see pp77, 78). But numerous hazards out-of-doors can also take a significant toll on health and well-being. Air pollution from heavy industry, motor vehicle exhaust and power stations can result in chronic coughs, asthma and increased vulnerability to the acute respiratory infections that are the single largest cause of death in infants and young children.[18]

lead

The impact of lead on children's health can be particularly damaging and has probably been underestimated.[19] Studies in some cities have shown that a considerable proportion of the child population is suffering from behavioural problems and impairment of learning ability and fine motor coordination because of exposure to lead. The impact of lead continues into adulthood; a study of young adults who had been exposed to higher levels of lead in their infancy found that they tended to be under-achievers: they had a lower standing in school, increased absenteeism, smaller vocabulary and lower grammatical reasoning scores, poorer eye-hand coordination and longer reaction times.[20] About 80–90 per cent of airborne lead that can be traced to source comes from motor vehicles using gasoline with a lead additive, still a common practice in many countries in the South. And since poor nutritional status and a poor home environment may potentiate the effect of lead exposure for many children, there is an urgent need for regulation and the replacement of leaded fuels.[21]

In many urban neighbourhoods, children face serious health problems from hazardous chemical wastes dumped untreated into water bodies or on land sites. Not only chemical industries, but metal, petroleum, pulp and paper, transport, electrical equipment and leather and tanning industries, as well as hospitals and some commercial enterprises, can produce significant quantities of toxic waste.[22] Most urban centres lack effective systems to monitor the generation, collection, treatment and disposal of toxic wastes, and to limit environmental impacts. Businesses, as a result, have little incentive to invest in 'good practice'. Many of these problems can be reduced and controlled without major expenditure if local authorities are willing to take an active role in giving priority to the health needs of children and communities.

- *Assess the health risks presented by various contaminants; involve local residents in identifying and reporting illegal dumps and polluted streams.*
- *Restrict polluting industries in the vicinity of residential areas; and give low-income groups access to land and housing in areas free from hazards.*
- *Establish and enforce regulations controlling and reducing industrial emissions and contamination, and promote the use of processes to maximize recovery and re-use of waste materials.*
- *Reduce vehicular pollution by promoting public transport, restricting traffic in residential areas, requiring annual road checks, and promoting the use of lead-free fuel.*

Other environmental health factors

- *Prevent children's injury and exposure to disease through adequate provision for play.*
- *Facilitate emergency access and prevent injury through provision of all-weather roads and paths.*
- *Support access to safe housing sites.*
- *Prevent epidemics and educate the public through special attention to environmental health and hygiene in clinics, schools and other public facilities.*

Regulation and coordination

There is generally a variety of public, private, voluntary and community-based agencies and organizations involved in the provision of water, sanitation, garbage collection and other activities important for good health. Local authorities must help to ensure that they work together cooperatively and also with health service providers.

21 WHO 1996, op cit Note 19

22 Hardoy, J E, Mitlin D, Satterthwaite, D (1992) *Environmental Problems in Third World Cities*, London: Earthscan

[23] Rispel, L, Doherty, J, Makiwane, F and Webb, N (1996) 'Developing a Plan for Primary Health Care Facilities in Soweto, South Africa Part 1: Guiding Principles and Methods', *Health Policy and Planning*, 11(4): 385–393

Municipal regulations can have an important impact on environmental health. Less demanding regulatory codes for infrastructure, for instance, can facilitate the provision of water and sanitation to low-income communities. High standards of hygiene for schools and childcare centres can help to ensure that disease is not spread from child to child, and on into the community. Strictly enforced regulations to control pollution can reduce a number of health risks. Wherever possible, regulations that seek to raise health-related standards should be accompanied by the advice and assistance necessary to enable people, institutions and businesses to meet these standards.

THE PROVISION OF COMPREHENSIVE, INTEGRATED HEALTH SERVICES

The health problems of low-income communities are closely tied to their living conditions and must be tackled in that context. But health care services are also essential, and in order to be useful, they must be well coordinated, easily accessible, affordable to all, culturally appropriate, and relevant to the health needs of low-income households.

Planning and coordinating comprehensive health care coverage

At both community and city levels, planning for health care coverage should assess the overall need for services and find equitable solutions that benefit those most in need. In determining need, the full range of existing services must be taken into account. Coordination of services will allow scarce resources to be used where they are most needed and avoid duplication.

coordination of services

Promoting the effective cooperation of various partners can be a demanding task. In Soweto in South Africa, for instance, five separate authorities were providing different aspects of health care. Planning for consolidation and simplification meant pushing for close cooperation among agencies, all of which wanted to protect their separate interests.[23] There are also the difficulties inherent in the large and often increasing role of private health providers, which by their nature, can only offer treatment for which there is an economic demand. And yet, private health services are an important part of any city's health promotion strategy, and their efforts must be supported. NGOs also function at times as health providers, and while their contribution is important, they can become a hidden form of privatization, substituting for what should be free public sector services. Local authorities must ensure that the often complex mosaic of provision in a given urban area does not end up excluding those with the greatest need.

restructuring health care in Dakar

To meet the most basic health care needs of poor children and their families, the focus must shift towards economical primary care. Basic health care delivery should be primarily through well-distributed small local clinics or health centres, which can respond at relatively low cost to the vast majority of health care needs. Dakar, in Senegal, has worked towards restructuring a top-heavy health care system. In 1985, the city

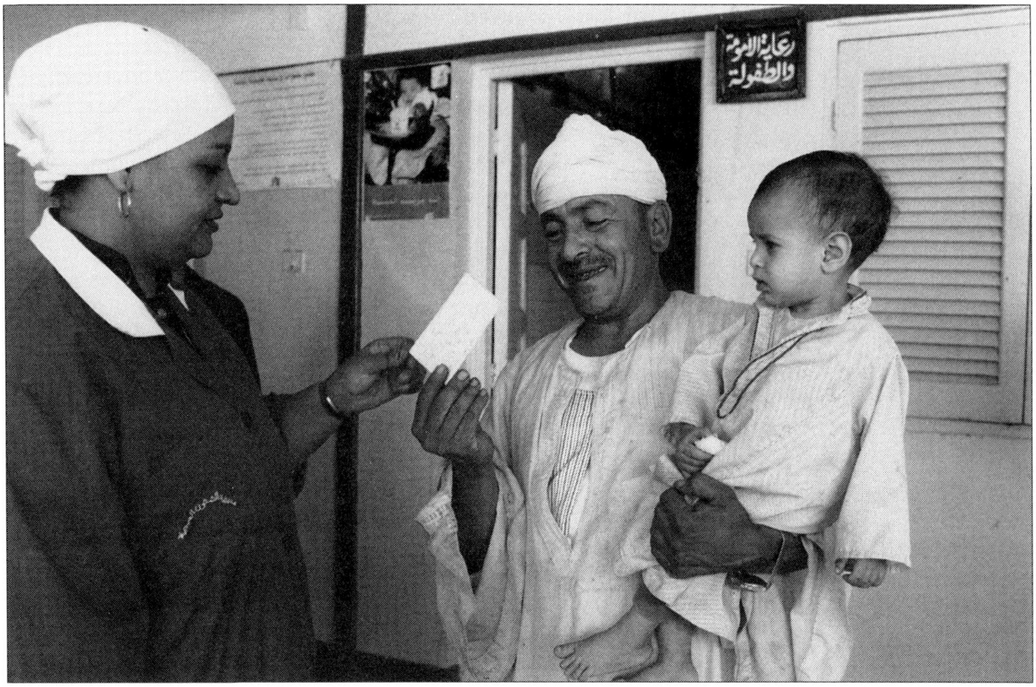

Health services should be easily accessible, well-coordinated, affordable to all and relevant to the health needs of low-income households. A man and his son at a UNICEF assisted health centre near the city of Asyut, Egypt. UNICEF 1996, Nicole Toutounji

had three major hospitals and a traumatology centre, but only a few local health stations. Over a decade the municipality moved to an emphasis on local care. Six smaller hospitals were built, along with 18 health stations in different parts of the city and four maternity centres in poor neighbourhoods. Each centre is managed by a health committee of elected neighbourhood representatives who work in collaboration with the head doctor. The income generated by each centre is managed by the committee to provide for the needs of the facility, including the provision of virtually free care and medication for the poor.[24]

cooperation between levels of care

For community health care to be comprehensive, there must be strong cooperation between different levels of provision. Too many urban deaths occur, in spite of the availability of services, because people are sent from one facility to another with no real coordination or follow-up, and with no-one taking final responsibility for the care of often seriously ill patients. Lower tiers of service are frequently underused because of drug shortages and a reputation for poor quality care, and as a result hospitals can be swamped by patients with illnesses or injuries which should be treated by lower levels.[25]

distance from clinics

The expense of higher tier care will be more appropriately targeted if hospitals can serve as a supportive base and staging post for community services. Patients can be referred from clinics when necessary up to the next level of care, and feedback from professionals at more specialized levels can be a useful source of information for clinic health workers. (At the same time it is important to recognize that a hospital may be the closest health facility for residents living in the vicinity. Hospitals should ideally include outpatient clinics which can provide primary preventive and curative care, without necessitating expensive emergency room treatment.)

[24] Marcus, M (1995) *Faces of Justice and Poverty in the City*, Paris: European Forum for Urban Security

[25] Lorenz and Garner 1995, op cit Note 7

26 Rispel et al 1996, op cit Note 23
27 Ebrahim, G J (1985) *Social and Community Paediatrics in Developing Countries: Caring for the Rural and Urban Poor*, Houndmills, Basingstoke, Hampshire: Macmillan

Planning for local provision must take careful account of physical accessibility. Distance has a significant impact on the utilization of health services, and preventive care is the first to be ignored if it cannot easily be reached. Those who most need it will be most sorely affected. Frail old people, busy mothers, and small children too sick to walk need resources close to home. Another factor is population density. If local clinics serve too many people, they tend to become too complex and impersonal to function well. Although basic health care facilities are most essential, diagnostic services, rehabilitation, emergency care and acute care should also be readily accessible to low-income communities. There is no one formula for provision; distribution of services will have to be adapted to local conditions. In Soweto, South Africa, the goal of health planners was a maximum distance of two kilometres for basic health services;[26] in Kwun Ton near Hong Kong, by contrast, because of high population densities, health centres were set up to serve households living within a hundred metres.[27] The goal must be to determine the most effective way of using resources to respond to those in greatest need.

- *Assess the overall need for health care services within a given community, and identify ways to achieve a more equitable distribution of services, giving priority to those with the greatest need.*
- *Reallocate resources away from top-heavy health care systems and towards economical preventive primary care.*

Focusing on prevention

Treating injury and disease and managing chronic health problems are integral to the services of any local health centre. But prevention must be a central focus of community-based primary health care. In part this is a function of a healthy environment, as discussed above; in part it calls for attention to adequate nutrition and to education, which will be discussed in more detail below. But it also means preventive health services. These are focused primarily on maternal and early child care, and on sexual and reproductive health care.

cost-effective preventive care

In general, the earlier in life that preventive health measures are taken, the more effective they are. Children who are born of healthy, well-nourished mothers, who are breastfed, whose growth is monitored, and who are immunized against tetanus, measles, and other diseases for which immunizations are effective, have a critical advantage that benefits them throughout life. These measures are tremendously cost-effective, and contribute over time to the development and well-being of the whole community.

obstacles to using preventive care

Many factors can keep parents and children from making use of preventive care, even when it is available. The curative emphasis of much medical practice is partly a response to what users have come to expect. Regular attendance at clinics for preventive care means spending time and money when there appears to be no immediate call for it. Particularly for those who are unaware of the long term investment that such care represents, this may seem a wasted effort. There is often a tendency to wait until there is a clear need for medical attention. Seventy-four per cent of all paediatric admissions to hospital in Nigeria, for instance, were found to be for illnesses that could easily have been prevented.[28]

Rather than offering special preventive care clinics for ante-natal care, reproductive health and the monitoring of under-fives, which may meet weekly or monthly, it has been found useful in many communities to integrate such services with curative care. When growth monitoring, immunization, ante-natal care and so on are available on a daily basis, and as a natural adjunct to curative care, more mothers and children will be reached, and the value of preventive care is more likely to become clear over time.

integrating preventive and curative care

- *Make prevention the primary focus of community health care services.*
- *Encourage community members to take advantage of preventive services by integrating them with curative care.*

Integrating primary health care with other services

Coordination in health care should not be limited to formal facilities. Even when primary health care facilities offer relevant and affordable care, there are many people in low-income urban communities who are not reached by these services. Some people are suspicious of formal health facilities and reluctant to make use of them. Cultural constraints may prevent women from leaving home. Preventive care may be considered a waste of time and money. Time constraints may overwhelm many people. One solution is the kind of outreach services that can be offered by community health workers, which will be discussed in the next section. Another approach is an active attempt to integrate health care with other services. Child care facilities are a good example (see p154). By providing basic health care for young children through their child care centre, the burden on mothers is lightened and some continuity of care can be assured. Schools are another important focus for health care outreach (see p176). An excellent example of successful preventive care made available through schools and child care centres is the dental health programme in Santos, Brazil, which has educated parents and teachers in dental hygiene, made toothbrushes and toothpaste available to all children, and applied topical fluoride to those children most inclined to get cavities. The programme has surpassed the goals of the World Health Organization, and 68 per cent of all children examined in 1995 were without any dental decay.[29]

childcare

schools

community centres

Integrated services can be physically simplified by placing facilities adjacent to one another in the community or in the same building. Health clinics, for instance, might be located within a general community centre, in the local school, or share a building with social welfare services, adult education or a community development office (see pp56, 167).

Coordination is important not only to make sure that health care is reaching those who need it, but because peoples' needs cannot be compartmentalized into separate domains. Ill health, for example, affects the capacity to work; education affects the use of health services and the level of community hygiene. Liaison between health and social welfare workers, and between health workers and teachers, is important to ensure that problems are approached holistically. The coordination of

[28] Denn, P and Ebrahim, G J (1986) *Practical Care of Sick Children: A Manual for Use in Small Tropical Hospitals*, London: Macmillan

[29] City of Santos (1996) 'Santos na Habitat II: Integrated Children's and Family Program', The City of Santos, SP, Brazil

holistic provision

services acknowledges the interdependence of all facets of human and community development. No single initiative in isolation has the capacity to make a significant difference to community well-being. In some cases, health care provision has actually become a built-in component of broader community development schemes. In Hyderabad, India, for instance, the municipality has established the Urban Community Development project, drawing on both community, NGO and state government resources, and providing health centres, child care services, adult literacy, nutrition centres, self-help housing schemes and sanitation drives as integrated parts of a whole development scheme.[30] More recently in Calcutta, a collaborative, people-centered, decentralized urban system was established for coordinating the delivery and monitoring of all basic services to children. The system depends on community level administrative units which, in order to ensure their success in addressing local needs, are guided by people-elected counsellors and monitored by the community.[31]

- *Ensure that there is adequate communication and follow-up of cases between different levels of health care provision.*
- *Increase the use of primary preventive health care services by integrating them whenever possible with other services within the community such as child care centers, schools, community development centres.*
- *Where possible, aim for the physical proximity of different services.*

Involving community outreach workers in health provision

the advantages of using local health workers

Local health auxiliaries, often volunteers, can be a vital component of the health delivery system, serving as an important link between the community and health centre staff. Because they know individual families and understand the intricacies of community life, they are in a good position to respond to local needs and identify potential problems. Community members who are suspicious of health care services or intimidated by them may respond far better to the home visits of familiar local community members.

Community health workers, with regularly updated basic training, can take over a number of procedures that will allow more highly trained professionals to make more cost-effective use of their time. Regular home visits, growth monitoring, vaccination, the distribution of contraceptives and the provision of health education can be some of the responsibilities they assume. They can ensure attention for those most in need of care, and least able to attend a health centre. They can also accompany people to clinic visits, and ensure that instructions are followed. Through their home visits they can identify factors in the home that may be undermining health. They can also become an important source of information on the availability of other services, and can serve as a vital link in responding to domestic abuse.

Local women are likely to be particularly good health workers. They tend to have informal health care knowledge and to share it with other women, to be more involved in the needs of children and other community members, and to be active in the many spheres of daily life that

[30] Boyden, J and Holden, P (1991) *Children of the Cities*, London: Zed Books
[31] Government of West Bengal, (1995) *Calcutta Plan of Action for Children*, Calcutta, Institute of Local Government and Urban Studies (ILGUS), Department of Municipal Affairs, Government of Bengal and Calcutta Municipal Corporation

Young people can be valuable additions to the local health team. In Suba, Colombia, high school students, as part of their curriculum, do several weeks of community service as trained health monitors. UNICEF, Ellen Tolmie

most influence health. The reproinsas of El Mezquital, for example, received training over the course of a year, primarily geared towards detection and prevention, and have become providers of basic health care and education for the families they serve. A survey conducted after four years found that 90 per cent of those questioned knew their local reproinsa, and had benefited from her services.[32]

Community health workers are often volunteers. If reimbursed at all, they usually get little more than a modest stipend. It may be difficult for them to meet their income needs, and attrition can be high. Local health authorities should find ways to support their long term commitment. If they can be compensated adequately, their accumulated knowledge and experience will not be lost to the community. In El Mezquital, again, small pharmacies and grocery stores were established, allowing reproinsas to generate an income for themselves. If direct payment is not a possibility, back-up and support for such initiatives are important in order to ensure the livelihood of local volunteers.

El Mezquital reproinsas

- *Train local health auxiliaries as a liaison between community members and local health clinics.*
- *Find ways to compensate these outreach workers through either direct pay or support for income generating possibilities.*

Including traditional practitioners and other dispensers of medical care

In many cities a high percentage of the low-income population seeks

32 Espinosa and Lopez Rivera, 1994, op cit Note 13

encouraging collaboration

health care from traditional practitioners. Where possible, their collaboration with the formal health delivery system should be encouraged. This is more effective than setting up an antagonistic relationship that requires community members to choose between their accustomed practitioners and the local health centre. Traditional healers and birth attendants should be provided with the necessary training and equipment to make them an effective part of the health team, and encouraged to refer difficult cases to medical professionals.

local pharmacists

Another common resource that people turn to are local pharmacies or patent medicine stores. In the minds of many, medicine is what is needed when someone is ill, and the pharmacist may be the first person consulted in the event of illness or accidents.[33] In Bangladesh, working mothers said that when their children were ill, they were most likely to pick up medicine from a pharmacist without first consulting qualified health workers, because of heavy constraints on their time.[34] This can be a dangerous practice when there is a lack of adequate information, or when drugs are being sold illicitly. Recent research in Africa has demonstrated the futility of attempting to alter this pattern.[35] This informal source of health care advice should be acknowledged and built on by offering basic training to those who sell medication, and enlisting them as allies in the provision of primary health care.

- *Provide traditional healers and birth attendants with the necessary training and equipment to make them an effective part of the health team.*
- *See p63 on the training of traditional birth attendants.*
- *Offer basic training in preventive and curative health care to all those who sell medication.*

The design and management of health facilities

Local and cultural factors should be taken into account in planning for health facilities, so that they feel welcoming to people who might otherwise be intimidated by formal care. Such issues as privacy, the arrangement of waiting spaces and the placement of toilets may have implications which can only be determined locally.[36] Although a health clinic cannot tackle a community's environmental health problems, the handling of its own hygiene issues can be an instructive example to the community at large. There should be adequate containers for the disposal of rubbish, well-maintained toilets or latrines, clean drinking water and facilities for hand washing. The waiting room can also serve as a good display space for information and teaching materials on hygiene and other health issues.

Maintenance, efficiency and forethought are essential to the effective use of scarce resources in any health care centre. Generic drugs are a better investment than expensive brand-name alternatives. Drugs must be kept in appropriate conditions, supplies must be monitored and reordered, equipment must be maintained, and funds must be carefully managed. In part this is a matter of training: the lack of middle management skills has been recognized as a barrier to improved health care in many countries.[37]

[33] Hardoy, J E, Cairncross, S, Satterthwaite, D (eds) (1990) *The Poor Die Young*, London: Earthscan
[34] Cameron, S, Kandula, N, Leng, J, Arnold, C (1998) *Urban Childcare in Bangladesh*, Save the Children (USA)
[35] Missair, A (1998) 'The Illicit Sale of Pharmaceuticals in Africa: "The Dangerous Solution"', Unpublished research
[36] Hart, R H, Belsey, M A, Tarimo, E (1990) *Integrating Maternal and Child Health Services with Primary Health Care*, Geneva: World Health Organization
[37] Ibid

- *Take cultural preferences and the needs of parents with young children into account when designing clinics.*
- *Ensure that hygienic practices at the clinic serve as an example for the community, and make educational material available within the waiting room.*
- *Encourage the use of generic drugs rather than expensive brand names.*
- *Train staff to manage health resources efficiently, and budget adequately for annual operating expenses.*

maintenance and management

cultural preferences

generic drugs

Hospitals that meet the needs of children and their caregivers

Hospitals can be frightening, impersonal places, dedicated more to the efficiency and convenience of staff and administrators than to the comfort and reassurance of fearful children and anxious parents. A number of measures can be taken to humanize hospital care. The following suggestions are adapted from a manual on the care of sick children in small Southern hospitals.[38]

- Children and parents should be treated as people, called by name, dealt with in a respectful, friendly and reassuring way, and informed as to what is going on.
- Staff should have greater responsibility for fewer patients, in order to ensure familiarity and positive rapport. This may mean reorganization of staffing structures.
- In many parts of the world mothers (or other caregivers) accompany a child during a hospital stay. This practice should be encouraged to reassure family and child, to reduce the workload of the staff, and to allow mothers to feel useful and involved. In order to avoid confusion and overcrowding there should not be more than one person at a time staying with the child. It is important to have supportive facilities for mothers – toilets, washing facilities, places to store possessions and to prepare meals.
- Children with infectious diseases should be kept in special wards or isolation rooms. High standards for hygiene should be maintained at all times, not only by hospital personnel, but by visiting family members.
- When isolation is not necessary, shared space of one kind or another is generally preferable. Contact with others has been observed to keep mothers and children from feeling anxious and isolated. Keeping children together also makes access to staff easier, and allows staff to keep an eye on all the children more easily. But it is important to allow for privacy. Curtains or moveable screens can be provided, or partial walls built between beds, all of which may face a central nurses' station.
- Children should have the chance to personalize space to give them a sense of belonging within the frequent anonymity of hospital surroundings, especially when they are there for more than a few days. At the very least there should be a place where they can keep their possessions or pin up drawings.

involving parents

shared space

privacy

cooking

[38] Denn and Ebrahim 1986, op cit Note 28

play

gardens

- A children's ward should have its own cooking facilities in order to ensure ready availability of food, especially for children who are extremely malnourished, but also because of the benefits to mothers of having a demonstration safe cooking site where principles of hygiene and nutrition can be learned together.
- Even in hospital children should have opportunities for play. When they are not too sick, play can distract them, create a relaxed atmosphere, become a way of coping with fear and anxiety, and even help to speed recovery. There is evidence that the provision of gardens within hospitals can be soothing and restorative for all ages.[39] The same spaces can give mothers, older children and adolescents the opportunity to congregate for informal discussion or practical education.

The guidelines provided by the baby-friendly and mother-friendly hospital initiatives are a valuable resource for adapting hospital practices to the needs of newborns and their mothers (see p65). By adhering to certain basic principles, hospitals can become formally accredited by these programmes (see resource list, p276).

- *Encourage local hospitals to take measures to support the comfort and reassurance of sick children and their families.*
- *Support hospitals to become accredited as 'baby friendly' and 'mother friendly'.*

Record keeping

data collection

patient held records

Health centres should keep good records not only to track the health of particular patients, but as a database for monitoring trends and evaluating service, in order to continually improve the level of care. The World Health Organization recommends home-based records for mothers containing information about their pregnancies, births and general health, as well as their children's growth charts, immunization records, and risk factors. Patient-held records ensure continuity of care, especially when the services of more than one health facility are being used. They also raise awareness of health problems and encourage a greater sense of involvement, control and responsibility.[40] In Thailand, a booklet has been developed for use by parents to record and monitor information on their children's immunizations, growth records and general health, as well as on their social and emotional growth. This encourages an integrated view of children's well-being.[41] Records should be designed with data collection in mind. When information is well-organized and coded, it should be possible to use older school children to collect and collate data.

- *Require health centres to maintain good records, not only to meet patients' needs, but to provide a good database for monitoring local health care.*
- *Encourage the use of patient-held (and parent-held) records to support continuity of care, and a sense of control and responsibility on the part of patients.*

39 Cooper Marcus, C and Barnes, M (eds) (1999) *Healing Gardens: Therapeutic Landscapes in Healthcare Facilities*, New York: John Wiley and Sons

40 WHO (1994) *Home-based Maternal Records: Guidelines for Development, Adaptation and Evaluation*, Geneva: World Health Organization

41 Herscovitch, L (1997) 'Moving Child and Family Programs to Scale in Thailand', UNICEF

Services for children with disabilities

Disabled children have a right to special care and assistance that will support their self-reliance and fullest development. Consistent, easily accessible support is likely to be more significant than a high level of specialization, and it is important to encourage low-cost community-based rehabilitation efforts. Local health workers with basic training in rehabilitation can receive back-up and technical assistance from more specialized centres, referring children when necessary for ongoing evaluation and input. Within the community, these local rehabilitation workers can provide a number of important services, in collaboration with parents and other community members, that do not require the routine involvement of experts.

local rehabilitation workers

The most basic service is support for parents in their attempts to care for children. Rehabilitation workers can ensure that secondary disabilities do not occur; they can help parents find ways to build on a child's strengths, compensate for weaknesses, monitor progress, and focus on achievable goals (see also pp86, 161). Community rehabilitation programmes can support workshops for designing and making low-cost appliances and aids, both for mobility and for general stimulation. With practical training and technical back-up, local workers and volunteers in poor communities worldwide have developed many creative solutions for responding to needs in ways that take local conditions into account, and make use of locally available materials. (See resource list, p278). Community rehabilitation programmes can also minimize the isolation of children with disabilities, serve as advocates for them, and work towards integrating them into the community. This will be discussed in greater detail in on p138.

building on strengths

advocacy

- *Make training available for community based rehabilitation workers who can provide support for parents and their children with disabilities.*

Mental health

Mental health has been a low priority in the health agendas of countries and cities in the South, but is increasingly being recognized as a serious problem. Mental illness encompasses far more than severe conditions such as schizophrenia. More common disorders, which make up 90 per cent of all mental illness, include anxiety, depression, insomnia, fatigue, irritability and problems with concentration, all of which can undermine the capacity to cope effectively with life.[42] This is not only an urban problem. Rural dwellers, coping with isolation and lack of opportunity, stimulation and services, face their own challenges to mental health. But children and adults living in the chronically stressful environments of urban poverty appear to be at particularly high risk for psychological disturbance.[43]

Unemployment, violence, overcrowding, challenging physical conditions, and the absence of strong social support systems can all undermine resilience and contribute to a sense of being overwhelmed. Many of the urban poor may be coping, in addition, with discrimination and hostility. Parents and other caregivers may feel anxious and helpless in the face of

[42] Blue, I (1996) 'Urban Inequalities in Mental Health: the Case of São Paulo, Brazil', *Environment and Urbanization*, 8(2): 91–99

[43] Parry-Jones, W L (1991) 'Mental Health and Development of Children and Adolescents in Cities' in Parry-Jones, W and Queloz, N (eds) *Mental Health and Deviance in Inner Cities*, Geneva: WHO/UNICRI/University of Naples, 13–19

urban stress

their circumstances, unable to summon the energy and involvement necessary to care for their children and tackle their daily challenges. Children may become withdrawn, fearful or overly aggressive in response to a range of difficult experiences.[44] Adolescents may be especially drawn to indulge in risky and self-destructive behaviour, and rates of delinquency are definitely higher in urban areas.[45]

social support

There are generally few resources for responding to the mental health needs of the poor. Nor, in most cases, can the emotional stresses of poverty and marginalization be realistically alleviated without addressing the larger circumstances in which they are rooted.[46] Having acknowledged these difficulties, it is still critical that local health authorities do what they can to respond to the mental health needs of children, adolescents and their families. At the very least there should be systems in place to identify those in particular need, along with training and support for teachers, primary health workers, and others likely to have regular contact with children and their families. Within the context of poverty, strong social support systems are likely to be the most important element in helping people to cope with depression and anxiety, and it should be a priority to promote any measures that enhance social support (p54).

For those suffering from serious mental illness, specialized mental health services should be made available. Responses must be sensitive to customary ways of understanding and expressing suffering; the ways that people make sense of their world and confront their difficulties can vary a good deal from one society to another. It is not effective simply to import models from the North. Therapy that focuses on 'talking it out', for instance, may be quite inappropriate in cultures that discourage the open discussion of feelings.[47]

Children's emotional difficulties should not be pathologized unnecessarily. Their responses even to traumatic events, such as being present during the violent death of family members, may require patient and understanding support more than specialized psychological treatment. Nor should support be professionalized to the point that only specialists are considered capable of dealing with troubled children. Rather than focusing on isolated symptoms, help should be geared towards finding ways to encourage stability and hope in children's lives. Save the Children makes the following recommendations for children who have been involved in violence or otherwise traumatized:

- Separation from family should be prevented whenever possible. Children without family should be placed where they can develop strong and trusting relationships with adults.
- Children should live wherever possible in normal community environments.
- They should have the opportunity to share their experiences with other children and young people.
- They should have access to people and activities that support their sense of identity, self-esteem and responsibility.[48]

44 Ekblad, S (1995) 'Helping Children Cope with Urban Environment Stresses in Developing Countries' in Harpham, T and Blue, I (eds) *Urbanization and Mental Health in Developing Countries*, Aldershot: Avebury, 103–123
45 Parry-Jones 1991, op cit Note 43
46 Queloz, N (1991) 'Urban Process and its Role in Strengthening Social Disadvantages, Inequalities and Exclusion' in Parry-Jones,W and Queloz, N (eds) *Mental Health and Deviance in Inner Cities*, Geneva: WHO/ UNICRI/University of Naples, 31–36
47 Richman, N (1996) 'Principles of Help for Children Involved in Organised Violence', Save the Children UK, Working Paper 13
48 Ibid

ADEQUATE NUTRITION FOR ALL

Lack of adequate nutrition is the single most significant health problem for young children. When children are malnourished, their bodies' defenses are weakened, they get sick more easily and their illnesses are more severe. When they are sick their appetites are poor, and the food they take in is less well absorbed. And so the cycle of hunger and infection perpetuates itself. Recent figures from UNICEF indicate that almost one third of children in developing countries are moderately or severely malnourished.[49] Fifty-five per cent of all young child mortality in countries of the South is attributable to malnutrition.[50] Pneumonia, for instance, one of the single largest causes of child death, is strongly associated with malnutrition.[51]

Inadequate nutrition affects not only children's general health but their development on every front. Children who are routinely undernourished are likely to be stunted mentally as well as physically, and their capacity to learn will be affected.[52] Connections have also been made between chronic malnutrition and vulnerability to psychological stress.[53] Malnourishment has implications not only for the children who experience it but for future generations. Mothers who are poorly nourished and debilitated are unlikely to have the energy to provide the level of care their children require. They are also more likely to give birth to sickly and underweight children, thereby helping to perpetuate poverty and disadvantage.[54]

Some reasons for malnutrition

Malnutrition is not always a simple matter of insufficient food. Other factors play a role. There may be insufficient awareness of children's nutritional needs. Calorie intake may be adequate, but children may lack protein or certain critical micronutrients. Breastfeeding, the ideal approach to early nutrition, may be undermined by social pressures, advertising for infant formulas, or the mother's need to work. Over 40 per cent of working mothers interviewed in Dhaka, Bangladesh, said they had given up breastfeeding because of work.[55] Even when children are adequately fed, repeated diarrhoea can cause malnutrition. For hundreds of millions of urban children, parasites such as hookworm, roundworm and whipworm consume nutrients and cause or aggravate malnutrition, as well as damaging the tissues in which they live and causing other problems.[56]

Cultural factors often have a role in children's malnutrition. In some societies, men eat first and there may be little left for women and children. Boys, too, are often given more to eat than girls in the belief that they require more, or because their development is regarded as a higher priority. Women, who usually take children's needs more seriously, may not have much influence within the household; various studies have shown that children's nutritional status benefits when women have greater decision making power.[57]

When all the adults in a household work, there is little time to shop for food or to cook. Families may rely on street food, which is often

49 UNICEF (1998) *The State of the World's Children 1998*, New York: Oxford University Press

50 Pelletier, D L, Frongillo,E A, Habicht, J P (1993) 'Epidemiological Evidence for a Potentiating Effect of Malnutrition on Child Mortality', *American Journal of Public Health*, 1993(83)

51 Rossi-Espagnet, A, Goldstein, G B, Tabibzadeh, I (1991) 'Urbanization and Health in Developing Countries: a Challenge for the Health of All', *World Health Statistical Quarterly*, 44(4): 186–244

52 Landers, C (1989) 'A Theoretical Basis for Investing in Early Child Development: Review of Current Concepts', UNICEF International Child Development Centre

53 Ekblad,1995, op cit Note 44

54 Engle, P L, Menon, P, Garrett, J L, Slack, A (1997) 'Urbanization and Caregiving: A Framework for Analysis and Examples from Southern and Eastern Africa', *Environment and Urbanization*, 9(2)

55 Cameron et al, 1998, op cit Note 34

56 Cairncross, 1992, op cit Note 16; and Satterthwaite, D, Hart, R, Levy, C, Mitlin, D, Ross, D, Smit, J, Stephens, C (1996) *The Environment for Children*, London: Earthscan

57 Engle et al, 1997, op cit Note 54

household politics

time constraints

contamination

inadequate cooking facilities

monitoring

adequate and nutritious; but for stalls too close to roads there may be problems of lead contamination from vehicle exhaust fumes. In other cases, unclean containers may contribute to contamination. In most of the dwellings of low-income families facilities to store food are inadequate and it often becomes contaminated by flies or spoils rapidly. It may be difficult for caregivers to clean bottles, cups and feeding utensils without plentiful water and sufficient fuel supplies to heat it.[58]

Young children can hold only a limited quantity of food in their small stomachs. They need frequent small meals rather than one or two large meals a day. If meals are difficult to prepare, this may not happen. Cooking facilities can be inadequate, or fuel too expensive, to allow for frequent cooking. Frequent feeding is especially critical when basic foods are bulky rather than concentrated, and when large amounts are needed in order to meet nutritional needs. Once children are malnourished, they may lose their appetites and be unwilling to eat even what is made available. Special attention may be necessary to encourage them to eat and to take an interest in their surroundings.

Any comprehensive response to malnourishment on the part of local authorities and their partners must first determine what the local issues are. Undernourished children must be identified so that their needs can be responded to. In Campinas, Brazil, social and health workers are required to notify the local Health Office of any cases of undernourishment, in the same way they would report contagious disease. The children then receive special care, and the family is observed.[59] Effective responses are likely to include a combination of support for breastfeeding, education in basic hygiene, nutrition and food preparation, feeding programmes, elimination of parasites and support for local initiatives that improve household food security.

- *Through community based data collection, determine what the local issues are that result in malnourishment for children, and plan accordingly.*
- *Identify malnourished children and make special care available to them.*

Support for breastfeeding

Breast milk cannot be improved upon as a food for infants. It contains the ideal combination of nutrients for growth and development, and also protects infants from disease and infection during their vulnerable early months.[60] Infant formula is nutritionally inferior to breastmilk, and under the wrong circumstances it can even be dangerous. When formula is overdiluted, infants will receive insufficient nourishment. When mixed with unclean water, allowed to stand unrefrigerated, or fed to infants in unsterile bottles, it can quickly cause diarrhoea. Bottle-fed babies in poor communities are significantly at risk, and are 14 times more likely to die from diarrhoeal diseases than babies who are exclusively breastfed.[61] Every effort should be made to encourage women to breastfeed their children, especially during the critical early months (see also Chapter 4, p65).

58 Satterthwaite et al, 1996, op cit Note 56
59 Personal communication, Raquel Rolnick, 1998
60 UNICEF (1998) *The State of the World's Children 1998*, New York: Oxford University Press
61 De Zoysa, I, M Rea, J Martines (1991) 'Why Promote Breastfeeding in Diarrhoeal Disease Control Programmes?', *Health Policy Planning*, 6: 371–379

The one circumstance under which breastfeeding might be discouraged is when mothers have HIV/AIDS. There is a 14 per cent risk that infants may become infected through their breastmilk. This creates a serious dilemma for an infected mother, especially if she lacks access to safe, clean water for the sanitary management of bottle feeding. The risks of breastfeeding must be weighed against the often greater risks of not breastfeeding.[62] Mothers need to discuss their options with trained health personnel, and to make their decisions based on local conditions and the support they can draw on. In some cases it may be possible to have the infant wet-nursed by a woman who is not infected. (For more on HIV/AIDS, see below).

HIV and breastfeeding

- *Make every effort to encourage women to breastfeed their infants, especially during the critical early months (see p65).*

Community feeding programmes

Community feeding programmes can help to ensure that children are receiving the nutrients they need. The purchasing and preparation of food in large quantities can be a relatively economical way of ensuring that young children receive the nutrition they need. Child care centres and schools can be good sites for such programmes, because of children's daily attendance. With training and material support, child care providers can be assisted in making balanced meals available to the children in their care (see p154). Where there is space, school gardens can contribute produce, as part of their broader goal of environmental and health education (see p181). For those children who do not attend either school or child care, other sites in the community must be found for ensuring they get the food they need.

meals in child care centres

school gardens

Community feeding programmes should not be targeted solely at children. In Lima, Peru, during a period of particular economic hardship and rising malnutrition in the 1980s, a number of community kitchens were established, largely as a result of initiatives from community members. For the most part these kitchens have been run by groups of women who participate in decision making and rotate tasks. The average kitchen prepares over 100 meals a day, and has been able to maintain a critical level of energy and protein intake for community members as well as reducing the time that women had to spend on household tasks. Labour is donated and meals sold at cost, although some groups provide free meals for the worst-off households. These groups have often gone on to become agents of change within their communities in other areas as well, involving themselves in discussion groups, income generating activities, growth monitoring and other minimal health services.[63]

community kitchens

A similar programme in Mexico, originally targeted at under-five children, pregnant and lactating women, is supported by a national government agency which provides start-up funds and equipment, while communities supply the labour and operate kitchens on a cost-recovery basis. Over time a number of variations in the original programme have developed, responding to local realities in order to improve cost-effectiveness and assure that the initiative can be sustained. Support has come from different levels of government.[64]

62 UNICEF 1998, op cit Note 60
63 UNICEF (1994) *The Urban Poor and Household Food Security*, Urban Examples #19, UNICEF
64 Ibid

- *In communities where it is necessary, establish feeding programmes through child care centres, schools and other community organizations, or provide support for organizations that are running such programmes.*

Supporting household food security

lower food prices

Feeding programmes can be a critical support, but a more basic response is to help ensure that families can themselves provide the nourishment that they and their children require. Many poor urban households buy most of their food supplies from small local shops or stalls which lack both the capital and the space to buy in large quantities, and hence have to charge high prices. A number of measures can be taken to enable small shopkeepers to operate more efficiently and to lower their prices. In Cali, Colombia, the Carvajal Foundation provided training to shopkeepers to improve their business capacity, offered low-cost credit for business expansion, and built a warehouse from which shopkeepers could buy direct from the producers. This resulted in lower prices for consumers, higher quality products and higher profits for the shopkeepers.[65]

Growing food and raising livestock can be an important component of household food security even in cities. This is discussed in more detail on p51. Many urban schools are also involved in food production (see p181).

- *Support fair-price shops and urban agriculture.*

Provision of micronutrients

inexpensive supplements

The lack of relatively inexpensive supplements can have dramatic health impacts. Vitamin A deficiency lowers the disease resistance of many millions of children, and can contribute to early mortality as well as causing blindness and illness. Iodine deficiency also affects millions of children, lowering their IQs and often causing more serious physical or mental problems. Iron deficiency affects hundreds of millions, compromising physical and mental development and contributing significantly to maternal mortality. These and other micronutrient deficiencies can be significantly reduced at very low cost.[66] Supplements can be made available at regular clinic visits, through child care centres and schools, or through community feeding programmes.

parasites

- *Make micronutrients easily available where they are needed.*

Eliminating parasites

Dramatic reductions in the incidence and severity of parasitic infections can be achieved at low cost through community-based programmes for treating children (and families), reducing the risk of infection and transmission, and educating children and their parents on preventive and curative measures. School-centred programmes have a central role here (see p176).

[65] Cruz, L F (1994) 'NGO Profile: Fundación Carvajal: The Carvajal Foundation', *Environment and Urbanization*, 6(2): 175–182
[66] UNICEF 1998, op cit Note 60; WHO 1995, op cit Note 1

- *Reduce the incidence of parasitic infections through the availability of clean water and sanitation, through education in hygiene, and through the availability of medication.*

HEALTH CARE EDUCATION

Education is an essential component of preventive health care, for it helps people to take control and responsibility for their own health. One of the most significant determinants of health for a young child is a well-informed parent or caretaker.[67] Such educational efforts are frequently directed only to mothers. It is important to include fathers, since they often make decisions within the home that affect the well-being of children. Adolescent girls and pregnant women should also be included to prepare them for the challenges of parenting.

including fathers

Health education should be focused on the following priorities:

- raising awareness of the long term benefits of preventive care;
- basic hygiene, including that oriented to infant and early child feeding, and the management of their excreta;
- nutritional education, including an awareness of nutritional needs and the benefits of breastfeeding, safe management of bottle feeding when necessary, information about food preparation and storage, and an understanding of girls' equal need for nutrition;
- the care of illness, including oral rehydration therapy, and an awareness of when intervention is necessary. (A greater awareness of the symptoms of pneumonia, for instance, could dramatically reduce the incidence of this single largest cause of infant and child death);
- the promotion of healthy lifestyles and the avoidance of risky behaviours.

health education priorities

methods

Information sessions can be held through schools, child care facilities, at health care centres, local government offices, child and family centres, or informally within the home during regular visits by community health workers. Topics should be relevant to peoples' needs and presented in a hands-on way in order to ensure retention. Not too many ideas should be presented at one session, and advice on hygiene, management, and food preparation should always be relevant to local conditions, so that it can be easily applied at home.

The use of traditional health practices may in some cases contribute to health and well-being, while in others it is ineffective or even damaging. Health educators should recognize and support positive practices, while discouraging – with clear information – those that undermine health. (See p106 for a discussion of traditional practitioners.)

using the media

The potential of the media to contribute to health education must not be underestimated. In one South American country, a survey found that people were 25 times more likely to obtain their health information from television than from health workers. Media surveys have found that health information is one of the topics most frequently requested by the public.[68] Local health authorities should find constructive ways to make best use of this important tool.

67 This may be because education results in better child care practices, including better utilization of health care facilities, or it may be a function of improved maternal income, or both. The precise reasons are not clear – see Engle et al 1997, op cit Note 54

68 PAHO (1996) 'Healthy People, Healthy Spaces', Pan American Health Organization, Report of the Director

Health education for children

child to child

Children can be effectively educated to become aware of health issues, take responsibility for themselves and for younger siblings, and influence adults to change their practices. Experience has shown that child-to-child approaches to disseminating health information can be extremely effective. (See the resource list for various useful publications.)

school-health partnerships

Schools, where attendance is widespread, are likely to be the best location for establishing sound health practices. Local health centres, as part of their effort to integrate service provision and form effective partnerships, should become involved in health education and hygiene practices in local schools and child care centres. Involving children in the monitoring of environmental conditions at schools, for instance, or establishing the school as a model for good sanitation, can have an impact throughout the community. School children can be a resource for health centres in assisting with local research and evaluation, and disseminating health information to their families and to the community at large.

Education on HIV/AIDS

women, children and AIDS

In recent years a vital component of preventive care has been education on HIV/AIDS. In some countries this is a relatively new problem. In others, it is a public health issue that has reached catastrophic proportions, reversing the positive gains that have been made in health and survival in the last few decades. The situation is most serious in some countries of sub-Saharan Africa, and the epidemic is growing in Asia. Women of childbearing age account for half of all new infections, and many are under 25 years of age.[69] The effects of the disease are devastating and far reaching, affecting not only those who are ill, but inevitably their families as well. Even when mothers do not transmit the disease to their children at birth or through breastfeeding, their debilitation can make child care difficult or impossible.

The number of children orphaned by AIDS is a problem of growing proportions, especially in Africa. Expensive drug therapies make the disease almost manageable in wealthier countries. But only a fraction of the money spent worldwide on HIV/AIDS research has been put towards finding a low cost vaccine, the only reasonable solution for most poor countries. In the meantime, education is essential, and should use all available avenues: health providers, schools, the media, voluntary groups, public figures and the private sector must all play a role. (See also p119).

- *Support health education programmes as an essential component of preventive community-based primary health care.*
- *Use the local media as an effective means of education as well as other partners.*
- *Involve children in health care education within schools and through child-to-child approaches.*

69 Piot, P (1997) 'Fighting AIDS Together' in UNICEF (ed) *Progress of Nations 1997*

THE SPECIAL NEEDS OF ADOLESCENTS AND OLDER CHILDREN

adolescent health risks

Older children and adolescents are not as prone to disease as younger children, nor as dependent on others for meeting their basic needs. But they have some particular health problems that can be serious and life-threatening, and that call for particular responses. The range of issues and their importance vary from place to place, but surveys indicate that overall the chief health risks for adolescent girls, and the highest cause of death, are complications related to pregnancy, abortion and childbirth. For adolescent boys, accidents and violence are the principle causes of mortality.[70] In many countries substance abuse also presents a significant health risk for this age group, as do sexually transmitted diseases, which affect one in twenty adolescents worldwide.[71] Over half of all new HIV infections affect young people between the ages of 15 and 24.[72] Because adolescence is a period of rapid physical growth, vitamin and mineral deficiencies are common in this age group. There is a strong need among young people for information and education, for health care that is respectful and non-judgmental, for emergency services, and for supportive environments that minimize their risks.

obstancles to health care for adolescents

There are many reasons why adolescents do not have access to the services they need. Because infants and young children are at higher risk, their needs take priority within health systems that are chronically short on resources. Adolescents may also dismiss health care as irrelevant. The sensitivity of some of their health needs may prevent them from seeking professional help and cause them to self-medicate, ignore their problems, or turn to unqualified people. Many adolescents work long hours or live outside of the family home; because primary health care is usually community-based, often focused on the family unit, it may be difficult for them to access it. The more exposed and vulnerable young people are, the less likely they are to have easy access to the health services they need. Health education is also likely to be a problem; there is often a social reluctance, for instance, to address issues of sexuality with young people out of a mistaken fear that it will encourage sexual activity.

Assessment and planning that involves adolescents and responds to their needs

Adolescents will frequently reject decisions and interventions made on their behalf without their involvement. It is critical that they be closely involved in establishing priorities for their own health care. The needs of different groups are likely to vary: girls and boys, different ethnic groups, young people in school and those in the workplace, those living with family and those on the streets, will all be facing different realities. Health authorities and voluntary groups should take into account the perspectives of various groups of adolescents in order to understand how best to offer them support. Adolescent involvement is particularly useful in identifying successful programmes that can be built on.

70 UNICEF (1997) *Youth Health – For a Change: A UNICEF Notebook on Programming for Young People's Health and Development*, Working draft
71 Ibid
72 UNICEF (ed) (1998) *The Progress of Nations 1998*, New York: UNICEF

There is a critical need among adolescents for health care that is respectful and non-judgemental, for information relevant to their needs, and for supportive environments that minimize their risks. They should be involved wherever possible in helping to establish priorities for their own health care. Young people below an AIDS awareness billboard in Port-au-Prince, Haiti. UNICEF 1995, Nicole Toutounji

Youth-friendly health services

reproductive health

In addition to the routine check-ups, preventive care, and the treatment of common diseases that should be available to all children, adolescents may need access to care for problems related to drug use, and to treatment and advice for the care of sexually transmitted diseases. They need a full range of reproductive care, including adequate birth control and sensitive, respectful, counselling. Services should emphasize the prevention of unwanted pregnancies, and health authorities must ensure that adolescent girls have alternatives to the unsafe abortions that are the only solution for so many. (67 per cent of those seeking hospital care as a result of septic abortion in Lagos in 1983 were girls between 11 and 20 years of age.[73]) If pregnancy is taken to term, there must be full prenatal care with the recognition that adolescents are at a higher risk for complications (see also p60).

For many in this age group, and especially for those living on the street, health care needs will best be met by outreach services or drop-in centres (see p218). In South Africa, the Youth Information Centre Pilot Project offers health services exclusively for adolescents and is designed to help them make informed decisions in their lives. Staff are young and casually dressed, and facilities include private counselling rooms and space for young people to socialize, along with music and videos.[74]

drop-in centres

In most cases it is not economically realistic to support parallel health care systems, and young people will find it necessary to turn to health centres serving the general population if they are to receive adequate care. To make health services more welcoming to adolescents, it is important that medical staff be alert to their concerns, non-judgmental in dealing with their health problems, and respectful of their need for confidentiality. Health workers should be trained to respond to the problems of adolescents, both in terms of technical competence and in effective communication, and training should come from those who have themselves been successful in working with young people.

medical staff

Health education for adolescents

Adolescents and older children need accurate information about sexual and reproductive health, the ramifications of alcohol, tobacco and drug use, the nutritional needs of their rapidly growing bodies, and basic hygiene and disease prevention. It is important not to assume that apparently streetwise young people are knowledgeable about health issues. Interviews with incarcerated youth, for instance, indicated that less than half of them knew that sexual abstinence reduced the risk of HIV infection.[75] Unfortunately, much of the educational material available is in printed form, and useful only to those with good literacy skills. Even adolescents who are functionally literate may not be sufficiently comfortable with the written word to make good use of pamphlets and other material.[76] Direct contact is often necessary, with information that is concrete and reinforced through discussion.

There is little evidence that information by itself is effective in changing risky behaviour. To make healthy choices, adolescents need a range of skills – the capacity to resist peer pressure, to think of the long term, to weigh options, to deal with conflict and to make responsible decisions. To have an impact, this kind of education must come from people whom adolescents trust and respect. Some of the most successful programmes have used peer educators. The Undugu Society in Kenya has found that girls who have left their life on the streets have been most effective in discussing sensitive issues with their old street friends.[77] A comprehensive analysis of drug prevention programmes in the United States found that those involving the active participation of young people were significantly more effective; the content of programmes was found to make little difference in the absence of a participatory and interactive approach.[78]

73 UNICEF 1997, op cit Note 70
74 Transgrud, R (1997) 'Adolescent Sexual and Reproductive Health in Eastern and Southern Africa: Building Experience', paper prepared for USAID/REDSO
75 Cited by Bond, L S (1992) 'Street Children and AIDS: Is Postponement of Sexual Involvement a Realistic Alternative to the Prevention of Sexually Transmitted Diseases?', *Environment and Urbanization*, 4(1): 150–157
76 Ibid
77 Ochola, L (1996) 'The Undugu Society Approach in Dealing with Children at Risk to Abuse and Neglect' in Verhellen, E (ed) *Monitoring Children's Rights*, The Hague, Boston: Nijhoff
78 Tobler, N S (1997) 'Meta-analysis of Adolescent Drug Prevention Programs: Results of the 1993 Meta-analysis', NIDP Research Monograph, US Department of Health and Human Services

peer education

For adolescents attending school, health education can be built into the curriculum (see p176), and counselling made available. For those at home, in the workplace or on the street, other solutions must be found. Local health authorities must work closely with organizations that have contact with various groups of young people, offering them the support and technical back-up that they need. Safe places for adolescents, of the kind described on p128, are a natural place for offering health education and counselling.

media

In some countries, the entertainment media have been used successfully to communicate health issues to adolescents. A video and comic book on HIV/AIDS prevention was found to be very effective in Brazil, some popular songs in the Philippines increased the rate of telephone calls to a youth hotline, and in India a TV drama serial was felt to have an influence on attitudes towards early marriage for girls.[79]

Broader levels of support

The challenging health issues of adolescents are closely tied to their social life, their connections with family, their access to education, and the degree of hope they feel about their lives. Information and health care will do little to affect risk-taking behaviour if it is not backed by supports that make alternatives realistic, and by environments that minimize risks. Warnings about the dangers of substance abuse, for instance, will have little impact for children who live dangerous lives and are focused on immediate survival. Efforts to prevent the spread of sexually transmitted disease will be wasted if children depend on selling sex for food and shelter. Detoxification for drug dependent adolescents makes little sense unless there is support and back-up during and after the process.[80] To address the health needs of children and adolescents effectively means to address the larger social and economic issues in their lives.

- *Where possible establish special adolescent health services that are responsive to their particular needs and designed with their involvement.*
- *Train health workers to respond sensitively and non-judgementally to the concerns of young people.*
- *Make education available that offers health-related information, but also supports long term thinking and responsible decision making; wherever possible use peer educators, and stress participatory approaches.*
- *Make use of the media for education on issues relevant to adolescents.*

[79] UNICEF 1997, op cit Note 70
[80] Ennew, J (1994) *Street and Working Children: A Guide to Planning*, London: Save the Children

7 Neighbourhoods for Children

Local neighbourhoods should provide a secure and welcoming transition to the larger world - a place where children can play safely, run errands, socialize and learn from those around them. It is important to remember that girls have an equal need for play, companionship and community life. These girls dance to tape recorded music in Bom Jardim, Fortaleza, Brazil. 1996 Janet Jarman

The CRC stresses the importance to children and adolescents of safe, supportive neighbourhoods. It recognizes their right to play and recreation, and to participation in the cultural life of their communities; their right to associate with others, to have access to information, and to be prepared for responsible life as citizens in a free society. To support these rights, they are guaranteed protection from discrimination and from violence of any kind.[1]

Too many communities fail to offer this level of security and support. Around the world urban children and adolescents speak of their fears and their desire to live in peace and safety. For many children this is a more pressing concern than even the need for food or health care. It is a concern, too, for those who are committed to supporting strong and responsible citizenship. Children who grow up in environments that provoke fear and limit social interaction are handicapped by this distortion of community life, and are less likely to develop the understanding and skills fundamental to civic involvement.

When cities are secure and lively places, they can be the finest expression of human culture, encouraging a quality of interaction that stimulates creativity and fosters civilization in its best sense. When they

[1] CRC Articles 2, 15, 17, 29, 30, 31

fear and insecurity

are permeated by fear and anxiety, the potential for this achievement is lost and cities become quite literally 'uncivil.' When people feel threatened and insecure they hesitate to use public space and withdraw instead into increasing isolation. Businesses falter, services deteriorate, community life is undermined and the range of opportunity narrows for everyone. The disintegration of a lively street and community life increases the likelihood of antisocial activity, and so the problem feeds upon itself.

exclusion

Fear and insecurity are fed by the disparities that characterize so many cities. The frustrations generated by injustice and exclusion can foster aggression both towards the self and others. Alcohol and drug use, family violence, delinquency and vandalism are natural expressions of anger and hopelessness.[2] So are apathy and resignation, which foster an atmosphere of insecurity. When conditions are too difficult, solidarity tends to disappear, leaving in its place hostility, suspicion and confrontation over scarce resources and opportunities.[3] Differences between people can be exacerbated by want, and chronic levels of stress can cause even minor incidents to escalate out of control.

positive measures

Finding lasting solutions to violence and insecurity means nothing less than eliminating poverty and exclusion through housing policies, education, job opportunities and changes in the judicial system. But within the context of these more comprehensive efforts, there are some practical measures for responding to the insecurities of community members. These must be part of an integrated and informed effort to promote an active community life and a culture of non-violence. In this chapter we will review some approaches that local authorities can take to help create the secure, stimulating communities that promote children's rights. Many of these measures can be carried out by residents themselves, with support and technical assistance. Others will require the more active intervention of local authorities, always with the involvement of residents.

HOW SUPPORTIVE COMMUNITIES AFFECT CHILDREN'S DEVELOPMENT

In early childhood, the home environment is the centre of life, and the place where most learning happens. But as children become more competent, the larger world becomes increasingly important. Ideally, a neighbourhood should be a place where children can play safely, run errands, walk to school, socialize with friends and observe and learn from the activities of others. When neighbourhoods provide a secure and welcoming transition to the larger world, children can gradually test and develop their competence before confronting the full complexity of a city.

Especially within the flux and variety of urban life, local neighbourhoods can be complex environments, calling for more sophisticated skills, understandings and choices than are necessary within the household. There are new sights and sounds to take in, strange faces and unfamiliar situations to respond to and new rules to be learned. Discovering how to negotiate these challenges is an important part of any child's growing competence and independence. It also provides the opportunity for

[2] de la Barra, X (1998) 'Poverty: The Main Cause of Ill Health in Urban Children', *Health, Education and Behavior*, 25(1): 45–49

[3] Moser, C O N (1996) *Confronting Crisis: A Summary of Household Responses to Poverty and Vulnerability in Four Poor Urban Communities*, Washington DC: The World Bank

children to begin to understand, accept and ideally to enjoy differences, a critical part of their development as tolerant, responsible citizens.

But when neighbourhoods are dangerous, threatening places, children will be limited in the use they can make of them, or forced to take risks that are inappropriate for both their bodies and minds. Fear of traffic, of violence and of bad company trap in homes many children who cannot hope to meet the full range of their social and physical needs. This appears to be a growing phenomenon, particularly in the affluent areas of cities around the world. In the United States and Britain, observers have noted that children are increasingly restricted in their access to spontaneous neighbourhood play. Instead, they are kept inside watching television, or, for those who can afford it, taken to a variety of programmed activities such as organized sports and special lessons.[4] These activities are valuable in their own way, but are not a substitute for the benefits of unstructured play with peers for young children's physical, social, intellectual and emotional development (see p122). Nor can they replace the growing sense of involvement that children gain from their access to local neighbourhood life.

restrictions

In poor neighbourhoods of cities in the South, where household life more frequently spills out into public space, children tend to have better access to the world outside their homes. It is not unusual to find them playing freely in the streets, part of the social fabric of busy neighbourhood life. But it is important not to romanticize this. While children enjoy more spatial freedom, they may be playing among open sewers, on dangerous catwalks or amid piles of rubbish and hazardous debris. Too often they are taking their chances with traffic. In many cities parents complain that they have no choice but to let their children run free given the small size of their homes. When families live near busy commercial districts or areas of high crime, parents fear for their children's safety, and are anxious that they will become attracted to street life. This is a particular concern when the neighbourhood itself offers few stimulating activities for older children.

freedom

hazards

Children are less able than adults to screen out negative stimuli, and their sense of security can be undermined in many ways. Neighbourhood tensions, ethnic violence, theft, rape, vandalism, bullying in the schools, drug abuse, police brutality and corruption all contribute to making children and adolescents feel that they live in a precarious and threatening world. Research has shown that children growing up in violent communities are less socially competent and academically motivated, and tend to be less controlled in their own behaviour.[5] When children become accustomed to violence, they can lose the capacity to empathize with victims, and are more likely to take on the role of aggressor themselves.[6]

The insecurity faced by many urban children may not be enough to endanger them. But it can undermine faith in the social order and the sense of community belonging. Even less threatening behaviours affect the quality of neighbourhood life and narrow the range of possibilities that are available to children and youth. Vandalism of public property, for instance, can end up curtailing children's access to a range of facilities and programmes. Researchers in Chawama, Zambia, noted that vandalism and theft put an end to evening classes and to a range of programmes and recreational opportunities for women and young people at local schools and community centres.[7]

[4] See for example Hart, R (1984) 'The changing city of childhood: implications for play and learning', *Catherine Molony Memorial Lecture*, City College Workshop Center, New York; and Hillman, M (1995) *One False Move: A Study of Children's Independent Mobility*, London: Policy Studies Institute

[5] Barbarin, O and T d Wet (1997) 'Violence and emotional development in black townships of South Africa: an ecological approach', Presentation at the Urban Childhood Conference June 1997, Trondheim, Norway

[6] Newell, P (1997) 'Children and Violence', *Innocenti Digest #2*, Florence, UNICEF International Child Development Centre

[7] Moser 1996, op cit Note 3

A number of measures can help communities to integrate children into neighbourhood life in a safe and positive way. It is in part a question of attitude: people must understand the significant benefits of making communities work well for children. Although for the most part children are accepted as a natural part of neighbourhood life, they are not always made welcome in the public sphere, where adult concerns and preferences are given priority. Broad-based education on children's rights can raise awareness of children as people with legitimate concerns. Local authorities can also foster a change in attitude through the attention they give to public space. It is a small matter, for instance, to install a drinking fountain at a height that small children can reach, but it can send a powerful message. Active intervention on the part of local authorities may also be necessary to combat discrimination against minority groups, girls and those with disabilities.

raising awareness

COMMUNITY INSECURITY AND SOCIAL FEARS

There is a growing consensus that urban violence and community insecurity cannot be dealt with through repression alone, but that preventive measures are critical to achieving effective results.[8] Insecurity is most effectively combated when community members feel a sense of ownership over their own neighbourhoods. Local authorities can encourage and coordinate the kinds of community wide strategies that help to prevent crime and promote security.

preventive measures

Public space as a support for social cohesiveness

Strong social bonds are fostered by the regular activity of residents in common space. Community ties may grow more easily in low-income neighbourhoods where people have reasons to depend on one another, and where they are less likely to meet all their needs within the confines of their homes. In contrast, more and more well-to-do people around the world live cut off from their neighbours in walled compounds or high security buildings. The mobility afforded by private cars further reduces dependence on their local communities. Poor communities can also be plagued by fear, but the more frequent presence of residents on the street and in public space can support a rich community life, and make neighbourhoods more suitable places for children's play.

using public space

This phenomenon works both ways. The presence of children in public space helps to stimulate positive interaction between adults. Caregivers checking on their children share a common concern. And when adults keep an eye on one another's children, this can develop into other forms of cooperation. Some communities have found that children's play can be a strategy for dealing with ethnic strife in trouble-torn areas.[9] It cannot be stressed too strongly that a neighbourhood where children's activities are encouraged and supported is likely to be a safer and better place for everyone else as well. Building strong social bonds is part of a self-perpetuating process that can strengthen local development on every front.

play as a strategy

8 Vanderschueren, F (1998) 'Towards safer cities', *Habitat Update*, 4(1): 1–6

9 Menary, S (1990) *Play without frontiers: A policy document on community relations in children's play*, Playboard, Belfast, Northern Ireland

Local authorities can contribute to this process in a number of ways. In Chapter 5 we discussed initiatives that can encourage friendly ties between close neighbours – the improvement of common space, attention to cultural patterns, measures to minimize hostility, and the involvement of residents in planning and management decisions (see p72). The same principles apply to the larger community.

defensible space

The theory of defensible space suggests that the physical characteristics of residential settings have an influence on criminal activity.[10] The size of buildings, their relation to one another and to the street, the quality of public space, can all contribute to differences in crime rates from one neighbourhood to another. The deciding factor is the degree of control that residents have over the space outside their dwellings. The frequent use of outdoor space and the social interaction that accompanies it increase the neighbourhood's capacity for informal surveillance, and tend to inhibit anti-social behaviour. Any factors that encourage people to extend their activities beyond the interior of their dwellings are positive from this perspective. Well-lit streets and alleyways, front porches, windows looking out onto the street, and inviting public space can all contribute to the active community presence that makes neighbourhoods safer for children.

building walls

A common response to insecurity has been to wall off areas from the surroundings, an approach most frequently associated with the gated communities of the wealthy. This may improve the situation for immediate neighbours, but it can also create neighbourhood islands that in the end decrease the overall level of safety and civility. Higher walls are not the solution to crime. A less exclusive approach is to close off one end of a street in order to create a cul-de-sac. This reduces through traffic and at the same time has been found to increase residents' sense of ownership (see p133).

local management

Local governments may lack the resources to implement major physical changes, but efforts should be made to support residents in modifying their own environments to increase their level of control. By employing residents in the maintenance and management of local facilities, municipalities can both provide jobs and heighten the sense of ownership, which can be instrumental in reducing vandalism.

privatization

There are worldwide trends towards the privatization of public spaces. This can bring in financial resources, but the investment is generally uneven and results in a tendency towards exclusion and segregation. Unless measures are taken to ensure that privately owned and developed spaces are available without discrimination to all local residents, they may have the effect of undermining public life and restricting the kinds of social interaction that are essential to building vital and safe communities.

- *Support measures that encourage increased community use of streets and public space – such as street lighting, benches, pleasant common space, areas for children's play, and support for cultural events, forums and local festivities.*
- *Hold residents meetings to discuss positive approaches to local control, and assist residents in modifying their local environments.*
- *Employ local residents for management and maintenance of local facilities.*

[10] Newman, O (1972) *Defensible Space*, New York: Macmillan and Co

- *Before permitting the privatization of any public space, assess the potential impact for local residents; include residents in the planning process; and ensure that privatized spaces remain available to local residents without discrimination.*

Police protection, law enforcement and community alternatives

corruption

mob justice

Poor neighbourhoods are most likely to be victimized by crime, but the urban poor tend to have inadequate protection, few resources for legal representation, and little chance of finding justice within inaccessible, inefficient and often corrupt systems. Lack of faith in the police is widespread, often with good reason. An internal report from one state in Brazil, for instance, found that 80 per cent of the police force was corrupt.[11] The ineffectiveness of the formal system encourages many people to take the law into their own hands. The establishment of vigilante groups and the acceptance of mob justice can have the effect of escalating the level of violence. In some cases, local criminals are ceded a level of legitimacy and protection within their own communities in order to guarantee in return their protection of the local area.[12]

police training

Addressing inadequacies within law enforcement is essential in reducing insecurity and restoring public confidence. Police forces and systems of justice must be trustworthy, accessible and responsive, and law enforcement must be a bottom-up effort, not a top-down response. Cali, Colombia has experimented with a number of measures; all police have been required to take training courses on human rights and on citizen relations; police have been concentrated in areas with the highest level of crime; each precinct makes regular reports to the mayor on trends in violence; and finally, the city has promoted the establishment of conciliation centres in different neighbourhoods, where issues that might otherwise lead to violence can be worked out with mediation.[13]

youth involvement

mediation

In New Haven, in the United States, a city with a high level of violence, the police chief has over the last five years involved a board of young people in interviewing all prospective police recruits. They have now been involved in hiring more than a quarter of the police force. The members of the youth board are elected from within their schools, or are recommended by other board members and voted on by them. The process has led to a number of police and youth friendships.[14]

Dakar, Senegal, has established a system whereby small neighbourhood disputes are taken to local police stations to be solved by friendly negotiations. The municipality has encouraged an association of young lawyers to set up legal information centres, and to organize public talks on legal themes. A particular focus is informing women of their legal rights.[15] In a mid-sized city in France, a small police sub-station was established opposite a local gathering place which was often the source of trouble at night. The duty officer became familiar with residents, conversed with passers-by, and helped to settle disputes as they arose.[16]

Uganda has developed a truly grassroots approach to community security and law enforcement. Local democratically elected 'resistance councils', linked to local government, have become the first institution

[11] Marcus, M (1995) *Faces of Justice and Poverty in the City*, Paris: European Forum for Urban Security
[12] Ibid
[13] Ibid
[14] Felson, L (1997) 'Youth in action', *Doing Democracy*, Winter 1997
[15] Marcus 1995, op cit Note 11
[16] Glowacki, F, M Marcus, G Mennetrier, C T Mennetrier, C Vourc'h (1996) *Urban Security Practices*, Paris: European Forum for Urban Security

that people turn to in cases of violence or crime. They, in turn, report to the police. The council deals with many cases itself, particularly civil law cases involving such issues as debt, damage to property, land problems and common law. They practice effective mediation and are able to deliver justice quickly and free of charge, lightening the load of the criminal justice system, and improving neighbourhood security and cooperation with the police.[17]

On the island of Reunion, where the capital city is plagued by crime, poverty and high unemployment, 'Houses of Justice and Law' have been opened in particularly difficult areas. Trained community volunteers offer a conciliation-mediation service to help citizens find peaceful solutions in crisis situations. Aggressors are expected to repair the damage done to victims.[18]

Vigilante justice is no solution to insecurity, but there are certainly more constructive community responses, and local authorities should support these by all means possible. Neighbourhood watches, for instance, should be given formal support by local authorities.

domestic violence

Children and women are most vulnerable to harassment and violence, especially domestic violence; but may find formal systems impenetrable. Municipalities must make strong efforts to ensure that appropriate protection and justice are easily available, and also to overcome the entrenched attitudes that make such protection especially necessary. The issue of domestic violence is discussed on p81.

harassment of minorities

Ethnic minorities, immigrants and refugees are also at particular risk of discrimination, harassment and violence. Because of their marginalization and cultural differences they may be especially fearful of police and other authorities. Attempts by minority groups to create their own informal systems of protection may serve only to heighten tensions. Local authorities must ensure that discrimination is addressed on all possible fronts – within schools, in access to services and housing, in the labour market and in the media. There should be a minority presence within all official agencies. There must also be a concerted effort on the part of police to ensure that these groups feel protected. In Dallas, Texas, a city with many ethnic groups, police have teamed up with minority teenagers in a programme to combat fear and violence. Teams of teenagers, Asian, Latino, African-American and Indian, patrol with police after school hours, offering as well such services as drilling peepholes in the doors of intimidated residents, inspecting residential fire alarms and distributing health and safety information in several languages.[19]

positive measures

- *Provide special training for police, legal workers and judicial staff to sensitize them to the rights of women, children, minorities and the poorest groups.*
- *Make police stations, courts, and local government offices easily available to all community members, and staff them with people, including women and minorities, who are responsive and respectful of community members' rights and concerns.*
- *Encourage familiarity between police and community members by assigning police officers to specific neighbourhoods; involve community members, including young people, in interviewing prospective community police.*

[17] Vanderschueren, F (1996) 'From violence to justice and security in cities', *Environment and Urbanization*, 8(1): 93–112
[18] Glowacki et al 1996, op cit Note 16
[19] The American News Service (1997) 'Young Dragons Chase Away Nighttime Fears in Dallas', *Doing Democracy*, (Winter 1997): 8

- *Make information about legal rights and about the availability of legal services easily accessible to all; seek the support of volunteer lawyers or law students to make free legal aid available to those who cannot afford formal advice or representation.*
- *Work with communities to institute procedures that can supplement or be alternatives to formal systems.*

Encouraging local involvement

safety coalitions

Neighbourhood insecurity affects everyone, and it should be the business of all to respond. Local safety coalitions can be an effective and constructive response. Such coalitions should include, aside from local citizens, law enforcement officials, representatives of the criminal justice system, health, education and welfare services, community organizations, and the private sector.[20] These coalitions can keep abreast of problem situations, uncover relevant information, diagnose the factors that contribute to local crime, and address conditions in ways that take into account local realities and the concerns of citizens. A local coordinator can be appointed to facilitate meetings, mediate between different groups, brief officials, ensure the involvement of local citizens, and uphold respect for human rights.[21]

public discussion

Public discussion of issues related to security can stimulate the public to take an active role. El Agora, an NGO in Cordoba, Argentina, has developed a series of activities, including forums involving people from all walks of life, to promote security in bars, cinemas and coffee houses; the proposals generated are publicized through the media.

- *Establish effective local safety coalitions within communities including, along with law enforcement officials, representatives of the criminal justice system, health, education and welfare services, representatives of community organizations and the private sector.*
- *Encourage public discussion of local security issues.*

Safe havens for children and youth

When children and adolescents live in violent households and communities, they need people and places that they can turn to for relief. Neighbourhood safe havens can be a critical resource, filling a number of important needs. They can:

- be safe places to go to, in order to relieve the stress of living in unsafe environments;
- provide a range of social and recreational activities for young people whose opportunities might otherwise be seriously limited;
- be a place to learn positive skills for decision making and coping;
- make information, support, discussion and referral to other services available to young people, addressing their problems holistically, and offering a cross-sectoral approach to long term solutions;
- offer quiet space for children whose homes are too crowded, noisy or poorly lit to allow them to study easily.

[20] Vanderschueren 1998, op cit Note 8
[21] Marcus 1995, op cit Note 11

Safe havens can be established in churches, schools, health centres or sports facilities; or they can be set up in store fronts, dwellings, or any available space the community can offer. In some cases in Mexico, young people have built their own centres.[22] Care must be taken to ensure that safe havens are not too closely tied to formal institutions, which may be overly controlled by adult authority figures. It is important that there be genuine youth involvement both in creating and running a safe haven in order to ensure an atmosphere where they feel comfortable. Young people should be involved in finding and setting up a place, and in ongoing management, including making the rules and choosing the activities. Facilities of this kind are usually set up by NGOs, but local authorities can play an important role in helping to make space available, offering training for youth workers and ensuring cooperation with health services and other local agencies.

youth involvement

Older children and adolescents need role models and opportunities for growth, and these may be hard to come by in urban communities torn by violence. Adults who work with young people in such settings must genuinely like children and adolescents. They must be accepting of youth, respectful of their ideas and priorities, and willing to listen non-judgmentally. At the same time, they must take seriously the responsibility of serving as role models for young people who may be confused and in need of direction. In many cases, older adolescents have been found to be ideal for this task.

role models

- *Support the establishment of 'safe places' for children and adolescents in violent neighbourhoods, where they can find safe recreational and social opportunities, as well as access to other services and agencies within the community.*
- *Provide training for youth workers who can support young people in learning positive skills for coping and decision making.*
- *Involve children and young people in the planning, building and management of their own space.*

Harnessing the energies of alienated youth

gangs

Children and adolescents are not only the victims of community insecurity; they can also cause fear in others. Many urban young people join gangs, or are drawn into the drug trade and the use of violence, as a way of gaining identity and respect in a world that may offer few constructive alternatives. Gang membership does not necessarily imply criminal activity – for some it can be a less ominous expression of youth culture and belonging. But organized gangs frequently represent a real threat to urban inhabitants. Experience in different countries indicates that more than 30 per cent of all crime and violence in urban settlements can stem from petty gang crime.[23] In Cali in the early 90s, for instance, an estimated 136 gangs were considered to be responsible for much of the city's crime.[24] In the first half of 1993, one in every ten deaths in Cali was thought to be carried out by adolescent gangs.[25]

Experience indicates that most gang members have limited options. Their schooling may have been poor or non-existent, and they are likely

[22] Hill, B (1996) 'Safe places for youth: programming, strategy and examples as identified through interviews with participants of the World Youth Forum of the UN system', UNICEF Report, December 1996

[23] Personal communication, Erik Vittrup, Community Development Programme of UNCHS(Habitat) in Costa Rica and Multi-Country Programme in Central America,1997

[24] Guerrero, R (1993) 'Cali's innovative approach to urban violence', *The Urban Age*, 1(4): 17

[25] Feuerstein, M-T (1997) *Poverty and Health: Reaping a Richer Harvest*, London: Macmillan

to have minimal opportunities for employment. Their poverty and lack of opportunity is further mocked by exposure to consumer goods, advertising and extreme disparities, all of which contribute to resentment and frustrated desires. Often they come from families in crisis, and for many the gang fills a social and emotional vacuum. Physical and sexual abuse during childhood, family violence, poverty, exclusion, police harassment and discrimination have left many of these young people without a sense of belonging, and may have undermined their capacity for trust and empathy. These adolescents struggle for survival and identity in groups that may turn to violence or self-destructive behaviour as a 'normal' means of expression.[26]

the positive side to gang culture

Those who work successfully with young urban gang members have found there is a positive side to gang culture, expressed through energy and creativity. The very characteristics that make them a threatening presence in a neighbourhood can sometimes be redirected in productive ways. Gang members have been noted to have a strong sense of solidarity and a willingness to confront accepted values. They tend to be extremely territorial and to protect their physical space from outside threats. There have been many successful attempts to harness these gang behaviours in the service of the community, and to develop future community leaders.

In Costa Rica, Belize, Mexico and El Salvador youth projects have been developed to address this situation with remarkable results. With very little investment, these projects have achieved marked changes in the community environment. Security has increased, and new leaders have emerged with a different vision of urban community leadership. As these adolescents become productive community members, they begin to provide a new kind of role model for many other rootless children.[27] In Mexico City, attempts were made through an action research project to tap into the creative energies of young gang members. A Saturday evening radio programme was established to play their music, read their writing, and give them opportunity to speak openly about topics that interested them. They also organized rock concerts and set up archives for their photography, poetry and other arts. Although they were subsequently pushed off the air, at the time of this report the research group was continuing to explore valid ways to support the creative efforts of these young people.[28]

finding alternatives

Vandalism, drug use and criminal activity may in many communities be the only alternatives to boredom and lack of opportunity. Young people need the chance to spend time together in involving and productive ways, and to form contacts with caring adults. In the United States, a compilation of studies from around the country has demonstrated a dramatic link between crime rates and investment in recreation and open space.[29] In Phoenix, Arizona, when recreational facilities were kept open in the summer until late at night, juvenile crime rates dropped by 55 per cent. In Philadelphia, when police helped neighbourhood volunteers to clean up vacant lots and plant public gardens, burglaries and thefts in the precinct dropped by 90 per cent. Such examples are not unique to the USA. In Cali, Colombia, children were invited to give up their war toys in return for an ID card that gave them free access to city recreational facilities. Four gangs gave up their real weapons and signed formal commitments to become involved in social rehabilitation. Within a year,

26 Garbarino, J (1998) 'Stress in children', *Child and Adolescent Psychiatric Clinics of America*, 7(1)
27 Erik Vittrup, see Note 23
28 Castillo Berthier, H (1993) 'Popular culture among Mexican teenagers', *The Urban Age*, 1(4): 14–15
29 Trust for Public Land (1994) *Healing America's Cities: How Urban Parks Can Make Cities Safe and Healthy*, San Francisco: The Trust for Public Land
30 Guerrero 1993, op cit Note 24

1200 gang members became involved in a programme which made job training, continuing education and recreation available to them in return for their weapons and a commitment to non-violence.[30] Local authorities must ensure that neighbourhood surroundings support the play and recreation needs of all age groups.

Kuleana Pizzeria

Young people also need constructive opportunities for employment, and for job-related training. A fine practical solution is the Kuleana Pizzeria in Mwanza, Tanzania, where young apprentices learn how to prepare ingredients, make bread and pizza, maintain a clean kitchen, wait on tables, manage sales and keep accurate accounts. Besides giving young people protected on-the-job training, the pizzeria also serves as a welcoming meeting place for children, providing space for theatre, games and art, as well as informal education on child rights and sexual health.[31] There is more information on such opportunities on p220.

- *Find productive ways to channel the energy of young people by supporting opportunities for recreation, self-expression, skills training and protected employment.*

Responding to drug and alcohol abuse

Criminal activity on the part of young people has been strongly linked to substance abuse because of the behavioural changes induced by drugs and alcohol, and because of the expense and frequent illegality of obtaining these substances. Responding to this is a critical element in any attempt to address community insecurity. We have already discussed the effectiveness of participatory educational efforts with youth for dealing with a range of risky behaviours (p120). But it is worth considering particular approaches to the stubborn problem of drugs.

successful programmes

In 1998, representatives of successful drug prevention programmes from around the world participated in a forum. In preparation, they ran workshops with their youth participants, asking them to discuss and evaluate their programmes. Drawing on these discussions, a typology of approaches to drug prevention was developed, along with an evaluation of each approach. The programmes were divided into educational efforts, those involving a live-in setting, and those focused on managing the leisure time of young people.[32]

The educational programmes all had a more or less participatory quality – either through peer-to-peer education or counselling, or through the use of theatre and other community-based events as an approach to drug education. Sometimes programme content was determined by adults. But when young people were more closely involved in the development of material, it was felt to have a greater impact on their audiences. Such programmes tend not to be heavily resource-dependent and can even operate without a permanent space, but they require the time and effort of youth workers skilled in involving young people in constructive ways.

Live-in approaches focus on isolating young people from the harmful circumstances that pushed them into drug use, building their skills and self-respect, and providing opportunities for success. The Whakapakari Youth Programme in New Zealand offers boys 14 to 17 years of age a

[31] Street Kids International (1995) *Participatory Methods: Community-based Programs*, Toronto, Canada: Street Kids International

[32] Sabo, K and S Iltus (1998) 'What do young people around the world think about prevention programs?', Prepared for Youth Vision Drug Prevention Forum, Banff, Alberta, Canada, April 1998, UNDCP

wilderness experience where reliance on one another replaces their dependence on drug and solvent abuse.[33] Isolated from the pressures of urban life, participants hunt, fish, cook, counsel each other, and help run cultural and physical fitness sessions.

The success of these live-in approaches depends on the amount of time spent in a programme and the level of support after leaving it. The more participatory examples contributed best to the goal of establishing responsible decision making. Because of the costly need for facilities and full time staff, programmes like this can only reach a small number of young people at any one time. Even when they are effective, they cannot be seen as a large-scale solution to the drug problem.

The alternative activity approach appears to have the potential for reaching the greatest numbers. By filling the free time of young people with compelling activities such as football, motor sports and art, it diminishes their opportunity to be caught up by drug use. Many such programmes allow young people to dream about success and work hard for it. The Tahuichi football academy in Bolivia reaches thousands of children and adolescents. Commitment to the sport creates a new value system, and drug use clearly conflicts with young people's desire to achieve and to be in the best possible condition. Some programmes are designed and run by young people themselves, but the larger programmes, which call for complex management, tend to be top-down. But because they give children an opportunity to work together constructively and to achieve, they contribute to a sense of belonging and personal direction.[34]

sports programmes

young people in the drug trade

Drug use is not the only issue. Young people can also be pulled into the drug trade because of the need to survive on the street, or to contribute to the family economy. Without alternative means of livelihood for families and adolescents, this problem is difficult to combat. When young people run into trouble with the law because of drug peddling, constructive responses are essential. Most of the traditional repressive measures have not been effective in reducing future problems, but instead have served to alienate young people further from their communities, and to reinforce negative behaviour (see p230). Nor does punishment for these young people solve the drug trade issue – they can always be replaced. Instead, local authorities must work closely with higher levels of law enforcement to tackle organized crime.

- *Establish approaches to drug education and prevention that stress participation and the availability of constructive activities.*
- *Ensure that young people involved in drug peddling have positive alternatives for earning a living.*
- *Respond to youthful offenders in ways that do not reinforce negative behaviour (see Chapter 12).*
- *Work closely with higher levels of law enforcement to tackle organized crime.*

Measures that respond to insecurity in an immediate way – whether by educating the police, installing street lights, or creating safe havens for children – do not address the underlying causes of violence and crime. True prevention must include longer term efforts outlined in other parts of this book: the provision of schooling, jobs, adequate housing and the

[33] Discussion at Youth Vision Jeunesse Drug Abuse Prevention Forum, April 14–18, 1998

[34] Personal communication, Selim Iltus, Children's Environments Research Group, 1998

reform of the judicial system. Only by reducing poverty and social exclusion can the issue of insecurity be honestly addressed.

RESPONDING TO TRAFFIC

In densely settled urban areas, traffic is a major obstacle to children's safety. In South Africa, traffic accidents are the leading cause of death for children over one year of age.[35] The developmental incapacity of young children to cope with traffic is discussed on p29. The presence of heavy traffic can be exacerbated by badly maintained streets which contribute to unpredictable patterns of traffic movement. The lack of pavements or properly marked crossing zones also increases the dangers for children. The quality of neighbourhood interaction is also at stake. Research has shown that people who live on streets with heavy traffic are less likely to know their neighbours.[36]

closing street to traffic

One effective approach is to close streets off to through traffic. Vehicles can still enter and leave, but the volume of traffic will be considerably reduced. This modification was first adopted on a wide scale in the Netherlands. But it is equally relevant to any densely built residential area. Once a street has been closed in this way, it has been found in many places that neighbours feel a new sense of ownership and often begin to improve the area as an extension of their household space. Parents feel more comfortable releasing children for play, and relationships between households are more likely to develop. This solution is not an option for all streets – through traffic is essential to a city's functioning. But even on streets with home businesses and a busy commercial life, residents can find ways to cut down on traffic. Devices such as speed bumps or barriers can also be used to slow traffic down or to reclaim small areas adjacent to the path of traffic. While traffic danger is reduced by such strategies, it is by no means removed. Even when vehicles are not speeding through a neighbourhood, reversing and parking can still cause accidents. The important principle here is to make it very clear which areas are for traffic movement and which are not, both in policing traffic and in educating and monitoring children.

speed bumps

involving residents

In the city of Leicester in Britain, the city council took a highly participatory approach to the issue of traffic calming, bringing together engineers, housing officers, parks and play officials, local planners and residents in an effort to make several city streets safer for children's play. Door-to-door interviews, public meetings, newsletters, and collaborative design that included residents and children resulted in plans for improvements that received broad support.[37]

'improvements' that don't help

A *lack* of improvement may have the same general effect. In some informal settlements, community members have refused to have their badly rutted streets upgraded and paved by the municipality, recognizing that an improvement for motorized traffic is not necessarily an improvement in the quality of life for their children.[38] Municipalities must be alert to such insights and initiatives, and find ways to build on rather than override them.

Not all solutions are long term. In the crowded centre-city slum of Jamestown in Accra, residents string canopies over the streets to allow

[35] Kibel, M A and L A Wagstaff (eds) (1995) *Child Health for All: A Manual for Southern Africa*, Capetown, New York: Oxford University Press

[36] Appleyard, D and M Lintell (1972) 'The environmental quality of city streets: the residents' viewpoint', *Journal of the American Institute of Planners*, 38: 84–101

[37] Adams, E and S Ingham (1998) *Changing Places: Children's Participation in Environmental Planning*, London: The Children's Society

[38] Personal communication, David Satterthwaite, 1998

for music, dancing and festivities on special occasions. In some cities, and there are good examples in Argentina, Bolivia and Mexico, local authorities have taken the lead in closing some residential streets to traffic on weekends. Mexico City has even provided support for weekend activities on these closed-off streets.[39]

- *Support local demands for redirecting or limiting the speed of traffic moving through residential neighbourhoods; do not improve traffic flow without consulting residents.*
- *Where suitable, and with local involvement, install clearly marked pedestrian crossings and traffic calming devices such as speed bumps and cul-de-sacs.*

OPPORTUNITIES FOR PLAY AND RECREATION

the importance of play

Provision for play and recreation is not a priority in most municipalities. Where there are high levels of poverty and a desperate need for health, education, housing and other basic services, investment in play may appear to be a frivolous use of limited space and resources. But even in the poorest neighbourhoods, children and their caregivers make it clear that safe play is high on their list of concerns. The desire for play is not a frivolity, but a deep-rooted developmental drive which, when met, contributes to growth and competence on every level (p22). This is not limited to younger children. Recreational opportunities for adolescents support their physical and social development, and their constructive integration into the community. Girls' needs, and those of children with disabilities, must especially be taken into account.

Supporting the play of younger children

simple requirements

There are a few simple requirements for young children's play: physical safety, social security, diverse and stimulating physical surroundings, the presence of other children, a lack of temporal pressure and the proximity of adults. These qualities seldom call for expensive equipment and facilities. Research has consistently found that children would rather play in streets, sidewalks, back alleys and empty lots than in formally designed playgrounds, segregated from the world of adults.[40] Children are resourceful and creative in their capacity to find involving activities within the everyday fabric of neighbourhood life. They play ball in the streets, skip rope on sidewalks, somersault off construction materials, and create ingenious playthings and intricate games of skill using whatever comes to hand. Even a poor neighbourhood with no formal play provision can function as a rich, stimulating environment for children, supporting intense involvement in peer culture and the development of many skills.

obstacles to play

But there are unquestionably serious obstacles to safe play in many urban neighbourhoods, including the environmental hazards, traffic and social insecurity discussed above. A lack of awareness of the importance of play is itself a factor. Even when efforts are made to address these issues, there may still be insufficient space and opportunity for a full

[39] Personal communication, Alfredo Missair, 1998

[40] Moore, R (1985) *Childhood's Domain: Play and Place in Childhood Development*, London: Croom Helm

range of play within the neighbourhood and more formal provision may be necessary. In most municipalities, if provision exists at all, it tends to be limited to spaces that primarily meet the needs of older boys and young men. There is little recognition that boys and girls of different ages, interests and abilities have a range of needs that call for thoughtful, creative responses.

For the youngest children, the most valuable play spaces are those closest to home. Even the best-equipped park will not be used frequently if it is not nearby. Instead, children will be limited to doorways, alleys, gutters and streets close to home where they can easily turn to familiar adults. Efforts by local authorities should focus on ready access rather than elaborate provision. Residents should be supported in improving all available pockets of land to meet the needs of young children. Even the smallest of such spaces can be an important contribution. A low fence or wall can protect children from stepping out into danger and double as seating for parents. Small children appreciate clean sand for play and climbing or balancing equipment which can be simply made from local materials. Vegetation can provide diversity in a limited space. Children are fascinated by the animal world even at the scale of insects and birds, and their contact with nature in early years is the route to their responsible caring and enjoyment of nature as adults.[41] These 'play gardens' would also be appreciated by the aged or infirm.

By the age of four or five, children begin to require more space to accommodate their need for running, jumping, climbing and other forms of active play, and such space should still be close enough for easy access. In many cases, areas for play can be located within local school grounds, and double as a valuable play and learning opportunity during school hours as well as after school hours (see p180). In communities with little

Formal provision for children's play too often consists of a few pieces of dilapidated equipment in otherwise barren playgrounds. Even in such settings, children are resourceful and creative in their capacity to find involving activities for themselves. But without great expense a space like this Peruvian playground could become a pleasant gathering place for community members, as well as offering a richer range of play for local children. UNICEF, Antmann.

[41] Chawla, L and R Hart (1988) 'The roots of environmental concern', *Proceedings of the 19th Conference of the Environmental Design Research Association*, EDRA, Washington DC

open space, fixed playground equipment such as slides and swings may be the most efficient solution for accommodating a variety of gross motor activities.

We will not attempt to recommend the construction of particular play equipment, for there are already detailed books on the subject (see resource list, pp278, 280). Besides, this should ideally be a response to the resources and creativity in a particular community. In the small city of Laprida, Argentina, for instance, as part of an annual week set aside to celebrate play, an impromptu playground for children was created in the corner of a local plaza with the support of the municipality, using hospital scrap. A hospital bed became a seesaw, for example, and an X-ray table was converted into a slide.[42]

safety standards

Consideration should be given to the safety of playground equipment. When large numbers of children play in close quarters on equipment that is poorly designed or installed, there is the potential for serious injury. At a minimum, equipment should be separated by a safe distance and surrounded by materials such as sand, wood chips or gravel which will absorb much of the impact of falls. Authorities should refer to national safety standards.

loose parts

maintenance

Communities are encouraged to aim for a richer range of play than can be accommodated by fixed equipment alone. Areas for informal ball games and wheeled vehicle play, for digging and constructing, for experimenting with various materials and loose parts, as well as for quiet activities and pretend play, will satisfy a much wider range of interests and activities. Richer and more diverse environments do not require heavy investment in equipment, but do call for strategies for management and maintenance and perhaps protection from vandalism. Community-based organizations or community members may themselves be able to take on these functions. Spaces for children's play should never be planned for children only. When there is ample vegetation, along with seating and tables, these spaces can become pleasant for relaxation and socialization for all ages.

indoor play centres

Opportunities for children's play need not only be outdoors. Communities can support play centres, often with staff, which provide rich environments for younger children, as well as a chance for parents and caregivers to learn together about the developmental benefits of play for their children (see p162). Such centres could be a part of the kind of family development centres described on p55. For recommendations on responding to the play needs of children with disabilities, see p138.

- *Emphasize easy access and diversity of space for play rather than elaborate provision.*
- *Locate space for play away from dangerous traffic and pollutants.*
- *Support residents in improving all available and appropriate pockets of land.*
- *Ensure that equipment such as swings and slides meets safety standards.*
- *Support the full repertoire of play through the creation of varied play environments and opportunities.*
- *Ensure that responsibility for management and maintenance is clearly established.*

[42] Personal communication, Nilda Cosco, IPA Argentina, 1998

- *Ensure that areas for play are also pleasant places for adults to relax and socialize*
- *Support indoor play centres for young children, especially in communities where outdoor play is difficult*

Supporting play and recreation for older children and adolescents

As they grow older, children begin to value organized games and sports which often require larger amounts of space. Children and adolescents are ingenious in tailoring play to the places they can find. Where possible, authorities should support them in their creative use of local space, and help to ensure that the solutions they have provided for themselves are safe, and continue to be accessible.

school facilities

Space for games and sports may be available within local school grounds, and we have described methods for gaining maximum use of limited space (p180). School authorities should be encouraged to make school grounds available outside of school hours. But urban schools often lack the space for sports, and may themselves depend on community provision. Many low-income communities have a football field, most often a barren plateau. This area could be a better resource for the whole community if it provided for a range of games and sports, as well as areas for free use and socializing by all age groups. Such areas need toilets and water for washing and drinking. Like smaller neighbourhood parks, they could include seating and tables, perhaps with chessboards painted onto them. Ideally, they should have staff who can maintain the site and provide support or training for children. Responsibility for management and maintenance could also be shared among community-based organizations; sports clubs, schools, childcare centres and so on. The challenge is to balance special interests with the more general need for open space for all residents. When there is no space within a neighbourhood to serve these needs, it is necessary to look further afield to open areas within the larger city (see p142).

community parks

recreation and community identity

Recreational activity can contribute to community identity, drawing people together in constructive, mutually satisfying ways. As discussed above, recreation and team sports provide a stimulating and legitimate alternative for young people who might otherwise turn to antisocial and self-destructive behavior. It is important to bear in mind the frequent resistance of young people to being organized by others, and their need to feel a sense of ownership over their own space and activities. They may prefer to have their own space for recreation to plan and manage, even if it is extremely simple. This might be part of the 'safe spaces' described on p128. When facilities must be shared, adolescents should be involved in decision making, scheduling and management. Adolescent girls are likely to have different concerns and priorities from boys which must also be weighed (see below).

- *Support the informal solutions that children and adolescents devise for their play.*
- *Upgrade existing facilities such as football fields to serve a wider range of uses.*

- *Support the use of school grounds by the larger community outside of school hours; see p18 for the optimal use of schoolyard space.*
- *Give older children and adolescents as much control as possible in the planning and management of their recreational space.*
- *Bring together youth organization representatives in the city to evaluate their situations collectively, and to plan local initiatives.*
- *Encourage youth organizations to include youth with disabilities in their membership and their concerns.*

Responding to girls as well as boys

Authorities must not assume that their responsibilities end when boys have access to recreation. Girls have an equal need for play, companionship and community life, but in many parts of the world their opportunities are far more limited. In part, this is because of work demands placed on them in their homes. There is also a greater concern with girls' safety because of fears about sexual harassment or molestation. Spatial restrictions on girls' freedom are often a formal part of cultural or religious custom. By the time they reach early adolescence, it may be considered inappropriate and even shameful for girls to play or socialize outside the home. This does not mean they no longer want and need such opportunities. Save the Children Fund staff in Dhaka, Bangladesh, found that when they brought girls together for an action research project, the girls would quickly take advantage of the chance to be together, and after closing windows and doors, would rearrange the space so that they could dance.[43]

restrictions on girls' freedom

Because girls' rights to leisure, play and association with others are so frequently ignored, special attention must be given to advocating for them and with them before those in control of public space and recreational facilities. Local authorities must help to ensure that girls are involved in assessing their own needs, that suitable spaces are available to them, and that families are encouraged to allow their daughters free time for activity outside the home.

- *Ensure that the needs of girls as well as boys are considered in local planning of recreational space; and involve girls in assessing their needs and in planning suitable responses.*
- *Encourage parents to allow their daughters the time and freedom for recreation and leisure.*

Responding to children with special needs

Children with disabilities are often the most marginalized in any community, and it takes active involvement to support their integration as community members. This may entail such physical measures as modifications for mobility, but more than anything else it calls for public acceptance of the right of all children to participate fully in community life. Local authorities must foster this awareness.

[43] Personal communication, Andy West, Save the Children UK, 1998

From the earliest age, children with disabilities should be welcomed into the community – through child care provision, school attendance and informal play. If children do not have direct contact with one another, they are being taught that segregation is normal and acceptable. Play is especially important, because it is through play that children form friendships. Play workers (see below) can help both adults and children become more comfortable in accepting children who have been hitherto isolated. Ways can be found to address the problems that might keep a child marginalized, whether they be issues of physical access, the reluctance of parents, or the need for physical aids to overcome practical problems. In responding to special needs, municipalities should work closely with parents, community rehabilitation workers and children themselves.

supporting the integration of children with disabilities

Not all children with disabilities are confident playing with others. In some cases there may be a need for play areas that enable them to develop at their own speed and to achieve a measure of physical competence until they are comfortable joining in the play of children with different physical capabilities. Municipalities have an important role in supporting the construction of play and recreation spaces which afford the greatest degree of accessibility to children regardless of their special needs. Although there is a wide range of play equipment designed specifically for children with physical disabilities, providing for special needs does not necessarily imply costly investment. (See resource list, pp276, 278, 279).

accessibility of play space

- *Ensure that the needs of children with disabilities are met; work with community members to build ramps, smooth roadways, develop wayfinding devices for blind children, and to construct play equipment that encourages the participation of children who are blind or limited in mobility.*
- *Ensure that parents of children with special needs, and the children themselves, are involved in planning for play.*
- *Consider the special needs of disabled children in building child care centres, school, health centres, as well as play areas and sports facilities.*
- *Appoint a municipal disabilities specialist to be involved in all local planning initiatives.*

Finding and protecting community space for play and recreation

Especially in crowded squatter settlements and in residential areas in the middle of cities, space is a significant issue. Municipalities should seize and protect every available piece of land to make recreational opportunities available for children and their families. Unused railroad beds, creeks, informal markets, pedestrian pathways, can all be cleaned and upgraded at low cost to make them available for safe play. If the municipality cannot afford to upgrade land, it should allow local groups to develop it for recreational use. In Cairo, with the assistance of community development associations, and with support from PLAN International and local authorities, residents cleared several small garbage dumps to create green areas and space for children's play. The local associations collect a small fee for maintenance.[44]

upgrading land for play

in Cairo

[44] Personal communication, Lalitha Iyer, Plan International, 1997

in London

Another example of such cooperation is the pocket park developed in Bermondsey, London, by the Eveline Lowe School. The park was once a bomb-site, overgrown, unsightly and inaccessible. Through negotiation with local authorities, the school gradually took over the site and developed it to provide recreational space not only for the children in the school, but also for other nearby residents. A pond, seating, play structures, extensive planting, and even an outdoor cooking area turned the site into an asset for the whole neighbourhood.[45]

Regulations should be in place to allow what space there is within a community to remain accessible to children without discrimination. Local authorities must be aware of the constraints that privatization may place on poor children. If left entirely to market forces, open spaces can become segregated and exclusionary, and the children of the poor are often the losers.

avoiding unnecessary improvements

Because professional planners often favour neat functional divisions, there is a tendency towards increased segregation of children from adults through the creation of specific recreational facilities. It is important to be cautious about such 'improvements' since many poor neighbourhoods may already cater to a rich play life. When vehicle use is low, for instance, and play can occur safely in the streets and public spaces, children are exposed to the variety and stimulation of neighbourhood life, and the benefits go beyond anything a formal playground can provide.

Some of the least stimulating play environments are found in planned middle-class housing developments with homogeneous tracts of lawn or concrete. It is important that communities recognize their strengths and weaknesses in this regard, and find ways to protect the qualities and spaces that enrich their children's lives, at the same time as they work to eliminate hazards and broaden opportunity. Local officials can help communities avoid the undesirable segregation of children through a systematic policy of integrated public space planning for all ages.

finding space outside the neighbourhood

When there is a lack of usable space in crowded city neighbourhoods, communities need the support of local authorities in finding other solutions. Most cities include areas of underused space owned by local or national government, or by the private sector. There may be large ornamental open grounds no more than a few blocks from the most crowded residential areas whose lack of use is never questioned. Vacant land sites reserved for future infrastructure can be made available on a temporary basis. Parade grounds, school grounds, parking lots unused on weekends or evenings, market places not in daily use, may all serve as recreational space during at least some part of the week. If such areas are inventoried and assessed for their potential, communities lacking access to recreation can be supported to make use of them.

- *Upgrade any available space with community help for recreational or play use; give local clubs and organizations the chance to improve and manage vacant municipal land.*
- *Protect children against discrimination and privatization in their use of space.*
- *Take care that community 'improvements' do not damage the quality of play; assess the way children are using space before making changes.*
- *Support residents of overcrowded neighbourhoods by finding space for recreation in adjoining areas of the city.*

Access to green spaces

Residential communities need areas of natural growth where people can relax together, and which satisfy the need for contact with nature. The restorative powers of the natural world have been well-documented, and should be available to all, especially those living under the stress of urban poverty. Given the enormous demand for space in low-income communities, it is not surprising that green areas for community use are so rare. There is an important role here for municipalities.

contact with nature

A natural environment with a range of vegetation offers children the best opportunities for free play. Ready access to natural areas is especially important to poor urban children, who may experience no other alternatives to the noisy squalor of city life.The significance of such areas was demonstrated by the impassioned efforts of a group of children in a poor urban community in Guayaquil, Ecuador to save a natural area adjoining their settlement. This overgrown green space belonged to a neighbouring college and had been enjoyed by the children for years. Over time, they had developed an intimate network of paths and they treated both the land and the wildlife within it with reverence and pride. When the children heard that the college planned to build on the land, they attempted, with the support of a community-based organization, to preserve the area. They failed to secure the land, however, in part because there was no recognition by the municipality of the value of such spaces to the growth and development of children.[46]

- *Ensure that the provision of green space in the city provides equitably for the needs of the rich and the poor.*

Play workers and supported opportunities for play

An effective way to improve the quality of children's play, especially in crowded urban areas, is through the training and support of 'play workers'. There are likely to be a number of individuals in any community who are interested in helping children and youth find opportunities for play. It only requires a small amount of training and support from local authorities to allow such informal helpers to become effective agents of community development for and with children.

improving local play provision

Play workers should understand children's desire for competence and see their role as supporting rather than directive, helping them find the opportunities they need. They should operate as close as possible to the communities they serve, and should ideally be based in a local school or community development centre. Play workers can serve as advocates for children's play needs in local planning processes. They can train parents and other residents to serve as play workers, work with them to assess and improve local play provision, and help to deal with hazards in the neighbourhood and traffic dangers, before moving on to a new community. In this way, a small cadre of play workers in any city can do a good deal to help low-income communities meet their children's need for play.

In a number of European cities, play workers have been associated with 'adventure playgrounds' which offer challenging opportunities within a restricted area. These are generally fenced-off spaces where

[45] Personal communication, Eileen Adams, 1998
[46] Espinosa, M F (1997) 'Working children in Ecuador mobilize for change', *Social Justice*, *special issue on children and the environment*, 24(3): 64–70
[47] Roger Hart, field trip

advocating for children

adventure playgrounds

play workers set the stage for children to create their own play environments. Work materials are provided and a tool shed made available to the children. The play workers do not direct activity, but remain available as supporting staff to deal with questions children may have and occasionally to deal with minor first aid. One ward in Tokyo has created a few such areas in the middle of its city parks where children build dams in small streams of water, construct play houses and cook simple meals on fires with the play workers and parents. In one the most densely populated areas of the world, these are precious moments of release for a population noted for its long working hours and serious pursuit of education.[47] Many children in low-income areas of cities find similar opportunities spontaneously in areas near their homes, but when such opportunities are limited or dangerous because of traffic or other constraints, adventure play areas with the support of play workers can offer an appealing alternative.

- *Improve the quality of children's play through the training and support of play workers, who, in turn, can train community members to become actively involved in supporting children's play.*
- *Where informal opportunities for creative and spontaneous play are limited, consider the adventure playground approach as an alternative.*

Community participation in the planning of recreational space

addressing local needs and preferences

If the assessment and planning of neighbourhood recreational space involves community members, it is more likely that creative, economical solutions will be found to the problem of limited space, and that local needs and preferences will be addressed, and that responsibility for management and maintenance will be more readily accepted. The planning process should include children and young people, for the issue concerns them deeply. For a discussion of promoting community participation in the planning process, see Chapter 14, p264. For more discussion of children's involvement, see below.

CHILDREN'S POSITIVE INVOLVEMENT IN THE COMMUNITY

A range of measures can be taken to ensure that children have the opportunity to be productive and welcome members of the community, sharing in traditions and activities, and contributing on their own behalf to local life and culture, and to local planning and decision making. This implies safe, secure public spaces, activities that are welcoming to children, an absence of discrimination and an acceptance of children as citizens.

Children's participation in religious, cultural and artistic life

Involvement in a community's cultural and religious life is an important element of children's membership in society. In some cases, the active involvement of children may be responsible for stimulating and sustaining cultural life, especially when the pressures and diversity of urban living challenge the survival of traditional arts and knowledge. Schools and community organizations, with the support of local authorities, can find ways to keep traditions alive for children. In the low-income neighbourhood of Ga-Mashie, in the inner city of Accra, Ghana, for instance, the community organization, CACIPO, provides access to tribal arts for local children. Through this group they are able to learn woodcarving, bead work, cane weaving and traditional textile design as well as a range of performing arts. The level of their achievement, especially in the area of dance and drumming, is extraordinary, and through the efforts of this organization children are now playing a significant role in maintaining the vitality of their cultural heritage. These activities are part of a larger programme designed also to offer counselling, literacy training and medical care.[48] The use of traditional art forms may also become a vehicle for children's involvement in other areas. In Sri Lanka, for instance, children employ the song, dance and puppetry forms of their Buddhist culture to communicate to their families and communities the health and environment messages of the Sarvodaya movement.[49]

stimulating cultural life

traditional arts

In Argentina, many communities have worked to recover local traditions which began to disappear under the constraints imposed by military government. In the low-income community of La Boca in Buenos Aires, over 40 local organizations, including child care centres, soccer clubs and church groups, have banded together to celebrate the traditional February carnival each year. Many local children and community members are involved in months of preparation with various art and theatre groups. With the support of local authorities, traffic is diverted from some streets during festival time, sound equipment and stages belonging to the city are set up for performances, and food and drink are sold in kiosks in the street.[50]

recovering local traditions

cultural patterns

The cultural life of a community is expressed not only in its celebrations, but also in its physical surroundings (see p74). The fine-grained environment established over time contains opportunities for people to carry out the customary patterns of their lives. In Bhaktapur, Nepal, for example, small Hindu shrines were traditionally built into the walls of homes, where children could carry out religious rituals with their families. A recently built housing project in the city did not include such shrines.[51] Those involved in decision making should be alert to the implications of such apparently minor factors in children's lives, and through participatory planning, should ensure that neighbourhood surroundings permit children to experience their cultural identity through daily activities.

Low-income Puerto Rican neighbourhoods in New York city have built group traditions into the fabric of community life by reclaiming and planting vacant lots to serve a variety of cultural and social uses. These gardens include vegetable plots, art work, religious shrines and 'casitas', or little wooden houses. Used for informal relaxation, and as space for performances, special events and religious fiestas, they serve as a refuge from the busy urban surroundings, and also as a vital link to traditional Puerto Rican culture. Classes are held in traditional music and arts, and community members can learn about the cultivation and medicinal uses of plants. The architecture, plant life and social activities all contribute to the celebration of a distinct culture within the mosaic of the larger city.[52]

48 Personal communication, Makkenzy-Golightly, CACIPO, Accra, 1997
49 Hart, R (1997) *Children's Participation: The Theory and Practice of Involving Young Citizens in Community Development and Environmental Care*, London: Earthscan/UNICEF
50 Personal communication, Nilda Cosco, IPA Argentina, 1998
51 Roger Hart, field trip
52 Winterbottom, D (1998) 'Casitas, gardens of reclamation: The creation of cultural/social spaces in the barrios of New York City', Presented at the 29th Annual Conference of the Environmental Design Research Association, St Louis, USA

The neighbourhood is an ideal domain for learning the skills of citizenship. When there is a high degree of local autonomy over the planning and management of the environment, there can be many informal opportunities for participation, the best of them resulting from children's own desire to be helpful. Here children become involved in laying sewer pipes in the community-managed Orangi Pilot Project, Karachi, Pakistan. Arif Hasan, OPP, 1997.

In many urban areas different cultural and religious groups live side by side, sometimes in comfort, but often in uneasy and even hostile tension. Such tensions can most effectively be addressed during childhood, and familiarity with the cultural and religious life of groups other than their own can help to build tolerance, interest and acceptance. The challenge is to support groups in retaining their own cultural identity, while encouraging tolerance and respect for others. Activities in schools are no substitute for cultural life within the neighbourhood, but schools nonetheless have an important role to play, especially in communities of more than one group. Rather than avoiding cultural events as potentially divisive, schools can recognize and celebrate the traditions of every group

When children and adolescents have the opportunity to investigate and inform others about issues they consider important, they gain confidence in their own capacity to contribute. In many cases they may be the best source of information for other young people. Here young people learn the basics of video production in Maputo, Mozambique. UNICEF 1995, Ruth Ayisi

equally, at the same time providing background information to encourage understanding. In Paranoa, a low-income community in Brasilia, Brazil, a local school organizes frequent festivals to celebrate the community's various ethnic groups, those with both native and African roots. Community groups can play a similar role. The Philippine Educational Theatre Association in Manila trains facilitators to work with children from marginalized groups to make theatre about their concerns, and thereby to foster understanding and tolerance across the many cultural groups of the Philippines.[53]

- *Support the public celebration of religious and cultural festivals and events.*
- *Support the efforts of groups to preserve their customs and patterns of living within the local community through participatory planning.*
- *Take a strong stand against discrimination of any kind in the management of public events, spaces and all public institutions.*
- *Provide training for teachers, community workers, play leaders and others in responding sensitively to cultural, religious and ethnic differences, and in celebrating these differences with children.*
- *Ensure that members of all local groups are involved in the planning and use of community space.*

Clubs and organizations for children

It is common throughout the world to find out-of-school organizations or clubs for children. They frequently focus on social and moral develop-

[53] Hart 1997, op cit Note 49

ment, and commonly work on projects offering service to the community. In recent years, many of these organizations have become increasingly participatory, giving children the opportunity to determine what activities and projects they will initiate. While they may have specific goals, such as helping children to learn to read or to find employment alternatives, they are also places where children can find a friendly ear and a place to relax and play.

participation in Ecuador

In Ecuador, the National Programme of Working Children (PMT) is an example that has involved thousands of children through local clubs in regular participatory action projects.[54] PMT has established centres in poor urban areas called 'Alternative Spaces' where children, many of whom do not attend school, are able to play and learn, and also to act on issues related to their rights. The goal is to convince these children that they are citizens with the capacity to create their own futures. Each year elected representatives from individual centres attend regional and national conferences where they identify the theme of the CRC that the national programme will address that year. Back in the local centres, children use participatory action research to identify local problems related to the theme. First they design small-scale projects, with advice from staff, which they can carry out themselves in their own communities. They then discuss, with groups of children from other centres, what larger actions their city might engage in. A network of local community organizations supports these efforts, along with government institutions and influential professionals at the municipal level. In each community a close working relationship is established with local political leaders, who are invited to attend presentations by the children to discuss with them the ways that the city can be helpful.[55]

working with adolescents

Clubs and organizations can be particularly important for adolescents, who seek out opportunities for meaningful social contact with their peers (see also Chapter 2).[56] For this age group the place of adult helpers is on the sidelines. They should always be available to listen, but should as far as possible be non-judgmental about the shifting values and interests of the young people. This does not mean they should ignore issues of morality or values. On the contrary, they need to encourage discussion on these important issues, so that young people find support in forging strong values that are a product of their own serious consideration.

Schools may be good sites for clubs, since they are often underutilized after hours and have many resources a children's organization needs. But working children often perceive schools as unfriendly environments.[57] And if the school is negatively associated with a high level of authority, it may be less than conducive to participatory activity. Given the record of these kinds of organizations, it is likely to be a good investment in community life for any municipality to help create spaces where young people are able to spend time together and decide on joint activities.

- *Support the creation of participatory clubs for children and young people, and wherever possible, make space available for these organizations.*
- *Allow children through their organizations to take an active part in community affairs.*
- *Provide training for both male and female youth workers who can be non-judgemental and supportive role models for young people.*

[54] Espinosa 1997, op cit Note 46
[55] Hart 1997, op cit Note 49
[56] Ibid; and Bryce-Heath, S B (1994) 'The Project of Learning from the Inner-City Youth Perspective' in F A Villarruel and R M Lerner (eds) *Promoting Community Based Programs for Socialization and Learning*, San Francisco: Jossey Bass
[57] Blanc, C S and contributors (1994) *Urban Children in Distress: Global Predicaments and Innovative Strategies*, Florence, Italy: UNICEF International Child Development Centre and London: Gordon and Breach

- *Involve young people in the planning and management of their clubs, girls as well as boys.*

Access to information

Children's right to information (Article 17) must be actively supported by local authorities. Care must be taken, however, that it is not used as justification for the political manipulation of young people. Children and adolescents need access to information that promotes their health and well being, makes the resources of the city more available to them, acquaints them with their own rights, and supports their efforts as active learners. Information is traditionally thought of as being available to children through school. But not all children attend school, and not all schools give children access to the resources they need. Not all children are literate, nor do they share the same language. In making information truly accessible, these factors must be kept in mind.

using the media

The mass media are an important source of information for most urban children, and can be used most constructively. In Cali, Colombia, for instance, local television broadcasts messages on tolerance, weapon carrying and responsible driving. Information on health issues may be most effectively disseminated through comic strips, radio and television, as well as through personal contact. Authorities must ensure that children's need for information is made a priority in the programming of local media.

violence and the media

Many observers are concerned that the violent content of film and television contributes to deviance in children and adolescents, and a number of studies argue strongly that watching violence stimulates aggression.[58] Another concern is the degree to which the media target children as consumers. Access to film and video appears not to be difficult, even for poor children. A study in one of the poorest neighbourhoods in Accra found that 75 per cent of the audiences in the popular local video centres are children and adolescents, and 60 per cent of the children interviewed preferred watching violent action films. Some paid for admission with money they had earned; others used their food money or resorted to petty theft.[59]

The Committee on the Rights of the Child, which monitors international compliance with the Convention, has raised the issue of tendencies within the mass media to incite ethnic violence and discrimination. Children, they argue, have the right to information which promotes tolerance and understanding between groups, and programming which runs counter to this objective should be ended.[60]

Local libraries should be available to all children, not just those in schools. They can be repositories for books and periodicals, but also for public service announcements, health related publications and the like. All reports and research on the community should be made available in the library alongside the more traditional library publications. There are many interesting examples of 'alternative' libraries for those without easy access to regular libraries. In Manila, for instance, street workers take library carts full of books out into the community. In Olongapo, also in the Philippines, The Working Committee for Street and Urban Working Children has a library trailer where working children can go

58 Boyden, J and P Holden (1991) *Children of the Cities*, London: Zed Books
59 Tagoe, G T (1985) 'Children and Adolescents and Video Films and Discotheques: A Study of the Jamestown and Mamprobi Areas of Accra', University of Science and Technology, Kumasi Faculty of Social Sciences, thesis
60 Hodgkin, R and P Newell (1998) *Implementation Handbook for the Convention on the Rights of the Child*, New York: UNICEF

libraries

when they have a few hours off from scavenging or vending in the market. In Caracas, Venezuela, the Bancos de Libros programme enables adults to borrow small boxes of books to operate their own mini-libraries in communities which have neither primary schools nor libraries. Some of these volunteer librarians offer informal literacy classes on their doorsteps, allowing their students to take books home for further study.[61]

Another good approach to bringing information to children is the 'green mobile' in Buenos Aires, sponsored by a workers' union. This van brings toys and games to urban children, as well as films and videos on urban environmental education. It moves from one location to another, usually for two hour visits, but sometimes longer for special events. It functions as a miniature community centre, is used as both a resource centre and a database, and provides interactive games and play props which teach practical solutions for environmental problems. In 1996, the green mobile served 3,500 children from public schools and community organizations, and presented workshops on water, air, garbage, urban flora and fauna, and nutrition.[62]

Buenos Aires 'green mobile'

Children also have the right to participate in creating and disseminating information. In many cases they may be the best source of information for other young people. In Paranoa, Brazil, the arts curriculum in a local school has given students the opportunity to make videos on topics they consider important. One video by pregnant girls and teenaged parents in the group dealt with the problems of being pregnant and having children when one is young, and it was disseminated to other young people.[63] The radio programme for young gang members in Mexico City, described above (p130), was an important opportunity for these young people to discuss charged issues in a responsible way. In El Salvador, adolescents in the northern town of Victoria, with the support of one adult, take this a step further, and actually manage the local community radio station, one of 12 in the country. They deal not only with practical details of operating the equipment, but are responsible for programme content and for ensuring that local residents are kept informed about issues that concern them.[64] There are hundreds of good examples of newspapers produced by children.[65] Groups of children in Nepal, for instance, have recently become involved in creating street newspapers on the walls of their cities as a way of exercising their rights, and informing others of issues they find important.

keeping others informed

radio

newspapers

- *Ensure, through a variety of media, that children and adolescents have access to the information they need in order to manage their lives successfully.*
- *Support local programming that makes use of the constructive potential of the media.*
- *See p119 for recommendations on making health information available.*
- *Support the availability of books and other resources for children who are not in school.*
- *Support opportunities for young people to be instrumental in creating and disseminating information themselves.*

[61] R Hart, field trip
[62] Personal communication, Nilda Cosco, 1998
[63] Hart 1997, op cit Note 49
[64] S Bartlett, field trip 1996
[65] The Bureau of Young GRAPEs, (1996) *We're in Print: The Whole Story by Kids for Kids*, New York: City University of New York, Graduate School

Encouraging an acceptance of participation by children

Democratic responsibility is acquired through practice, and can be fostered from an early age. Children and adolescents can be encouraged to ask questions, to join in discussion and to add their contribution to that of adults in a range of local actions. As they grow older and their capacity for involvement develops, children will tend to take an increasingly active role in their own communities, given the opportunity.[66] Municipal staff working directly with community organizations can remind them of children's right to have a voice, and to be introduced gradually by their elders into responsible citizenship. They can also take an active role themselves in tapping children – girls as well as boys – as a resource.

Children's right to have a voice can be a contentious issue, especially in societies or groups where obedience and deference towards adults are the expected behaviour. It makes little sense to promote children's rights in this area without the support and involvement of parents and community members. If parents feel they are being undermined, they may well resist angrily and be unwilling to be receptive to any aspect of the Convention. This will be particularly true if parents have little understanding of their own rights. Children are more likely to enjoy the right to take an active role in their own lives with the support of their families if the following conditions are met:

children's right to participate

- first give parents the chance to understand and experience themselves as rights-bearing individuals;
- give parents the opportunity to discuss in groups the ways that the Convention might be understood and implemented at local level;
- teach children to express their views in ways that do not violate the expectation of respect for adults;
- encourage both parents and children to recognize that responsibilities are an important component of rights, and that active participation in planning, decision making and community management are basic to citizenship in a society built on rights.

gaining the support of parents

The neighbourhood is an ideal domain for learning the skills of citizenship. When there is a high degree of local autonomy over the planning and management of the neighbourhood environment, there can be many opportunities for participation, the best of them resulting from children's own desire to be useful. The radio station described above was not initially organized for young people; they were simply the community members who were available and willing to work when the station was established. The important thing is that their willingness was recognized and supported, and they were taught the necessary skills to take a responsible role.

children's desire to be useful

The most obvious way to involve children is through those projects that most immediately affect them, for instance in the planning and management of spaces for play and recreation. Since children know best what they want and can experience at first hand the results of their efforts, they will usually be eager to contribute. But there are also many other areas where their efforts can be welcomed and encouraged. The National Programme of Working Children in Ecuador (discussed above

[66] Adams 1998, op cit Note 37; Hart 1997, op cit Note 49

on p145) has demonstrated that children can conduct research, run pollution prevention campaigns, and plan and carry out such projects as bridge building to improve local access to facilities.[67]

Another excellent example of the use of participatory research with children is the international Growing Up In Cities project (GUIC), which has involved children in seven countries in action research on their own communities. Not only have they gathered information, but they have followed it up with a range of initiatives for improving their environments, including design and planning activities, community organizing and working to secure commitments from local government bodies.[68] (See resource list for a manual outlining their tested methods.)

- *Encourage awareness of children's right to participate, and be responsive to the need for parental and community support.*
- *Encourage children's presence at local meetings and planning sessions;*
- *Ensure that community organizers are trained to support participation, especially the involvement of children.*
- *See also pp172, 181, 202, 259.*

Children as catalysts for change

The involvement of children in their own communities can be far more than a learning opportunity. If taken seriously, it can have a powerful political impact. In some cases children begin to take the lead, often in surprising and unexpected ways. Their notions of fairness and justice may be unaffected by cynicism, apathy or 'practical' considerations, and their priorities can be different from those of adults.

Children's Movement for Peace, Colombia

In Colombia, where people have been increasingly disillusioned and intimidated by routine corruption, atrocities, killings, kidnappings and illicit dealings, the Children's Movement for Peace is credited with being the catalyst that has begun to turn the country in a new direction. In October 1996, more than 2.7 million Colombian children, aged 7 to 18, took part in a special election, in which they were asked to choose which of their rights were most important to them. The children voted overwhelmingly for their right to life and to peace, and the nation's adults were obliged to respond. This children's movement has been significant not only nationally, but at the most local level. Their right to participate in town meetings was established as a legal right. This effectively revived the interest of entire communities in making better use of these meetings, and strengthened local democracy.

Children and adolescents have increasingly become a presence in local municipal debates, and their systematic representation in all municipalities is being gradually established. Their involvement in local affairs has emerged as both a means and an end in promoting peace, even in the most violent communities and municipalities. Instead of being faced with the defeating choice of joining armed groups, or quietly acquiescing, children now have the opportunity to work actively for peace. They, their communities and their country are profoundly better off because of their involvement.[69] Those working with children and adolescents must be aware that their participation may lead in some new and unexpected

[67] Hart 1997, op cit Note 49; Espinosa 1997, op cit Note 46
[68] Driskell, D (in press) *Creating Better Cities with Children and Youth*, Paris: UNESCO
[69] Cameron, S (1998) *Making Peace with Children*, UNICEF Colombia

directions, and as far as possible be prepared to support the idealism of youth.

MOVING BEYOND THE LOCAL COMMUNITY

Many opportunities within cities are not possible at neighbourhood level, and should be made available at little or no cost to all young people of the city, especially those in poverty. Brazil has been notable in providing such opportunities. In the city of Santos, the municipality organizes a number of children's activities that create an environment rich in culture. Children's dramas are staged and there are classes in dancing, painting and other cultural activities, as well as a wide range of recreational opportunities. Sports schools have been organized which use city facilities or hire them from other organizations. Classes in surfing and other sports have been made available to more than 4,000 children, and priority is give to children with few options for leisure activities.[70] In São Paulo a labour union has helped fund a swimming pool for 3,000 children, and through the municipality children from poor communities can belong to a classical orchestra and contribute to the artistic life of the city. In Copacobana, the wealthy beach front of Rio de Janeiro, the full length has continuous public provision of popular recreational facilities used by the poor as well as the rich. Swimming as well as volleyball, exercise areas and a continuous running track are available to young people without cost.[71]

opportunities in Brazil

Young peoples' urge for new experience, greater independence and familiarity with the larger city should be encouraged in positive ways, to foster an awareness and appreciation of the larger society. Maps and brochures identifying resources for young people within reach of a city's mass transit stops can be designed through participatory research with teams of children and youth from different neighbourhoods.

Children's involvement in governance and decision making can also be supported beyond the community level. In a number of cities, children and adolescents are now included in councils and committees at city level which focus on the rights of children, and provision for their needs (see p259). It is important to ensure that they are not token members, and that they are included as active and experienced representatives of local community groups.

children and city government

- *Ensure that the cultural and recreational facilities and opportunities of the larger city are available without discrimination, and with financial support when necessary, to young people from low-income communities.*
- *Provide older children and adolescents with the information necessary to make full use of the city's resources.*
- *Involve children and adolescents, as representatives of their local organizations, in city level committees that focus on children's interests.*

70 City of Santos (1996) 'Santos na Habitat II: Integrated Children's and Family Program', The city of Santos, SP, Brazil
71 R Hart, field trips

Child care can be an ideal entry point for other vital services such as health care, supplemental feeding and parent education. Such integrated care programmes simplify life for overburdened parents, and the cumulative effects for children can be significant. Here children in Bangkok benefit from a UNICEF centre's feeding programme. UNICEF, Sean Sprague

8 Child Care

The realities of urban poverty can interfere seriously with the ability to provide optimal care for young children. Changes in family structure, women's work patterns, and challenging living environments mean that many children are deprived of the conditions that best support their development during their most vulnerable years. The Convention recognizes that the children of working parents have a right to appropriate child care, and also requires that the State ensure children's health and full development (Articles 18, 24, 27). These services should not be conceived of separately, and no child care setting should limit its function to keeping children from harm while parents work. Child care can productively be used as a touchpoint for providing infants and young children with the range of opportunities they need in order to thrive during these important early years. Investment in affordable, high quality, comprehensive child care will make a significant difference to children's long term development and the stability of their families.

Institutionalized early child care may seem an anomaly in cultures which have traditionally turned to extended family for such support. But realities have changed; the survival strategies of urban families in poverty often mean that there is no adult in the home to care for young children, since subsistence generally depends on paid work outside the household. Using older siblings for child care is not a real solution, for it usually means denying them an education. Nor is it generally reasonable for mothers to take young children to work, unless care is provided on the site. Alternative care arrangements are critical to success in many cases.

Even when there are adults at home during the day, the pressures and constraints of urban poverty may seriously limit the quality of care available for young children. When physical space is crowded and possibly hazardous, and when a mother or grandparent is overburdened by the demanding chores of daily survival, the possibilities for stimulating play and interaction may be limited indeed. Alternative care during the day can provide relief for burdened parents, become a source of information and support, and encourage children's positive development through attention to health, nutrition, intellectual and social growth during these critical years.

a range of child care options

Although early childhood care and education is a proven source of support for families and children, adequate funds are seldom available for widespread formal responses.[1] Nor should it be assumed that centre-based programmes are the best solution for all children. Child care centres in poor urban communities almost always have their own share of problems. Especially for the youngest children, family-based options within the community may be preferable. Centres have been found more likely to provide positive support for development when children are over two years of age, and when they attend for only part of the day. Non-formal solutions and community based programmes must be an important part of any child care system.[2]

THE ROLE OF LOCAL AUTHORITIES

Municipal support is critical in the city-wide development of comprehensive child care facilities. By providing training, technical back-up and material assistance, local authorities can ensure a high quality of child care, provide employment opportunities for women, and create an entry point for other services. Formal support is essential, making optimal use of national funds and coordinating the efforts of community groups and informal community resources.

Assessing the situation

A first step is assessment at the most local level. To plan adequately it is necessary to know:

- which children are currently being left alone, in the care of young siblings, or taken along to work;
- which children are in need of developmental support or intervention;
- what child care arrangements already exist in the community, whether formal or informal;

1 Kagitçibasi, C (1996) *Family and Human Development Across Cultures*, Mahwah, New Jersey: Lawrence Erlbaum
2 See Myers, R (1992) *The Twelve who Survive: Strengthening Programmes of Early Childhood Development in the Third World*, London: Routledge, for a comprehensive review of different kinds of programmes in countries of the South

- what level of support these arrangements need in order to meet children's needs adequately;
- which women, not currently working, might choose to work to improve their families' situation if good child care were available;
- what kind of support caregivers at home need in order to provide good care for their children.

- *Make a comprehensive assessment of local needs, provision and untapped resources for child care, drawing on the knowledge of local residents.*

Tapping community resources

grandmothers in Dhaka

Any plan for child care within a community should make use of the informal arrangements that already exist, the institutions and facilities within the area, and the untapped knowledge and skills of community members. By providing training for local women, upgrading local facilities (either private homes or community space), providing access to materials for use with the children, and ongoing support for caregivers, it should be possible to establish high quality care with the maximum use of existing community resources. A recent study by Save the Children (USA) in Dhaka on the child care arrangements of garment workers found that a surprising number of children (42 per cent) were cared for by their grandmothers. What was most needed was not the provision of alternatives, but information, education, appreciation and occasional support for those already providing care.[3] Other elderly persons, or those who are unemployed, might equally be willing to provide child care with this kind of support.

- *Provide technical support and material assistance for existing and potential child care solutions.*

Integrating child care with the provision of other services

a comparative study from Colombia

Child care is an ideal entry point for other vital services, which too often are delivered through separate programmes whose schedules may even conflict. A study in Colombia demonstrated the value of an integrated approach: three groups of poor undernourished children were provided with different levels of care, and compared to a group of children from well-to-do families. The first group received health care alone, and after two years showed little change. The second group was given health care and supplemental feeding, and their growth caught up to that of the well-to-do children. The third group had health care, nutrition and a stimulating play environment, and caught up both physically and intellectually with the control group.[4] Training and enrichment programmes for parents can be a valuable supplement to integrated care. A study in Turkey found that when mothers were trained to understand and support children's development, this added substantially to the long term benefits of integrated care.[5]

When a range of services is provided through a child care centre, it can

[3] Cameron, S, Kandula, N, Leng, J, Arnold, C (1998) *Urban Childcare in Bangladesh*, Save the Children Fund (USA)
[4] Morley, D and Lovel, H (1986) *My Name is Today: An Illustrated Discussion of Child Health, Society and Poverty in Less Developed Countries*, London: Macmillan
[5] Kagitçibasi, 1996, op cit Note 1

simplify life greatly for overburdened parents. The ongoing relationship with young children and their families makes it possible to establish continuity in the provision of services, and the cumulative benefits can be significant. This very continuity allows the value of various supports to become evident over time. Where families might otherwise attend a clinic only in case of illness, for instance, the improved health of children in child care programmes can demonstrate the importance of preventive care.

coordinating services

Integration of services can be established in various ways. Nutritional support can be a part of the regular daily programme in any child care arrangement. Regular medical check-ups, immunization, welfare reviews and classes for parents can be made available through outreach from health centres. When facilities are planned, efforts can be made to locate child care adjacent to other services, for instance in a local community centre. Local authorities can help to ensure joint planning, coordination of relevant services, and the support of community and NGO efforts through technical back-up and material assistance (see pp55, 257, 261).

sharing space

- *Use child care facilities as an entry point for the provision of integrated services for children and families.*

Establishing standards for child care

Any environment where young children regularly spend time must meet some basic standards for health, safety and psychosocial development. There may be national codes for child care centres, but because conditions can vary widely it is advisable that local authorities, with the support of early childhood experts, develop a set of standards that are locally relevant. In order to ensure compliance, there should be some form of official oversight. Those whose job it is to ensure that standards are being met should also serve as a resource for child care providers, offering access to advice and support.

locally relevant standards

Providing a safe and healthy environment

Environmental standards in any child care centre must promote health and safety, establish the capacity of adults to provide high quality care, and be fully able to support the needs of as many children as might be present at any one time. The possibilities for disease transmission are always higher when a number of children are together, and this must be kept in mind in determining local standards.[6] Inadequate toilets or hand washing facilities, for instance, may allow parasites or disease to spread quickly from child to child, and from there through the community.

preventing disease transmission

At a minimum, every child care centre should have regular and plentiful supplies of clean water, sufficient toilets suitable for young children, facilities for changing and washing children, and for doing laundry and dishes, prompt and regular garbage removal, well-ventilated rooms and the capacity for hygienic storage and preparation of food. Where possible, facilities should be planned with the use of young children in mind – when children are able to wash their own hands and dispose of rubbish themselves, this helps to instil an early awareness of healthy habits. A well-appointed child care centre is an important model

[6] Satterthwaite, D, Hart, R, Levy, C, Mitlin, D, Ross, D, Smit, J, Stephens, C (1996) *The Environment for Children*, London: Earthscan

for environmental health, and a source of education on basic hygiene for both children and their families.

Staffing requirements

emergency back-up

The ratio of staff to children should depend on the age and needs of the children, but also on the experience and capacity of the caregiver. Even with a small number of children, it is important that a caregiver have some back-up, even if it is a less experienced helper. If a child is hurt or sick, or if for some reason it is necessary to leave the premises, someone must be present to call on for help.

- *Develop standards for child care provision that are relevant to local settings and that will promote children's health and safety, and their psychosocial development.*
- *Ensure that those who monitor child care standards can also serve as a resource for child care providers.*
- *Support child care centres to become models of environmental health and hygiene for communities.*
- *Ensure that staffing requirements recognize the skill and experience of caregivers, and the need for back-up in case of emergency.*

Cultural continuity

sensitivity to family practices

When different cultural groups live side by side, as is often true in urban settings, child care outside of the family can raise significant issues. Daily caregiving routines for young children reflect the values of those who care for them and convey to children a particular approach to life. If the beliefs and practices of child care providers are distinctly different from those of the family, this could be confusing; even a loving caregiver can inadvertently teach behaviour that might be considered unacceptable within the family. When infants and toddlers cannot be cared for by providers who share a cultural background with the child's family, it is important to ensure that providers can respond with sensitivity to differences, and can involve parents in finding ways to create continuity between family routines and the child care setting. Especially for slightly older children, this can form the basis for tolerance and understanding, and can make the difference in easing the transition from home to the formal school system.[7]

Some beliefs about child rearing may violate children's rights and be developmentally damaging – for instance a belief that children should be beaten if they disobey. Child care providers have the opportunity through example and discussion with parents and other family members to challenge and influence damaging child rearing patterns from within the context of the local culture and community.[8]

- *Provide training for child care providers that enables them to respond with sensitivity to cultural differences, and to address damaging child care practices through supportive dialogue with parents.*

[7] Myers, R G (1997) 'Removing Roadblocks to Success: Transitions and Linkages between Home, Preschool, and Primary School', *Coordinators' Notebook: An International Resource for Early Child Development*, (21, 1997): 1–19

[8] Arnold, C (1998) *Early childhood – Building our Understanding and Moving Towards the Best of Both Worlds*, Redd Barna/Save the Children Fund (USA)

Providing for play

In any setting that caters to a number of young children, particularly where numbers are high, there is a need for efficient management and careful supervision. But it is important that children's developmental needs do not take second place to the child care provider's need for order and efficiency. Caregivers should be sensitive to children's hunger for exploration, variety, unstructured play and free choice, and to the developmental benefits of making these possible. Opportunities for play should be varied, stimulating, geared for a range of interests and ages, and sufficient to meet the needs of all the children (see p22, 84). It is valuable for children to learn to share, but not ideal that they spend their playtime waiting to take turns. Rather than investing scarce resources in a few expensive toys or pieces of equipment, it is preferable to use found materials and simple handmade toys and equipment which can be easily available in sufficient quantity. (See resource list).

materials for play

- *Train care providers to be aware of the developmental benefits of exploration, variety, unstructured play and free choice.*
- *Ensure that toys and materials are sufficient to provide for the numbers of children attending a facility.*

SOME MODELS FOR CHILD CARE PROVISION AND SUPPORT FOR EARLY CHILD DEVELOPMENT

Provision for child care for early child development can take a number of forms that will vary depending on local needs and conditions. We will describe some basic models, using local examples for illustration.

Family-based child care

Child care provided by a neighbour in her home is likely to be the most common form of care outside the family. This tends to be an informal arrangement, but it is not unusual for local authorities or community organizations to support home-based child care networks, and to ensure, through training and oversight, that they meet a high standard. One such network was established in the densely populated community of Tecun Uman in Guatamala City with the support of UNICEF. Five community women each received a month of training in early childhood development from social workers, psychologists and nutritionists. Their homes were upgraded to provide the water, toilets and play space necessary for ten children each, and they were give a small salary when they began to provide care. A support team developed a weekly curriculum and compiled lists of children's songs and games, and pamphlets on nutrition and development. These home care mothers were then able to train others, using the printed material and their own experience. Within a few years 250 children were receiving high quality care in 25 homes that were part of this ongoing network.[9]

examples from Latin America

[9] Espinosa, L and Lopez Rivera, O A (1994) 'UNICEF's Urban Basic Services Programme in Illegal Settlements in Guatamala City', *Environment and Urbanization*, 6(2): 9–31

Attention to hygiene is a critical feature of care in child care centres, where infection can spread rapidly from child to child. Even if water is not piped to the centre, there should be sufficient quantities kept on hand to ensure that children can wash after toileting and before eating.

The home-based Hogares do Bienestar (Homes of Well-being) programme in Colombia was designed to reach children under seven who were malnourished or lacked minimum requirements for growth and development, and to provide care in homes in their own neighbourhoods. The community identified the children in need, determined the number of such homes required, and selected mothers to implement the programme. Through government and private financing, mothers were trained and their homes upgraded to allow for the care of approximately 15 children in each home. At the time this programme was reported, it was providing care for almost 400,000 children in Colombia.[10] Some home-based facilities have also provided a broad range of assistance for parents. The Day Care Homes of Venezuela, established in the 1970s, in addition to providing child care and nutritional and health back-up, also offered parenting education classes and legal services to acquaint parents with their legal rights and responsibilities towards children.[11]

[10] Landers, C (1989) *Early Childhood Development: Summary Report*, Florence, UNICEF International Child Development Centre

[11] UNICEF (1979) 'Urban Examples for Basic Services Development in Cities: The Infant and the Young Child – A Focus for Assistance and a Stimulus for Family Improvement', *Urban Examples #3*

- *Support home-based child care networks, and ensure, through training and oversight, that they meet a high standard.*
- *Provide support for home-based providers to upgrade their homes to meet the needs of groups of children.*

Rotating care within the community

When women have flexible work arrangements, they can arrange to share child care with other mothers or caregivers on a rotating basis. Such arrangements may be quite informal, but again there are cases where authorities have provided a training and support framework. Project Entry Point in Nepal developed such a programme for women engaged in subsistence farming or other income generating activities. Although this was a rural programme, its approach would be equally appropriate for an urban area. Mothers organized themselves into groups of five or six, and received a basic kit of materials and four intensive days of training, designed to respect traditional practices while introducing new information.[12] Since the 1980s the programme has developed in a number of interesting ways. Some groups persuaded their communities to provide them with centres which they still run on a rotating basis. Others selected one or two mothers to run the group for them, and compensated them for this. The pioneers of the programme recently provided training to an urban programme in Bangladesh.[13]

an example from Nepal

Centre-based child care

Larger centres for child care can serve most easily as a focus for integrated service provision within a community. The Anganwadi centres of India, first developed at the end of the 1970s, were designed to serve a population of approximately 1,000, and were considered to be child welfare institutions, coordinating a range of services. Anganwadi workers were local women who received four months of training, and were supported by a supervisor in charge of 20 Anganwadis. Growth monitoring and feeding programmes ensured that extra food was going to the children who needed it rather than to other family members. Health care was offered in collaboration with local primary health centres, which provided the supervision of an auxiliary nurse. Pre-school education for children from three to five emphasized stimulation of children's curiosity and learning on all levels. Adult education focused on nutrition and food preparation, domestic hygiene and child development. The overall impact of such centres is difficult to measure, but can be significant in providing the basis for community change and development.[14]

India's Anganwadi centres

- *Provide the support and coordination for child care centres to become bases for community change and development.*

Care based at place of employment

For many women, child care at their place of work is the ideal solution. For those with young infants, this proximity can make a difference in the mother's ability to breastfeed her child. When health and other services are available through the child care centre, mothers can more easily manage the many demands on their time. Employers benefit from decreased absenteeism and tardiness and a higher level of commitment from workers.

In some countries legislation requires employers to provide child care for their workers. In India, since 1970, child care on site has been required for women workers in various categories, such as factory work and contract labour. The Mobile Creche Programmes, developed to provide care for the infants and young children of women working (and sometimes

[12] Landers, 1989, op cit Note 10
[13] Personal communication, Caroline Arnold, Save the Children Fund, Bangladesh, 1998
[14] MacPherson, S (1987) *Five Hundred Million Children: Poverty and Child Welfare in the Third World*, New York: St Martin's Press

living) in the hazardous conditions of construction sites, were established within many high rise buildings under construction, and were moved when women moved on to new sites. Children attended from their earliest weeks, and malnourished children were given an initial medical check-up, weekly visits by a doctor, special feedings and the close supervision of a nutritionist. The unhygienic surroundings of the construction sites provided a challenge for care providers, and they responded with measures that could be practiced at home by the family. Cloth hammocks, easy both to wash and store, were used for rest times. Careful attention was paid to essential play and early learning experiences, using inexpensive and indigenous materials such as old saris, kite paper, wooden beads, stones, leaves and flowers. Parent education classes focused on nutrition and food preparation, but also on adult literacy and political topics.[15] These centres often became the focus for broad-based community development, helping older children to be integrated into schools, providing training for young women as child care workers, entering into problem-solving discussion with parents and other community members, and working towards the improvement of living conditions for all.[16]

care on construction sites

The groups operating these creches have tended to be NGOs and voluntary groups, and have not always received support from employers and contractors. A Delhi survey of creches on construction sites found that in many cases a lack of resources resulted in poor physical conditions, untrained staff, and inadequate equipment and activities for children.[17] Local authorities are responsible for monitoring compliance and ensuring that employers are fulfilling their legal obligations. Although most women do not work in the formal sector, it is important to ensure that those who are legally entitled to child care from their employers are receiving it, and that it meets appropriate standards.

- *Enforce legislation requiring employers to offer work-based child care.*
- *Monitor provision to ensure high quality.*
- *Coordinate work-based child care with the provision of other services.*

Parenting support and enrichment services

Care at home may be preferable for very young children. Breastfeeding makes a significant contribution to infant health and nutrition (see p112), and it is widely agreed that the security of consistent primary caregivers (not necessarily the mother) is an important foundation for children's emotional and social development, especially in the first year or two of life. This may be difficult to achieve in child care centres, especially if there is a high staff turnover.

building on the knowledge of caregivers

Even when families are able to provide care for young children at home, many can still use support and guidance. Successful efforts have been initiated around the world to expand the understanding of parents and caregivers about their role. These programmes should never be carried out simply as instruction. Parent educators should be trained to listen as much as to inform, and to recognize and build constructively on caregivers' own knowledge and concerns. Accepted socialization practices, as well as the many pressures experienced by parents in poverty, must be taken into account, so that helpful strategies can be

15 UNICEF 1979, op cit Note 11
16 MacPherson, 1987, op cit Note 14
17 Ibid

developed collaboratively. This will be far more effective in encouraging the assimilation of new information than a purely didactic approach. Most parenting programmes have been aimed at mothers. When there is a male head of family, however, he often has a disproportionately powerful role as decision maker, and it is ideal if he can be included, as well as any other caregivers in the family. Home visiting programmes can be enhanced by occasional group meetings in the community, which can offer practical and emotional support for parents struggling with minimal resources and multiple stresses.[18] Parents from low-income neighbourhoods can also be trained, so that they can themselves become para-professional parenting workshop leaders.

involving fathers

parent groups

Community members trained to work at the local level are more likely to be trusted by local residents. This enables them to supplement regular workshops with direct household visits. Families struggling to raise children under difficult conditions and with minimal resources can benefit greatly from information and advice offered by an experienced child care outreach worker.

home visits

Community health centres, social welfare departments and local schools could all serve as the base agency for such efforts. Ideally, a community should have a place which can serve as a family development centre – a setting which could not only house resources and services of various kinds, but where community members could meet to discuss a range of issues, including those related to their children's development (see p55).

family development centres

- *Promote the availability of maternal care during the first two years.*
- *Establish programmes to provide support and guidance to parents and other family caregivers.*
- *Wherever possible bring groups of parents together for mutual support.*
- *Train parent educators to build constructively on existing child care practices.*

responding to the isolation of children with disabilities

Support for parents of children with disabilities

Home-based support is especially important for the parents of children with disabilities, who may find themselves isolated, especially where there is a stigma attached to disability. For parents burdened by multiple demands, the strain of providing appropriate care for a child with disabilities may be overwhelming. Too many children spend their days in dark rooms without stimulation, dependent on others for every aspect of their care. Through lack of attention, they may over time become increasingly limited in their capacities. Simply sitting in one place, for instance, may cause a child with physical handicaps to develop contractures which will increasingly limit motion.[19] The intellectual and social development of a child with cognitive disabilities may similarly atrophy with a lack of stimulation, the result of unwitting neglect.[20] Although they are deeply concerned, some parents may have no conception of the child's real potential to acquire many skills, and to function well with some assistance. They may be ashamed of the child, and try to keep her hidden or, in attempting to protect her from harm or ridicule, they may overprotect her. Even parents who fully understand a child's potential

18 Myers, 1992, op cit Note 2
19 Werner, D (1987) *Disabled Village Children: A Guide for Community Health Workers, Rehabilitation Workers, and Families*, Palo Alto, USA: The Hesperian Foundation
20 Brown, W, Thurman, S K, Pearl, L F (1993) *Family-centered Early Intervention with Infants and Toddlers: Innovative Cross Disciplinary Approaches*, Baltimore: Paul H Brookes

may find that they are seriously limited in their capacity to provide what she needs.

It is critically important that parents and caregivers receive the support and information they need to respond knowledgeably to their child's condition, and to encourage and facilitate their interaction with the world. Efforts should be geared towards building on their strengths and compensating for their weaknesses. Early and consistent stimulation is essential. Modification of the home environment is also important and can best be achieved in collaboration with the family in their own dwelling. When children with disabilities need day care, authorities must ensure that providers, like family members, have the support and assistance they need (see also pp86, 109, 138).

- *Ensure that parents and caregivers of children with disabilities receive the support and information they need to respond knowledgeably and effectively to their children's conditions, and to ensure their optimal development, both at local health centres or rehabilitation centres, and through home visits.*

Toy libraries and play centres

Toy libraries or play centres can be especially valuable for children with limited access to play opportunities. They can lend out toys, and also serve as a rich environment for play, making shared resources available to large numbers of children. These centres should ideally be part of a more comprehensive community resource which might serve as a general family development center (see p55). The most critical element in any play centre is the staff. They should be trained in group dynamics, have an understanding of child development, and be able to educate parents, teachers and others in supporting children's play. Even one well-trained play worker can reach many children with the assistance of trained volunteers.

staff training

Play centres have special significance for children with disabilities, and programmes should be thoughtfully designed to integrate these children. Where resources make it impossible to serve the needs of all children in the community, those with disabilities should be given priority. Training sessions for parents and teachers of children with special needs can provide emotional support and a chance to share daily problems. Play centres can also lend out specially designed toys, equipment and furniture to maximize children's access to play at home. In some cases a mobile toy library makes the most sense. Lekotech of Buenos Aires, for instance, has fitted out large trucks to take toys and equipment to those families that most need the service.[21]

giving priority to children with disabilities

- *Support the establishment of toy libraries and play centres to meet the play needs of young children in low-income communities.*
- *Provide training for play workers so that they can make rich opportunities available to children, and help parents and caregivers to promote their children's optimal development.*
- *Ensure that attention is given to the needs of children with disabilities.*

21 Personal communication, Nilda Cosco, IPA, Argentina, 1998

Nursery schools and pre-schools

Many parents and educators see formal preschool education as an essential preparation for children, especially where schooling is competitive. In low-income communities as far apart as Accra and Dhaka, mothers of young children speak of the critical necessity of entering their children in paid preschool programmes to ensure their success when they enter the formal school system.[22] There is an increasing tendency to formalize learning in these establishments through an emphasis on rote learning and memorization.

Up to a certain point young children enjoy the sense that they are in 'real' school, and take pride in the skills they learn in such settings. But the developmental requirements of young children are broad and varied. They need an active physical involvement in the world around them, the chance to experiment with a rich variety of materials, the opportunity to exercise their imaginations, and access to spontaneous play with other children (see p22). These kinds of opportunities will do far more to stretch their minds and expand their abilities than will a premature pressure to acquire academic skills. Young children *can* learn their numbers and letters, but this may imperil their capacity later on to make use of a wide variety of learning strategies and problem-solving techniques (p171). Pre-schools and nurseries should be encouraged to offer a well-rounded programme, and to focus their efforts on the development of the whole child.

the danger of stressing formal education too soon

- *Encourage pre-schools to offer well-rounded programmes which focus on the development of the whole child, rather than just the early acquisition of formal academic skills.*

[22] Bartlett, S and Hart,R, field trips

Small, locally based schools promote a sense of ownership and involvement on the part of both children and adults, and they can become vital centres of local life. When schools are within walking distance it also encourages attendance, especially for girls. These girls walk to school in a low-income colonia on the outskirts of Nuevo Laredo, Mexico. Janet Jarman, 1996

9 Schools

The Convention recognizes the right of all children to equal opportunity in education, and specifically to free, compulsory primary schooling, with reasonable access to secondary and higher education (Article 28). According to the Convention this education must be focused on children's full development, and should support the personality and talents of individual children. In addition to preparing children for a livelihood, education should encourage respect for parents, cultural identity and human rights, and should foster a knowledgeable, caring response to the natural environment (Article 29).

Education, as envisioned by the Convention, is not limited to the acquisition of academic skills, but must help children to be competent, caring, responsible members of society. This has implications for the way that learning is defined, and for the place of schools within the community. In this chapter we will describe the qualities of schools that support the Convention's goals, and that are relevant to the needs of urban children and their families.

Experience has demonstrated that investment in education, and especially primary education, can yield significant benefits to society in the form of improved health, better incomes, and heightened productivity. The World Bank found that the returns from investment in primary education are about 27 per cent higher than from most other areas of social investment.[1] Education is frequently presented as the optimal solution to the problems raised by poverty, exclusion and inequity; and those in poverty are encouraged to see school as the 'way out' for their children. Contemporary urban life requires increasing levels of formal knowledge, and the full range of skills provided by a good education are basic to a viable future.

the unfulfilled promise of schooling

Although there have been overall global gains in the numbers of children receiving a basic education in recent decades, real progress is extremely uneven. Nor does increased coverage necessarily mean an improvement in quality. For many children schooling has been an unfulfilled promise. In many poor countries those who start school frequently leave after the first few years, often because of the inadequacy of the schooling. In Bihar, India, where an estimated 50 per cent of children leave school before their fifth year, the low quality of education is the primary reason given for dropping out.[2] Highly centralized national bureaucracies, poorly trained and underpaid teachers, incompetent management, lack of supplies and rundown facilities are major obstacles to a good education. Many of those who do attend school may find that it does not appreciably expand their options in life. In Latin America, over 80 per cent of low-income students fail to master reading comprehension.[3] In Brazil, children take an average of 12 years to complete eight years of schooling.[4] For many children, school is a frustrating experience, completely divorced from the concerns of their lives. They can become bored and disillusioned by the lack of stimulation, and may find work to be a more challenging option.

But even when resources are limited, school should not be a waste of time. Nor should it be a way out for the few, a filter through which only the brightest and luckiest will pass. Education must be a real option for all children, relevant to their individual needs and to the life of their communities. Rather than being 'privileged territory', schools can become vital centres of local life, a means for expanding the aspirations of the entire community, and a foundation for integrated development.

THE ROLE OF LOCAL AUTHORITIES IN FOSTERING SCHOOL-COMMUNITY LINKS

Responsibility for education covers several domains – from the building of schools and the ongoing funding of school programmes to the training and hiring of teachers, the setting of curriculum and the monitoring of standards. Control over these various functions can reside in a number of levels, from the most central to the most local. But if schools are to be responsive to local needs, and to fulfill their potential as a focus and generator of local development, they must have deep roots in the communities they serve. Local government should use its authority to ensure maximum control at the community level. The recommendations in this chapter represent goals that local authorities and communities can aspire to, whether through direct allocation of funding, through coordi-

[1] Dall, F P (1995) 'Children's Right to Education' in Himes, J R (ed) *Implementing the Convention on the Rights of the Child*, The Hague: Martinus Nijhoff
[2] Hassan, A (1997) 'School Dropouts and the Myth of Child Labour in India', Presentation at Urban Childhood conference, 9–12 June, 1997, Trondheim, Norway
[3] Boyden, J, Ling, B, Myers, W (1998) *What Works for Working Children*, Stockholm: Radda Barnen and UNICEF
[4] Rizzini, I, Rizzini, I, Munhoz, M, Galeano, L (1992) *Childhood and Urban Poverty in Brazil: Street and Working Children and their Families*, Florence, Italy: UNICEF

nation of services and resources, or through advocacy and collaboration with higher levels of authority.

local control and outside funding

Although local control is critical to vital community-based schools, decentralization can also exacerbate differences in quality and affordability between richer and poorer cities and communities. Some central financing should be maintained in order to ensure a reasonable degree of equity across school jurisdictions. When there are large influxes of refugee or transient families, for instance, local communities are more than ever likely to need outside funding to cope with the increased educational burdens. It is also important to accept the fact that the 'community' may not be a closely knit and homogeneous group of people with shared values (see p263). Especially within rapidly changing urban areas, the concerns of disparate groups must be considered, and local authorities must ensure that vulnerable and marginal households are not excluded.

assessment

To provide effective schooling for all a community's children, it is essential that educational needs and resources be accurately assessed. This should be undertaken at the most local level, with the technical support of the city's education agency and local school administrations, and through community-based discussion and decision-making described on p264. This is necessary in order to guarantee that the needs of all children are recognized, including those who have difficulty attending school. It is not sufficient simply to determine the numbers of children attending; it is also important to consider the kinds of provision being offered within the school as perceived by parents and children.

Representative school planning and management

involving parents

The Convention emphasizes the primary responsibility of parents for the development of their children. It follows that parents should be closely involved in decisions about their children's education, and that there should be cooperation between parents and school administration on the nature of schooling. This is a highly practical measure. Experience around the world has shown that schools improve in quality when they involve parents and community members. This has received tangible recognition in Brazil, where the central government has experimented with providing funding directly to schools, provided they have a participatory governing body that includes parents.[5]

democratic space

School as community space, and community as school space

Schools should come to be seen as 'democratic spaces' which all families have an equal right to become involved in. Particularly for communities without a community centre, a primary school can serve a number of functions. An excellent example is the Centro Des Formacao do Educador Popular Maria da Conceicao in Recife, Brazil, which is simultaneously a pre-school, day care centre, primary school, a professional training centre for teenagers, a community development centre and a meeting place centre for the entire community. Since the entire centre is concerned with community development, children spontaneously become involved, and even initiate community projects.[6]

5 Personal communication, Ladislau Dowbor, 1998

6 Hart, R, Dauite,C, Iltus, S, Kritt, O, Rome, M, Sabo, K (1997) 'Developmental Theory and Children's Participation in Community Organizations', *Social Justice*, 24(3): 33–63

For low-income families who often lack access to essential family services, there is great value in bringing these all together in one place. Where space allows, the school can be an ideal site for coordinated provision of such services as reproductive health planning, health care, social welfare, child care, adult education and employment. These overlapping uses can promote a broader concept of education. It can also help limited community resources go as far as possible, as when sports fields are used after hours by community members. Because the school belongs to everyone, it can be the most neutral location for local meetings and decision making (p266). School administrations may resist use by the public because of control and security issues. Administrative offices and records should be kept secure, and full responsibility taken by community groups for their use of these facilities.

coordinated service provision

supporting community use of school space

Initially, adults who have had little or no formal schooling may be intimidated by the formal setting. But local government and community organizations should fight this image through a concerted coordination of services and democratic inclusiveness. Policies that separate functions for the poor and marginalized will serve only to maintain their separation from the mainstream of the community. When they are the base for essential services, schools may start to be perceived as more relevant, approachable institutions.

The community can also become school space. Schooling does not have to take place only on one site, especially when resources are limited. When the community contains recreational facilities, a library or a meeting space, these can serve as invaluable extensions to a school with limited facilities.

- *Promote the inclusive and participatory assessment of local educational needs, resources and provision.*
- *Establish a representative community school governance board for all schools, including both parents and school staff, to make decisions regarding educational ideology, school finances, curriculum and design or modification of the school environment; make all meetings open to the community; and ensure that the interests of marginal families are represented.*
- *Involve children in appropriate areas of planning and management within the school.*
- *Wherever possible plan schools to serve as sites for a range of integrated community services, or to be closely linked with such services; and support local control and management of facilities in order to facilitate shared use.*
- *When schools are short on space or have limited facilities, make other resources within the community available to them.*

MAKING EDUCATION TRULY UNIVERSAL

In all cities there are children who, for a variety of reasons, do not attend school. When local assessment has revealed why they are not attending, measures can be taken to respond to the situation.

Making schools affordable

the many costs of schooling

Affordability is an insurmountable barrier for many. The Convention mandates a free primary education, but in many cities school fees are a fact of life. Even where fees are not charged, the costs for books, school uniforms and transportation can be prohibitive for poor families. Without proper supplies, children may feel stigmatized in school and become unwilling to attend. When school-age children would otherwise be contributing to family survival by earning money or helping at home, the true costs are even greater. Special efforts must be made to provide children from poor families with free books, uniforms and supplies, and where necessary with scholarship aid and transportation vouchers.

financial aid

Through collaboration of municipal agencies with NGOs, the small city of Olangapo has managed to raise a number of scholarships from a variety of sources. One woman in a very poor community raises money from a more prosperous adjacent neighbourhood to support scholarships for 20 children. Parents whose children receive this aid sign contracts agreeing to their child's regular school attendance, and the contributing families are given formal reports.[7] Similar programmes in Brazil are having excellent results; trained volunteers visit the family when children drop out of school, and if the reasons are financial, temporary aid is made available in return for the parents' commitment to keeping their children in school.

Including working children

Ideally, children should be free to attend school unburdened by conflicting obligations. But under conditions of poverty it continues to be a fact of life that many children will be working. It is critical to ensure that they have access to the education they need to keep open their options for the future. This issue will be discussed on p203.

Educating girls

Gender disparity in education is a form of discrimination against girls that must be vigorously targeted by local authorities and policy makers. Education for girls has been closely linked to increased opportunities, to maternal and child health, to falling birth rates, and to social progress in general.[8] Experience has shown that as enrollment becomes more balanced, girls grow in confidence, participate more freely and speak up for themselves. Their success as participating members of society is closely related to their access to an appropriate education.[9] Although progress has been made in access to basic education, gender gaps continue to be high at all levels, particularly after the first three years of school. Recent figures indicate that two thirds of the illiterate adults in the world are still women.[10]

Poverty and cultural constraints are the major obstacles. Contributing to household survival, especially through work in the home, is most frequently thought to be a daughter's responsibility. A survey in India found that in 57 per cent of slum households, girls had left school

7 Blanc, C S and contributors (1994) *Urban Children in Distress: Global Predicaments and Innovative Strategies*, Florence, Italy: UNICEF International Child Development Centre and London: Gordon and Breach
8 UNICEF (1998) Girls at Work, New York: UNICEF
9 Ibid
10 Dall, 1995, op cit Note 1

because of the burden of household work.[11] In many cases education is considered inappropriate or unnecessary for girls, given their likely role in life. The access of girls to the public realm may also be limited by religious beliefs and the fear of harassment or molestation. Especially when schools are at a distance, parents may be unwilling for their daughters to attend.

responding to parental concerns

Any measures taken to make schooling more accessible, more affordable and more flexibly responsive to family schedules will help to promote the attendance of girls. But in addition, school authorities must be sensitive to parental concerns and to the particular needs of girls, making it clear that they take them seriously. Change needs to occur throughout the whole of society, not just within schools. In Brazil, for instance, where girls' overall school achievement is now better than boys', they continue to get paid less when they enter the workforce.[12]

Responding to children with disabilities

Too often, children with disabilities are kept out of school on the assumption that education is wasted on them. This is a clear violation of their rights. All reasonable efforts must be made to ensure these children access to appropriate schooling in an environment that supports their sense of autonomy.

mainstreaming US special schools

Some specialists advocate 'mainstreaming' children with disabilities into regular local schools in order best to integrate them in their own communities. Others argue that they should have the benefit of programmes and facilities tailored to their particular learning needs. There can be both educational and economic benefits to bringing together children with similar needs for equipment and specially trained staff. But there are also important advantages for both disabled and typical children when they learn together in their own communities.

In an ideal world it would be possible to provide adequately within community schools for the needs of all children, regardless of their special requirements. But in most cities attempts to meet this ideal will be frustrated by lack of resources. Even in wealthy countries, communities can resist the financial burden of providing fully for children who have severe handicaps, learning problems or behavioural disorders. It is important that the rights of children with disabilities be recognized and properly represented both to school officials and to the wider community. Within the school, teachers can do a good deal to ensure that children with disabilities are accepted and included. This is a critical age for learning tolerance, and the school can be an ideal setting for tackling the prejudices of the larger society. There are some excellent resources available to support teachers in their efforts (see resource list, p280).

Including minority children

Many children of minority groups, including refugees, migrants and transient residents, may miss out on education because of the fear of ostracism, harassment or marginalization in schools, or because schooling is not offered in their own language. Authorities may not even consider

[11] Balakrishnan, R (1994) 'The Sociological Context of Girls' Schooling: Micro Perspectives from the Slums of Delhi', *Social Action*, 44 (July–September 1994)

[12] Dowbor, L (1986) *Aspectos economicos da educacaõ*, Saõ Paulo: A'tica Ed

provision for these groups to be their responsibility. The Convention, however, guarantees these children freedom from discrimination and the right to an education which respects their cultural identity. Local officials, school boards, and school personnel must take an active role in guaranteeing this right.

investment

- *Increase investment in schools, so that fees are unnecessary.*
- *Find ways to provide children from poor families with free books and uniforms, and, where necessary, with scholarship aid and transportation vouchers; where appropriate make financial assistance contingent on parents' commitment to keeping children in school.*

parental awareness

- *Raise parents' awareness of the benefits of education for their daughters, and their disabled children, involve them in planning and decision making, and ensuring that their concerns are addressed.*
- *Train teachers not to give boys preferential treatment.*

advocacy

- *Where there is strong resistance to the participation of girls in the public realm or to the mixing of the sexes, consider single sex classrooms.*
- *Support the availability of affordable child care services to free older sisters for school.*
- *Ensure that capable advocates or advocacy groups are supported in negotiating the best educational solutions for children with special needs; and work closely with health and rehabilitation services, social services and the relevant voluntary organizations within a community in order to come up with the best plan for each child.*

teacher training

- *Make training and support available for teachers, through contact with more experienced teachers, health workers and others who can assist them in working with their students with disabilities.*
- *As far as possible, include children themselves in decisions that affect their schooling.*
- *Ensure that children of minority groups have access to schooling which is free from discrimination and respects their cultural identity.*
- *Ease the transition from home to school by training teachers to understand and respect the background and culture of the children they teach, to encourage communication with parents, and to ensure that questions and concerns are addressed.*
- *Through the school's curriculum address issues of diversity with children, and work proactively against discrimination (see p173).*

EDUCATION THAT PROMOTES CHILDREN'S RIGHTS

schools as instruments of ideology

Schools are not just places where children learn to read and write. They are powerful transmitters of ideology. The quality of the interaction between children and teachers, the choice of skills taught, and the materials and methods used are important messages in themselves. When schools teach about democracy in undemocratic ways, for instance, or use curricula that represent the perspectives of old colonial powers, it is unlikely that children will develop a sense of their own efficacy and that

of their communities. It is important for authorities to acknowledge that schools are tools of socialization. The messages that they transmit must be compatible with the rearing of confident and responsible young citizens.

Educating children for citizenship in a democratic society means giving them opportunities to exercise their own rights and responsibilities. Here, children in a 'New School' near Armenia, Colombia, vote to elect their own student council, which will oversee all student activities including the school garden and daily maintenance. UNICEF 1990, Ellen Tolmie

Child-centred education

Different children, as well as different age groups, have different ways of learning, which should be accomodated through flexible and child-centred approaches. In the early grades, for instance, children often require concrete examples to grapple with abstract concepts. As an old Chinese proverb says, 'I hear and I forget; I see and I remember; I do and I understand'. But education within the classroom is often limited to rote learning with little opportunity to learn by doing. Some skills, such as the memorization of multiplication tables, can benefit from rote learning, but a child's deeper understanding is best supported with examples from the real world and with the opportunity to discover the best avenue for his or her own learning. When children become actively involved in the learning process, they are more likely to become curious lifelong learners. This calls for teachers to be flexible and creative facilitators of children's learning, rather than simply a delivery system for information. For this they need training, resources and ongoing support (see p183).

Making education child-centred also involves recognizing the major transitions that many children have to make to adapt to formal schooling. Efforts should be made to ensure that these transitions are comfortably negotiated, so that children can acquire the self-confidence necessary to become successful learners.[13]

[13] Myers, R G (1997) 'Removing Roadblocks to Success: Transitions and Linkages between Home, Preschool, and Primary School', *Coordinators' Notebook: An International Resource for Early Child Development*, (21, 1997): 1–19

Education for livelihood

relevant curricula

Curricula are commonly set at the national level and are frequently irrelevant to the needs of local communities and contemporary life. The content of local education should be compatible with local realities, and relate to the livelihoods that children have a realistic hope of pursuing. If schooling is alien to the understanding and goals of parents, it will be harder to ask them to forego the loss of income and domestic work that results from their child's school attendance. Curricula can be developed or modified with teachers and can include the perspectives of children and parents. Relevance to local earning opportunities should not preclude the possibility that some children may wish to pursue education further, and their primary schooling should also prepare them for this.

Education for sustainable development and urban regeneration

Agenda 21, the global plan of action for sustainable development, argues that children should be active participants in identifying and acting on local environmental issues. Because so many of the issues addressed by sustainable development have their roots in local realities, Agenda 21 also calls for the creation of 'Local Agenda 21' action plans. Any city with such a programme should coordinate closely with schools to make children's involvement an integral part of both the production and implementation of their Local Agenda 21.

locally based environmental education

The sustainable development and regeneration of urban areas cannot be realized unless the general public has a caring and informed attitude towards the local environment. To promote such an attitude, it is important to encourage and build on urban children's familiarity with their surroundings.[14] Generalized texts produced in some distant city cannot foster this familiarity. The urban habitat that children know best is the neighbourhood they experience everyday which, through their involvement in locally based education, they can come to know in a deeper and more concerned way. School officials should bear in mind that environmental education is pointless if the school itself engages in wasteful or destructive practices. Ways of involving children in responsible practices will be discussed in more detail below (see p181).

Education for citizenship in a democratic society

Educating children as responsive citizens means giving them an understanding of their own rights and civic responsibilities. An obvious approach is to incorporate the Convention into school curricula. But just as schools should be models for environmental care, so should they also serve as examples in fostering democratic attitudes. Teaching about democracy is futile if the school does not exercise democratic principles in its daily interactions with children and their families. It has been argued that rights become most meaningful in the process of efforts to achieve them.[15] Children can gain an understanding of their right to play and recreation, for instance, through their involvement in improving the school grounds; and of their right to good health by promoting hygienic conditions within the school.

14 Chawla, L and Hart, R (1988) 'The Roots of Environmental Concern', *Proceedings of the 19th Conference of the Environmental Design Research Association*, EDRA, Washington DC

15 Holland, T (1998) 'Human Rghts Education for Street and Working Children: Principles and Practice', *Human Rights Quarterly*, 20: 173–19316 Hart, R (1997) *Children's Participation: The Theory and Practice of Involving Young Citizens in Community Development and Environmental Care*, London: Earthscan/UNICEF

Colombia's New Schools

Colombia's New Schools offer an excellent example of truly participatory schooling.[16] These schools are largely in rural areas, but their philosophy could well be applied in urban areas. Mixed aged groups for learning, a flexible programme, and cooperative organizations within the school enable children to function as a coordinated democratic community. In addition to graduated progress through a national curriculum, children are expected at each age to carry out community projects designed by and executed with their peers. These might range from social projects, such as an analysis of the transportation problems of children living at a distance; to environmental projects, looking into such issues as the success of recycling strategies in the community. Children's committees manage successful school gardens, worm farms and fish farms. If this level of involvement is undertaken seriously, it will not be perceived by parents as irrelevant to their children's education.

There are many barriers to this kind of democratic schooling. To overcome the threat it initially poses to teachers who fear a challenge to their authority, the New Schools make teacher training itself more democratic, with teachers supporting one another as their schools become more democratic centres for learning. In many of the New Schools the community actions of the children have brought the school closer to the activities of the local village government. It is more difficult to find examples of such a relationship in urban areas, because local urban government is generally not that local. But, wherever possible, it should be integral to every school's programme to expose children to the workings of local government, and to find ways to support their participation (see pp149, 259).

Respecting children's language and culture

The Convention requires that education support the child's identity and promote respect for his or her culture. To be equally accessible and relevant to all cultural groups, schooling should be offered in the languages children use in their homes and communities. This is complicated when a country's dominant language is not that used locally, and even more complicated when more than one language is spoken within the school area. Children's future options may be limited if they do not speak the dominant language.

advantages of using the local language

But use of local languages, especially in the early primary years, may encourage the attendance of children who would otherwise drop out, and will make it easier for schools to establish a good working relationship with the community. Many countries have found it practical and effective to use two languages in the classroom, enabling children to prepare for a future that is either local or distant. Recognizing and respecting the language and culture of all children in the school is also an important way of addressing tensions within the community at large (see p143).

Eliminating stereotypes from the curriculum

the power of images

The ways that girls and women are portrayed in learning material can perpetuate gender stereotypes and discourage girls from setting high goals. Often the heroic figures they learn about are men, and if girls are represented at all in picture books, it will often be running errands and helping around the home. This material may reflect reality in many places, but teachers and school boards must be alert to the power of such images, and do all they can in the selection and presentation of material and role models to encourage girls to take an active role in life and to realize their own potential. The same principles should be applied in dealing with attitudes towards minorities and those with disabilities.

Teaching life skills

children as an informed source for parents

A range of skills is necessary to navigate the complexities of daily life in the city. Especially for children whose parents may not themselves be adept, it is important that these skills be learned at school. Children can also then serve as a source of information for their parents. Awareness of legal rights, information about registering for the vote, familiarity with local services, bureaucratic requirements and government procedures, knowledge of basic health and nutrition, the ability to handle personal and family finances, should all be a part of primary school education, especially when students are unlikely to continue into secondary school.

Promoting a culture of non-violence

physical punishment in schools

The Convention prohibits the use of all forms of physical and mental violence against children (Article 19). A growing number of countries have prohibited the use of physical punishment in schools, including South Africa, China, Burkina Faso, Botswana and most of Europe, but it continues to be a routine means of disciplining and controlling students in much of the world.[17] Beatings, threats and public humiliation can be a factor in keeping children, and especially girls, out of school.[18] Bullying and other forms of violence among children in school may also be ignored or even condoned.[19] When violence is established in this way as an acceptable response, its presence in society is perpetuated. Research has shown that violent and humiliating forms of discipline may be a significant factor in the development of violent attitudes and actions later on.[20] If children are to participate actively in a democratic society, they must learn in school as well as at home that there are more productive and humane ways of providing guidance, solving problems, and relating to other people than through violence.

For children who have learned through experience that violence is the natural response to conflict, it may be necessary to provide alternatives through education. In South Africa, where violence has been for many a daily fact of life, a School Mediation Project educates children and teachers about the nature of conflict. Training stresses tolerance as the basis of true democracy, and points to the importance of honouring and respecting the needs of others. Conflict resolution techniques such as mediation, negotiation and arbitration are now taught to all older students in two of the country's provinces.[21]

17 Newell, P (1995) 'Respecting Children's Right to Physical Integrity' in Franklin, B (ed) *The Handbook of Children's Rights: Comparative Policy and Practice*, London/New York: Routledge, 215–226; and Newell, P (1997) 'Children and Violence', Florence, UNICEF International Child Development Centre

18 Boyden et al 1998, op cit Note 3; and Balakrishnan 1994, op cit Note 11

19 Tattum, D P and Lane, D A (eds) (1988) *Bullying in Schools*, Stoke-on-Trent, UK: Trentham Books

20 Newell 1997, op cit Note 17

21 EDev News (1993) *Education for Development Bulletin*, 4(1, March 1993)

- *Help children become involved, self-motivated learners by allowing classrooms to be rich and stimulating environments, by making a range of resources available, by training teachers in child centred education, and encouraging teachers and children to learn from one another (see pp179, 181, 182).*
- *Ensure that curricula prepare children effectively for local livelihood possibilities, as well as for further education.*
- *Help children to understand their rights through education on the CRC, and through practical efforts to work towards their rights within the school and the community.*
- *Expose children wherever possible to the workings of local government, and find ways to support their involvement in planning and decision making (see pp149, 259).*
- *Foster respect and understanding for the cultures of all children within the school (see p143), and wherever possible offer schooling in the languages used by the children.*
- *Train teachers and other staff in schools to recognize and respond to stereotyping and discrimination within the classroom; encourage girls, minorities and those with disabilities to realize their potential.*
- *Integrate into the curriculum an active involvement in the local environment, including, for instance, research into school hygiene issues and community environmental health.*
- *Support schools to serve as models of sound environmental practice, and to encourage active involvement in the local environment; involve schools in the development and implementation of Local Agenda 21.*
- *Ensure that children have the information and skills they need in order to handle the complexities of daily life in the city.*
- *Prohibit the use of violence in the school, either between children, or as a means of discipline; and teach conflict resolution techniques within the school.*

SCHOOLS AND HEALTH

Schools are an ideal setting for promoting the health of children, and through them, the health concerns of the entire community. Schools can educate children towards a healthy lifestyle, help to address their immediate health needs, and provide them with healthy surroundings which can serve as a community model for environmental care.

Provision for basic health and hygiene

toilets

Schools should be adequately served with water, sanitation, drainage and waste removal. Without provision for basic hygiene, they can become the means through which infectious disease is transmitted throughout the community. Too many schools lack adequate toilets, often because of lack of upkeep. Some schools have no toilets at all. Children in parts of Accra must leave the school and pay for the use of toilets in the community.[22] Inadequate sanitation and water provision in schools can have significant implications not only for children's health and the cleanliness of the school grounds, but also for attendance. Girls especially are unlikely to attend if toilets and facilities for washing are not available. For girls who are menstruating, the lack of facilities and privacy can be deeply humiliating. A healthy school environment also implies the thoughtful management of outdoor space, and this will be discussed on p181.

girls' attendance

For many children the school may be their first encounter with working toilets, running water, smoke-free rooms and clean surroundings. This can have a powerful impact on their vision of what is possible in the world and even in their own communities. It is important that schools expose children to the potential for hygienic living and give the whole community a standard to aspire to.

Health services for school children

collaboration with local health services

School-aged children are not considered a high risk group in terms of health, but a number of problems, such as malarial fevers, intestinal parasites and undernourishment can affect their health and make learning difficult or impossible. Children who are hungry, debilitated or ill are unable to summon up energy and concentration. A study in Jamaica found that children with moderate whipworm infection scored 15 per cent lower than uninfected children at school; when retested after treatment these same children did almost as well as uninfected children.[23] Regular visits by health personnel can ensure that these problems are identified and responded to.

Education for a healthy lifestyle

hygiene
nutrition

sex education

School-age children develop lifelong habits, and schools can be an important influence and source of information for promoting healthy lifestyles. Information about daily hygiene, nutrition and environmental care are important from the earliest school years (see p116 on health education for and through children). But substance abuse and sexual risk-taking should also be addressed. Because of late starts in school and the frequent need to stay back, many children even in primary school face these issues in their daily lives, especially in urban areas. In addition, it is recognized that an early introduction to responsible decision making is important to good health education. There are often fears that sex education may encourage early sexual activity. On the contrary research indicates that children who are informed are more likely to make responsible decisions (see also p119).[24]

- *Ensure that schools have adequate water provision, sanitation, drainage and solid waste removal, and can serve as community models for environmental health.*
- *Provide health services for children in schools through local health services; and promote collaboration between teachers and health workers.*

22 Bartlett and Hart, field trip 1997
23 World Bank (1993) *World Development Report 1993: Investing in Health*, Washington DC: Oxford University Press
24 UNICEF (1997) *Youth Health – For a Change: A UNICEF Notebook on Programming for Young People's Health and Development*, working draft

- *Provide balanced, well-targeted school feeding programmes to address nutritional deficiencies, and act as an incentive for school attendance.*
- *Have children help with record keeping for periodic check-ups and screenings.*
- *Make health education part of the curriculum, focusing on daily hygiene, nutrition and environmental care, and ensuring that children are well informed and capable of making responsible decisions about drug use and sexual activity.*

THE PHYSICAL ENVIRONMENT OF SCHOOLS

Material environments influence human activities, and schools are no exception. Their size, where they are placed and the way they are arranged affect learning, and how children relate to one another, to adults and to the community. School buildings can foster a sense of belonging, the opportunity to relate with others, and the chance to be engaged in self-initiated activities. But they can also promote a rigid approach to learning and an authoritarian relationship between teachers and pupils, as well as discouraging interaction among students, and between school and community.

environment influences behaviour

The quality of education is not defined by the expense of a school building. Many exciting, effective schools operate under serious physical constraints, some of them meeting in buildings without walls, or even under trees. Large amounts of money are also being spent in many cities to build new school facilities, and some of these are impersonal barracks-like facilities, lacking in warmth, variety and stimulation. In their very design they violate the principles of child-centred and community-based education.

Available resources should be spent in ways that promote the most effective education and allow schools to become vital centres for community development. This means that the goals of the school must be clear, and that the physical environment must be planned to support these goals. For example, in order to encourage the involvement of parents, schools must be close to where they live and must be physically welcoming for them – too often schools can be forbidding places for 'outsiders'. Something as simple as a small common space and a few chairs near the entrance of the building can communicate to people that their presence is welcome. This kind of planning can only happen at the local level, although there are guidelines that can help in decision making.

physical environments that support school goals

Location

Decisions on location should involve community members together with departments of water and sanitation, health, parks and recreation, and social welfare agencies. A number of factors must be weighed. Location should minimize the risk to children from traffic, crime and other dangers. It should allow for the provision of clean water and adequate sanitation. The school should ideally be within walking distance for all children. When children have to use transportation to get to school, costs

distance affects attendance

go up and poor children are more likely to be excluded. Distance is also a significant factor in the attendance of girls. A study in Egypt showed that when schools were three or more kilometres from home, girls' enrollment stood at 30 per cent. When the school was within 1 kilometre, 70 of girls attended.[25] A central location promotes a sense of ownership and involvement on the part of children and community members, and this will enhance the quality of schooling in numerous ways. Keeping schools local has implications for school size, which will be discussed below. The school site, or land nearby, should ideally allow adequate space for outdoor physical play and recreation. When there is enough space for the operation of an urban farm or garden, and ideally for a biodiverse landscape, the school can serve as a training ground for the principles of sustainable development (see below, p181).

The size of primary schools

The tendency in urban areas is to create large schools. But small schools which accomodate 300 children at most, and ideally fewer than that, have been found to be preferable for children for a number of reasons:[26]

small schools encourage involvement

- They are within walking distance for more children.
- Small schools encourage a sense of belonging. Staff are more likely to know all the children, and children are more likely to know one another and to see other students outside of school. It is easier to be 'lost' in a large institution, especially for children who are shy.
- Small schools encourage recognition of children's special needs. Staff are more likely to recognize problems, to have an informed interest, and to share their observations with one another and with parents.
- The Convention emphasizes the participation of children in all matters concerning them, and it is important for children to have voice in the management of their school. This is more workable in a smaller institution.
- Smaller schools can more easily establish a close relationship with the surrounding community, and relate the school curriculum to the daily lives and experiences of the children. The likelihood of parent involvement increases, and the possibility that the school can serve as a centre for a variety of other functions promoting child and community welfare.

small classes

Many of the advantages of small schools apply also to small classrooms. Teachers are more able to give individual children the attention they need; girls may be more comfortable in smaller groups; and small classrooms help in accomodating diversity. But because teachers' salaries are the single largest cost that a school faces, class sizes in publicly funded schools tend to be over 30 and can reach as high as 100. To some degree the benefits of learning in a smaller group can be achieved by rethinking the mode of teaching. Instead of dealing with the class as a unit, teachers can work with some children while others work together or on their own. This is more easily managed when there are classroom aides, volunteers,

[25] UNICEF (ed) (1996) *The Progress of Nations 1996*, New York: UNICEF

[26] Barker, R G and Gump, P V (1964) *Big School, Small School: High School Size and Student Behavior*, Stanford, California: Stanford University Press

or the possibility of team teaching, and when classrooms can be easily rearranged (see below).

Design, construction and furnishing of schools

Decisions about the physical design and furnishing of schools must reflect local conditions, materials, resources and priorities. But some basic principles may help in planning buildings that encourage flexible and participatory approaches to education:

encourage flexibility and active learning

- Classrooms can vary in size and can serve different functions, with children moving from one to another for different purposes.
- Instead of being single purpose spaces, classrooms can allow for a number of different activities, depending on the age and level of the children – areas for quiet reading, research, group work, making things, and so on.
- When seating is movable, children can work alone or in groups of different sizes. Chairs or stools are easier to move around than benches. Materials such as jute sacking or scraps of carpeting can also make the floor a more comfortable place for working or reading.
- A blackboard and teacher's desk at the front of the classroom encourage a focus on the teacher as the only resource for learning. If the teacher can move around to different learning areas, giving assistance to groups of children working at different projects, this will allow children to be more actively involved.
- When building materials, such as concrete, make it difficult to display children's work and interesting resources on the walls, there are various solutions, such as installing strips of wood from which to hang materials.
- Instead of serving only for transit, hallways can serve as common space for meetings or informal interaction.
- Direct access to the outdoors from classrooms enables children to make better use of the outdoors as a learning resource.

GSS classrooms, Bangladesh

The GSS classrooms in Dhaka, Bangladesh, apply many of these principles at low-cost. Within a simple corrugated iron building, teachers have created a rich learning environments with the participation of the children. Children make use of different parts of the classroom for different activities; a reading area, mathematics area, arts and crafts area, play area. Work by the children and the teacher fill the walls and ceiling. The impression is that of a busy building site with everyone intensely involved in their activities.[27]

- *Locate schools within communities, whenever possible within walking distance of the children who will attend them; find sites that allow for provision of clean water and adequate sanitation, and that minimize risks from traffic, crime and other dangers.*

[27] Hart, R, field trips 1998

- *Wherever possible, promote small schools and small classes; make aides and volunteers available to teachers, or consider team teaching approaches.*
- *Avoid design and layout solutions that promote inflexible and authoritarian approaches to learning.*

School grounds as landscapes for play and learning

Most schools, even in urban areas, have some outdoor space, but it is rarely thought of as being significant to school function. Schoolyards often look like military parade grounds, and are used primarily as places to assemble or to 'let off steam'. It is possible, with the collaboration of teachers, children and their parents, to transform a school's outdoor environment to allow for a wider range of activity.

Play, games and sports

accomodating a range of needs

From earliest school years up to adolescence there is a continuum of recreational needs, from the unstructured, spontaneous play of younger children, through child-organized games and pastimes, to more conventional sports. Individual children's needs depend on age, temperament and the mood of the day, and during free time they should be able to choose between structured team sports, spontaneous active play, and quieter pastimes. With ingenuity and careful planning, even small school grounds can support a range of choices without major cost.

In many parts of the world, swings, slides, and other fixed equipment are considered to be basic components of school playgrounds. Such equipment is by no means essential to children's play experience, but in the limited space of urban schoolyards, it can provide a relatively high concentration of physical activity. For more information on the benefits, drawbacks and safety issues of fixed equipment, see p135.

using limited space

sports

Ideally, every schoolyard should contain sufficient space for locally popular sports and games. When space is tight, activities can share the same piece of ground; a sand pit for play, for instance, can double as a long jump; and overlapping ground lines can be drawn to allow for different games. Children should be involved in laying out the games area, since they understand the needs, and which games will conflict with each other. When space constraints make organized sports impossible, it is important to try to find alternative space within the community. Participation in mainstream sports events with other schools is an important experience for older primary school children, and their exclusion is another form of marginalization.

unstructured play

variety

Active play should not be limited to organized sports and games. Younger children especially desire free unstructured play, and like to design their own games and pastimes as they learn to function in groups. Active and imaginative play can be promoted through the provision of props, movable items and simple building materials in even the most minimal schoolyard. Research has shown that children dislike traditional school grounds characterized by asphalt and open, boring space with a lack of shelter and seating. They like grounds that have different levels, trees, shady areas, wild areas, animals, and places in which to climb, hide and explore.[28] Moore and Wong have documented the transformation of a schoolyard in the urban United States from a boring asphalt yard to a lush natural environment containing trees, ponds, gardens, hideaways, and play equipment constructed without cost from logs, rocks and found objects. In spite of the resistance of elected officials, children and school staff collaborated with community members to create a place that was treasured by all. Children's experience in the schoolyard changed from boredom and anti-social behaviour to a new fascination with nature, and with their own capacity to create a place of beauty and hope.[29] Such biodiverse environments also have educational benefits.

Many children, and especially young adolescents with their emphasis on peer relations, need small protected spaces where they can sit and converse. Schoolyards often cater primarily for physical activity, leaving children who do not wish to participate pinned up on the periphery of the site. A simple solution is to allow for niches of different sizes and with different heights of seating for children of all ages. This is easier in a richly planted schoolyard. Larger areas of this kind can also be used as outdoor classrooms. Pupils in any climate can benefit from periodic changes in the learning setting. This might be difficult for lessons requiring many different resources, but it is useful for discussion groups where children can sit informally to work on problems together.

quiet spaces

Schoolyards as sites for learning and models for sustainable development

In urban schools where outdoor space is limited, the emphasis should be on safe and pleasant play space, ideally with some greenery. When schools have more space, far more is possible. Natural and diverse environments best suit many of children's play and leisure needs, and can also become demonstration sites for the basic principles of sustainable development and urban regeneration. A biodiverse school landscape serves not only as a rich microcosm for children to learn a wide range of environmental knowledge and skills, but as a training ground for environmental management.

biodiverse schoolyards

Even if there are no large areas left after allotting the necessary space for organized games and sports, there may be small peripheral locations where vegetation can be planted or simply allowed to grow. The more diverse the vegetation, the more diverse the wildlife it will attract. Children and staff together can be involved in researching and planning plantings. Children can investigate the climatic and soil qualities required for different plants, and map their distribution. With a little help, they should be able to measure the acidity of the soil, grade its quality and identify the plants and trees that could survive on the site.

gardens

There are many ways for children to be actively involved in daily management and monitoring of the school environment. Where space is not an issue, a large garden can be an important learning opportunity and also contribute significantly to food provision. Even in crowded city schoolyards space can be found for a few intensely planted raised beds of herbs and vegetables. A compost area and worm farm can be natural additions to an urban garden, and composting materials can be brought from the community and from children's homes. Rotating tasks can include recycling and composting, and the tending of gardens. Records

[28] Titman, W (1994) *Special Places, Special People: The Hidden Curriculum of Schoolgrounds*, Godalming, Surrey: World Wide Fund for Nature

[29] Moore, R C and Wong, H H (1997) *Natural Learning: The Life History of an Environmental Schoolyard*, Berkeley, California: MIG Communications

environmental care

experimenting with technology

should be kept to monitor food production, plant quality and wildlife. Other ideal features when there is sufficient space would be alternative energy technologies, including a windmill and a solar energy collector. Water can also be collected in tanks, perhaps on a school roof, and energy sources can be monitored by the children as part of their ongoing investigation into sustainable development. Where equipment is available, climate and air pollution should be monitored and records kept. Children can also do school energy audits.

- *Promote the most effective use of available outdoor space at school in order to allow for unstructured play as well as organized sports and games, and quiet interaction as well as physical activity.*
- *Allow vegetation to grow freely in schoolyards, and where there is sufficient space, support gardening and composting, and use schoolyards as places to experiment with alternative technologies such as windmills and solar energy collectors.*
- *Be sure that children are actively involved in the decision making, daily management and monitoring of the school environment.*

Maintenance

involving children and parents

No matter how well a school is designed and built, it will not function smoothly if it is not well managed and maintained. Dilapidated, rundown facilities are demoralizing for both students and teachers. Maintenance costs must be adequately budgeted for. Much of the regular cleaning and maintenance of the school can involve the children. A time set aside for sweeping, yard maintenance, and the kinds of environmental management tasks described above can be a regular part of the daily schedule, and involve even the youngest children. When the school has an active relationship with parents and other community members, many of the larger maintenance and repair tasks, including repainting, can also be done in a participatory way, and can involve the children. A well-kept school can be a resource and a source of pride for the whole community. Allocation of funds for the ongoing upkeep of the school should be decided by the democratically elected school board.

- *Provide adequately in school budgets for the costs of regular maintenance, and encourage participation of children and community members in maintenance tasks.*

ACCESS TO INFORMATION: LIBRARIES AND RESOURCE CENTRES

Many schools in the South lack even the most rudimentary libraries and resources, and municipalities must make this a priority. True education stresses learning rather than teaching, and encourages the learner to take an active role, with teachers in a guiding and supporting role.

Access to information is central to this process. When the 'New Schools' of Colombia made the changes necessary to become more progressive and child-centred, their average annual increase in costs was 10 per cent per school, all of which went towards purchasing good reference resources.[30]

sharing resources with the community

When a community does not have the resources for more than one library, the primary school library can also serve the community. Arrangements may be necessary to ensure that this works well. Community use may have to be restricted to after-school hours, and the collection may have to be expanded to serve a wider range of needs. Materials specifically for the school may need to be set to one side. If a community library is the only information resource available to the school, teachers should be free to borrow enough materials to allow for classroom-based research.

local media as a resource

Books and other printed matter are not the only learning resource. The world has become increasingly dependent on other information technologies, and children should have access to as much as possible of this rapidly expanding domain. If schools can afford video and audio equipment and computers, these resources should be heavily used, not only for their capacity to deliver information but so that children become familiar with them. For the majority of schools with limited funds, access to technologies may depend on the assistance of other groups within the city. The local media can be an especially valuable resource, and authorities should encourage active partnerships between schools and local radio and television. Time on air can be made available to school groups, who can work together with media personnel to produce their own shows. Community radio stations can be based in local schools, and children can play a significant role in gathering and disseminating information that is relevant to the whole community. See also p148.

- *Recognize the importance to active learning of access to information; support investment in books and other learning aids, and ensure that children have access to as wide a range of technologies as possible, not only through direct investment, but through partnerships with the media and other groups in the city.*

TEACHER RESOURCE CENTRES

teachers learning from one another

Strong schools require capable, creative and committed teachers. Too many teachers are expected to take on this challenging work with minimal training, inadequate pay, no regular support and little professional recognition. In order for teachers to sustain their commitment and to continue growing professionally, they must have on-going support. This need not take the form of formal further education. In fact, teachers learn best from other teachers, and they need a time and place for the regular exchange of problems, ideas and materials.[31]

These activities are best carried out at a permanent location which can house materials and resources for teachers – a good solution is a resource centre serving teachers from about 10 to 20 schools. Such a

[30] Hart, 1997, op cit Note 16

[31] Personal communication, Dr Heidi Watts, consultant in continuing education for teachers in India and the United States

centre could contain a master library of resource materials that can be copied or borrowed, and also equipment for the reproduction of locally produced teaching materials. Ideally, this could extend to the level of a 'community press', enabling teachers to reproduce children's research reports or news accounts for distribution to the community. For economic and administrative reasons this centre could be next to one of the primary schools.

A specially trained staff person would be required to maintain the library and resources, schedule meetings, facilitate special training sessions and be available to guide and respond to teacher discussion groups. If funds are not available for a centre, another solution is a rotating series of teacher workshops at each school. Even with a central resource centre, there are benefits to having on-site workshops within each school. Such workshops could encourage the staff of all primary schools to participate in the teacher network, not just those from the more progressive schools. They can also give the staff of the host school a chance to discuss, on-site, how to deal with many of their unique problems, particularly those concerned with the physical environment of the school.

- *Support teacher resource centres, where groups of teachers from a number of schools can discuss their problems, share ideas and make use of equipment and shared materials.*
- *Hire a specially trained person to run this centre, schedule meetings and serve as a regular adviser and resource for all area teachers.*

SECONDARY SCHOOLS

The Convention does not mandate free secondary education, but it does require that it be made available and accessible to all children. Secondary school attendance in the South, however, is still out of reach for the majority: in the least developed countries only 22 per cent of boys and 13 per cent of girls attend.[32]

the benefits of secondary education

There are some far-reaching benefits to broad secondary education. The capacity to think about abstract concepts becomes more highly developed as children enter adolescence. In order for societies to grapple thoughtfully with issues of civil responsibility or political power, it is important that a critical mass of citizens be exposed to the kind of thought and discussion that can best be promoted at secondary level. Although the net gains from primary education are more significant overall, it is important that all societies move progressively towards providing good secondary schooling for greater numbers.

Many of the principles discussed with regard to primary schools also apply to secondary schools. Like primary schools, they should attempt in their management, curricula and physical environments to be relevant to the students and communities they serve. There are, however, some important differences. Secondary schools are likely to draw students from a wider area and as a result be less closely related to a particular community. This may mean less active involvement by parents. On the

32 UNICEF (1998) *The State of the World's Children 1998*, New York: Oxford University Press

other hand, an older student body should, with appropriate support, be capable of taking on a much wider range of responsibility in school management. Adolescents are generally ready to move beyond their communities, and to be more focused on their peers and on preparation for adult life. Secondary schools have the potential to be not only centres for formal learning, but also a physical base for other aspects of adolescent life, and a transitional zone for entering the larger world. Students can be given opportunities to test their growing competence in productive and rewarding ways. Space for sports and informal gatherings, and for a range of support services relevant to this age group, can constructively be housed within schools. Even when a strong secondary school serves as a focus for many facets of adolescent life, it must not be seen as a substitute for adequate space in the community for young people of this age. Many adolescents will not attend the secondary school, and even for those that do, there is a need for space that is outside the domain of adults (see pp128, 137, 145).

school as a 'transitional zone'

School-work connections

Although this discussion may be relevant for many children in primary school as well, it is particularly pertinent for students in secondary schools, for whom combining work and school may be a more appropriate option. There are a number of ways in which schools can act as a bridge to the world of work. One critical role is providing support for children who are already working. Combining work and school is a tremendous challenge, and the school can help children to meet it more successfully. Familiarity with the demands of a child's working life can make school personnel more responsive to scheduling and other problems that a working child faces. Teachers are in a good position to identify children at risk of dropping out of school because of work, or who are moving into harmful work. The school's active involvement, in cooperation perhaps with a local children's rights committee may also help to ensure better conditions and scheduling for children at work. When schools include large numbers of working children, they might consider hiring a staff person to act as liaison between children's workplaces, their families and the school. (See also p203).

providing support

links with employers

identifying children at risk

Technical and vocational training courses and programmes have been a common way of introducing students to employment skills. But training is too often based on capital-intensive, modern production processes that may have little relevance to local employment.[33] Improvement in efforts to provide practical employment-enhancing educational opportunities for young people is essential to educational reform. Supervised apprenticeship programmes through the school system can help to ensure training that is more relevant to the local economy. Constructive partnerships between the school system and employers can allow for visits to a wide range of jobs for students. This can shatter stereotypes and expose young people to new possibilities. It may also help to ensure that those children who must earn are engaged in protected work experience that will most benefit them in the future.

training programmes

[33] Boyden et al 1998, op cit Note 3

Non-formal alternatives may provide the most practical solutions in some situations, perhaps on a temporary basis. Local authorities should support such solutions, and ensure that a transition to the formal system is possible. In Lahore, Pakistan, a shopkeeper holds classes for neighbourhood children. UNICEF 1992, John Isaac

- *Support the student body of secondary schools to take on a wide range of responsibility in the management of their schools.*
- *Within secondary schools, when possible, make space available for sports and informal gatherings outside of school hours, and for a range of support services relevant to this age group.*
- *Encourage schools to monitor the situations of their working students and to establish connections between schools and employers to facilitate scheduling and ease the burden on children.*
- *Allow children to visit a range of employment opportunities during their school years so that they can plan in an informed way for their futures.*
- *Support the development of high quality technical and vocational training programmes and apprenticeship programmes relevant to local employment opportunities.*

NON-FORMAL EDUCATION

Efforts should always be made to adapt the formal school system to children's needs and to ensure equal access; but there are inevitably situations in which non-formal approaches may provide a better solution, sometimes on a temporary basis. Regular schools may be unable to provide the support and flexibility that some working children need. Even when schools can be flexible in terms of scheduling, children who have been working for years, or who have dropped out for other reasons, may need help making a transition back into the formal system. School may be completely alien to the experience of some families, and parents may have little interest in making the commitment to send their children to school. Some children, bored and frustrated by regular school, or perhaps traumatized by bullying or violent disciplinary methods, may be unwilling to attend. In these situations and many others, non-formal programmes can provide an important alternative.

Because they are not hampered by the constraints and expectations of the formal system, some of these programmes have been able to develop innovative and creative ways of reaching children and addressing their right to an education. An ingenious approach that is not remotely 'school-like' was developed in Brazil. In São Paulo, in settlements which house some of the city's poorest and most excluded inhabitants, there are permanent circuses, established some years ago by the local ministry of childhood. Local children, many of whom do not attend school, are drawn to the tents, eager to be a part of this venture. Learning circus skills requires close attention and serious discipline. Nor is it only performance that these children learn. Performers need costumes and props; audiences need refreshments. A number of studios or workshops have been set up around the tents, and here children acquire the wide range of skills necessary to produce a circus; at the same time they learn responsibility, commitment, teamwork and attention to detail – skills that will stand them in good stead in the rest of their lives. At any one time this project is able to involve thousands of children, and many of them have gone on to become instructors.[34]

São Paulo circus-schools

Although such creative efforts (not all of them so elaborate) are frequently the work of NGOs and community organizations, local authorities have a significant role in providing support and ensuring coordination between non-formal efforts and the formal system. In the case of the circus, for instance, authorities could make training and support available to instructors to ensure that academic skills are also learned; they can ensure that formal schools are a real option for children who elect to move on into them, and that the transition is smooth. They can also find ways to ensure that the training provided by the circus is made relevant to other local employment opportunities.

supporting non-formal alternatives

In Chapters 10 and 11 we will discuss some alternative programmes that have met the needs of working children and children on the street, in some cases making it possible for them to successfully re-enter regular schools (see pp210, 220).

- *Support non-formal alternatives for schooling in situations where the formal system is unworkable.*
- *Establish connections between non-formal programmes and the formal system, to ensure that programmes have access to the resources of regular schools, to work towards the accreditation of non-formal programmes, and to facilitate children's transition to the formal system where this is desired.*
- *Encourage regular schools and teachers to learn from the innovations of non-formal programmes.*

[34] Personal communication, Nilda Cosco, IPA Argentina, 1998

Unsuitable and hazardous work has a direct impact on children's health and development, but also harms them indirectly by depriving them of positive opportunities for growth and learning. Responses must take into account not only their immediate protection, but also the larger issues that continue to make their work a necessity. This child carries bricks in Butawal, Nepal. UNICEF 1993, Shehzad Noorani

10 Working Children

We live in a world where, with few exceptions, the rich become richer while the poor struggle for survival. Within the global market economy, ownership and control of resources are increasingly transferred to those who are already rich, while the costs, both economic, social and environmental, are disproportionately borne by the poor and disenfranchised. One of the manifestations of this inequitable system is the number of working children who contribute to both local and global economies at a significant cost to themselves and their futures.

The issue of children's work is causing growing international concern. There are determined efforts to respond to the issue by setting high international goals and standards, while at the same time acknowledging the need for progressive solutions. These efforts are especially valuable for their insistence that child labour is not impervious to committed action. But there is a limit to the capacity of international meetings, international agencies, and even national governments, to develop detailed plans of action for responding to the rights of working children. Although children's work is an expression of large economic forces and political trends, it actually occurs in the context of the most local realities. Local governments are on the front line here, as on so many issues.

Practical responses can only be developed at the local level, weighing both the extent of the problem and the options and resources available within a given city.

The Convention contains a number of provisions pertaining to children's work, and which together provide a framework for policy and action. Most explicitly, the Convention requires that children be protected from all exploitative and hazardous work, and from work that interferes with their education and development. In order to ensure this protection, State Parties are required to set minimum ages for employment, and to regulate working conditions (Article 32). But this provision cannot be read in isolation. The Convention also recognizes the right of children to the means for survival (Article 6). The uncomfortable reality is that children's work is often the only apparent avenue to their survival and that of their families. In the context of poverty, and in the absence of welfare systems that guarantee a livelihood for children and their families, work remains the most viable option for many children and adolescents. Responses to this cannot deal only with their immediate protection, but must also tackle the problems that make their work a necessity. Protective legislation can only be successful in the context of practical, sustainable alternatives for children and their families. The Convention calls for authorities to support parents, when necessary, in their efforts to ensure their children's optimal development and adequate standard of living (Articles 18, 27). It also guarantees access to free, relevant, high quality education, a critical element in resolving the issue of child work (Articles 28, 29).

the broad implications of the Convention for children's work

These provisions, like many others in the Convention, are understood to be subject to the availability of resources, and hence to progressive realization.[1] Until these goals can be fully implemented, some children and adolescents will continue to work out of necessity, and cannot be ignored. While governments progress towards eradicating inappropriate child labour, they must continue to support those children who are presently working, listen to their concerns and ensure their access to education, a high standard of health, rest and leisure, and acceptable working conditions (Articles 12, 24, 28, 31, 32). By drawing on a range of constructive examples, this chapter will discuss how local government can respond to the complex web of concerns raised by their obligations towards working children.

THE IMPLICATIONS OF WORK FOR CHILDREN'S DEVELOPMENT

Work has always been an important avenue of learning and socialization. Children have a powerful desire for competence, and this is expressed and satisfied through work as well as play. In the best of all worlds, work for children would be a choice and a positive opportunity, one element in a balanced life. Instead, it defines and limits the lives of many poor children. Under the pressures of poverty, the burden of children's work can quickly outweigh the benefits. It is important not to define as unacceptable those activities that are central to a child's learning and identity as a responsible human being. But it is also important that socialization not be used to

[1] Himes, J R (1995) *Implementing the Convention on the Rights of the Child: Resource Mobilization in Low-income Countries*, The Hague: Martinus Nijhoff/UNICEF

justify work that is in fact grindingly repetitious, demanding, harmful or limiting to a child's potential.

children's vulnerability

For millions of poor children around the world, work takes a heavy toll physically, emotionally and intellectually, and the younger they are, the heavier the toll. Children are subject to all the occupational hazards and diseases faced by adults, but they are frequently more vulnerable because of their growing bodies, their lower threshold for toxics, and their lesser ability to respond effectively to hazards such as rapidly moving machinery. When children grow up in serious poverty, they are likely to be poorly nourished and in precarious health to begin with, and the demands of work create an additional health burden. Children working long hours suffer from excessive fatigue, and may have inadequate time for meals. Their rundown state can make them especially susceptible to infectious disease, and their work conditions may expose them to added risk of infection. Stunted growth is common among working children. In many cases, injury results from fatigue and an inability to concentrate. Children need more rest than adults, and long working hours can result in a lack of attention or stamina that can be lethal in certain circumstances.

hazardous conditions

In some occupations, children are exposed for long hours every day to toxic fumes or industrial waste. Others do work that strains and damages their eyesight. Children frequently perform work that is too demanding for their size and strength. This, combined with the effects of repetitive actions, can result in musculo-skeletal damage that is permanently distorting. Some work situations expose children to unprotected machinery, the risk of explosions and industrial accidents. An ILO survey in the Philippines found that more than 60 per cent of working children were exposed to hazardous conditions in their work. Of these, 40 per cent experienced serious injury or illness.[2]

Many children endure less visible forms of exploitation. Some of the grimmest hazards are those faced by children who are exploited for sex. In Mumbai, India, 80 per cent of young prostitutes were found to have sexually transmitted diseases, and 60 per cent had AIDS.[3] Sexual exploitation also has significant emotional ramifications, and girls (and boys) who have been abused in this way are often psychologically scarred by the experience. Young domestic workers, a large and virtually hidden population, again mostly girls, are also both physically and emotionally at risk. They work long exhausting hours in isolation, and are often victims of beatings, verbal abuse and sexual molestation.[4] Even girls working in their own homes can be subjected to responsibilities too burdensome for their strength and emotional maturity.

loss of opportunity

Unsuitable and hazardous work has many direct effects on developing children, but it also harms them indirectly by depriving them of positive experiences. Time spent working is time taken away from the education, play and rest necessary to their optimal development. When children's work prevents them from making use of opportunities for learning and growth, it reduces their chances in life and contributes to the perpetuation of increasing poverty from one generation to the next.

It has been customary in discussions of children's work to classify as unacceptable child labour, any work undertaken by a person under 18 which is exploitative, hazardous or detrimental to development. We will also use the term in this way, but with the understanding that the line

[2] ILO (1996) *Child Labour: Targeting the Intolerable*, Geneva: International Labour Office
[3] Gilada, I S (1997) 'Child Prostitution: a Blot on Humanity', Indian Health Organization
[4] Blanc, C S and contributors (1994) *Urban Children in Distress: Global Predicaments and Innovative Strategies*, Florence, Italy: UNICEF International Child Development Centre and London: Gordon and Breach

between unacceptable child labour and more benign child work is by no means always clear. Work that is intolerable for a six year-old may be quite manageable for someone who is 16, but somewhere between those ages the distinction will be less clear. Sitting at a loom for 12 hours a day is unacceptable for a child of any age, but the same activity for two hours, balanced by schooling, rest and play, could be an invaluable way to learn a skill. The implications of most work changes with the circumstances – with the child's age and maturity, the demands of school, the conditions at the workplace, the climate, the child's health, the cultural setting, the family circumstances.

variables to weigh

The new ILO Convention and Recommendation, likely to be adopted in 1999, focuses on the most intolerable forms of child labour and will provide helpful guidance in determining the areas of work most urgent to address.[5] Forced and bonded labour and sexual exploitation cannot be considered acceptable under any terms, and should be eliminated in the shortest possible time. Detrimental work by very young children and particularly vulnerable groups, especially young girls, is also increasingly viewed as intolerable in most international circles.[6] But most children will continue to work in areas not addressed by this Convention, and it is important to decide what level of support, attention and protection should be made available in these situations. The age issue must be addressed, and efforts should be especially focused on the youngest children. The ILO Convention No.138 suggests a minimum age for employment of 15, and this is an important goal to work towards. Most countries have established age limits for work of either 12 or 14. Interventions for children below these legal age limits should be directed through the family wherever possible, and must respond to children's right to an education. For older children and adolescents it makes sense, within the context of the local culture, to focus on the acquisition of work skills and the opportunity for protected employment.

intolerable forms of labour

THE CHALLENGES FACING LOCAL AUTHORITIES AND THEIR PARTNERS

In order to respond to all the requirements of the Convention, local authorities must work towards three simultaneous goals:

three simultaneous goals

- removing from work the youngest children and those in the most hazardous and developmentally damaging situations, while at the same time ensuring that they and their families are not thereby forced into more precarious situations;
- preventing the influx of children into inappropriate work through broad-based efforts to eradicate poverty, support family stability, and create relevant, accessible and affordable education for children;
- supporting those children who, for the present must continue to work by listening to their concerns, improving their work conditions, and ensuring their optimal development.

[5] UNICEF (1997) 'Social Mobilization and Child Labour', Background paper for International Conference on Child Labour, Oslo, 27–30 October 1997
[6] ILO 1996, op cit Note 2

In developing a plan of action, local authorities face significant challenges – chief among them their own limited resources, the limits inherent in national legislation, and the range of often conflicting perspectives on the appropriateness of work for children. But they are also best placed to establish processes that are inclusive and comprehensive. The implications of a progressive approach to eliminating child labour can only be established in the local context. Authorities must develop and implement plans of action that are linked to the social, cultural and economic realities of their own cities. While there can be no single blueprint for action, the following guidelines, broadly based on the Convention's requirements, can be helpful in establishing a general direction.

CREATING A FRAMEWORK FOR ACTION

Existing legislation in many countries requires government agents to monitor the situation of working children, and to remove from work children below the legal age. These national laws, along with laws establishing ages for compulsory school attendance, are often the only frame of reference that local authorities turn to in determining their policies towards working children. Such legislation is an important way of setting national goals, but it is an inadequate framework for effective and comprehensive local approaches to the issue of child labour. It may actually interfere with the capacity of local authorities to respond flexibly and progressively to the concerns of local children and their families. The prohibition of child labour, as Fyfe points out, can paradoxically make it harder to protect working children, since if work is illegal, little can be done to improve it.[7]

Authorities seldom have the resources for adequate enforcement. Informal enterprises and well-hidden family work are particularly inaccessible to control. When large numbers of children are working, enforcement becomes unrealistic and authorities may turn a blind eye. This laissez-faire approach may be reinforced by a recognition of the importance of child work to family survival and to the interests of employers. When laws are enforced, on the other hand, children may be removed from work without adequate attention to the realities of their lives, which can cause considerable harm to both families and children, destroying a precarious economic equilibrium, or pushing children into more hidden and damaging work.

the dangers of enforcement

National laws clearly have their place; they establish important goals, they help to ensure that schooling is made available, and they may be especially useful as a tool of last resort for dealing with employers or families who are unwilling to remove children from damaging and exploitative work. But they must be one among a number of tools, part of a more comprehensive municipal strategy that weighs local realities in order to address this issue in all of its complexity. Putting an end to harmful child labour means an intensive investment of resources not only into inspection and enforcement, but also into education and the permanent improvement of the lives of the poorest and most excluded families and groups. But few municipalities in poor countries have the capacity for a truly comprehensive response to their obligations (see Chapter 13).

[7] Fyfe, A (1989) *Child Labour*, Cambridge, UK:Blackwell/ Cambridge MA, USA:Polity Press

Instead, they must make difficult choices in allocating limited resources, and this inevitably means compromise. To focus on child labour violations that are most visible and disturbing could mean ignoring less visible but no less harmful practices. To invest heavily in inspection and enforcement may mean that less is available for education. To respond to the short term rights of working children for support and protection could mean fewer resources to put towards long term strategies for poverty reduction. And yet all of these are legitimate and necessary responses to the rights of children and their families. To reconcile the various requirements of the Convention demands a balanced approach with action on all fronts, and calls for the investment not only of budgetary resources, but of all the human and organizational resources that can be mobilized.

finding a balance

Mobilizing broad-based social support

When children's work is common, it can easily become taken for granted, and abuses can more easily flourish. Because the situation is deeply rooted in the local economy, it is likely to be resistant to regulation, and top-down approaches are seldom effective. The assumption is often that nothing can be done. The whole of society is complicit in this – from parents who depend on their children's contribution and employers who profit from the low-cost labour, to the general public which benefits from low prices and tacitly accepts the disparities that underlie poverty and deprivation. Poverty and its implications are often tolerated not so much out of cruelty as out of ignorance and fear, and these can be effectively addressed.

Broad social consensus is essential to real change. Without it, interventions are unlikely to be understood and supported. Sometimes a change in awareness is necessary even among those closest to the children. When a group of mothers in Turkey was invited to visit their children at their places of work, most of them afterwards withdrew their children.[8] The support of local government is essential in building a broad base of awareness and cooperation. The Convention is a valuable framework for helping to establishing such a social movement. But in order to be truly useful, its relevance at the local level must be debated and developed. The dialogues that the Convention can generate are likely to result in greater awareness and in changed attitudes towards children, and these are the best guarantee that exploitation and damaging work will be recognized and challenged by civil society. The breadth of the Convention ensures attention to the whole range of issues affecting working children and to the many ways their rights can be violated by the work they do.

Public awareness can be raised through the schools, through parent education and through targeted media campaigns. Research into child work involving the participation of community members can itself be a useful form of mobilization (see p196). One-time public events can also be useful. The head of the local government in Muktagacha, Bangladesh, used a carefully planned festival on National Children's Day to build social support for working children in the town. For three months his staff coordinated the efforts of volunteers, schoolteachers and children's organizations in identifying working children, and

mobilizing support in Bangladesh

8 ILO 1996, op cit Note 2

helping them fill out registration forms with information about their families, work histories and schooling. Some children were fearful that their employers would fire them if they took part. But because the event was a festival for all working children, it became difficult for employers to object.

On the festival day, children were organized into occupational groups and asked to descibe their working lives. Employers, police and local political leaders were excluded from these sessions so that the children did not feel intimidated. Journalists were invited, but asked not to identify individual children. On the basis of the information collected, authorities were able to publicize the conditions of working children and start developing a long term strategy, as well as taking some immediate safety measures such as the provision of eyeglasses for welding and gloves for battery-making work with acids.[9]

- *Find effective ways to raise public awareness on the rights of children, and specifically on their right to be protected from harmful and exploitative work.*
- *Encourage public dialogue on the implications of children's rights for local conditions and local assumptions about child work.*
- *Involve the media in mobilizing public awareness.*
- *Support public events and campaigns to broaden peoples' understanding of the situation of working children.*

Establishing working partnerships

building networks of support

In order to develop a workable, comprehensive and coordinated strategy, it is essential that local authorities enlist the practical assistance of all groups and stakeholders that have a contribution to make. Local government is well-placed to serve as the convener of different groups and to build coordinated networks. These should include NGOs, employers, trade unions, religious organizations, schools, health officials, police, labour inspectors, and most of all children themselves and their parents. These kinds of partnerships are critical not only in establishing a strategy, but also in planning and implementing specific programmes and interventions.

a collaborative effort in Brazil

The experience of Montes Altos in Minas Gerais, Brazil is an excellent example of a collaborative intervention. With the initiative of a strong woman, the local secretary of education, and through the joint decision of coffee farmers, unions, community organizations and municipal government, children were removed from their traditional coffee-picking jobs. The municipality provided classrooms, and parents agreed to send their children to school. Knowing that the children were well-kept and fed at school, parents actually worked more effectively and produced more than they had formerly with their children's help. The children received schooling and food, the parents earned more money, farmers had a more efficient harvest, and support for the mayor was strengthened.[10]

Children's work is a contentious issue, and the perspectives of various stakeholders are likely to differ considerably. Officials, labour

[9] Personal communication, Muktagacha planning department, 1998

[10] Personal communication, Ladislau Dowbor, 1998

unions, employers, parents and children may have quite different goals and priorities. Although discussion and negotiation between groups with different perspectives may be difficult, it is essential to the development of realistic solutions. Reconciling divergent perspectives can generate creative new responses. In order to work effectively for change, mutual understanding and respect are critical.

reconciling different perspectives

In Chapter 14 we describe the kinds of bodies that can work collaboratively with local government to advocate and monitor the achievement of children's rights (see p260). Such coordinating councils, established as the broadest possible group for addressing the concerns of children, can play an important role in working towards consensus on practical local solutions for working children. This will inevitably involve discussion of thorny issues of inconsistency between national laws, the Convention and the reality of children's lives in the city. Open debate will reveal the often impossible dilemmas that municipal governments have to face, and will allow the responsibility for solutions to be more broadly shared. It is important that the council not become narrowly focused on the legal and the pressworthy issues of children's work but keep the broad interests of children at the core of its dialogues.

developing a plan

The council should advise local government in assessing the situation of local working children and in developing a comprehensive plan. They need to bring local regulations into compliance with national legislation, to raise general awareness of the rights of working children, to monitor violations of working children's rights, and to evaluate progress. Cooperation with local school systems is important, for schools are well-placed to help assess needs and evaluate the progress of specific interventions. Another important function for the council is to advocate for the concerns of working children at higher levels of government.

For discussion of involving children in working partnerships, see p202.

- *Establish a broad coalition of partners who can provide practical assistance in developing and implementing a comprehensive local strategy for action.*
- *Encourage discussion and negotiation between groups with different perspectives to ensure the development of inclusive and realistic solutions.*

Assessing and evaluating the situation of children at risk

In order to respond appropriately, local authorities and their partners must collect adequate information for assessing the situation of working children. It is not sufficient to collect data only on children who are wage earners. Vast numbers of children, most of them girls, work without pay in their homes and the homes of others, and must also be taken seriously. Nor is it sufficient simply to list the numbers of working children. There must be information about working conditions, how these conditions affect children's health and development, what is currently being done to improve their situations, how these efforts can be strengthened, and what needs and rights are not being met. A useful assessment tool, points out Vesna Bosnjak (UNICEF, Brazil), is to arrange on a continuum the various working situations of children in a given community or city, from beneficial activities that promote learning and self-confidence, to the most harmful and exploitative situations.[11] This can be helpful in identifying those children who need priority attention.

Data on working children can be difficult to collect, given the suspicion that both children, parents and employers may have towards authorities, and given also the range of opinion on what constitutes inappropriate work.[12] Reasonable results can only be achieved through highly cooperative efforts involving working children's NGOs and all relevant government departments, as well as children and their families. In the interests of consensus it is also a good idea to invite the press to be a partner in the cause. Significant progress has been made in using household surveys as a source of information about working children and their families.[13] UNICEF and ILO together have developed the Rapid Assessment Process, an approach to investigating the dynamics and impact of child work within a given community that makes use of surveys, interviews, focus groups, mapping and observation. It includes interviews with local authorities, representatives from various city agencies, business people, community leaders, street educators as well as families and children.[14]

A number of cities in the Philippines have found that participatory action research involving a broad spectrum of the community can do a great deal to galvanize interest in and action for working children.[15] In Olongapo, it led to the formation of the city working committee on street children.[16] Children's perspectives on their own situation can be most useful in data collection. The recent Rädda Barnen survey of working children in the Philippines, Ethiopia, Senegal, Bangladesh, Peru, EL Salvador, Guatemala and Nicaragua provided useful insights that could not have come from anyone but the children themselves.[17] It is essential in collecting information from or with children, to be aware of the real fears they often feel towards their employers; they may be reluctant to disclose information, and this should be respected. As in any attempt to gather information from or with children, there are some important ethical and practical considerations which will be considered in more detail on p255.

- *Ensure that there is an adequate body of information, not only on the numbers of working children, but on their working conditions and on the range of existing responses to their rights and needs.*
- *Support participatory data collection methods, drawing in particular on the perspectives of working children themselves.*

MAKING CONSTRUCTIVE USE OF LAWS AND REGULATIONS

Because of inadequate resources for inspection and the lack of political will, national laws prohibiting child work frequently go unenforced. When an official response does occur, it can be insensitive, forcing

[11] Bosnjak, V (1998) 'Child Labour: The Ten Commandments, UNICEF, Brazil
[12] Black, M (1993) 'Street Children and Working Children', *Innocenti Global Seminar Summary Report*, UNICEF International Child Development Centre
[13] ILO (1996) *Child Labour Surveys: Results of Methodological Experiments in Four Countries 1992–93*, Geneva: International Labour Office
[14] UNICEF1997, op cit Note 5. For more information, authorities should contact the UNICEF office in their country
[15] Rialp, V (1993) *Children and Hazardous Work in the Philippines*, Geneva: ILO
[16] Porio, E, L Moselina, Swift, A (1994) 'Philippines: urban communities and their fight for survival' in Blanc, C S (ed) *Urban Children in Distress: Global Predicaments and Innovative Strategies*, Florence, Italy: International Child Development Centre of Unicef & London: Gordon and Breach
[17] Woodhead, M (1998) *Children's Perspectives on their Working Lives: a Participatory Study in Bangladesh, Ethiopia, the Philippines, Guatemala, Nicaragua and El Salvador*, Stockholm: Radda Barnen

children out of existing jobs and into worse situations. The move by the United States government in 1992 to prohibit the importation of garments produced by child workers in Bangladesh, for example, led garment manufacturers to fire 50,000 children, mostly girls, most of whom moved into domestic work and other more hazardous forms of employment such as stone crushing and prostitution.[18]

Expanding the concept of enforcement

a progressive approach to compliance

Given the proven limitations of inspection and enforcement, a major challenge for local authorities is to persuade employers to become partners rather than adversaries in the struggle for improved conditions. Under this expanded definition of enforcement, specially trained inspectors would function not only to monitor violations, but would offer employers advice and support in moving towards compliance, as well as serving as a resource for children and their families. Rather than removing children from work and upsetting an often fragile equilibrium, a progressive approach can be taken which focuses first on improving working conditions, and then on creating better alternatives for children and their families. Programmes can be developed, for instance, which initially allow the continued employment of children in return for fewer hours, better physical conditions, and opportunities for play and recreation. Provision for health care and relevant education can be arranged in collaboration with employers, NGOs and the government agencies involved. Employers can move gradually towards phasing children out of work in ways that support their future opportunities and the stability of their families. The adoption of voluntary codes of conduct, and of social labelling to inform consumers about the conditions under which a product was made, can increase the incentive to hire adult workers and improve conditions for children.[19]

an example from Pakistan

A progressive approach was initiated in Sialkot, Pakistan, where up to 8,000 children were reported to be working in sporting goods factories. Sialkot's factory owners, in collaboration with human rights organizations and sporting goods companies, worked out a plan to move children off the factory floors over an 18 month period, to hire their parents and older siblings in their place, and to provide new schools and social programmes to broaden opportunities for the city's young people.[20] Follow-up investigations are demonstrating the importance of ongoing attention after the initial statement of good intentions. Reporters visiting Sialkot a year and a half later found that adults have taken the place of children on the factory floors. But the outcome has been mixed. The schools that were promised have yet to materialize, many children are bored and restless, and some would prefer still to be working. Local activists feel that the manufacturers were only interested in improving their international image. It is essential that continued pressure be brought to bear.[21]

Enforcement has generally been seen as a response that can reasonably be targeted only at the formal sector. Although children employed in this sector (a small minority of all working children) have the advantage of being relatively accessible to view and to influence by local government, there are ways to ensure that this oversight is available to

[18] Stalker, P (1996) 'Child Labour in Bangladesh: A Summary of Recent Investigations, UNICEF
[19] UNICEF 1997, op cit Note 5
[20] Islam, S (1997) 'Carrots, not Sticks', *Far Eastern Economic Review*, March 27
[21] http://news.bbc.co.uk/hi/english/world/s/w_asia/newsis_78000/78953.stm, April 1998

children in other areas as well. The willingness of employers in the formal sector, for instance, to adopt voluntary codes of conduct can have a ripple effect on their dealings with sub-contractors in the informal market.

reaching the informal sector

Broad awareness of the issues can result in a growing level of social pressure on informal employers to raise their standards. Employers will often find that it is in their own best interests to improve the situation of the children who work for them. They may fear that children who have received some education will become challenging troublemakers; but if employers themselves are involved in this initiative, children's improved self confidence and skill is likely to work in their favour.

registering compaints

An important aspect of the effective enforcement of legislation lies in ensuring that children and their parents are aware of their legal rights and are easily and confidentially able to register their concerns and complaints. Local authorities can provide suitable sites for registering complaints within community offices.

- *Train inspectors not only to monitor violations, but to offer employers advice and support in moving progressively towards compliance.*
- *Negotiate for improved working conditions, shorter hours, access to schooling, health care and recreation for working children.*
- *Promote adherence to voluntary codes of conduct and social labelling.*
- *Use all avenues possible to expand enforcement and oversight within the informal sector.*
- *Provide permanent and easily accessible sites where parents and children can register complaints about work conditions.*

Targeting the intolerable situations

determining priorities

Not all situations lend themselves to gradual improvement. When children are exposed to hazardous work, authorities are responsible to protect them. Establishing a continuum of local work conditions, as described above, can be a useful tool in helping to identify those children and situations most in need of intervention. The youngest children and the most damaging work conditions should always be the priority. Any such intervention must take into account the larger context of these children's lives, and must ensure that alternatives are made available for them, and where necessary, their families.

An excellent example of such a comprehensive municipal strategy is the 1995 campaign in Kathmandu, Nepal, launched by the NGO Child Workers In Nepal (CWIN) to address the plight of 200 boys working as 'tempo' taxi conductors. An initial survey revealed that 90 per cent of the boys were migrants, over half of them illiterate. 65 per cent were under the legal working age of 14, an asset for employers because they could be hired for little pay. Children worked from 11 to 15 hours a day, and all were found to have significant exhaust-related health problems from perching over the exhaust pipes of these highly polluting vehicles.

Building on this research, CWIN, in collaboration with local government, police and traffic officers, and the trade union of tempo workers, developed an awareness programme leading up to National Children's Day. Drivers were informed that an effort was under way, children were invited to workshops to introduce them to alternative living situations and sources of employment, and the public was made aware of the initiative. The 'rescue' operation took two days. A few drivers resisted, but most went along with what had become an unstoppable movement, thanks to collaboration with the government and with the press. About 50 tempo conductors, some as young as eight years of age, were brought to a transitional home run by CWIN, where they stayed while their options were discussed. Because most of them had families, attempts were first made to understand the cause of their separation and to reunite them. Those who could not return home had the choice of going to a children's home or being sponsored at a boarding school. For those aged 14 to 16 the focus was on finding another job that allowed for recreation, at least two hours of education each day, and minimum wage. Children were allowed to stay in the transit home of CWIN for a period of about 3 months and if necessary, for up to a year. Because this process is still under way, it is difficult to know how many children have been successfully reunited with their families. Generally, CWIN has a success rate of about 80 per cent with such rehabilitation. The results of this project are being communicated to all relevant municipal offices through regular memos. CWIN hopes to assist the remaining tempo conductors and to address systematically each of the other hazardous occupations in the city.[22]

a 'rescue operation' in Nepal

Not all children in unacceptable forms of work are accessible to action. Children in some of the most damaging and exploitative work, such as prostitution or drug trafficking, are perhaps the most difficult to reach. In some cases children on the streets may be pulled into illicit work not only out of the need for survival, but in response to various enticements. In the case of many young prostitutes, their families may actually be complicit in the arrangement, having accepted payment up front, or expecting a share of the earnings.

prostitution and drug trading

Because so much prostitution and drug trading is controlled by organized crime rings which reach beyond local areas, getting to the roots of the problem must involve national and international efforts. Local strategies must focus on guaranteeing children's health and safety. Enforcement is not sufficient, for that can drive illicit activity further underground, making children less accessible. It is critical to be able to reach these children regularly to provide medical services, and to engage in the kind of one-to-one dialogue which offers the greatest hope of pulling them out of what may be highly lucrative activities. Some successful approaches for responding to the needs of these children will be discussed in the chapter on street children (p222).

Longer term local strategies for eradicating the problem are also critical. Efforts to raise public consciousness can be highly effective in tackling child prostitution. A good example comes from Pagsanjan, a tourist town in the Philippines, where a council for child protection, involving local government officials, concerned local residents, church groups and children's groups, adopted a variety of creative methods to educate the public about the tourist sex trade and its implications for their children. Schoolteachers were trained to detect children at risk and to warn their classes about the dangers of paedophiles. Health professionals volunteered time to educate children about the dangers of AIDS. Children themselves were involved in theatre activities and rallies against the exploitation of children. The council also organized exhibits of photographs taken for

tackling the tourist sex trade

22 Personal communication, CWIN information officer, 1998

western magazines showing Filipino children involved in sexual acts with Caucasian men. This shocked parents who had not questioned the intentions of their children's foreign 'friends'. The community became more aware of its problem and the entire relationship with tourists changed. The estimated number of child prostitutes fell from about 3,000 children in the mid 1980's to about 300 children by 1993.[23]

- *Determine, within the spectrum of local realities, which children most urgently need intervention.*
- *Ensure that children are removed from hazardous conditions with careful attention to alternatives for them, and where necessary, their families.*
- *Use broad public awareness as a tool in combating intolerable forms of employment, especially in such cases as prostitution where official action may drive it underground.*

FINDING PRACTICAL ALTERNATIVES FOR CHILDREN AND THEIR FAMILIES

Any local agenda for responding to children's labour must include as a primary goal the provision of practical alternatives for children and their families. Families must be able to support themselves without relying on their children's unacceptable work, and children must have access to a relevant education. Both children and families must be involved in decisions that affect them.

Involving and supporting families

Most children work because of the poverty of their families. Unless the perceptions and economic realities of families are taken into account, solutions cannot be realistic or sustainable.[24] A range of ways must be found to reduce family dependence on children's work, especially through improved opportunities for adult employment. Making credit available can also be a significant intervention, especially in areas where family debt is paid through children's bonded labour.[25] In Chapter 3, we discussed the measures that local authorities can take to support the economic viability of families. Such supports must be made available not only to those with working children, but to all poor families in order to prevent their children from entering the workforce.

Although child work is most frequently a response to the need for survival, it is not always perceived as a last resort by urban parents. Sometimes work is seen as a more practical measure than schooling, which may prepare children only for scarce jobs in the formal sector. Especially when available schooling is poor in quality, child work may be regarded as the more realistic preparation for life. Parents can also perceive it as a way of keeping children from delinquency. A survey in Delhi found that only 4.6 per cent of parents interviewed felt that child labour should be eliminated. Instead, they wanted improved working conditions and wages.[26]

[23] Rialp, 1993, op cit Note 15
[24] UNICEF 1997, op cit Note 5; and UNICEF (1997) *Strategies for Eliminating Child Labour: Prevention, Removal and Rehabilitation* Background papers for International Conference on Child Labour, Oslo, 27–30 October 1997
[25] Badiwala, M (1998) 'Child Labour in India: Causes, Governmental Policies and the Role of Education', http://www.geocities.com/College Park/Library/9175/inquiry1.htm
[26] UNICEF (1990) *The Invisible Child: A Look at the Urban Child in Delhi,* Delhi: UNICEF Middle North India Office

Many children consider paid work to be the most effective avenue to independence and respectability. Official responses must take children's desire for self-determination into account in their attempts to realize their best interests. A boy sells newspapers in the city of Loja, Ecuador. UNICEF, Jeremy Horner

Aside from general support for families and communities, more focused interventions may also be necessary. Under ideal circumstances, parents or their surrogates should determine what is beneficial for their children, along with the children themselves. But it is important to bear in mind the injustice and difficulty of expecting desperately poor parents to protect their children from the realities of earning. Parents in poverty are often forced into decisions against their better judgement or without adequate knowledge of the implications or of the available alternatives. When interventions on behalf of working children are necessary, they should to the maximum degree possible be planned and implemented together with family. Ideally, interventions should give children and their families greater control over their lives, rather than reducing the control they already have. Family involvement contributes to a better understanding and analysis of the problem, and also gives parents and other caregivers the opportunity of becoming better informed. Solutions developed collaboratively are more likely to gain the understanding and cooperation of parents, and hence to be lasting.

There has been regrettably little documentation of ways of supporting parents in this endeavour. A notable rural exception is a demonstration project by Action Aid in Nepal, which carried out participatory action research on the daily spatial and temporal patterns of children's work. With their highly visual data, they were able to work together to find alternatives that would allow children the time for schooling.[27] Another family-centred response is the Projecto Compartir in Tegucigalpa, Honduras, a community-based intervention for children working in the streets who still have contact with their families. Through job training, family counselling and community organization, the project provides assistance for families before their children end up on the streets.[28]

[27] Johnson, V, Hill, Ivan-Smith, E (1995) *Listening to Smaller Voices: Children in an Environment of Change*, Chard, Somerset UK: Actionaid

[28] de la Barra, X (1998) 'Poverty: the Main Cause of Ill Health in Urban Children', *Health, Education and Behaviour*, 25(1): 45–49

family assistance

Except in hazardous situations requiring urgent action, children should never be removed from their jobs unless there has been discussion with both them and their parents. When the family's survival or stability is at stake, transitional programmes should offer immediate alternatives which can generate at least as much income for the family as the child was previously bringing in. Cash assistance to keep children in school is another important support. For instance, the Support to Families programme in Santos and other cities in Brazil, having identified the families of children at risk, offers financial assistance in return for which families sign a contract with City Hall, promising to keep their children in school. At the same time the programme offers access to other public services and supports families in reorganizing their lives.[29]

parent groups

Parents of working children can offer valuable support to one another. The Association of Mothers of Working Children, initiated by the social research center CISOL in Loja, a city in the Ecuadorian Amazon, was established to strengthen the ties between working children and their families. But it also became a mutual support group for women who were together able to identify their chief problems and to work together to begin addressing them.[30] Boyden, Ling and Myers describe the work of the Bonded Labour Liberation Front in Pakistan, which involves parents through committees attached to schools in the attempt to enable children to leave their work in brick kilns and elsewhere and to attend schools. Involving parents in this way can be an important part of a strategy to mobilize increased political support for adequately funded schooling of decent quality.[31] When such parent groups exist they should be represented on any coordinating or oversight council for children.

- *Support the economic viability of all poor families in order to prevent their children from entering the work force.*
- *Ensure that interventions on behalf of working children are planned and implemented with the knowledge and involvement of their families.*
- *Make poor families aware of the full range of options and services that are available to them, and support them in making use of these.*
- *Promote the formation of organizations for parents of working children.*

Supporting the involvement of children on their own behalf

Children, like parents, have a perspective on their work, and it may have little in common with the official agenda. Most working children have little choice about whether or not they will work. But for many children, being a paid worker is the most obvious route to independence and respectability. In policy makers' discussions of child work, domestic work for the family is commonly presented as preferable to wage labour, which is considered more likely to result in exploitation. But work within the home is unpaid and often undervalued. Children often claim to prefer the paid work of the marketplace to the less visible and unpaid drudgery at home. They may be more highly valued and better treated, even within the family, when they are paid workers.[32]

Working children can often be their own best spokespeople. Increasingly, they are forming organizations demanding access to

[29] City of Santos (1996) *Santos na Habitat II: Integrated Children's and Family Program*, The City of Santos, SP, Brazil
[30] Personal communication, Espinosa, M F 1998
[31] Boyden, J, Ling, B, Myers, W (1998) *What Works for Working Children*, Stockholm: Radda Barnen and UNICEF
[32] Nieuwenhuys, O (1994) *Children's Lifeworlds: Gender, Welfare and Labour in the Developing World*, London /New York: Routledge

organized child workers

improved working conditions, and in some cases defending their right to work. In Latin America, organized groups of working children are increasingly recognized as protagonists of their own rights.[33] There are also examples from Asia and Africa of children organizing to represent their own concerns as workers who contribute to the economy.[34] When working children are educated about their rights, they can more effectively participate as their own defenders. Blanchet presents the example of an ILO-IPEC project in Indonesia. Two hundred children working in factories under often hazardous conditions were trained to present their concerns to local and national government leaders, to the media and NGOs. As a result, 13 factories removed about 1,500 children from hazardous work, and extended to them wage, insurance and leave benefits that were previously available only to adults.[35]

The very act of organizing themselves to address their situation can have an enormous impact on the growth and self-confidence of working children. At the same time, their priorities may clash with official goals that stress minimum age requirements for work and compulsory school attendance. It is important that local authorities not respond in a confrontational way, but work closely with children's organizations to find common ground and to develop programmes and solutions that are compatible with both the children's long term best interests and their desire for self-determination.[36]

- *Encourage and support the formation of working children's organizations, especially for older children.*
- *Work closely with these organizations to find common ground and to develop programmes and solutions that are compatible with both the children's long term best interests and their desire for self-determination.*

Improving the quality and accessibility of education

Research and experience have established strong and complex links between the quality and accessibility of education and the prevalence of child labour.[37] Over the long term, the lack of education is fundamental to the perpetuation of poverty and the ongoing pressure on families to put their children to work. But there are short term connections as well. The lack of appropriate educational opportunities is widely considered to be a key factor in children's availability for labour.

Experience in the state of Kerala, in India, for instance, suggests that it is accessible, high quality education, rather than the enforcement of labour legislation, that has led to a remarkably low child work rate.[38] But formal education is too rarely offered with a regard for the economic constraints or working schedules of the poorest. In some cases it may push children into the work force, because of the need to earn school fees.[39] Nor is schooling always found to be relevant to their perceived needs. If education is to be a realistic alternative to child work, it must be not only affordable and accessible, but must also represent a better investment for the future than the skills that can be acquired through work. Otherwise it is likely to be rejected as a solution.

[33] Cussianovich Villaran, A (1997) *Some Premises for Reflection and Social Practices with Working Children and Adolescents*, Rädda Barnen

[34] See for example Marcus, R and C Harper (1996) *Small Hands: Children in the Working World*, Save the Children Fund UK; Dallape, F (1987) *An Experience with Street Children*, Nairobi, Kenya: Undugu Society; Dallape, F and Gilbert, C (1994) *Children's Participation in Action Research*, Harare, Zimbabwe: ENDA

[35] Blanchet, T (1996) *Lost Innocence, Stolen Childhoods*, Dhaka: The University Press

[36] UNICEF 1997, op cit Note 5

[37] See for example Boyden, Ling and Myers 1998, op cit Note 31; and Himes, J, Colbert de Arboleda, R V, Garcia Mendez, E (1994) *Child Labour and Basic Education in Latin America and the Caribbean*, Florence: UNICEF International Child Development Centre. The background papers from UNICEF for the Oslo conference on child labour are also pertinent – see Note 24

[38] Badiwala1, 1998, op cit Note 25

combining work and school

Most children in poverty, and especially those who are already working, would like access to schooling that is truly responsive to their needs. Recent research by Martin Woodhead with 300 working children in Bangladesh, Ethiopia, Central America and the Philippines found that two thirds or more of the children in each country believed that combining work and school was the best option in their present circumstances. It is important to emphasize that these comments focused on 'present circumstances'. Woodhead suggests that improved family circumstances, reduced poverty, better schooling and prospects for better jobs might alter their views.[40]

In some cases, combining work and school is a reasonable alternative. More flexible responses to the needs of working children, including shorter school hours and evening shifts, have been used in many places to make this feasible. When children are not working long hours, and when the quality of schooling is good, initiatives like these can be a valuable approach. But too often compromises are made, and poor quality education is combined with excessive work burdens. Night shifts of school for exhausted children can be useless in terms of any real educational achievement, as well as being detrimental to health. Research shows that the number of hours of attendance contributes vitally to the effectiveness of schooling.[41] Attempting to squeeze a few hours of mediocre instruction into days already overburdened with work will do little to address the developmental needs of children, or to motivate low-income parents to take education more seriously. Double shifts can also lower the overall quality of schooling – the time in school for children is decreased, and the teacher load made heavier. More flexible scheduling may also have the effect of pushing more children into the labour market.

On the other hand, when schooling is found to be worthwhile, families will make sacrifices to ensure that it is possible for their children. CIN ASHA, an organization in Calcutta, managed over a two year period to mainstream 1,500 child labourers from a squatter settlement into formal schools. A study of 200 of the families looked at the adjustments made within households to accomodate the children's return to school. It was found that parents took up a 40 per cent increased workload; grandparents took on more domestic chores; there was a reduction in gambling and alcoholism on the part of fathers; and food habits of the family changed to reflect the loss of income.[42] The Montes Altos experience must be recalled here (see p195); when parents knew that their children were constructively occupied at school, they themselves were able to work more productively.

Designing high quality school programmes that are truly adapted to the needs of low-income families calls for collaborative efforts on the part of school authorities, working children and their parents. Children could be permitted, for instance, to attend schools outside their home communities but more convenient to their place of work. Employers must be involved, to ensure that children have sufficient time for school. Teachers must be encouraged to make working children welcome in their classrooms. Working children may be more assertive than other pupils; they may arrive late, and may be dirty and untidy. If they are humiliated by teachers and other students, they are less likely to continue attending.[43]

Although every effort should be made to integrate working children comfortably into the regular school system, in some cases non-formal

39 Boyden, Ling and Myers 1998, op cit Note 31
40 Woodhead, M (1998) *Children's Perspectives on their Working Lives: a participatory study in Bangladesh, Ethiopia, the Philippines, Guatemala, Nicaragua and El Salvador*, Stockholm: Radda Barnen
41 Boyden, Ling, Myers 1998, op cit Note 31
42 Pappu, K (1997) *Elimination of Child Labour and its Impact on Families*, Presentation at Urban Childhood Conference, 9–12 June 1997, Trondheim, Norway
43 Boyden, Ling, Myers 1998, op cit Note 31

alternatives may make sense as a transitional measure. If children have never been to school or have dropped out, they may need support in coming to think of themselves as capable of formal learning. Initially, a formal school setting may reinforce their belief that school is not meant for them. Older children, for instance, may find themselves placed with far younger children, using materials that are poorly suited to their level. A fine example of a transitional programme is the summer school created in 1996 in Santos, Brazil, with the aim of pulling back into the school system children and adolescents who had dropped out. Of the 1,800 children who participated in 'pedagogical first aid' and such activities as theatre and music, 70 per cent were successful in rejoining the formal school system.[44]

non-formal alternatives

In some cases non-formal alternatives may provide the only practical solution, especially where formal education is truly not accessible, or when alternative livelihoods cannot be found. Children's work may be too far from the nearest school, or may move frequently. Work may be so periodic or unpredictable that even flexible school hours are impractical. Non-formal schools for scavengers in one of the two enormous dumps of Mexico City, or in the centre of roundabouts for the shoeshine boys of central New Delhi have been just a few of the creative ways that basic learning has been brought to children with extremely limited options. In Calcutta, the Institute of Psychological and Educational Research (IPER) took special measures to ensure that children were not too tired to learn. Instead of holding night schools, they offered the formal primary curriculum on Saturdays and Sundays, and supported these sessions with home teaching programmes.[45]

Non-formal alternatives may develop creative and innovative approaches that the formal system would do well to emulate. But when non-formal schooling is not connected to the state system, it may be more difficult for children to move on to higher levels of education or receive formal accreditation. Local authorities should liaise with the formal system to ensure a smooth transition for children who want to continue their education. The support offered by local government to non-formal alternatives should ideally go beyond encouragement and occasional assistance to entering formal partnerships with organizations responding to special educational needs. This can give them legitimacy and the right to make use of the formal system's resources, and can help to take these solutions to scale.

Schooling need not be only a way to supplement or replace work; it can also be actively used as a preventive measure. In the north of Thailand, the Daughter's Education Programme (DEP) provides a participatory residential programme for girls who are at risk of becoming prostitutes or child labourers. In addition to being offered a high quality basic education and a range of marketable skills, girls have the opportunity to learn to live and share with others, to function as a supportive team and to express themselves clearly. Many of them go on to become community development workers and to help other girls like themselves.[46] See the resource list for DEP's newsletter (p282).

- *Provide incentives for low-income families to choose schooling over work as the best alternative for children (see p170).*

[44] City of Santos 1996, op cit Note 29
[45] Boyden, Ling, Myers 1998, op cit Note 31
[46] DEP (1996) 'The Development of Youth Participation: An Experience of the Development and Education Programme for Daughters and Communities' in National Council for Child and Youth Development (ed) *Youth Participation in Thailand*, Bangkok: NCCYD

- *Modify regular school programmes to fit the needs of working children and their families, without compromising the quality of their schooling; involve working children and their parents, teachers and employers in arriving at solutions.*
- *Support non-formal programmes as an alternative for children where necessary, and ensure that they are connected to the formal system to give them legitimacy and to allow for smooth transitions to formal education.*
- *See also p219 for a discussion of schooling for children on the street.*

SUPPORTING CHILDREN IN THE WORKPLACE

Few local governments have the resources to end child labour within their jurisdictions in the short term. The need for progressive change is broadly accepted. But as long as any children are required to work, they have a right to the support of their local governments. An obvious measure is ensuring their access to schooling, as discussed above. It is also essential that their health needs be addressed. Even when good primary health care is available for families within communities, it may not be easily accessible to working children. Health services should be available, when necessary, near their places of work, and during hours that are possible for them. (See pp100, 218).

healthcare

Opportunities for exploration, imagination and joyful movement are also critically important to working children, keeping open the channels of creativity and growth. Local authorities must support all possible ways of making play and recreation available to children who are pushed by circumstances to take on adult responsibilities (see p136).

recreation

Not all interventions for children in the workplace are resource-intensive. In many cases simple measures, together with coordination and assistance to existing efforts, can make dramatic differences. Children and adolescents involved in different kinds of work often require support that is specific to their situations. The following are examples of interventions that have been effective within certain broad categories of work.

Children employed in the informal sector

Most work for urban children is in the informal sector, in small workshops or enterprises, vending, scavenging, carrying loads, or doing any of the numerous other jobs possible within a given city. These children are usually outside the reach of formal regulation, and helping them can take ingenuity and persistence. Successful efforts require cooperation between relevant government departments and the NGOs which most directly serve these children. The best of these efforts are highly participatory, helping children to meet their immediate needs, and to increase the level of control they have over their circumstances.

In Olongapo, in the Philippines, children can join groups related to their particular work (as plastic bag vendors, jeep cleaners, barrow pushers at the market, and so on). These cooperatives allow them to support one another in improving conditions, rather than working in competition. The inter-agency group behind this effort has worked from the beginning in close partnership with the mayor and several municipal agencies, and through their joint efforts children have been able to find housing and to obtain publicly raised scholarship funds for schooling. In response to the children's expressed need for a safe place to keep their money, special bank accounts have been opened. One child in each group manages the accounts, co-signing checks with the organizing street worker. Concrete ways have also been found to upgrade working conditions. For example, a man who rents barrows to the barrow boys allowed his storage hut to serve as a meeting place where they could meet, have a warm drink, and receive informal help with their reading early in the morning.[47]

cooperative children's groups

In many cases the working conditions of children are the direct responsibility of municipal authorities, since their workplace is the public domain. Many children spend long hours every day on city streets with no amenities to meet their basic needs. The 'adequate standard of living' recognized as a right by the Convention cannot be assumed to refer only to conditions at home. Public space, for these children, is a significant part of the living environment. Toilet facilities and water for washing and drinking must be easily accessible. Children must have places where they can sit when they are tired without fear of being turned away or treated as a public nuisance. Local authorities may prefer to have children in school or at least off the streets, but as long as it is necessary for them to work, it is in the interests of all that their basic needs be met.

Lack of water and sanitation will keep few children off the streets, but its presence will contribute to the level of civility for all. Being able to stay clean and use a toilet in privacy are essential to dignity and self-respect for many children and adolescents. These are important traits to support, because it is out of self-respect that children learn to respect the rights of others. For girls who are menstruating, access to sanitation may feel especially critical. An excellent example of the provision of sanitary facilities are the Sauchalaya complexes in a number of cities in India. Over 100 have been installed, for instance, at railway stations by the Sulabh Social Service Foundation. These complexes include bathing and laundry facilities as well as toilets and urinals. Children, disabled persons and those who cannot afford to pay may use these facilities free of charge. Round-the-clock service by an attendant is funded by users who pay.[48]

toilets and washing facilities

Working children on the street should be able to see police as the source of protection and support that they ought to be, rather than as enemies to be evaded even when no wrong has been done. If children are treated as criminals, they are more likely to behave as criminals. The courtesy and responsiveness of police and other officials can promote a general atmosphere of mutual respect. In some cities police receive training in the Convention (see also p252) and in ways of responding positively to the situation of children working on the street. In both Bombay and Olongapo, children were issued with ID cards that included the name and phone number of a policeman who had agreed to be their particular friend and advocate in case of trouble.[49] This issue will be discussed further with regard to street children on p218.

police

[47] Personal communication, Olongapo street worker, Reach Up 1998
[48] Roger Hart, field trip
[49] Personal communication with SPARC and Reach Up street workers

Official figures show that more boys work than girls - but these figures ignore the hidden and often unpaid work of girls. For many millions of girls the daily burden of work interferes with opportunities for schooling, play and rest. A girl at home in Davao, Philippines. UNICEF 1996, Shehzad Noorani

A large number of working children in cities are unable to afford the cost of transport to return to their families and homes on the outskirts at night. Instead, they sleep near their place of work and swell the population of children living outside of family. They become at the same time more vulnerable to theft and harassment, and are perhaps more likely to turn to illegal behaviour. Providing free transport passes could contribute to keeping them community-based, and protecting them from the many risks of sleeping rough.

For a discussion of children living on the street, see p212).

- *Provide assistance to organizations which support children working in the informal sector.*
- *Ensure that the public domain, where so many children work long hours, meets their basic needs for drinking water, toilets, and places to sit and rest.*
- *Ensure that police are trained and required to respect and protect the rights of children working in public space.*
- *Where practical, provide working children with free passes for transport to enable them to return home at night.*

Children working at home

Children's work at home is seldom considered the concern of local authorities. Under reasonable circumstances, household responsibilities are a valuable part of children's lives, and cannot be considered exploitative. But in conditions of poverty, when children's contribution may become critical to family survival, household workloads can increase to the point of being harmful. This is particularly so for many millions of girls, whose lives may be completely circumscribed from an early age by the demands placed on them at home or, for many married adolescents, in the homes of their in-laws. Their daily chores can be too strenuous for their growing bodies and may compromise their opportunities for schooling, play and rest. Their isolation contributes not only to their invisibility within society, but to a lack of self-worth in their own eyes.[50] Although parents and other family members may not intentionally exploit their daughters, the net effect can be as damaging to health and development as the overtly exploitative forms of child labour more commonly targeted by reform.

the invisible burdens of domestic work

It is important to raise awareness of the fact that these girls are working children, even though they earn nothing. Children's domestic workload must be taken into account in identifying families in need of formal assistance. If support of various kinds is available for families to keep their children out of the labour market, it should also be available when family survival depends on inappropriate workloads for children at home. Outreach workers should determine with parents whether all available options have been explored. The long term benefits of education should be discussed, and wherever possible, ways found to expand the educational opportunities of girls working at home (see p168).

The provision of basic municipal services can do a great deal to lighten the burdensome work loads of many young girls. When child care is available within the community, for instance, older sisters may be freed up to go to school. When water is available close by, it saves many hours of heavy carrying and may protect immature bodies from permanent damage. When effective transportation is available to working parents, it can decrease the number of hours during which a child has full domestic responsibility. Local authorities must be aware of this dimension when allocating resources. Alleviating the domestic workload of children should be a factor in any cost-benefit analysis of service provision. In some cases, specific interventions can make a dramatic difference. A group of mothers' associations in Burkina Faso was able to reduce girls' domestic workload and increase their time for school and study by investing in labour-saving equipment such as shared grain mills and presses.[51] Authorities must encourage and support all such efforts to reduce domestic workloads.

ways to lighten the load

- *Take the domestic workload of children into account in identifying those families in need of support and formal assistance.*
- *Consider the impact on the workload of many young girls that investment in improved water provision, affordable child care, and other basic services could have.*
- *Investigate labour saving devices for reducing domestic work loads.*

Domestic work in the homes of others

Millions of children worldwide, especially girls, are employed as domestic helpers in the homes of better-off families. These girls are often migrants from rural areas, sent to live with relatives or distant connections in the city in order to give them access to broader opportunities, or to repay a

[50] Friedman, S A (1998) *Girls at Work*, New York: UNICEF

[51] Iberia, A (1993) *Report on a Visit to Cecil Province: Increased Participation of Mothers in Daughters' Education*, UNICEF, Burkina Faso

the abuse of 'fostering' arrangements

family debt. It is not uncommon for these 'fostering' arrangements to be abused, and for children to become essentially unpaid servants, dependent on people who may have little concern for their welfare. Even relatively caring employers may fail to recognize the emotional needs of young girls separated from their families for the first time.

isolation

These girls have little control over their lives, and their isolation and dependence put them at high risk for loneliness and depression, exploitation and abuse. When they belong to different ethnic groups from their employers, a common phenomenon in Latin America and the Philippines, this may increase their vulnerability. According to various studies, girls in domestic service work extremely long hours for low pay, often performing arduous chores.[52] There are no fixed hours, and time off can easily be cancelled. Scoldings and beatings are not uncommon, and girls are frequently exposed to sexual harassment and molestation by the men of the household. If they become pregnant, they may be dismissed and forced into prostitution.[53]

The fact that their work takes place within private homes limits the possibilities for monitoring and intervention. One approach has been to find places where they meet during free time. Staff from Visayas Forum, a Manila NGO, observed that girls often gathered together in the city's parks. Although they had set up their own informal support networks, with older domestics caring for younger ones, they were receptive to the help and encouragement of the NGO. A group of girls from one park, for instance, established themselves as a formal association of service workers to support one another and monitor the situation of those facing particular difficulties. With back-up from the NGO, they were able to deal with emergencies themselves.[54]

Another strategy is to appeal directly to the employers. Shaisab, an NGO in Dhaka, Bangladesh sends staff members into upper class neighbourhoods and persuades employers to release their servants for a few of the least busy hours each day. Small groups of girls gather for literacy classes in garages or under stairwells. This improves their long term options, and also relieves the isolation of these young workers.

improving long term options

Ideally, programmes for domestic working girls should go beyond literacy to provide them with routes to a better future. The director of the Women and Child Labour Resource Center in Nairobi, Kenya says that in their city these girls are thrown out helpless onto the street when they become pregnant, which happens not infrequently by the time they are 14 or 15. Without an education they have few options beyond prostitution. To prevent this, the organization has established a six month course which girls can attend during mornings or afternoons, depending on their employers. The course includes basic literacy, cooking and an introduction to such skills as typing and tailoring. The centre occasionally serves as a refuge for girls who are being abused. The organization also plays an important role in informing the public and local authorities on the conditions of young domestic servants.[55]

- *Ensure that employers are informed of the rights of children working in their homes.*
- *Support the provision of opportunities for schooling and training in marketable skills, and encourage employers to allow girls to make use of these.*

52 Blanc, 1994, op cit Note 4
53 Black, M (1993) 'Girls and Girlhood: Time We were Noticed', *New Internationalist*, (240): 4–7
54 Personal communication, director of Visayas Forum, 1998
55 UNICEF (1997) *The State of the World's Children 1997*, New York: Oxford University Press

- *Encourage the formation of support networks of girls in domestic service.*
- *Support the provision of refuge for girls who have been abused or turned into the street.*

Protected opportunities for employment

Adolescents should have opportunities for work that pays fairly, supports their learning and increases their options in life. In Recife, Brazil, the Projeto de Praia (Beach Brigade Project) trains adolescents to work as tourist guides. They receive US$50 monthly, a daily meal, and a scholarship to study English.[56] In Lima, the national movement of working children (MNNATSOP), along with its supporting NGOs, recently signed an agreement with the city mayor to establish 100 part time gardening jobs for local children. They will work four hours a day, attend school for another four hours, and will receive a salary and social security for medical care. There are plans to extend this programme to provide up to 600 part time jobs through the city.[57] Bringing such programmes to scale is a significant goal, since even excellent initiatives tend to reach very few young people relative to the enormous need.

Young people with disabilities have a particular need to be prepared for employment that supports their dignity, self-reliance and integration within the community. PROMOVE Rehabilitation Centre in São Paulo, Brazil, provides training for young people with a wide range of special needs – physical, mental and emotional. The goals of the programme are holistic, and focus on the development of these young people as self-confident and productive human beings. They also work towards acquiring professional skills in such areas as baking, hairdressing, gardening, graphic arts and printing. When the course is over, the Centre helps to place students in jobs. In Bangalore, India, the Association of the Physically Handicapped (APH) runs training programmes for young people with physical disabilities in engineering trades, technical drawing and horticulture. They have also created special workshops for manufacturing braces, calipers, special shoes and other mobility equipment, along with training courses to enable young people with disabilities to work in these units.[58] Local authorities should support such initiatives, and make incentives and assistance available to other employers to adapt jobs and equipment for particular capacities.

training for young people with disabilities

Many of the most successful programmes creating work opportunities have been designed for older children living on the street, and will be discussed on p220. For a discussion of technical and vocational education, and of school/work connections, see p185.

- *Support, assist, and help to bring to scale opportunities for training and protected employment for young people over primary school age.*
- *Establish and promote programmes for young people with disabilities to prepare them for employment that supports their dignity, self-reliance and integration within the community.*
- *Make incentives or assistance available to employers to adapt jobs and equipment for particular capacities.*

56 Personal communication, Raquel Rolnick, 1998

57 fabrizio@enda.sn (1998) *Two Good News for Organised Working Children of the Third World*, edited and distributed by HURINet (the Human Rights Information Network)

58 Moll, K (1991) 'Working with Disabled People in Bangalore, South India', *CBR News*, (9)

Experience demonstrates that the most successful programmes for street-based children are those that accept them on their own terms, and support them in their efforts to take an active, responsible role in their own lives. Here a street worker from a Guatemala centre enjoys a warm exchange with some boys. UNICEF Dennis Budd Grey

11 Street-based Children

The highly visible issue of children and adolescents living and working on the streets of the world's cities has attracted global attention, and remains an ongoing source of pressure and concern for local authorities. This chapter attempts to define responses that are consistent with children's rights, and to describe some models for action that have been found useful in different places.

There is no question that the most important and effective response is prevention. Through general support to families in poverty, it is possible to address many of the factors underlying family disintegration that propel children into a life on the street. Access to employment for adults, support in times of crisis, relevant schooling, strong child care programmes, and efforts to address the roots of domestic violence can all be effective measures to keep families intact and able to fulfil their responsibilities to their children. These measures have been discussed repeatedly throughout the book. (See pp50, 54, 81, 152, 164).

But while cities work towards reducing poverty and family stress, children already on the street cannot be ignored, and their rights must be vigorously defended. Most of the provisions of the Convention are relevant for children living outside of family in the public domain. At issue are their survival, their healthy development and long term well being, as well as their full range of civil rights. They have the right, like all children, to dignity, to health and education, to protection from abuse, exploitation and violence, and to a voice on their own behalf. Perhaps most basic is the obligation of government not to discriminate against these children and to act in their best interests (Articles 2 and 3).

the rights of street-based children

Because of their visibility, and the level of international concern for children on the street, some of them may be better served than many who endure more hidden hardships, such as domestic workers.[1] Programmes run by NGOs may in some cases give street children better access to health care and other services than is true for many children in illegal settlements.[2] They may earn more than other working children – in the Philippines, children earn up to $3 a day scavenging on the streets, more than the average per capita GNP in the country.[3] And because of their relative independence, these children may have more opportunities for play and leisure than children who attend school and work at home, and more chances for self-determination than those whose choices are made for them by parents.

advantages of visibility

the other side of the picture

But there is another side to the picture. Many of these children may have 'chosen' their life on the street, but only as an alternative to realities which can include extreme poverty, disintegrating families and high levels of abuse. A street worker in Guatemala estimates that 75 to 80 per cent of the children she deals with have been sexually or physically abused.[4] Once on the street, these children live dangerous and marginal lives. Their immediate health and well-being is threatened, and also their long term opportunities. The social stigma they suffer can be the cause of humiliation, rejection and even threats to life. This may be compounded for girls, whose presence on the street is often a disturbing violation of accepted gender roles. Researchers in Colombia found that, when asked about their needs, street-based children spoke of psychological supports, relationships and a role in society more than of food or shelter.[5]

The literature on street children often distinguishes between street-based working children who still live for the most part with their families, those whose links with family are more tenuous or occasional, and those who are truly on their own, having either broken their ties with family or having been abandoned. It is tempting to rely on such categories in order to reduce the complexity of the problem, but from the perspective of those who work with children and adolescents in many cities, these distinctions may be unrealistic or may serve no useful purpose.[6] The boundaries between categories are often fluid and shifting.

Many children retain family ties even when living on the street, and return home if time and distance make it possible. Others may have left home temporarily because of abuse or family insecurity. In some cases even those who 'live' at home may be working on the streets for such long hours that they need services and support that can only be available outside of their home communities. Consequently, we are including in this chapter all those children who require direct support of various kinds, in addition to, or in place of, the support that might be funnelled through their families or communities. Of necessity, almost all street-based children work in one way or another for their survival. Many of their work-related needs have been discussed in the preceding chapter.

[1] Rajani, R (1997) 'Street Children Hijack the Urban Childhood Agenda', Presentation at Urban Childhood Conference, June 1997, Trondheim, Norway
[2] Baker, R (1998) *Negotiating Identities: A Study of the Lives of Street Children in Nepal*, University of Durham, Durham
[3] UNICEF (1997) *The State of the World's Children 1997*, New York: Oxford University Press
[4] Lajoie, R (1998) *Shelter from the Storm*, Amnesty Action, Summer 1998: 6–8
[5] Ennew, J (1994) *Street and Working Children: A Guide to Planning*, London: Save the Children Fund
[6] Glauser, B (1990) 'Street Children: Deconstructing a Construct' in James, A and Prout, A (eds) *Constructing and Reconstructing Childhood*, London: Falmer Press

Here we will consider the broader range of supports that children and adolescents may need when they live a large part of their lives in the public domain.

THE RESPONSIBILITIES OF LOCAL AUTHORITIES AND THEIR PARTNERS

common responses:

Children and adolescents living and working in the public space of the city have customarily been viewed as a nuisance and a threat. Not only do they resort at times to illegal or uncivil behaviour, often in response to the constraints they operate under, but they also generate fear and discomfort among those who are better off, a reminder of realities that many would prefer to ignore.[7] Local authorities are frequently under considerable pressure from the business community and the public to find ways to 'deal' with the issue of street-based children.

incarceration

harassment

violence

In many parts of the world, the response has been to remove children forcibly from the streets, often to incarcerate them, and sometimes to resort to violent measures. According to a number of studies, harassment is a constant reality for these children, and their most pervasive fear is of violent death.[8] Gross abuses are often quietly sanctioned by local authorities and commercial interests. Not only do children find it necessary to protect themselves from the hostility of the public, but even from those who should be offering them protection. From numerous countries there are reports of street children being beaten, tortured and even murdered by police, para-military groups and private 'security' forces. In Rio de Janeiro, almost 1,400 children were reported slain in 1994 alone.[9]

rehabilitation

Another common response has been to view street children as being in need of rehabilitation. In some cases this may be appropriate, for many of these children have been victims of abuse within their families, subject to harassment, violence and trauma while living on the streets, and may well be troubled by substance abuse and addiction. Too often, however, well-meaning attempts to 'rehabilitate' children and adolescents fail to take into account the understanding these young people have of their own situations. Reasons for being on the street vary with each child. Responses must be based on an understanding of their personal histories and their own assessments of their situations. The sense of freedom may be intensely important to many of these children, and the sole compensation for the other difficulties they face. Taking this freedom away is not a constructive response. And when a child has strong ties to a group of peers, removal from this support may be the emotional equivalent of separation from family. Authorities are obligated by the Convention to ensure that any measures taken are in the best interests of these children, protecting not only their right to survival and development, but also respecting their right to an active role in shaping their own lives.

In most cases NGOs have been more successful than government agencies in offering the flexible provision necessary for addressing the issues of street-based children. Often different organizations respond to different needs. But the struggle for funding can lead NGOs to be less well coordinated and collaborative than might be desirable.[10] Cooperation is vital to offer a comprehensive and integrated response to

[7] Aptekar, L and Abebe, B (1997) 'Conflict in the Neighborhood: Street and Working Children in the Public Space', *Childhood*, 4(4)
[8] Ibid and Connolly, M (1997) *The Health Matters for Street Children and Youth*, Newmarket UK: Global Gutter Press
[9] Marcus, R and Harper, C (1996) *Small Hands: Children in the Working World*, Save the Children Fund, UK
[10] Löw, U (1998) 'A World of Violence: the Daily Battles of Nairobi's Street Children', *UNCHS Habitat Debate*, 4(1): 20–21

the situation of street-based children and youth, and local authorities can take a critical coordinating role. They must ensure, first of all, that there is adequate assessment and awareness of the needs, using the guidelines described on p196. In the light of children's needs, authorities should evaluate the coverage provided by existing organizations, determine what support these organizations need, and find what areas remain to be addressed. A coordinating committee can support cooperation and ensure more efficient coverage. Local government is often seen as the enemy in efforts to help street children. But with supportive links, organizations assisting street-based children should be able to work in close, productive collaboration with officials from health departments, education, the police force, juvenile justice and social welfare. In Kathmandu, Nepal, for instance, the Children At Risk NetWork Group (CAR-NWG) invited senior police officers to debate strategies for helping street children.[11] In Mwanza, Tanzania, cooperation between the local police and Kuleana, a children's rights organization working with children on the street, has resulted in a dramatic drop in the number of children in the local lock-up facility every week.

cooperation between authorities and NGOs

The responsibility of local authorities does not end with coordination. Street-based children are local citizens, and their needs, like those of other city residents, should be reflected in local policies and budgetary allocations. Only when local government is fully involved and committed can the effective responses of NGOs and community groups be taken to scale.

A significant responsibility of local government is to raise public awareness, and to encourage the involvement of civil society in developing solutions. In the Philippines, the city of Cebu celebrates an annual festival in which community organizations, NGOs and local personalities, in partnership with the authorities, support the artistic presentations of street children. The opportunity to see these children in a more positive light tends to alleviate the tensions and public hostility.[12] In Santos, Brazil, city authorities made an agreement with a local radio station to establish a weekly programme, produced by young people on the street, with the support of an NGO. Through interviews and discussion, a range of local issues are raised on this programme, including violence, health problems and policies towards children. In listening to these thoughtful young people, the public has gradually come to a different understanding of their situation, and one not shaped by fear.[13]

raising public awareness

- *Ensure adequate assessment of the needs of street-based children, using the guidelines described on p196.*
- *Evaluate the coverage provided by existing organizations, determine what support these organizations need, find what areas remain to be addressed; and match the cost of meeting these needs with potential funding sources, whether private or public.*
- *Establish a coordinating committee to support cooperation between agencies and organizations and to ensure more efficient coverage of needs.*
- *Raise general awareness among the public of the condition and rights of street children, of their civic responsibility towards them, and of the long term costs of failing to respond to their needs.*

11 Personal communication, Rachel Baker, 1998
12 Together Foundation 'Best Practices: Building Communities of Opportunity', www.together.org
13 Personal communication, Ladislau Dowbor

SUPPORTS FOR CHILDREN AND ADOLESCENTS ON THE STREET

Street-based children in different cities face different needs and realities. But some basic responses can be adapted to local conditions. Proven strategies have been developed, many of them place-based and focused on the availability of integrated support for children. The most successful programmes have been those that accept children on their own terms and support them in gaining control of their lives, rather than taking that control out of their hands or encouraging dependence. Many good programmes respond to children's needs in a progressive way, first helping them to satisfy their immediate practical needs, and more gradually making available opportunities for counseling, education and training, protected work and, whenever appropriate and possible, reunification with their families.

Training street workers

working 'with' rather than 'for' children

Reaching out to street children requires sensitive, non-judgemental professionals who can serve as a link to the range of services that children may need. Street workers work 'with' rather than 'for' children, learning to identify with them and helping them to assess their situations, meet their needs, and work towards their goals. In some cases, they were themselves street-based children, and are able to draw on their own experience and understanding. Especially for girls, it has been found helpful for male and female workers to operate in pairs.[14] These workers ideally have a reputation as trusted and caring adults whom children can approach on their own terms. They generally move about between the places where children gather, carrying with them first aid supplies or materials for informal education. Street workers are generally attached to NGOs, but training can be made available through municipalities to ensure that they are professionally prepared to deal with the issues they will face. Baizerman stresses that training should be experiential, and conducted on the streets by experienced street youth workers. Youth workers should know how to listen to and talk with children and youth, as well as with police, health officers and other officials; and should be able to support the potential and right of youth to take an active, responsible role in their own lives. Continued support, supervision, group discussion and reflection should be available to help prevent burn-out from this taxing job.[15]

- *Provide training and support for youth street workers who can deal sensitively with street-based children and serve as a link to the range of services and supports they may need.*
- *Draw on the skills and knowledge of experienced street workers in providing this training.*

[14] Ennew, J (1994) *Street and Working Children: A Guide to Planning*, London: Save the Children Fund

[15] Baizerman, M (1996) 'Youth Work on the Street: Community's Moral Compact with its Young People', *Childhood*, 3(2): 157–167

Shelters and drop-in centres

Many organizations run shelters or drop-in centres where children and adolescents can go to meet their basic needs: places where they can wash

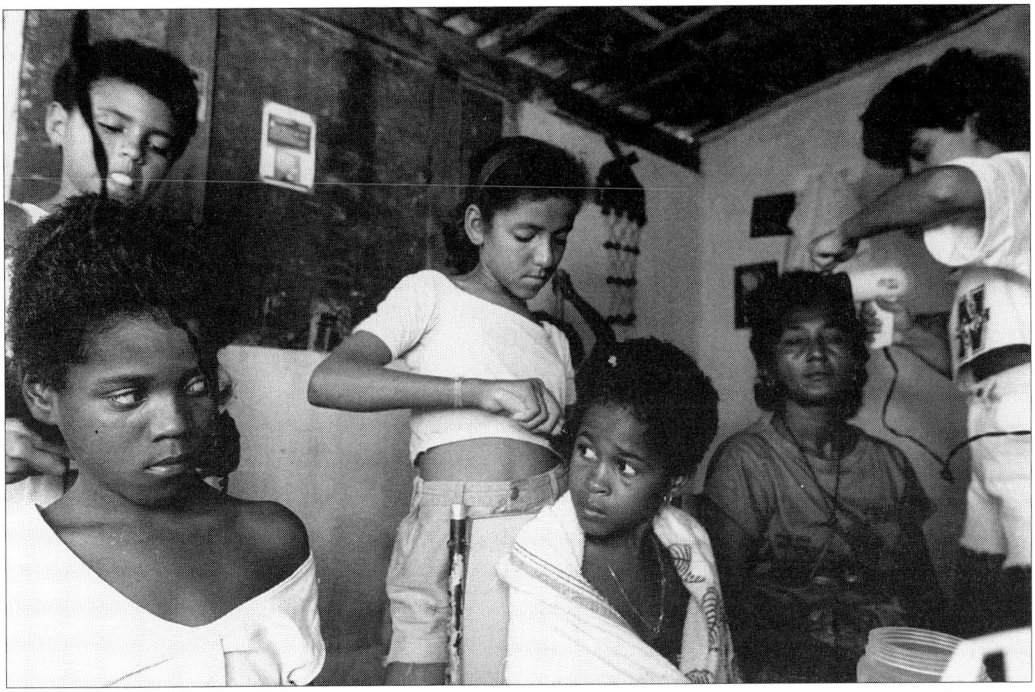

Opportunities for training and meaningful work can be a valuable preventive measure when there is a risk of children turning to more hazardous livelihoods on the streets. These girls at Casa de Pasagem in Recife, Brazil learn hairdressing, and at the same time discuss schooling and health issues. The Passage House, Recife, 1996

and have access to toilets, cooking and laundry facilities, first aid and basic health care, where they can safely keep the money they have earned, or also just rest or pass the time in friendly surroundings. Such centres can serve as a clearing house for information, and a focus for some of the services and activities described in more detail below. In Katmandu, the CWIN programme has such a centre called the 'Common Room' which includes a variety of resources which children can use up to nine hours a day.[16] Some centres provide sleeping facilities, but in many cases they are daytime resources only. Even when open at night, they are generally not intended to serve as living quarters for children, or to encourage complete dependence on the organization. On the contrary, through their use of the resources available through such a centre, children are able to work towards improving their own situations and strengthening their independence. In many centres children pay a small sum for their food and sometimes for other services, an acknowledgement of their dignity as self-supporting individuals.[17]

Not infrequently, local authorities have required drop-in centres to move to the periphery of cities as part of an attempt to get children off the city streets.[18] This defeats the purpose of these centres, which is to offer children the supports they need in the busy city centres where they can earn a living, however meagre.

- *Support the establishment of drop-in centres which can serve as a base for meeting the practical needs of children on the street, and support them in finding ways to improve their situations.*
- *Permit these centres to function where they will be most accessible to the children who need them.*

16 Personal communication, CWIN information officer, 1998
17 Ennew, 1994, op cit Note 1
18 Vanderschueren, F (1996) 'From Violence to Justice and Security in Cities', *Environment and Urbanization*, 8(1): 93–112

Access to health services

health problems

obstacles to receiving care

A lack of hygiene and preventive care, along with exposure to drugs, violence and exploitation, leave street-based children vulnerable to many health problems. They are likely to suffer from respiratory infections, skin diseases, wounds and other injuries, tooth decay, parasites, gastrointestinal conditions and emotional problems, as well as high rates of sexually transmitted diseases, and drug-related problems.[19] In parts of Africa, many street children have been orphaned by AIDS, and are themselves HIV positive.[20] Street-based children need access to emergency care and first aid as well as to regular preventive care and disease management. They need information and health education, and in many cases counseling, so that they can take greater control of their own well-being. All these issues are discussed in more detail on p117. In most cases appropriate health care is hard to find. Even if a clinic exists close by, expense may keep children from using it. Many health centres require birth certificates, vaccination records and parental consent before they will provide treatment. Street-based children often feel unwelcome in health facilities, and frequently have good reason to distrust officials and formal institutions. The care and services made available to them must take this into account, and must be easily accessible and affordable, non-judgemental and respectful of their desire and capacity to manage their own lives. Health services for children on the street are most frequently provided by NGOs, whose efforts should be supported by the local government health agency.

Because these young people lead dangerous lives, they may be even less impressed than most adolescents by the long term dangers of hazards such as drug use and HIV/AIDS. Their health education must focus on the immediate problems that dangerous activities pose for their day-to-day life. The fact that the debilitation associated with AIDS can undermine daily survival strategies may be more of a deterrent than the fact that it will ultimately cause illness and death.[21]

- *Support efforts to make affordable, accessible and non-bureaucratic health care services and education available to children on the street.*
- *Train health workers to be non-judgemental, supportive and respectful of children's desire to manage their own lives.*

Street-based children, police and the law

Because street-based children occupy the public domain, police can reach into every corner of their lives. For many of these children, police harassment and violence figure as their most significant daily problem and greatest fear. But the police can serve as powerful allies if they are appropriately trained and encouraged. As part of their basic training, police should be educated to understand children's rights and to accept that these rights extend without exception to children on the street.

Cooperation between police and the organizations that work with street children is an important goal. Too often they function in opposition. Where police are corrupt and hostile, this is inevitable. But where police are willing to accept a more positive role as supporters of children's

[19] Baker, 1998, op cit Note 2; and Connolly 1997, op cit Note 8
[20] de la Barra, X (1998) 'Poverty: the Main Cause of Ill Health in Urban Children', *Health, Education and Behavior*, 25(1): 45–49
[21] Ennew, 1994, op cit Note 14

rights, cooperation can ease the pressure on both sides. Street workers should be involved in police training in order to communicate some understanding of their goals and methods. In Bombay, cooperation with the police took the novel form of employment for some older street-based children. At times, vehicular and pedestrian traffic reaches dangerous levels, and police trained adolescents to assist them in controlling traffic during peak hours. After six days of training over a six month period, these adolescents were given uniforms and put to work for the city. The programme was so successful that police extended it after its first year.[22]

cooperation with police

Many children and adolescents on the street run into trouble with the law because their survival strategies involve illegal activity. In many cases they are in the grip of organized crime, which makes use of children on the street for prostitution, drug peddling and theft. Care must be taken to focus the control of crime on adult criminals rather than their child pawns, and there should be cooperation with higher levels of government in this regard. Ideally, through the training of police officers and raised public awareness, unwarranted and discriminatory arrests of children can be avoided. And through easier access to the basic necessities for children on the street, the incidence of petty crime will be reduced. If children are arrested, they should have ready access to trained legal advice and advocacy before being unnecessarily sentenced, or forced to endure weeks or months of pre-trial incarceration.

conflict with the law

- *For recommendations on children in trouble with the law, see p225.*

Schooling for street-based children

The recommendations made with regard to education for working children hold true for children on the street: the schooling made available to them should be convenient, flexible and responsive to their needs (see p186). Some street-based children may want, at some point, to enter or re-enter the formal school system, and should be encouraged and assisted in this. But initially, their needs may be better served by non-formal responses that take account of their working schedules, and particular strengths and weaknesses that result from their circumstances. These children, for instance, may be missing certain basic social skills, may have trouble adapting to rules and routines, and may lack fundamental concepts and skills essential to formal education.[23] At the same time they will probably have acquired other skills, and a capacity for self-determination which can be constructively built on. Municipalities should offer support and technical assistance for schooling programmes for street children, and should help to ensure that a smooth transition to the formal system is possible. When children do attend formal schooling, teachers may need training or skilled back-up; the problems prompting street children to run away from school placements have often been observed to arise from the inexperience and lack of understanding of the staff.[24] For older children and adolescents, especially if they have spent many years on the street, a transition into formal schooling may be particularly difficult, and technical and employment oriented training may be more practical (see p220). These programmes should include training in literacy and numeracy.

[22] Ibid
[23] Ibid
[24] Baker, 1998, op cit Note 2

- *Support programmes that provide relevant and responsive education for street-based children, and ensure coordination with the formal school system.*

Educating street-based children in their rights

rights education as problem-solving

Fundamental to the education of street-based children is the goal of helping them to see themselves as legitimate members of society with the rights and responsibilities of citizens. Holland, a human rights education trainer, points out that we all try to make sense of our lives and the realities we confront. These self-chosen explanations become the framework within which we cope on a daily basis. For children on the street, who have lived difficult and marginal lives, the abstract concept of rights may have little bearing on their understanding of their situation. They may feel, for instance, that it is pointless to attend school, because they are incapable of formal learning, and are better off acquiring real life survival skills. A superficial knowledge of their rights will do little to change their self-image or the way they respond to the world. Instead, Holland argues, a good human rights education should help them to gradually reframe their understanding of their personal experience, and to act out of a conviction of their own worth. The notion of rights can only become meaningful as they actively attempt to solve the problems associated with acquiring their rights, whether by helping to build and organize a place where they can gather and eat, or by learning to read and handle numbers.[25]

- *Support opportunities for street-based children to gain an understanding of their rights through active participation in initiatives which address the problems in their lives.*

Skills training and income generation

a constructive alternative

Often children are most interested in acquiring skills that can be immediately applied to their livelihood. Job training and good employment opportunities for older children offer an alternative to harmful or illicit work while at the same time respecting their independence and their need to support themselves. The cost to any city of supporting training and opportunities for work is a good investment, and a constructive alternative to providing policing, detention, incarceration and other unproductive responses to unwanted street activities.

A number of successful programmes have been established. The city of Santos, which established the Experimental School Generation 2001 as a resource for street-based children, offered, among other opportunities, the chance to join carpentry and printing workshops, and to share in the profits that were generated.[26] Street Kids International has developed a curriculum for NGO partners to teach basic business skills to street children, so that they can improve their existing work or establish small businesses with friends. One such NGO is the Youth Skills Enterprise Programme in Zambia, which has made training available to over 200 young people, and has loaned money to 100 to support them in starting their own micro-businesses, which range from running small

[25] Holland, T (1998) 'Human Rights Education for Street and Working Children: Principles and Practice', *Human Rights Quarterly*, 20: 173–193

[26] City of Santos (1996) 'Santos na Habitat II: Integrated Children's and Family Program', The City of Santos, SP, Brazil

kiosks to producing and selling knitted wear. A number of these businesses are thriving and growing, and have had a significant impact on both the participants and their families.[27]

small business

Adolescents can also be linked to business people acting as mentors.[28] Other young people can often be the most valuable mentors – Baker describes such a scheme in Kathmandu. Boys on the street were given the opportunity to apprentice as motorcycle mechanics. Some found the transition to a regular work routine difficult to manage, and decided to return to the streets, but others persevered. The critical factor appeared to be the support of a mentor, generally a mechanic slightly older than the participant who had been in the workshop for some time and was able to be an older brother figure.[29]

mentors

In some cities, entering formal employment depends on the possession of legal identification, which many street-based children may lack. Procedures must be established to help children acquire the paperwork they need. In Nepal, CWIN worked alongside government agencies to collect life history information from older street children. This was presented to the Home Office so that these boys could be granted citizenship cards, which are necessary for any civil service post and for most jobs paying a regular monthly wage.[30]

identification

- *Provide job training and employment opportunities for older children which provide them with skills and offer alternatives to harmful or illicit work, while at the same time respecting their independence and their ongoing need to support themselves.*
- *Link older children with mentors, and especially with young people to whom they can easily relate.*
- *Ensure that street-based children have the legal identification they need to obtain employment.*

Responding to the situation of girls on the street

Most children on the street are boys, but girls are present in growing numbers. It is commonly accepted that around 10 per cent are girls; but this is a generalization based on a few studies, and subject to the inaccuracies prevalent in research on street children.[31] Because of social constraints in many countries, girls' options for survival may be more limited, and they may be more emotionally vulnerable than boys on the street. Swift suggests that while boys can identify with daring male roles in their life on the street, for girls, there are few acceptable role models, especially in cultures which stress home and family as the only legitimate context for girls and women.[32] Girls on the street have been frequently observed to join up with groups of boys, and often to de-emphasize their sex by dressing and acting like boys.[33] Others, like the kayayoo girls who carry loads in the markets of Accra, band together for safety and support, and sleep in groups in market sheds which are used during the day for trade.[34]

Because of their smaller numbers there are generally fewer supports available for girls on the street. What programmes there are often focus on girls in prostitution. Some of these programmes perform a vital service (see below). But sexual exploitation, harassment and violence on the street are by no means exclusively a hazard for girls. Nor is prostitution an

[27] Street Kids International (1995) *Participatory Methods: Community-based Programs*, Toronto, Canada: Street Kids International

[28] Boyden, J, Ling, B, Myers, W (1998) *What Works for Working Children*, Stockholm: Radda Barnen and UNICEF

[29] Baker, 1998, op cit Note 2

[30] Personal communication, Rachel Baker, 1998

[31] Connolly, M and Ennew, J (1996) 'Introduction: Children out of Place', *Childhood*, 3(2): 131–147

[32] Swift, A (1993) 'A Passage Out of Hell', *New Internationalist*, (240): 13

[33] Blanc, C S and contributors (1994) *Urban Children in Distress: Global Predicaments and Innovative Strategies*, Florence, Italy: UNICEF International Child Development Centre and London: Gordon and Breach

[34] Agarwal, S, Attah, M, Attah, M, Apt, N, Grieco, M, Kwakye, E A, Turner, J (1994) 'Bearing the Weight: the Kayayoo, Ghana's Working Girl Child', Presented at the UNICEF Conference on the Girl Child, Ahmedebad, India

option turned to by girls only. Boys, too, may find it a lucrative and ready source of income. There is a danger that focusing on the sexual vulnerability of girls may end up defining and limiting the interventions that are made available to them, and stigmatizing them in the process.[35] Girls should have easy access to the full range of supports that are available for boys. In addition, however, girls face the possibility of pregnancy with all its attendant health risks (see p60). If they bring an infant to term, they must then cope with the overwhelming task of raising a tchild in the unforgiving environment of the street. Special supports should be made available to respond to pregnancy, childbirth and parenting on the street.

- *When there are girls on the street, be sure that female street workers are able to offer support and understanding.*
- *Ensure that girls have equal access to any services and programmes made available to boys. In addition to the other health services, ensure that girls have access to any services and programmes made available to boys and to reproductive health care services.*
- *When girls on the street give birth, ensure that services are available to meet their needs for shelter and follow-up support.*

Support for children who have been raped or sexually exploited

sexually active children

Many street-based children and adolescents are sexually active, and this can have different meanings in different situations. Some children turn to sex with their peers for comfort and a sense of belonging. For others, sex may be a source of income, and its significance will vary depending on their culture, background and a number of other factors. In some cases, however, children may be traumatized by rape or repeated abuse, or they may feel trapped by their dependence on prostitution, but see no alternatives for survival. These children need special help and support. Instead, they often fall through the cracks and find that there is nothing available for them. The situation of one child in Delhi is a case in point. After being raped, she was found crying by youth workers. They took her to the police, as required by law, and she was sent to the government hospital to be examined. There she was placed in the labour room with a woman giving birth. When she screamed in fear, the doctor forced her legs apart in order to examine her, in effect repeating the experience of the rape. The youth workers subsequently tried to find a place where she could stay. Various facilities for women turned her down because she was a minor, and children's centres rejected her out of fear that a raped girl would undermine the morality of their young clients. In response to this situation the non-profit group, Butterflies, created a facility especially as a crisis response centre for children who have been raped or abused. The centre and its telephone hot line are never closed, there is round-the-clock medical care, counseling, and access to advocates and lawyers.[36]

sexually exploited children

For children who have been sexually abused or involved in prostitution there may be need for longer term support than can be offered through transitional centres. The Casa de Passagem or 'Passage House' in Recife, Brazil, offers both a short stay home where girls can find immediate refuge, and a long term home which leads them to an independent

[35] van Beers, H (1996) 'A Plea for a Child-centred Approach in Research with Street Children', *Childhood*, 3(2): 195–201

[36] Personal communication, Butterflies street worker, 1997

future in work which both they and society find acceptable.[37] In many of these programmes, girls are encouraged to help friends still on the streets. A few years ago the girls of the Passage House conducted a survey of the knowledge of all the girls working in the streets of Recife about AIDS and its causes. In response to gaps in their knowledge, and after thoroughly interviewing medical experts on the issue, they drew and wrote cartoon-like sequences about what they had learned, and together with the director of the centre, edited a book which was made available as an educational tool for other child prostitutes. The Youth Skills Enterprise Programme in Zambia, described above, has demonstrated that making work alternatives available to children can be a successful way of ending their dependence on prostitution. A number of young people who have participated in this programme have mentioned the fact that they no longer need to engage in casual sex in order to support themselves.[38]

helping friends on the streets

- *Support the establishment of crisis response centres for street-based children who have been raped, abused or sexually exploited.*
- *Support longer term refuges for girls (and boys) who have been in prostitution, enabling them to work towards an independent future and alternative livelihoods which both they and society find acceptable.*

Other longer term interventions

Some programmes make longer term living situations available to children, as part of a strategy of working towards a better future off the streets, and possibly as an alternative to reunification with family (see below). The acceptance of life off the street can be a slow process, and some children may prefer to continue sleeping rough or moving between the homes of different family members and friends. The progressive approach offered by some programmes means that greater commitment and acceptance of structure and responsibility on the part of the child leads to a greater range of opportunities within the programme. World Vision's street children centre in Phnom Penh, Cambodia, located opposite the city market, houses about 50 children on an extended basis, while others may drop in during the day, or for a few nights. The centre provides meals, washing facilities and medical treatment to all, and counsellors are available for those who wish to discuss long term plans. Non-formal education is offered, and attempts are made to integrate children into the formal school system. Staff at the centre negotiated with a local school to waive the usual fees, and half of all children at the centre have been accepted back into the regular school system. For older children it is possible to learn a trade such as mechanics or tailoring. When short term visitors are engaged in hazardous work such as prostitution, centre staff discourage them from returning to their work, and try to find other options.[39]

a progressive approach

- *Support the establishment of longer term programmes for those children who are committed to finding alternatives to life on the street.*

[37] Swift, 1993, op cit Note 32
[38] Participant review process, Youth Skills Enterprise Programme, Zambia
[39] Paul, D (1995) 'Child Labour in Context', World Vision, Research and Policy Unit

Reuniting children with their families

Some street-based children can be successfully reintegrated into their families and communities, but this cannot happen if the original cause of separation is not removed. Dealing with the situation requires patience and sensitivity in understanding both the child's perspective and that of the family. Negotiations can theoretically be undertaken by a street worker familiar with the child. But, as Ennew points out, it may take an intensive effort which is beyond the scope and resources of most street projects. Because the roots of the original separation generally lie in economic difficulties or in the kinds of family dysfunction that are exacerbated by poverty, addressing the situation lies more within the realm of community development and poverty reduction efforts. Yet reuniting children with family must also happen on a case-by-case basis, and this fits uncomfortably with a community development model.[40] In many countries, children may have traveled great distances from home, and negotiations with family may be particularly difficult to achieve, since they will involve collaboration with organizations or authorities in other areas. The best person or agency to undertake this sensitive task will have to be determined on a local basis, making best use of the resources available. If a local community has a social welfare worker or family support centre (see p55), they might undertake this task.

Children's willingness to return home is not enough to guarantee success. It is important to ensure that they will be welcomed back. This can be difficult when their time on the street is a source of shame. Especially for rural families, city habits may be difficult to accept, and children may be seen as a source of disruption in a community. For children to be successfully reintegrated, they will have to find reasonable opportunities within the home community; either schooling or, for older children, training and appropriate work.

If children left home initially because of abuse of some kind, return to the family may be inappropriate. If it can be managed, it will have to involve the willingness and capacity of family members to change their ways of dealing with one another. The La Florida municipality in Chile runs a programme specifically for this purpose – to educate adults in avoiding family violence while reintegrating their children into the family.[41] If economic circumstances led to separation or abandonment, there is the need to discuss with family members how their situation might be improved, and to look for economic opportunities within the community. Successful reunification of children with family must involve the kinds of integrated community support that are necessary to prevent family break-up in the first place. It is also important to provide follow-up support.

[40] Ennew 1994, op cit Note 14

[41] Municipality, La Florida (1994) *Qué Hacer en Vez de. Material de Apoyo para la Crianza de Nuestros Hijos: Proyecto de Capacitacion de Padres para el Desarrollo Infantil*, Municipalidad de la Florida and UNICEF, Chile

- *When children and families wish to be reunited, ensure that the original cause for separation is addressed (See Chapter 3 and Chapter 10 for recommendations on providing support for families in economic difficulties).*
- *Help to find constructive opportunities for returned children within their home communities, and ensure that there is follow-up support within the home community for children and families that have been reunited.*

In most countries there is a high level of concern about juvenile crime, but little awareness of the many ways in which young peoples' rights are routinely violated through the justice system. Police arrest a boy in Cape Town, South Africa. UNICEF 1993, Benny Gool

12 Juvenile Justice

Article 40 of the Convention deals with children's rights with regard to penal law, and is one of the most detailed and prescriptive articles in the entire document. It recognizes that children and adolescents accused of crimes have a right to all the protections extended to adults, but it requires, in addition, that legal proceedings and dispositions be adapted to the age and developmental needs of the child. The Convention does not ban imprisonment, but calls for it to be a measure of last resort, for conditions to be humane, and for rapid social reintegration into the community to be a primary concern. Capital punishment and life imprisonment are not permitted. Wherever possible, judicial proceedings are to be avoided entirely in favour of other approaches that are sensitive to children's rights and their developmental needs. A number of other rights instruments have outlined in greater detail the standards that should be applied with regard to juvenile justice.[1] Unlike the Convention, however, none of these instruments is legally binding.

[1] These other instruments are United Nations Standard Minimum Rules for the Administration of Juvenile Justice 1985 (Beijing Rules); United Nations Rules for the Protection of Juveniles Deprived of their Liberty 1990 (JDLs); and United Nations Guidelines for the Prevention of Juvenile Delinquency 1990 (Riyadh Guidelines)

THE ROLE OF LOCAL AUTHORITIES

Local authorities seldom have control over the full range of procedures related to juvenile justice. In many countries, police forces, detention facilities, prison and court systems are functions of central government. But a number of municipal governments are developing their own policing capacity (for instance, Johannesburg and Buenos Aires). And in many cases, juvenile offenders may be handled at least in part by the local welfare system rather than the penal system. Where this is the case, local authorities are more likely to have a significant role.

The recommendations in this chapter will be more relevant where local authorities have a greater range of powers. But authorities at the local level must do whatever they can to ensure that children's rights are respected in the areas where they do have influence. They must reform conditions and procedures that come within their own jurisdictions, and support any efforts by non-governmental organizations establishing children's rights in the area of juvenile justice. They may be able to provide or facilitate alternatives to the options offered by the regular system, whether in providing housing for children awaiting trial, or opportunities for non-custodial sanctions. Regular meetings should be set up with representatives of all government agencies, and other groups involved in any way with children in conflict with the law, in order to discuss and coordinate their goals and activities.

It is also imperative that local authorities work in partnership with higher levels of government to tackle problems that cannot be fully addressed at the local level. In some countries, for instance, organized crime rings may use children for drug transportation and peddling because of their relatively protected status. Local authorities need the cooperation of central government to be able to respond effectively to the vulnerability of children in regard to organized crime.

prevention

Perhaps most significant for local government is the range of preventive measures that can be taken to reduce the likelihood of children getting into conflict with the law in the first place: adequate support for parents in challenging circumstances, the availability of high quality child care and schooling, measures to minimize violence and insecurity and to support strong community networks, and constructive alternatives for young people in high-risk situations.

COMMON VIOLATIONS OF THE RIGHTS OF CHILDREN IN CONFLICT WITH THE LAW

Systems of justice around the world vary in some important ways, but a significant number of them are guilty of routine violations of children's rights, and fail to offer even the protections extended to adults. Too many children are detained for behaviour that is not illegal, or that would not be considered an offence if they were adults. They may be 'guilty' of nothing more than homelessness or of being without the protection of an adult, and may be apprehended simply to clean up the streets. In Kenya, Côte d'Ivoire and the former Zaire, for instance, children are routinely arrested for homelessness or vagrancy, and in Nepal and the Philippines, arrests have been noted to increase dramatically before the visits of dignitaries.[2] Children may be arrested for suspected misconduct or for minor misdemeanors – begging, petty theft or riding a bus without a ticket. The number of children arrested who have actually committed significant offenses may be quite small. In India in 1988, serious crimes were found to account for less than four per cent of all juvenile offenses.[3]

There are overwhelming connections between being poor and in difficult circumstances, and being apprehended. A study of detention conditions in Egypt found that all the children interviewed came from poor backgrounds and histories of hardship.[4] In Nairobi, Kenya, 68 per cent of girls living on the street had been in official places of detention.[5] In Nepal, there are few street children who have not at some time been put into detention or custody centres.[6] The majority of those arrested may never, in fact, be convicted of an offense. In Pakistan, only 13 per cent to 17 per cent of the children brought to trial are found guilty.[7]

The rationale for arrest is often that it is in children's own interests to be removed from the perils of the street. In India, for instance, children can be apprehended if police consider them vulnerable to abuse or exploitation.[8] But this rationale carries little weight when no constructive alternatives are offered. Once they are apprehended, there is the potential for children's real needs to be addressed, but too often this is not the case. A UNICEF programme officer in Egypt claims that while the intention in classification centres is to separate the obviously innocent from those likely to be convicted, in fact many children who are guilty of little or nothing may spend months in grim conditions because of severely overloaded criminal justice systems and a lack of alternatives.[9]

After being apprehended children are sometimes held in juvenile detention centres, but in many countries they are placed in facilities that also house adults awaiting trial, often waiting months or even years for their situations to be addressed. In Lebanon, 90 per cent of all incarcerated children have not been convicted of any crime, but are simply awaiting a hearing; and in Jamaica children as young as 10 can be held with adults for indefinite periods of time.[10] These months or years can be a critical time in the development of a child or adolescent. A recent UNICEF report suggests that the most severe abuses may occur during this pre-trial phase of the justice process. First hand accounts from Turkey, Bangladesh and Pakistan describe the torture of children and adolescents held in police custody.[11] Detention centres are frequently overcrowded, squalid, and threatening to health. They are also likely to be psychologically damaging for children, who run the risk of rape and abuse, and are exposed, sometimes over long periods, to hardened adult criminals. Because of the supposed 'temporary' nature of detention facilities, there are often no activities available, and the deprivation for developing children who may be held for long periods can be extreme.[12] The difficulties of incarceration are often worse for minority children, who may experience hostility and violence from staff and other detainees, and be especially vulnerable to isolation and depression.[13]

While children under police custody await disposition, they cannot be sure of having contact with family or receiving legal advice. A 1993 study in Namibia, before reforms were introduced, found that 90 per cent of detained children were sentenced without legal representation.[14]

2 Blanc, C S and contributors (1994) *Urban Children in Distress: Global Predicaments and Innovative Strategies*, Florence, Italy: UNICEF International Child Development Centre and London: Gordon and Breach; Pradhan, G (1993) 'Child Delinquencies and Children in Adult Prisons in Nepal', *Voice of Child Workers: Newsletter of Child Workers in Nepal Concerned Center*, (17 and 18); UNICEF (1998) 'Innocenti Digest: Juvenile Justice', Florence, UNICEF International Child Development Centre

3 Blanc 1994, op cit Note 2

4 El Baz, S (1996) *Children in Difficult Circumstances: A Study of Institutions and Inmates*, UNICEF

5 Ochola, L (1996) 'The Undugu Society Approach in Dealing with Children at Risk to Abuse and Neglect' in Verhellen, E (ed) *Monitoring Children's Rights*, The Hague, Boston: Nijhoff

6 Pradhan, 1993, op cit Note 2

7 UNICEF 1998, op cit Note 2

8 Palme, L (1997) 'No Age of Innocence: Justice for Children' in UNICEF (ed) *The Progress of Nations 1997*, New York: UNICEF, 51–55

9 Bibars, I (1998) 'Street Children in Egypt: from the Home to the Street to Inappropriate Corrective Institutions', *Environment and Urbanization*, 10(1): 201–216

10 Palme 1997, op cit Note 8

11 UNICEF 1998, op cit Note 2

12 Ibid

13 Black, M and Smith, C (1997) 'Rights of Institutionalized Children', European Conference on the Rights of Institutionalized Children, Bucharest, Romania, UNICEF

14 Palme, 1997, op cit Note 8

harsh conditions

retribution rather than rehabilitation

There is little data available on conditions for children who have been sentenced to prison. Accountability is not high. UNICEF points out that most countries have records of immunization and school enrolment, but may have little idea of the numbers of children involved with the criminal justice system.[15] The available information is discouraging. Even in special juvenile prisons, conditions can be harsh. Prisons, like detention centres, are often antiquated facilities with little provision for health or comfort; high rates of disease result from overcrowding and insanitary conditions. The emphasis is frequently on retribution rather than rehabilitation, and even where physical punishment is forbidden by law, children can be subjected to brutal behaviour. In Egypt, children report beatings and other humiliating punishments.[16] In Nepal there are reports from children of torture, beatings and forced labour.[17] In the Gambia, Sudan and Guyana, whipping is still officially sanctioned as part of a child's sentence.[18] There is often little available in the way of education, contact with family, or efforts towards reintegration into the community. For children incarcerated with adults, the risks are even higher. It is hardly surprising that incarceration has been found ineffective as an antidote to delinquency. Instead, it exposes children to a range of antisocial and criminal experience, and offers them little in the way of positive alternatives.

Children convicted of crimes are not the only ones whose rights are violated by prison conditions. In some countries young children, many of them born in prison, live with their imprisoned mothers in conditions that seriously threaten their development and well-being. Reports from Rwanda and Nepal, for instance, speak of the alarming rate of hygiene-related illness and morbidity, and the utter lack of appropriate stimulation for these children.[19]

SOME BASIC PRINCIPLES AND MODELS FOR ACTION

In order to meet the provisions of the Convention in the area of juvenile justice, some fundamental principles must guide policy and practice at every level.

Raising awareness

In most countries there is a high level of concern about juvenile crime, but little awareness of the ways that young peoples' rights are violated through the justice system. Even the administrators and staff of correctional facilities may be unaware that their routine procedures violate international law.[20] All those having official contact with children and adolescents in the justice system, including police, lawyers, social workers, court personnel and the staff of detention centres and long term institutions, must be specially trained to understand children's rights, and to protect these rights with respect and compassion. Their dealings with children and adolescents should always be geared towards providing them with the support necessary for moving towards responsible life in the community. Cantwell argues for requiring judges and magistrates to

[15] Ibid
[16] Bibars, 1998, op cit Note 9
[17] Pradhan, 1993, op cit Note 2
[18] Newell, P (1995) 'Respecting Children's Right to Physical Integrity' in Franklin, B (ed) *The Handbook of Children's Rights: Comparative Policy and Practice*, London/New York: Routledge, 215–226
[19] Pradhan, 1993 op cit Note 2; UNICEF 1998, op cit Note 2
[20] UNICEF 1998 op cit Note 2

visit prisons and detention centres, so that they may be aware of the conditions under which children await trial and to which they may be sentenced. Local organizations should also have access in order to raise general awareness about these facilities and to encourage the provision of services for incarcerated children.[21]

- *Provide special training for all those having official contact with children and adolescents in conflict with the law, to ensure that they understand and are willing to protect children's rights.*
- *Encourage judges, magistrates and members of local civic organizations to visit prisons and detention centres.*

Apprehension, arrest and detention

rapid response for detained children

Where local policies support the apprehension of unattended children, without other cause, these policies must be reviewed and modified, preferably by a local committee for overseeing children's rights, and in collaboration with local law enforcement agents and social welfare workers (see p260). When children are not guilty of a crime, the police should immediately turn them over to more suitable agencies and organizations, or return them to their families, when appropriate.

When there is reason to believe that children have committed an offense, those guilty of minor misdemeanors should be rapidly separated from more serious offenders, and where necessary, referred on for appropriate services. This is not only in the interests of the children, but also prevents the misuse of overburdened judicial systems. The process for children awaiting disposition should be rapid. When children cannot be returned to family, perhaps because of the severity of the offence, detention conditions must be safe, healthy and responsive to the child's developmental needs. Legal advice must be readily available. The Youth Reautonomy Foundation in Turkey provides an excellent model for responding to the many needs of children and adolescents in detention. They provide advisory services directly from police stations, and have an office at the Juvenile Court building which provides children and their families with support during the hearing, finds employment for families when necessary and helps to provide for their material needs. The foundation has established separate detention houses for children, where they are taught by retired teachers and supplied with sporting facilities such as table tennis and volleyball. The foundation also runs seminars for volunteers, training them to provide useful services for these young people.[22]

legal advice

separate facilities for children

- *Review local policies and regulations to ensure that they do not permit the apprehension of unattended children without other cause.*
- *Establish screening and referral centres for children and adolescents who have been arrested for minor offenses.*
- *Ensure that children are not detained for long periods; that they are held separately from adults, and that living conditions are healthy, safe, and supportive of their developmental needs.*
- *Provide advisory services for children awaiting trial.*

[21] Cantwell, N (1998) 'Nothing More than Justice', *Innocenti Digest: Juvenile Justice*, (3): 16–17
[22] Informational brochure, Youth Reautonomy Foundation, Istanbul, Turkey

Sentencing

The response to any offense by a child or adolescent must take into account the maturity of the child, and must emphasize guidance, education and supervision rather than punishment. The goal must be the most rapid possible reintegration of the child into the community and, ideally, the family. There is increasing recognition of the value of alternative approaches, especially for those whose offences have not been serious. In Uganda, for instance, children's courts have been introduced, presided over by specially trained judges. There are limits on trial periods – cases not settled within three months are dismissed – and custodial sentences are a last resort.

alternative approaches

In some countries there are growing efforts to by-pass the court system entirely for young offenders, since the more common sentencing responses often serve only to alienate them further, and fail to deter them from crime in the future. An increasingly common response for less serious offences is a pre-trial screening: the child or adolescent in question meets with a social worker or court representative to determine an alternative, non-judicial course of action – generally some programme of counselling, restitution, life skills training and supervision.[23] Many Brazilian cities have established screening and referral centres which offer a number of integrated services as an alternative to incarceration. These include the availability of small residential homes where young offenders can live together away from the temptations of the streets, and with the support of advisory staff. Children are actively involved in the day-to-day running of the household and, with the help of staff, work to re-establish contact with family, to enter school, or to find employment.[24]

guidance

supervision

reparation

Responses that require young lawbreakers to acknowledge the consequences of their actions, and where possible to make reparation to their victims and the community, have been found to have very positive results. In a number of countries, in a scheme inspired by Maori tribal law in New Zealand, young offenders meet with their victims and hear about the suffering, loss or inconvenience they have caused. This approach has been found to reduce youth crime dramatically. In New South Wales, Australia there has been a 50 per cent reduction in the number of juvenile offenders in court, and a 40 per cent reduction in reoffending. Police in the Thames Valley in Britain claim that the number of young people reoffending had been lowered from 30 per cent to 4 per cent.[25] In the Philippines, a similar mediation scheme draws on the traditional village justice system to bring about amicable settlements between victims and juvenile offenders.[26]

mediation

peer juries

In the United States, communities in 30 states offer a scheme in which young offenders appear before a jury of their peers. This programme eases the load on the formal judicial system by siphoning off the misdemeanors and minor felonies that can clog the system and cause long delays. The peer jury solution is not necessarily an easy way out: one 13-year-old, who stole two packs of cigarettes from a store, was required to perform 28 hours of community service, send a letter of apology to the store, and write reports on both the health hazards of smoking and the effects of stealing on the community. He also had to serve eight times as a jury member on the peer court. In return for these often stiff judgements, offenses do not remain on the young offender's permanent record. Parents must consent to the teen court option and appear for the hearing.

[23] Cantwell, 1998, op cit Note 21
[24] Blanc, 1994, op cit Note 2
[25] Petty, C and Brown, M (eds) (1998) *Justice for Children: Challenges for Policy and Practice in Sub-Saharan Africa*, London: Save the Children Fund
[26] UNICEF 1998, op cit Note 2
[27] Weil, N (1996) 'In Teen Courts Young People Set their Peers Straight', *Doing Democracy*, Winter 1996

These courts have been funded by grants from local civic groups, local school budgets and municipal court budgets. Confidentiality laws regarding minors preclude hard data, but those involved in these systems claim dramatic results for the young people who go through them.[27]

UNICEF's recent report on juvenile justice, while acknowledging the value of such extra-judicial approaches, offers a note of caution. In a normal court of law the accused person is theoretically guaranteed the protection of due process. These alternative approaches, however, are based on the young person's willingness to acknowledge guilt. There is at least a chance that, in order to avoid the formal justice system, children may be pressured into admitting to offences they did not commit, and as a result become subject to far-reaching decisions by others regarding their well-being. Care must be taken with any such solutions to ensure that children are aware of their right to due process and legal representation.[28]

ensuring the right to due process

- *Protect the rights of children to due process and legal representation, and ensure that they are aware of these rights.*
- *Ensure that sentencing emphasizes guidance, education and supervision rather than punishment.*
- *Work towards the most rapid possible reintegration of the child into the community and ideally the family.*
- *Consider responses that require young lawbreakers to acknowledge the consequences of their actions and where possible to make reparation to their victims and the community.*

Improving prison conditions

improved conditions in:

Namibia

Non-institutional solutions are preferable for children and adolescents, but change can be slow. Existing conditions within prisons must also be improved so that basic needs for survival and healthy development in both mind and body are adequately addressed. In a number of countries there has been heartening progress. In Namibia, where as recently as 1993 children were routinely sent to adult prisons, they are now increasingly held separately from adults, and given access to a life skills course that teaches responsible decision making.[29] In Karachi, reforms over the last five years have involved young prisoners in learning vocational trades and at the same time improving their own prison environment. Nine hundred boys, from about 10 to 18, learn skills such as barbering, tailoring, cooking, electrical work and carpentry, and use them in part to serve one another and to improve their surroundings. They do their own cooking and cleaning, and have even constructed their own beds. These changes were brought about through collaboration between jail authorities, local philanthropists, NGOs and committees including government appointees. All funding was given by Karachi citizens. Efforts have also been made to improve conditions for very young children in prison with their mothers in Karachi. With funds from public donations and Rädda Barnen a Montessori school has been established, which is working towards the provision of play facilities and gardens for children who might otherwise never see the outdoors.

Pakistan

Rwanda

28 UNICEF 1998, op cit Note 2
29 Palme, 1997, op cit Note 8

Sometimes even small changes can make a difference to children incarcerated in grim circumstances. In Rwanda, as of 1997, 1,300 adolescents were being held for crimes allegedly committed during the civil war, separated from family in harsh and extremely overcrowded adult facilities, and lacking the most basic responses for their often traumatized psychological state. The TEP programme (Teacher Emergency Package), supported by UNICEF and UNESCO, has provided materials for setting up makeshift schools, as a first step in normalizing the situation of these young people and providing a focus for their days (see resource list, p284).

- *Where incarceration for children and adolescents cannot be avoided, be sure that conditions support their safety and their healthy development in both mind and body.*
- *Give children the opportunity for education and for acquiring useful skills while in prison, including skills in responsible decision making.*

Reintegration

support during re-entry

The ultimate goal of every phase of the juvenile justice system must be to reintegrate children and adolescents successfully back into the community, and to help them lead productive lives in the future. Support must continue through the often difficult period of re-entry. The conditions which may have pushed a child or adolescent into illegal behaviour are unlikely to have changed dramatically. Efforts must be made to minimize their risk of re-offending. If families are unable to provide the support and guidance their children need, other solutions must be considered. Counselling must be available to young people who are trying to pick up responsibility for their lives, and appropriate schooling or vocational training. The Youth Reautonomy Foundation in Turkey, described earlier, which provides services for young people awaiting trial, continues to offer support during the period after discharge, and focuses on resocializing juvenile delinquents by helping them to develop self-respect and confidence, and by encouraging tolerance and compassion towards others. Once children are discharged, they can make use of a youth house run by the foundation for ongoing support as they re-enter society.[30]

Taking appropriate steps to reduce the risk of reoffending should be part of a larger prevention effort in every community, offering support and opportunity to young people, and providing them with realistic and productive alternatives to delinquency and alienation.

- *Be sure that children and their families receive adequate support through the difficult period of re-entry into the community.*
- *If families cannot provide the support their children need to avoid reoffending, consider alternative living arrangements.*
- *Make counselling available, schooling and vocational training; for those who are old enough, help to find appropriate employment.*

[30] op cit Note 22

Part Three

Governance for Children's Rights

Part Three

As we have seen throughout this book, a concern for children's rights is not a narrow focus. It includes a concern for stable and healthy families as the means through which children's rights are most often fulfilled. It also involves a concern for the services and institutions that are necessary to support children and their families, to protect them from maltreatment and exploitation, and to involve them in decisions affecting their lives. It includes the rights of children and their families to make demands within representative and participatory political structures. The challenge is to establish a coordinated system of governance which can promote the economic security, social justice and environmental care that are essential for healthy communities and families and for the realization of children's rights.

Obligations towards children are most pressing at the local level. Violations of children's rights are generally experienced outside the oversight of national government and international agencies. Moreover, city and municipal authorities have increasingly become the primary governmental actors in the provision of basic urban services that affect children's lives. Local governments are on the front line and have the significant responsibility of responding to local conditions in ways that make children's rights a reality.

But governance at the local level is not a function of local government alone. Governance also includes all the other activities and processes that societies use to organize themselves, and the many and varied groups, institutions and organizations within civil society that contribute to meeting basic social needs. Local government cannot function effectively in isolation from these groups and activities. Local authorities must also operate within the framework imposed by higher levels of government, and within the context of international realities. When we consider the kinds of governance necessary for achieving children's rights, it is important to recognize all of these relationships.

In Chapter 13 we will clarify the range of responsibilities of local government, and the context within which it functions, including its relationship to community governance, to higher levels of government, and to the international framework. In Chapter 14 we will discuss the practical implications of children's rights for the structure, policies and practices of local authorities.

Local government serves as an important link between higher levels of government and global realities on the one hand, and, on the other hand, action at the most local level by organizations and groups within civil society. A low-income settlement in Jakarta. UNICEF, Sean Sprague

13 The Context of Local Government

In most countries, local governments are responsible for a wide range of tasks that affect the well-being of children and their families. It can be difficult to generalize, since there are significant differences from country to country in the scope of their responsibilities, their powers, and the degree of support they receive from higher levels of government and other sources of funding. This chapter describes some of these variations and acknowledges the challenges that local governments face in attempting to implement children's rights.

responsibilities of local governments

Although there are exceptions, local governments in urban areas are usually responsible for developing urban plans and implementing related codes and regulations. They also tend to be responsible for implementing codes related to health and safety within the built environment, and for other regulatory tasks such as pollution control. They are generally responsible for road construction and maintenance, solid waste management, street lighting and street cleaning, and they most often deal with the maintenance of parks, playgrounds, sports facilities and other public spaces. In addition, local authorities are usually responsible for water supply, sanitation, electric power, police and fire protection and public transport. Even where they do not provide infrastructure or particular services, they often have a major role in supervision and regulation. Where services are privatized, they often ensure quality and coverage, and control prices. In many countries, local governments have a growing role in providing primary education, health care and social assistance, often in association with national or provincial level ministries or agencies.

In some countries there is relatively comprehensive and well-funded government provision for the needs of children and their families. Decentralization reforms have in some cases reallocated responsibilities to local authorities as well as resources or the power to raise them locally. But even where resources are available to local governments, there are often significant numbers of children and families whose basic needs are not met. In some wealthier cities in the South, for instance, statistics show good overall provision; but in neighbourhoods where low-income groups are concentrated, provision remains inadequate, and large and often growing disparities in access to basic services are the norm.

decentralization

In other countries, local governments are provided with little or nothing to meet basic needs in spite of the responsibilities conferred on them by law.[1] In some cases these urban centres have democratic and accountable governments, but too little funding and too few professional staff to meet their responsibilities. Many of the examples of good practice in this book are drawn from such cities. These local authorities use their limited funding in combination with their power to draw on underused resources, to improve regulatory frameworks, and to work alongside other groups. Innovative collaborations with community based organizations, NGOs and other voluntary sector organizations, national or provincial government agencies, international agencies and private sector enterprises have been effective in helping to meet basic needs in these cases.

limited funding

There are differences between cities and countries not only in levels of provision, but also in the ways governments operate. At one extreme are government structures that are relatively democratic, accountable and transparent. At the other are dictatorships, or systems that remain structured along clientelist lines in spite of some democratic characteristics. Many government institutions regard the poor and their neighbourhoods as 'the problem', and there is little connection between their policies and priorities, and the daily lives and most pressing needs of most of the population.[2] In situations like this, most of the organizations that are effective in addressing children's needs lie outside of government, and it is here that a broader concept of 'governance', rather than only 'government', becomes so important. But even where private agencies are highly effective, they still need appropriate regulatory frameworks to ensure quality and safeguard rights, and their efforts can be strengthened by the kinds of coordination government can provide. Children's rights are an integral part of participatory democratic processes that cannot be comprehensively addressed by private agencies and civil society alone.

THE RELATIONSHIP OF LOCAL GOVERNMENT TO COMMUNITY GOVERNANCE

Whether because of lack of resources or lack of political will on the part of local governments, responding to the requirements of poor urban children and their families often becomes the function of informal

[1] UNCHS (1996) *An Urbanizing World: Global Report on Human Settlements 1996*, New York: Oxford University Press

[2] See for example Halfani, M (1997) 'Civic Associational Development and Public Sector Reforms in Tanzania: Disjuncture in Transforming Urban Governance', Paper presented at the GURI Conference on Governance in Action: Urban Initiatives in a Global Setting, Centre for Urban and Community Studies, University of Toronto, Toronto; Swilling, M (1997) 'My Soul I Can See: The Limits of Governing African Cities in a Context of Globalization and Complexity', Paper presented at the GURI Conference on Governance in Action: Urban Initiatives in a Global Setting, Centre for Urban and Community Studies, University of Toronto, Toronto

community institutions and initiatives. It is important to consider, for instance, the reality of who builds and manages cities. The conventional view is still that cities are built by private sector enterprises and public sector agencies, and managed by authorities. In reality, it is now common for between 30 and 50 per cent of an entire city's population in poorer countries to live in houses and neighbourhoods that have been developed without government approval, and with no contribution from public sector institutions in construction, financing, management or regulation.[3] The scale and nature of their investments is rarely recorded or reflected in official statistics, but in the poorer areas of most cities, the annual investment made by low-income households is many times the average investment per household made by city and municipal authorities. This is especially so if a realistic monetary value is given to the labour time people put into improving or extending their homes.

the bottom-up processes by which cities are built and managed

In most informal settlements, public agencies have also provided little or no investment in water, sanitation, drainage, roads, sidewalks, schools, health centres and other essential forms of infrastructure and services. Investments in public infrastructure and services in the poorest urban settlements are often generated locally, or negotiated directly with external bodies (NGOs, agencies from higher levels of government, international donors). In many urban centres, governance takes this form in most illegal or informal settlements even as more conventional patterns of local government provision prevail in other areas. More recognition must be given to the 'bottom-up' processes by which individuals, households and communities build and manage cities, for these have a greater influence for many children than the activities of local authorities. Even when governments do provide basic infrastructure and services, action at the community level is usually still necessary. The involvement of community members in the on-going management of schools, health centres and other services widely used by children and parents is critical to ensuring that local children's rights are adequately met.

In some cities, especially in Latin America, many low-income settlements have democratically elected community councils with extensive experience in setting up and managing community initiatives, and in negotiating with local authorities and other external agencies for infrastructure, services and land tenure. This is less common in sub-Saharan Africa, but even here many urban areas have important informal institutions such as the tribal structure, and community associations which raise funds to provide or improve schools or health centres, to manage roads, squares, markets, garbage disposal and cultural activities.

Strong, effective action at community level helps to ensure that the rights of children are addressed, and also builds the potential for more supportive, accountable and democratic government structures. The scale and scope of community action is much increased if municipal government is supportive. Municipal authorities can also achieve far more in meeting their responsibilities if they work cooperatively with the range of informal institutions and initiatives at the community level rather than ignoring or obstructing them.[4] Permanent channels of support for such initiatives should be set up and managed in ways that are transparent and accountable; local governments must establish formal lines of communication with community efforts, and find ways to support and coordinate with existing initiatives. They must help to ensure that marginalized

[3] Hardoy, J E and Satterthwaite, D (1989) *Squatter Citizen*, London: Earthscan; Lee Smith, D and Stren, R (1991) 'New Perspectives on African Urban Management', *Environment and Urbanization*, 3(1): 23–36

[4] Attahi, K, Carr, M, Stren, R (1992) *Metropolitan Planning and Management in the Developing World; Abidjan and Quito*, Nairobi: UNCHS (Habitat)

groups are included and their rights recognized, and where communities lack the solidarity and organization, local government must work to mobilize awareness and to encourage and support community involvement in planning and management. Experience to date points to some important guidelines for such efforts, and these will be discussed in more detail in the following chapter.

THE RELATIONSHIP OF LOCAL GOVERNMENT TO THE NATIONAL LEVEL

Decentralization policies of various kinds have been implemented in most countries in the South over the last 15 years, in many cases in response to a crisis of the central state.[5] But decentralization is not necessarily accompanied by increased local democracy or by more effective municipal governments. In many nations, the political, financial and technical capacity to define and implement initiatives remain with politicians, ministries or agencies at higher levels of government.[6] National governments usually establish the legal framework within which municipal and other government agencies operate in urban areas, defining their powers and duties, supervising their operations, regulating their sources of revenue and controlling the flow of investments into urban infrastructure, whether from national budgets or international agencies.[7]

Nor does the introduction of elected municipal authorities necessarily ensure more effective municipal governments. In some cases, higher levels of government restrict the power and funding available to democratically elected city authorities when opposition parties gain control.[8] Cities in Mexico, for instance, which have elected mayors from parties other than the PRI, which has long controlled national government, have faced difficulties in obtaining funding from higher levels of government.

Changes associated with decentralization are frequently more a delegation of responsibilities rather than any real devolution of power and funding, but there are exceptions. In some cases fundamental reforms at national level have given local governments more scope, more resources and in some instances, more power and more accountability. Brazil's 1988 constitution, for instance, included provisions for transferring power and autonomy to municipal governments and ensuring that they were democratically elected. Innovations in many other Latin American countries are also linked to democratization at national and local levels and some increases in power and resources at city or municipal level, including the replacement of appointed municipal leaders with elected officials.[9] The transition back to democratic rule in Chile in the late 1980s, for example, included the gradual strengthening of municipal governments, and municipal elections for local councillors and mayors began in 1992. There have been comparable changes in some Asian and African countries. In India, where municipal authorities come under the jurisdiction of state governments, the amendment to the Federal constitution in 1992 helped to define a considerably expanded role and a greater independence for municipal authorities.[10] In many Francophone African nations in recent years more attention has been given to the development of city and metropolitan government structures and to more democratic and decentralized frameworks.[11]

5 UNCHS 1996, op cit Note 1; Dillinger, W (1993) 'Decentralization and its Implications for Urban Service Delivery', Urban Management Programme Discussion Paper no 16, Washington DC: World Bank

6 Ramirez, R (1996) *Local Governance Models: Decentralization and Urban Poverty Eradication*, London: Development Planning Unit, University College London

7 Davey, K (1992) 'The Structure and Functions of Urban Government: The Institutional Framework of Urban Management', Birmingham, Development Administration Group, University of Birmingham

8 UNCHS 1996, op cit Note 1

9 Ibid

10 Mathur, O P (1997) 'Fiscal Innovations and Urban Governance', Paper presented at the GURI Conference on Governance in Action: Urban Initiatives in a Global Setting, Centre for Urban and Community Studies, University of Toronto, Toronto; Singh, K (1996) 'The Impact of Seventy Fourth Constitutional Amendment of Urban Management' in K Singh and Steinberg, F (eds) *Urban India in Crisis*, New Delhi: New Age International Ltd, 423–435

11 UNCHS 1996, op cit Note 1

One key aspect of an appropriate national framework for supporting effective urban government is the institutional means to reduce inequalities between wealthy and poor local authorities. Without this, decentralization may simply consolidate or exacerbate inequality and poverty, as the wealthier municipalities can raise the funding needed for infrastructure and services more easily than the poorer ones.[12] In cities and metropolitan areas made up of a number of separate municipalities, it is common to find large differentials between them in per capita incomes and in the revenues raised by their local authorities. Especially within large and rapidly growing cities, municipalities that are new and relatively weak administratively may have a high concentration of illegal or informal settlements and among the lowest per capita incomes. Their local governments will not be able to meet their responsibilities without mechanisms to transfer funding and other forms of support from elsewhere.

If national governments are to ensure steady progress towards the fulfilment of children's rights, they will have to permit stronger, more effective and more accountable local governments. They must also seek ways to support appropriate innovations by local governments and to encourage better coordination between local authorities and the various agencies from higher levels of government when there is joint responsibility for infrastructure, services, regulations or institutions. Local governments can help to encourage these trends by joining with other municipalities to lobby actively for a voice in national policy decisions, as will be discussed in the following chapter (see p269).

THE GLOBAL CONTEXT

Consideration must also be given to international forces and factors that affect the capacity of municipal authorities to ensure that children's needs are met. Almost all the world's governments have been able to reach agreement on the CRC, but they are probably further from an international framework to implement these rights within the world's lower income nations than at any time over the last four decades.

Global economic trends that affect poverty and children's rights

Within most of the world's wealthier nations, development assistance budgets have been cut in recent years, and the post-war consensus on the role of the United Nations and other international development agencies is being increasingly questioned. More fundamentally, there is no serious discussion among the world's most powerful economies and political blocs about two of the most critical issues in regard to poverty reduction.

- The first is the question of how to adjust the world economic systems to ensure greater prosperity for lower income nations, and more stability for both low and middle income nations. The assumption seems to be that free markets and private investment flows will allow the lowest income nations to gain greater prosperity. But the evidence

[12] Ramirez 1996, op cit Note 6

of the last few decades has shown that while some low-income countries have achieved greater prosperity, most have not.
- The second is the issue of how to find a balance in an increasingly globalized economy between market pressures and the rights of citizens to defend their interests and priorities. The assumption is that markets provide a 'level playing field' where producers and consumers can meet on an equal footing. But markets favour those with capital and political power and essentially disenfranchise those with neither. The implications of these inequalities are magnified when state structures fail to provide individuals and communities with the means to defend their interests against the illegal practices so often employed by powerful economic concerns.

market vs rights

Democratic systems should ideally provide a critical check against this. But even in democratic societies, citizen concerns rarely have equal weight with commercial concerns.[13] All local governments face difficulties in reconciling their social and environmental responsibilities with the need to attract new investment.[14] By expanding the market beyond the boundaries of the nation-state, the process of economic globalization has shifted power away from governments. Economic decisions made by transnational corporations have become increasingly influential in determining where economic growth takes place, and the social and environmental consequences of such growth.[15] There are worrying implications.

- As globalization forces governments to attract private investment, they cut budgets for social provision, wages, job security and often, environmental protection. There are numerous cities where business enterprises have obtained sites from which poorer groups were evicted with little or no compensation; where new enterprises have brought elevated levels of air and water pollution, and abuses of occupational health and safety; and where limited municipal resources have been concentrated on building infrastructure to serve business with little or nothing spent on improving provision for the low income population.
- Nor does economic growth, even when sustained over many years, necessarily ensure more attention to children's needs.[16] The global experience is of increased disparities and exclusion. In the last 50 years, as the world economy expanded five times, disparities in per capita income between rich and poor countries became three times greater.[17] The benefits of economic growth tend to remain highly concentrated, while the costs of that growth are generally distributed among those with the least income and political power.
- There is also the issue of debt. A large group of countries, most of them in sub-Saharan Africa, have suffered in recent decades from civil war, political instability, low per capita incomes and very poor economic performance. These countries lack the resources, production structures and trained personnel to provide adequate living standards for their citizens using their own internal resources, and their potential is further limited by the external debts they are obliged to pay. It falls to the population within those countries to bear the costs

13 Winchester, L, T Cáreces, Rodriguez, A (1997) 'Urban Governance from the Citizen's Perspective: The Defence of a Barrio in the City of Santiago: The Case of Bellavista', Paper presented at the GURI Conference on Governance in Action: Urban Initiatives in a Global Setting, Centre for Urban and Community Studies, University of Toronto, Toronto

14 de la Barra, X (1996) 'Impact of Urbanization on Employment and Social Equity', Presentation at World Resources Institute

15 Korten, D C (1996) 'Civic Engagement in Creating Future Cities', *Environment and Urbanization*, 8(1): 35–51

16 See Mehrotra, S and R Jolly (1997) *Development with a Human Face*, Oxford: Clarendon Press; Sen, A (1995) *Mortality As an Indicator of Economic Success and Failure*, Florence, Italy: UNICEF International Child Development Centre

17 UNDP (1994) *Human Development Report 1994*, New York, Oxford: Oxford University Press

of the economic and fiscal policies that reduce social expenditure in order to ensure repayment of such debts.[18]

But there is little discussion internationally of the kinds of adjustments to the world economic system that would allow these nations to develop the stable economic base essential to meeting their own needs. Nor have countries in the North, or international banking institutions, acknowledged the ethical issues surrounding loans made to undemocratic governments which have used them primarily to enrich themselves and their supporters and maintain their grip on power. There may be no simple linkage between economic stability and political structure, but it is surely impossible to expect the development and maintenance of democratic, participatory, accountable, transparent government structures within economies continuously in crisis.

debt crisis

Although the debt crisis faced by so many countries in the South attracts less attention than it did during the 1980s, it remains a major influence on the resources that governments are able to allocate to schools, health care systems and other essential supports for children. The pressure for governments to meet debt repayments, and the conditions set by the Bretton Woods institutions for providing help in doing so (including lower public expenditures and the elimination of subsidies), reduced the quality and breadth of service provision in many countries during the second half of the 1980s and the first half of the 1990s, and have helped to impoverish large numbers of urban households. Only with growing evidence of sharp increases in poverty in a large number of countries has some compensatory action been taken.[19] Although measures to reduce the impact of structural adjustment on the poorest groups have been promoted and funded by international agencies, their effectiveness is limited, especially in their capacity to support more effective, accountable local government.

The inappropriate development assistance framework

Two other aspects of 'the broader context' need highlighting:

- The low priority that most international donor agencies – both multilateral development banks and bilateral aid programmes – have given to projects or programmes that directly benefit children.
- The constraints that the current aid framework faces in supporting the kinds of community and municipal initiatives that this book has recommended.

Most 'official' development assistance agencies, that is, the official bilateral aid programmes of the world's wealthier nations (mostly from Europe, North America, Japan and Australasia) and the multilateral development banks (including the World Bank and the regional development banks) assign a low priority to services essential for child health and development. It is rare for primary schools, day-care provision and maternal and child-centred primary health care to receive more than five per cent of total commitments over the last 20 years, and in many inter-

[18] de la Barra, X (1998) 'Poverty: The Main Cause of Ill Health in Urban Children', *Health, Education and Behavior*, 25(1): 45–49

[19] Cornia, G, R Jolly, F Stewart (eds) (1987) *Adjustment with a Human Face: Volume 1*, Oxford and New York: Oxford University Press; Moser, C O N, Herbert, A J, Makonnen, R E (1993) 'Urban Poverty in the Context of Structural Adjustment; Recent Evidence and Policy Responses', Washington DC, Urban Development Division, World Bank: 140; Stewart, F (1995) *Adjustment and Poverty: Options and Choices*, London: Routledge; Woodward, D (1992) *Debt, Adjustment and Poverty in Developing Countries: Volumes 1 and 2*, London: Pinter Publishers with Save the Children

national agencies, far less than that has been allocated.[20] Most international agencies also give a low priority to the provision of safe, sufficient water supplies and provision for sanitation, drainage and garbage collection; it is also rare for these to receive as much as five per cent of any agency's commitments. Most international agencies give little or nothing to programmes that help low-income households obtain or build better quality housing.[21]

low priority to children and basic services

This chapter cannot consider in detail why this is the case. It would require a detailed analysis of factors both internal and external to the major agencies, and their relative importance from agency to agency. But certain factors can be highlighted.

the reasons why

- First, since the whole structure of official development assistance is set up to provide assistance to national governments, any priority to the needs of urban children is difficult if national governments do not themselves prioritize children's needs and rights or do not wish to use development assistance to support the programmes of city and municipal governments.
- Secondly, many bilateral agencies have long avoided support to urban areas because they believed that most poverty was concentrated in rural areas, and that urban populations were relatively privileged in terms of services. This assumption, based on misleading averages, is changing in many agencies, as the evidence on the ground contradicts their assumptions, but the change is recent and slow and has yet to be reflected in resource allocations.
- A third reason centres on structural limitations within official development assistance agencies. In most cases these agencies were set up to provide large capital sums and technical assistance. Their understanding of what supports development has changed fundamentally, but they still have to operate within structures shaped by this earlier conception of development assistance. It is very difficult for any agency to support a large number of relatively cheap community-based projects when their system is designed to handle a few large recipient-government implemented capital projects.[22]

All development assistance agencies are also under great pressure to keep down staff costs; there is still an assumption among government departments or their supervisory boards (and the public) that an efficient agency is one that spends as much money as possible with the lowest possible staff costs. Yet supporting community-based initiatives generally means spending much less – indeed, the less the better, since the cheaper the cost and the greater the cost recovery in any community initiative, the less the reliance on external funding to make it work. Supporting community-based initiatives also requires more staff time in supporting such initiatives, relative to the money spent.

Finally, since development assistance agencies were set up to provide recipient governments with funds for capital projects, decision-making systems remain concentrated within the agencies, and mostly in their headquarters. It is difficult to allow participatory decision-making within agencies with most of their staff in central offices in the North. There

[20] Satterthwaite, D (1997) *The Scale and Nature of International Donor Assistance to Housing, Basic Services and Other Human Settlements and Related Projects*, Helsinki: WIDER
[21] Ibid
[22] Hardoy, J E, Mitlin, D Satterthwaite, D (1992) *Environmental Problems in Third World Cities*, London: Earthscan

are also many contradictions between the scale and timing of conventional project-cycle oriented development assistance and the kinds of processes at neighbourhood and local level that ensure children's rights are met. All development assistance agencies have sought ways around this – for instance, by channeling funds through international NGOs or national or local NGOs. But the proportion of funds that can be channeled in this way is always limited. And development assistance agencies often impose conditions on these intermediary institutions that prevent them from being effective. This helps explain why many international, national and local NGOs also fail to support participatory actions and processes.

new channels of support

If donor agencies accept that in many countries it is action at the community and municipal level that needs to be supported, they must develop alternative funding channels to support community and municipal initiatives. To do so on any scale means a great increase in the number of initiatives that will receive support. This implies major changes to the systems by which projects are suggested, developed and appraised and funded within these agencies. It is impractical for most of this process to take place outside of a recipient country, yet few development assistance agencies have sufficient staff in recipient countries. Again, there are interesting precedents among some donor agencies that try to address this problem – for instance, more staff in agency offices within recipient countries or special local funds managed by embassies – but these still represent the exceptions, and the proportion of funding channeled through them remains a very small part of development assistance.

The impact of international forces on the daily lives of children and their families, and on the practice of local government is, of course, profound. Municipalities, operating under often serious constraints, must be resourceful and innovative in their responses. While they are limited in their capacity to influence these forces, they are not completely helpless. As in their relationship with national government, there is the possibility of mobilizing in an organized way with other municipalities, in order to voice their common concerns and to be recognized together as a force in the international domain. One method that has been proposed for the effective decentralization of development assistance, for instance, is the funneling of aid to sub-national networks of municipalities, which could serve as a mutual check on one another – this approach was discussed at the InterAmerican Development Bank meeting in Cartagena in 1998. By working efficiently and responsively with international sources of funding, while at the same time protecting the rights of their most vulnerable citizens, local governments can demonstrate their effectiveness as partners in people- and child-centred development. Their support of community management approaches and participatory budgeting, for instance, could serve as an indication of transparency and commitment to democratic ideals. For more discussion of constructive partnerships with higher levels of governance, see p269.

THE CHALLENGES FACING LOCAL GOVERNMENTS

Despite their wide-ranging responsibilities, then, local governments generally face significant constraints in their capacity to act effectively.

The lack of financial capacity

The extent to which most local governments can respond to the growing need for infrastructure and services depends on the extent of their support from higher levels. But many factors act to reduce this support, including, in recent years, the cuts in public expenditure which are part of neo-liberal economic policies and of structural adjustment programmes. It is still rare for local authorities to have any significant capacity to invest, as virtually all their revenues go to pay for recurrent expenditures. A review of available statistics on local government investment found local capital expenditures are often the equivalent of only a few US dollars per person per year.[23]

no funds for investment

Major capital investment commonly depends on provincial or national governments, or specially created development authorities, while the management and maintenance is often handed over to local authorities which lack the necessary funding and trained staff. In addition, agencies responsible only for capital investment have little incentive to build systems that are more easily and cheaply maintained.[24] The funding available from higher levels of government, or from international donor agencies, is often for new investments or facilities, but not for on-going maintenance or management. Hard-pressed local authorities often favour putting limited resources into staff for schools and other services, rather than into repairs or capital projects. This exacerbates their difficulties with external agencies which can only support capital investment.

no funds for maintenance

Regulatory frameworks

Municipal authorities may also be hampered by inappropriate and outdated regulations. Some local authorities have the discretion to change or adapt national regulations, but many do not. Infrastructure standards often make provision unnecessarily and unrealistically expensive, and thereby limit the number of people who can be reached, and the possibility of cost recovery from users. Building codes are meant to promote health and safety; but are frequently ignored because they demand unnecessarily expensive standards or materials. Regulations on land use and development can be particularly constraining. The administrative systems for ensuring that private developers and house builders meet these norms and codes are also generally understaffed and inefficient, and this again encourages most developers and builders to operate outside the law or resort to bribery to gain official permission. Managing the expansion of urban areas is particularly problematic for authorities, especially in rapidly growing cities, for there can be many different levels of power controlling the purchase, price and ownership of land.

restrictive and outdated plans and regulations

An example of the difficulties facing any local authority intent on good practice is provided by Fernando Carrion, who was appointed as head of the planning department in Quito, the capital of Ecuador in 1989:

> *What planning did we find? There was a 1967 regulation that provided zoning for 7,500 hectares; the city covered 18,000 hectares. It was designed for a pre-petroleum*

[23] UNCHS 1996, op cit Note 1
[24] Davey 1992, op cit Note 7

> *economy and it was still in effect. Then there was the Metropolitan Area Plan (1973) and really this only provided a design for the main roads and some statements of intent for the Andean Pact. The 1981* Plan Quito *was a diagnosis of all the city's problems and it concluded with a very general land use proposal that never came into effect. This is what we found in terms of planning, that and an absolute absence of information and trained personnel. Indeed, trained personnel had been expelled from the Municipality. So, we began from scratch.*[25]

Dealing with competing demands

competing needs of business and low-income groups

All city and municipal authorities have to reconcile competing demands for limited public resources. Landowners, business enterprises, upper, middle and lower-income populations will all want resources to be allocated in ways that favour their interests, with the wealthier groups inevitably being more powerful, better connected and usually better organized. Urban authorities generally face conflicts in seeking both to expand the economic base of the city and meet the needs of many low-income households. Improved provision for business often conflicts with improved provision for low-income groups. Most often it is low-income neighbourhoods that are cleared to make way for new commercial or industrial developments, which then receive the water, landscaping and municipal services that were never available to the former residents.

There are also conflicts between immediate economic growth and gain, and the goal of ecologically sustainable development. Economic growth within any city generally transfers increased environmental costs to the surrounding region from which resources are drawn and where wastes are dumped. For cities to progress towards the achievement of sustainable development, they must keep to a minimum these transfers of ecological costs.[26] They must also keep to a minimum the transfer of such costs to more distant people and ecosystems or into the future – these cost transfers tend to happen in wealthier cities as they pay more attention to the environments in their region.[27] This presents considerable institutional difficulties, since city authorities are officially responsible only to the citizens within their boundaries. Within a competitive world market, it is difficult for city officials to reconcile the need for new investment with a commitment to the full range of sustainable development goals, especially when those goals raise financial costs within the city in order to reduce environmental costs elsewhere.

Responding to the challenge

In order to function effectively within a framework that frequently presents more constraints than supports, local governments must make the best use of available opportunities and strengths. They must work, first of all, to improve the effectiveness of their own internal structures and processes. They must establish productive working relationships with

[25] Carr, M (1992) 'Metropolitan Planning and Management in the Third World: a Case Study of Quito, Ecuador' in UNCHS (ed) *Metroploitan Planning and Management in the Developing World: Abidjan and Quito*, Nairobi: UNCHS, 83–137

[26] Haughton, G and Hunter, C (1994) *Sustainable Cities*, London: Jessica Kingsley

[27] Ibid; also McGranahan, G, Songsore, J, Kjellen, M (1996) 'Sustainability, Poverty and Urban Environmental Transitions' in C Pugh (ed) *Sustainability, the Environment and Urbanization*, London: Earthscan, 103–134; and Satterthwaite, D (1997) 'Urban Poverty: Reconsidering its Scale and Nature', *IDS Bulletin*, 28(2): 9–23

the communities they serve, with the private sector, and with other partners, supporting existing initiatives, mobilizing civil society and drawing on the considerable skills, resources and commitment that exist in every city. They must also coordinate and organize with other local governments to negotiate in unison with higher levels of government and with international agencies and funding sources. The following chapter will outline some of the practical steps that local governments can take in order to work towards achieving children's rights.

PREFEITURA
DE ICAPUI
PRESTAÇÃO DE CONTAS DE Março DE 1992
DESPESAS
POR SECRETARIAS E CÂMARA MUNICIPAL
I ADMINISTRAÇÃO E FINANÇAS
• pessoal 9.620.769.08
• material de consumo 2.170.721.46
• serviços de terceiros 12.984.371.99
• investimentos -0-
II SAÚDE E SANEAMENTO
• pessoal 9.740.383.75
• material de consumo 19.059.188.57
• serviços de terceiros 11.974.015.00
• investimentos 2.654.834.00
III EDUCAÇÃO E CULTURA
• pessoal 23.960.710.68
• material de consumo 1.930.042.00
• serviços de terceiros 6.937.589.52
• investimentos 4.500.000.00
IV OBRAS E SERV. PÚBLICOS
• pessoal 4.715.682.68
• material de consumo 8.139.038.60
• serviços de terceiros 10.691.424.79
• investimentos 12.879.093.62
V DESENV. ECON. E SOCIAL
• pessoal 2.182.337.44
• material de consumo 2.274.728.20
• serviços de terceiros 11.072.191.30
• investimentos 99.000.00
VI CÂMARA MUNICIPAL DE ICAPUI 10.000.000.00
VII DESPESAS COM RECEITAS VINCULADAS 7.127.404.39
TOTAL DAS DESPESAS 174.713.518.07
RECEITAS
DE ONDE VEM O DINHEIRO DA PREFEITURA
I. FPM (Fundo de Participação dos Municípios) 80.700.654.67
II. ICM (Imposto s/circulação de Mercadorias) 53.281.430.25
III. ISS (Imposto s/Serviços de Qualquer Natureza) -0-
IV ROYALTIES (Indenização p/Ext. de petróleo) 23.812.219.81
V. VERBA DO SUS 4.268.139.00
VI. OUTRAS RECEITAS 10.209.222.58
IVVC 844.208.00
IPI 715.930.88
IRRF 472.252.94
IPVA 8.769.12
REC. UTILID. PUBLICA 610.514.00
TLL 45.000.00
EXTRAS 7.512.547.62
TOTAL DAS RECEITAS 172.271.666.29
RECURSOS NA PMI
SALDO 01.03.92 13.502.753.16
SALDO 31.03.92 11.060.901.38

Transparency and accountability are essential to good governance. Access to information should not be restricted to those in power, but must belong to the whole community as the basis for democratic action. Here, in the municipality of Icapui in north-eastern Brazil, the local government's budget is painted on the wall of the mayor's house and updated each month. A third of local spending is allocated to education. UNICEF, Ellen Tolmie

14 The Practical Implications for Local Government

It is ironic that the level of government of greatest importance for protecting urban children's rights also tends to be the level with the least power, the least resources and the least trained staff. The goals suggested for local authorities in this book will appear daunting, and perhaps unrealistic, to the staff of many municipal agencies and other institutions important for children. But what we attempt to outline are ways to improve policy, planning and practice in the face of severe budgetary and staff constraints.

providing a framework of support

Earlier chapters have described many specific measures that local authorities can adopt. Case studies have shown what scope there is, even with limited funding, for improving housing, infrastructure, healthcare, schooling and other services for those living in illegal or informal settlements. In order to function as a catalyst for change and development, overstretched and underfunded public institutions must not only allocate their own funds fairly, but must work to provide a framework of regulation, incentive and technical support that encourages and supports good practice among all the groups and organizations that can help to ensure that children's rights are met. Local authorities, in short, can help to ensure that the framework for effective and inclusive action is in place, and that the most constructive, synergistic use is made of all available resources, whether they be natural, financial or human.

INSTITUTIONALIZING THE CONVENTION FOR SUSTAINED ACTION

If local government is to promote children's rights, the principles and provisions of the Convention must be given formal recognition within the various frameworks of local action. Local plans of action must reflect the goals of the Convention; local regulations must be brought into compliance with it; and budget allocations guided by its priorities.

The need for a local plan of action

Clear, publicly negotiated and democratically determined policies and strategies promote accountability for government, and provide a framework for responding to changing conditions. The kinds of accomplishments described throughout this book should not be scattered and isolated efforts, but must be part of a systematic, integrated plan that is reflected in the structures and processes of local government. A local plan of action for children, using the Convention as a guide, and adapting both the Convention and any national plan of action to local realities, is an important component of effective and democratic municipal action.

Working on a plan of action for children's rights should not be viewed as a distraction from the broader work of government. On the contrary, a plan focused on the rights of children could mobilize society more effectively than a traditional plan, while covering most of the same issues. Moreover, a local plan of action based on children's rights would be compatible with Agenda 21, and with the Habitat Agenda, coming out of the UN City Summit in 1996, for these, too, are grounded in participatory democracy, social justice and sustainability.

partnerships

The development of a local plan should be undertaken collaboratively, with representatives not only from municipal government, but also from other sectors of society, and in partnership with the local body for overseeing children's rights. It should be based on local assessment and analysis, reflecting the issues as they are experienced by city residents in all areas. Making a local plan the subject of broad debate can be one of the most effective ways of raising public awareness, opening the door to disenfranchised groups, and moving towards participatory governance.

plans as processes

A local plan of action is not a one-time effort or document, but an ongoing process. It shapes the structures and practices of local government and its partners, and is in turn shaped by the practices it has initiated. The recommendations that follow should be seen as contributing to the development of a comprehensive and responsive long term local plan that will guide an effective local government in meeting its obligations.

Reforming the regulatory framework

National governments are required to bring their legislation into compliance with the Convention. Local government, in the same way, must ensure that municipal regulations support the implementation of children's rights. We have already spoken of the importance of revising outdated regulatory codes when they are unnecessarily restrictive (pp43, 245). Building standards, for instance, should support safety, but should not put legal housing out of the reach of all but the well-to-do. Standards for infrastructure should not eliminate the possibility for progressive solutions or innovative technologies. There are many ways in which the needs of children could be better served with more flexible regulatory systems.

regulations that support children's rights

There are also areas that may require tighter regulation. Child care providers and institutions housing children, for instance, should be required to meet basic standards to ensure the health, safety and psychological well-being of the children under their care (pp87, 155). Regulations regarding child labour and working conditions need to be carefully developed to respond to the local situation as well as to national legislation (p197). There should be formal procedures for responding to the maltreatment of children, whether in the home, at school or elsewhere. Strong regulation can ensure higher levels of transparency and accountability, not only within government but within the range of organizations and institutions that affect the lives of children. In our increasingly privatized world, as procedures pass out of the hands of government, it becomes even more important to require sub-contractors and service agencies to operate according to certain standards. The careful revision of local regulations should be undertaken by municipal authorities in collaboration with representatives of the local children's rights oversight group (p260), and proposed regulations should be subject to the review and approval of a full range of partners.

Making children's rights a priority in budget allocations

investing in children

The allocation of limited economic resources is the most concrete expression of a municipality's priorities. The Convention recognizes the valid financial constraints that limit the implementation of children's rights, and the need in many cases for a gradual realization of goals. But it also requires investment 'to the maximum extent possible' of available resources (Articles 4, 6). The interests of children cannot be an afterthought, but must be a primary consideration in all budgetary allocations (Article 3). This is not as radical a suggestion as it appears, since it is widely acknowledged that attention to children's well-being will be reflected in the well-being of the whole society.

Responsible fiscal management requires that resources be used efficiently. But many public spending choices result in extraordinary levels of waste. The common focus on curative rather than preventive health care, for instance, is a poor investment, and may make little difference to the long term health of the population (p94). Failing to provide adequate education results similarly in an enormous waste of human potential. Making children's rights a priority in spending means taking the long view and investing in the potential of human beings. Decisions about budget allocations should involve representatives from all groups.

- *Develop a local plan of action adapting the Convention and the national plan of action to local realities, and coordinating with the goals of Local Agenda 21.*
- *View this plan not as a one-time effort, but as an ongoing process that is regularly updated, and that requires the involvement of all local stakeholders.*
- *Bring local regulations into compliance with the provisions of the Convention, and ensure that this process involves a full range of partners.*
- *Make children's interests a primary consideration in budgeting decisions.*

RAISING AWARENESS OF CHILDREN AND THEIR RIGHTS AT EVERY LEVEL

Broad social understanding of children's rights throughout society is essential to using the Convention as a framework for change. Without this common understanding, rights-based arguments for initiatives targeted at children can generate misunderstanding and resentment. It is especially important that people accept the principle of non-discrimination, and that their understanding of children's rights extend to those groups that they might unconsciously exclude – the children of minority groups, girls hidden from public view, adolescents who may be considered adults, and the poorest and most marginalized children. A real acceptance of the Convention requires nothing less than a change in culture.

accepting children's rights can mean a change in culture

Making effective use of the mass media

The mass media are a pervasive feature of contemporary life, and few urban dwellers are not touched by their reach. In Brazil, for instance, more than 80 per cent of homes have television sets. Radio, television, printed matter, billboards, school curricula and even messages on T-shirts are powerful instruments not only for disseminating information, but for shaping attitudes and values both for good and ill. The commercial world has been enormously successful in using this capacity to its own advantage. But it can also be used to build society, and local authorities can find constructive ways to use these important tools.

constructive use of the media

Awareness of children's rights can be actively supported through various kinds of campaigns, and in all languages locally spoken. In Nepal, brochures, music tapes, photo panels, radio and television have been used to publicize the message of children's rights; some post offices have agreed to stamp an article of the Convention on all mail.[1] Schools are an obvious place to introduce the Convention (p172), and the Committee on the Rights of the Child has recommended its inclusion in school curricula.

[1] Hodgkin, R and Newell, P (1998) *Implementation Handbook for the Convention on the Rights of the Child*, New York: UNICEF

publicizing violations and progress

News Agency for Children's Rights – Brazil

Public awareness should be raised on the existence and content of the Convention, but also on the many ways that its provisions are routinely violated. When the population of a city is honestly informed of the situation of its children, it is like holding up a mirror, showing everyone the scandal that they live with. This can become a powerful stimulus for action. It is important also to publicize the positive steps that are taken, so that there is a sense that change is possible and worth working for. It is important to establish good working relationships with the media. In Brazil, the News Agency for Children's Rights (ANDI) performs an invaluable public service in this regard by promoting the development of a journalistic culture which takes an active role in investigating the situation of Brazilian children and youth. ANDI collects data relevant to the protection of children's rights, maintains an up-to-date database and offers suggestions, advice and encouragement to the media. (See resource list).

Training for all those who deal with children

codes of conduct

field experience for municipal staff

All those who have professional or official contact with children and adolescents should be specially trained to understand and respect their rights. School teachers, judges, police officers, prison staff, social welfare workers, doctors, health workers and others can have a considerable impact on the children they deal with, and should be guided in their daily practice by codes of conduct that comply with the Convention (see for instance, adolescent health section and the juvenile justice section). Even officials and professionals who do not make direct contact with children, such as city planners and policy makers, developers and investors, must understand how their work may affect children's rights. The decision to relocate those in an illegal settlement, for instance, may be a profound violation of children's rights if it is not conducted with their best interests in mind, and with the involvement of their families (p70). Exposure to the realities of urban poverty for children should be part of the training of every municipal official or representative. In Olongapo, in the Philippines, representatives to a committee for children were routinely invited to accompany researchers into depressed communities.[2] Another approach can be to encourage the rotation of staff between bureaucratic responsibility and fieldwork.[3]

[2] Porio, E, Moselina, L, Swift, A (1994) 'Philippines: Urban Communities and their Fight for Survival' in Blanc, C S (ed) *Urban Children in Distress: Global Predicaments and Innovative Strategies*, Florence, Italy: International Child Development Centre of UNICEF and London: Gordon and Breach

[3] Dowbor, L (1996) 'Urban Children in Distress', *Development*, 1: 81–84

Educating parents about children's rights

The Convention stresses that the family is the primary institution responsible for the fulfilment of children's rights. For this reason, parents and other caregivers should be a particular target in raising awareness of children's rights. A tendency has been to focus efforts on children, in the hope that the message will be communicated to parents. But child rearing beliefs are deep-seated, and it is unrealistic to expect that parents will change their ideas as a result of their children's comments. In cultures where children are expected to defer to adult opinion this may even have a negative effect. It is also unlikely to be successful when parents do not experience themselves as having rights.

Educating parents on the rights of their children should never be prescriptive. Instead, it should take the form of dialogues with groups of parents in which the provisions of the Convention are discussed in the light of local realities and child rearing beliefs, and with a clear acknowledgement not only of parental responsibilities, but of the parents' own rights as human beings. This is not a one-way process. Not only is it necessary to educate parents and family members about the Convention; it is also essential that parents contribute to developing an effective local understanding and interpretation of children's rights. These discussions are likely to require the moderation of group leaders, possibly social workers, who have been trained to listen to parents and their concerns, and to think collaboratively about how the standards of the Convention might apply in the local context (see also p149).

dialogues with parents

- *Make information about the Convention available in all local languages, using a range of media; incorporate information on the Convention into other government publications; and introduce the Convention into school curricula.*
- *Identify child-friendly journalists in all the media to ensure that both violations of children's rights, and positive gains for children are widely publicized.*
- *Train all those who deal with children to respect their rights, and establish codes of conduct for professional practice.*
- *Through discussion with various groups, including parents, establish the implications of the Convention for local customs and practice.*

IMPROVING THE QUALITY OF INFORMATION AND COMMUNICATION

Adequate information is essential to every level of government action. Without it, it is impossible to understand peoples' needs, to plan effectively, to target resources appropriately, to monitor the effectiveness of policies or to predict trends for the future. It is equally critical to the practice of real citizenship. Unless people are accurately informed, they lack the basis for participation. Accurate and relevant data is an essential resource for the management of cities, not an unnecessary or added exspense.

adequate information: essential to effective government

Authorities often work with insufficient data, much of it poorly organized, incomplete, inaccessible, inaccurate or obsolete. Available information is often scattered among agencies, has never been coordinated or integrated, and is seldom disaggregated by location, sex, age or ethnic group. The lack of an accurate overview results in inefficiency, costly overlaps, a lack of continuity and a waste of limited resources. Effective city management requires an information system that is comprehensive, detailed, well-coordinated and easily accessible to all stakeholders. Dowbor points out in his practical guidelines for such systems that information must be viewed not as another sector of municipal activity, but as an ongoing activity permeating all sectors and allowing them to coordinate effectively with one another; 'a permanent fluid that feeds a network'.[4]

[4] Dowbor, L (1997) 'Municipal Information Systems: Practical Guidelines', http://ppbr.com/ld

Establishing an integrated information system

up-to-date technology: a cost-effective investment

Experience indicates that up-to-date computer and communication technologies are the most cost-effective expenditure a local government can make. They are a powerful, efficient and relatively cheap means for coordinating and managing large bodies of information, a valuable planning tool, and a means for ensuring effective communication. In cities facing rapid, unpredictable change, such technologies as the Geographic Information System (GIS) can allow for detailed spatial analysis, geographically referenced, and the capacity to explore through computer modelling, the implications of different policy decisions.[5]

The creation of an information-rich environment requires the efforts of a core group with strong political support to take the initiative. Within every institution or agency there should be a person who can be part of the effort to establish an interactive information network. Local information systems should be coordinated wherever possible with national systems and other municipalities, as well as with a range of local partners – universities, business organizations, schools, the media and NGOs – to ensure democratic involvement and broad access as well as increased capacity.

The quality of information

disaggregation of data

The effectiveness of any information system depends not on the amount of data, but on its usefulness and accuracy. Indicators must be identified that are relevant to the local plan of action, that can present a realistic and comprehensive picture, that allows for comparability. Information is more useful if it is disaggregated. Conditions can vary enormously from one part of a city to another, and the impact can be different for children and adults, girls and boys, rich and poor, dominant groups and ethnic minorities. The main health risks for adolescents, for instance, are often hidden because statistics on morbidity or mortality focus on such large age groups.[6] If the needs of a particular group are to be fairly responded to, these needs must first be identified. Data should be broken down according to location, age, sex, religion, ethnicity, and socioeconomic standing.

It makes good sense to explore, assemble and analyse existing information sources before initiating expensive new data collection efforts. Recent studies in Accra and São Paulo have demonstrated that a relatively detailed picture of inequalities in social and environmental conditions can be produced, drawing on existing statistics.[7] A team in São Paulo, headed by Aldaiza Sposatti, used existing information to create a 'Social Exclusion Map' which depicted graphically the situation of city residents and became an aid for practical micro-planning.[8] Agencies may be more than willing to collaborate in this task if they know that they will benefit, along with others, in sharing a more complete bank of information.

Participatory data collection and analysis

Wherever possible, data collection should involve those whose lives are being surveyed. Especially in poor neighbourhoods, where there may be

[5] Cayon, E (1998) *Selected References on Geographic Information System (GIS) and Urban Issues*, Ibadan, Nigeria: UNICEF Nigeria; and ODA (1996) 'Computers in Urban Spatial Planning', *ODA Urbanization*, (2): 7–8
[6] Arrossi, S (1996) 'Inequality and Health in Metropolitan Buenos Aires', *Environment and Urbanization*, 8(2): 43–70
[7] Stephens, C, Akerman, A, Avle,S, Borlina, P, Maia, P, Campanario, P, Doe, B, Tetteh, D (1997) 'Urban Equity and Urban Health: Using Existing Data to Understand Inequalities in Health and Environment in Accra, Ghana and São Paulo, Brazil', *Environment and Urbanization*, 9(1, April): 181–203
[8] Dowbor, 1996, op cit Note 3

suspicion of authorities and a high degree of transience, this can create a more accurate picture. Participatory data collection and analysis can be the basis for discussing plans and actions with local community members, and should always involve the most vulnerable groups, including women and children. An excellent example of such community-based participatory data collection is described on p96. The last ten years have seen rapid progress in the development and use of participatory methods to work with communities in discussing problems, setting priorities, collecting and analysing data, and developing and monitoring actions (see resource list, p284). This includes many examples of the use of such methods with children and adolescents, especially in gathering information and insights that are important in understanding their lives and in monitoring the Convention.

involving children in research

Involving children in participatory action research is an effective way to gather information, and also a way to strengthen children's understanding of their world and to prepare them for active citizenship.[9] As with any age group, there are important ethical considerations. Children have the right to expect that information regarding their situation will be responsibly and objectively collected, that it will respect their own expert knowledge of their lives, and that it will be used in their interests and not against them. Ideally research should go hand in hand with action. If data collection is not to be closely followed by action, this should be made clear so that children do not have unrealistic expectations.

Making information open and available to all stakeholders

making information understandable to all

Access to information cannot be restricted to those in power, but must belong to the whole community as the basis for democratic action. Information must be both physically accessible, and able to be understood by all. This means finding different ways of presenting information. In Uganda, for instance, the government makes available copies of all legal statutes that refer to children, and a version is being produced that contains no legal jargon. The needs of different language groups and of those who cannot read must also be taken into account.

- *Make the acquisition of efficient new technologies a priority for investment.*
- *Establish a comprehensive and coordinated information network that includes the range of local partners as well as national systems.*
- *Make effective use of existing information.*
- *Develop context sensitive indicators relevant to the goals of the local plan of action and to the Convention.*
- *Disaggregate data in order to achieve a realistic analysis of conditions for all groups.*
- *Use participatory methods in problem identification and the collection and analysis of local data.*
- *Make information easily accessible and understandable to all groups.*

9 Hart, R (1997) *Children's Participation: The Theory and Practice of Involving Young Citizens in Community Development and Environmental Care*, London: Earthscan/UNICEF; Nieuwenhuys, O (1997) 'Spaces for the Children of the Urban Poor: Experiences with Participatory Action Research (PAR)', *Environment and Urbanization*, 9(1): 233–249

EFFECTIVE GOVERNMENT STRUCTURES AND PROCESSES

If local government is to work efficiently towards the realization of children's rights in spite of limited funds and capacity, it must coordinate and critically evaluate its own functions and processes, as well as forming new partnerships and even new structures.

Government bodies that are truly representative

hiring policies

Local agencies will respond more effectively to the concerns of all residents if they include representatives of marginalized or excluded groups. Hiring policies for government agencies and departments should ensure that women, minorities and the poor are well represented throughout the layers of local officialdom. Training should be made available so that members of excluded groups can reasonably compete for jobs.

Elected members of local government are theoretically representative, but deep-seated assumptions about social roles mean that women are seldom equally represented, in spite of the critical contribution they can make.[10] In response to the 1995 United Nations Conference on Women, in Beijing, significant changes were made in some countries to ensure more balanced representation. In Ghana, a proposal to ensure that 40 per cent of parliamentary candidates and 40 per cent of government appointees at the District and Unit Committee level are women has been endorsed, and parliamentary approval is pending.[11]

- *Encourage the formal representation of women, youth and other vulnerable groups in local government, if possible through quotas; and establish hiring policies for local government agencies to guarantee the representation of these groups.*

Assessing the functions and practice of individual agencies

child impact statements

This book has referred to numerous measures that can be taken by different local agencies to meet children's rights. Rather than responding to such suggestions through piecemeal addition and modification of programmes for children and families, each agency should initiate a comprehensive review of its functions and practices in the light of the Convention. This can happen even in agencies not generally thought of as serving children. A small working group within each agency, together with professionals familiar with children's rights and developmental needs (perhaps a member of the local child rights oversight committee, p260) can effectively evaluate agency practices. Child impact statements should become a routine component of the planning and assessment of all agency initiatives.[12]

- *Establish intra-agency review and evaluation processes with support from professionals familiar with the rights and developmental needs of children and adolescents.*

[10] Beall, J (1996) *Urban Governance: Why Gender Matters*, Gender in Development Monograph Series, UNDP
[11] (1998) *Women Legislators in Action*, 3 (2): 7
[12] Hodgkin, R and Newell, P (1996) 'Effective Government Structures for Children', London: Gulbenkian Foundation

- *Include child impact statements as part of the routine use of social and environmental impact studies in the planning of all agency initiatives.*

Achieving inter-agency and inter-municipal coordination

Service provision within urban areas has traditionally been sectoral. Particularly where provision is privatized. or assigned to independent public institutions (such as parastatals or provincial boards), it can become increasingly compartmentalized. In many cities, provision is also geographically fragmented because the urban region is divided administratively among many local governments, each with its own policy and investment programme. There are powerful reasons for moving towards more integrated approaches to service provision and regulation.

integrated responses to children's needs

Society's response to children and adolescents should reflect the fact that their rights are best addressed in integrated ways. A young child's requirements for health care, nutrition, developmental support and secure nurturance cannot be separated from one another. Nor is it possible to isolate an adolescent's need for health care from sex education and substance abuse prevention, or their education from vocational training and job placement. There are also economic reasons for coordinating provision. Limited resources can be used most effectively if they are shared, and if costly overlap is eliminated. We pointed earlier to an example from Soweto in South Africa, where an assessment of health care provision revealed that five separate authorities were involved in different, but overlapping, aspects of provision (p101).

Many initiatives can promote better coordination, including the creation of metropolitan planning and development authorities, the development of two tier systems of local government (municipal and metropolitan), inter-municipal cooperation (for instance by sharing capital equipment and professional services), and the amalgamation of municipalities. For example, San Salvador has a metropolitan area of 13 integrated municipalities. The Mayor's Council of the metropolitan area provides the mechanisms by which the municipal governments can coordinate.[13] There are many successes, as well as significant obstacles in the way of replicating such initiatives.[14] In recent years, the emphasis has been less on setting up overarching bodies with the power to ensure coordination, and more on developing processes to encourage coordination, such as the GIS system.

The coordination of services should happen on a systemic level, but it can also be effectively introduced in small-scale ways. In Manila, street workers from a particular community were given UBSP (Urban Basic Services Programme) funds to address issues not usually included in their programmes for street children, such as community upgrading and livelihood.[15] Community liaison workers can help to coordinate agency services at the local level (see p261), and community centres serve as the base for integrated local service provision (see p55).

One approach to ensuring the coordination of services for children is the creation of a separate agency for children's affairs. (This should not be confused with children's rights oversight groups, described on p260.) There is the risk, however, that the existence of such an agency could, in fact, marginalize attention to children by removing responsi-

[13] Lungo, M (1997) 'Governance, Urban Development Plans and Sustainability in Central American Cities', Paper presented at the GURI Conference on Governance in Action: Urban Initiatives in a Global Setting

[14] Davey, K (1992) 'The Structure and Functions of Urban Government: The Institutional Framework of Urban Management', Birmingham, Development Administration Group, University of Birmingham

[15] Porio, 1994, op cit Note 2

bility from other departments.[16] Separate agencies for children are only as good as the quality and commitment of their staff, and their effectiveness is limited by their political and administrative freedom to act. A system-wide awareness of children's rights is likely to be more effective.

- *Assess local needs in all areas, and identify overlaps or gaps in provision.*
- *Strengthen coordination between agencies through information-sharing and joint planning, and ensure that the goals and policies of different agencies are compatible with one another, with the Convention and with the local plan of action.*

Creating new partnerships

a partnership in Guatemala City

It is important to go beyond agency coordination and encourage a broad range of partnerships among diverse groups. Ideally, when all partners combine efforts, consensus on key problems can be worked towards, resources can be shared, and more will be achieved (see p194). Partners that should be routinely involved at both city and community levels include government agencies at all levels, political parties and unions, business and cultural organizations, academic institutions, community organizations, minority groups and the media.[17] In Guatemala City, an important institutional innovation in the attempt to improve conditions in marginal settlements was the establishment of a 'Committee for Attention to the Population of Precarious Areas' (COINAP) which included representatives from more than 20 public and private institutions, including several national ministries, the local governments within Guatemala City, local universities, NGOs and aid agencies and representatives of organizations in communities where projects were underway.[18] Cross-party alliances on basic social issues should be encouraged in such groups, so that progress is not reversed when there are changes in government.

It can be difficult for partnerships to work between groups with very different levels of power. When the rights of weaker groups, such as women, children, low-income groups and minorities, are not protected by well-enforced laws, there is little incentive for powerful vested interests to form partnerships with them. And if they do, powerful groups are unlikely to give equal voice to groups with little strength when negotiating compromises.[19]

- *Create partnerships between all levels of government agencies, social organizations, political parties and unions, business and cultural organizations, academic institutions, minority groups and the media*
- *Encourage cross-party alliances, so that progress is not reversed when there are changes in government.*
- *Increase the effectiveness of groups with little power through strong, well-enforced laws to protect their interests.*

16 Hodgkin and Newell, 1996, op cit Note 12

17 Dowbor, L (1998) 'Decentralization and Governance', *Latin American Perspectives*, 25(98): 28–44

18 Espinosa, L and Lopez Rivera, O A (1994) 'UNICEF's Urban Basic Services Programme in Illegal Settlements in Guatamala City', *Environment and Urbanization*, 6(2): 9–31

19 Satterthwaite, D (1998) 'Can UN Conferences Promote Poverty Reduction? A Review of the Habitat II Documents in Relation to their Consideration of Poverty and the Priority they give to Poverty Reduction', Washington DC, Woodrow Wilson International Center for Scholars, Occasional Paper Series, forthcoming

Involving children as partners

A recent report cites strong evidence in many countries of growing alienation on the part of young people from politics and the democratic process, while at the same time documenting the benefits of giving children more responsibility in this area.[20] Recently, in some countries concerted efforts have been made to bring children and youth into city-wide planning and advocacy processes, particularly in Europe. In France, there are close to one thousand municipal child and youth councils which meet regularly to discuss specific local concerns, and to develop and refine recommendations which are presented to the mayor. A representative from local government often serves at these meetings as an advisor, but in many cases the children prefer to organize themselves and call on technical assistance when they need it. On some issues, young councilors are asked to participate in various commissions of the local government. These councils have made an important breakthrough in establishing dialogue between children and local authorities, and have in hundreds of ways improved the quality of their cities and towns.[21] Council members are generally elected through their schools, but this model could be modified to include children and young people outside the formal school system. The emphasis should be on encouraging all institutional settings for children, from schools to youth clubs, to become more inclusive and participatory themselves, so that they can realistically contribute representatives to local government bodies.

children in city-wide planning processes

Examples of active child and youth involvement in local government are not limited to Europe. Rosario, Argentina, with the support of UNICEF, has created a Municipal Council of Children, and children have actively participated in decisions regarding the reorganization of traffic patterns and the design of green space. In India, there have been a number of experiments with children's Panchayats which function as shadow bodies to the adult Panchayats, or local government bodies. A most dramatic example, discussed on p150, has been the growing representation of children in municipal discussion and decision making in Colombia, one of the outgrowths of the Children's Movement for Peace.[22] Unfortunately, at the time of writing there has been no comparative review of these experiments.

A concern for any municipality seeking to involve children and adolescents in this way is the extent to which their parents and other adults have the capacity to become similarly involved. If there is not a broad culture of participation, the involvement of children is unlikely to be taken seriously. Adults cannot be expected to support the right of children and young people to participate if their own rights in this regard are ignored.

children's rights in the context of adult rights

- *Establish ways to involve children and adolescents in municipal decision making, building on their democratic involvement in community-based organizations, schools, and child and youth clubs.*

[20] Hodgkin and Newell 1996, op cit Note 12
[21] Hart, 1997, op cit Note 9
[22] Cameron, S (1998) *Making Peace with Children*, UNICEF Colombia

New structures for overseeing children's rights

The Convention requires that children's best interests be considered in all decisions affecting them, and this can include, directly or indirectly, most of the decisions made by local government. But children and adolescents have little social, political or economic power. It is essential, then, that there be bodies that can oversee the actions of local government and its partners for their effect on children and their adherence to children's rights. The establishment of such bodies indicates a willingness on the part of authorities to be held accountable.

various models

Various models could fulfill this function, from single ombudsmen acting as advocates and monitors for children's rights, to representative committees which ensure that the interests of children are addressed in local government activity.[23] The range of responsibility and power may vary from one situation to another, and could include some or all of the following:

range of responsibilities

- working to change public awareness;
- evaluating the situation of children;
- ensuring that the interests of children are reflected in regulations, standards, budget allocations and policy decisions;
- monitoring the practices of institutions, agencies and organizations responsible for children;
- investigating violations of children's rights;
- promoting communication among various agencies and organizations responsible for children;
- providing children and their families with a direct channel for legal information or assistance.

independent or appointed by government?

In some cases these entities may be appointed and funded by government. In others cases they are completely separate bodies. There are certainly benefits to be gained from working within the system, and developing a capacity for self-evaluation within government. But independence is often essential to ensure objectivity. The political realities of a given city will have to be weighed to determine the most effective local solution for monitoring the fulfillment of children's rights – but local governments are urged to recognize the constructive value of being monitored and evaluated by truly independent bodies. Some countries have established parallel systems. In Namibia, for instance, a Division of Children's Affairs has been established at national level within the Ministry of Local Government and Housing. But the constitution also provides for an independent ombudsman empowered to look into violations of children's rights.[24]

Brazil's Guardianship councils

The Guardianship system of Brazil is an excellent model for many of the functions of such oversight bodies. Every municipality is legally required to create a certain number of Guardianship Councils, depending on child population and the size of the territory. These councils, each composed of five professionals who are part of the local community and experienced with children, work closely with families and public agencies, and serve to facilitate the relationship between them. They are responsible for handling cases of children in need, at risk, or in conflict

23 Lansdowne, G (1997) 'Ombudswork for Children', *Innocenti Digest*, (3)

24 Hodgkin and Newell, 1996, op cit Note 12

with the law, and finding the best possible assistance for them. They can be approached directly by children, families, teachers, social workers and other officials to intervene in specific situations. The councils also work closely with municipal governments, advising on budget allocations and on any plans of action affecting children.[25] By 1994, 1,500 of Brazil's 4,485 counties had installed these councils.[26]

- *Support the establishment of oversight committees or bodies to monitor the activities of local government, and to advocate for children's rights.*
- *Determine the best method locally for ensuring the objectivity and independence of these groups, together with the capacity to work collaboratively with government.*

SUPPORTING COMMUNITY ACTION AND BUILDING CITIZENSHIP

We have described how, in the face of limited government capacity, many of the initiatives that most affect the lives of children and their families take place outside the realm of formal government. It is essential that local government both encourage and collaborate with these initiatives. A close, supportive relationship allows for creative solutions, rapid adaptation to changing conditions and transparent governance. Without such relationships government processes are apt to be remote, ineffective and even corrupt, and this will be reflected in the culture of the entire city. Some communities are active and successful in organizing themselves, but in many cases community involvement may need to be stimulated from outside, and local government can play a significant role here – not only in ensuring the political participation of residents, but in supporting the social and economic inclusion of all.

encouraging and stimulating local initiatives

Establishing connections between communities and formal government

Even when local government is well-organized and communities are strong, if communication between them is not good, government efforts on behalf of communities are likely to be poorly conceived, and community efforts will be inadequately supported. The formal channel between citizens and local authorities is generally through elected representatives to municipal government. But the area they represent is generally larger than the neighbourhood, which is the true unit of local governance. This link is strengthened if every neighbourhood has one or more elected councillors.

Authorities might also consider the use of community liaison persons to ensure communication between community groups and the formal structures of local government, and to work closely with elected representatives where these exist. These individuals could provide information on government agencies, bureaucratic processes and funding resources. They could serve as community advocates to municipal and other public

25 Rizzini, I, Munhoz, M, Galeano, L (1992) *Childhood and Urban Poverty in Brazil: Street and Working Children and Their Families*, Florence, Italy: UNICEF
26 Penne Firme, T (1994) 'Meeting At-risk Children where they Get Together' in Asquith, S and Hall, M (eds) *Justice for Children*, Dordrecht: Marinus Nijhoff

agencies; and could encourage coordination among various community-based organizations and with the different government agencies operating at the community level. They could attend community meetings, and monitor local development through observation and informal discussion with all sectors of the community. An enduring relationship between such workers and a given community could bridge changes in local government. Checks and balances are of course needed to ensure that the liaison officer does not reproduce or reinforce clientelist forms of political control.

community liaison officers

There are examples for such a position. In Lusaka, Zambia, DANIDA/UNCHS sponsors a training programme for municipal officials to provide such liaison between the municipality and communities, especially in issues related to the upgrading of squatter areas.[27] In Nasik, India, the Urban Basic Services Programme for the Poor (UBSP) included a UBSP cell within the municipal government, staffed by community organizers in charge of the liaison between municipal government and resident community volunteers. Frequent visits by these organizers to the specific communities, and monthly meetings of the resident community volunteers facilitated mobilization, participation, training, monitoring, evaluation and allowed for true municipal support of community management.[28]

elected community leaders

Many low-income neighbourhoods have developed their own forms of representative government, in which elected leaders have a critical role in representing the views of 'the community' in negotiations with municipal authorities, other state institutions and other external agencies (for instance funding agencies). External agencies must be careful not to undermine such arrangements. Many local authorities recognize the need for cooperation, and in some cases representatives of neighbourhood organizations operate as part of the formal structure of local government, for instance the Barangay Captains and executives in urban centres in the Philippines.[29] On the other hand, a local leader may represent only a certain power bloc rather than the interests of the whole community. Authorities must be aware of these issues, and while responding to existing structures, should be sure that all needs are represented and conflicts resolved.

Some cities have introduced direct ways of improving communications between city neighbourhoods and government agencies. In Cali, Colombia, in the early 1990s, every week a two hour public meeting took place in one of Cali's twenty communes or city sub-divisions between the mayor and his full cabinet and local leaders. The agenda allowed for flexibility so that relevant issues could be raised.[30] Such practices are a welcome attempt to improve access to city government, but should not be considered a replacement for other formal connections. A meeting every 20 weeks, valuable though it may be, is no substitute for daily communication and liaison.

- *Ensure that formally elected representatives to city government represent the neighbourhood level.*
- *Consider appointing a trained community development liaison person as a link between government agencies and each neighbourhood.*
- *Recognize and involve informally elected neighbourhood leaders.*

[27] Vanderschueren, F, Wegelin, E, Wekwete, K (1996) *Policy Programme Options for Urban Poverty Reduction*, Washington DC: The World Bank/Urban Management Programme
[28] Mehta, M (1993) *Convergence in UBSP: An Exploratory Study of Nasik and Aligarh*, sponsored by UNICEF, November 1993
[29] Davey, 1992, op cit Note 14
[30] Guerrero, R (1993) 'Cali's Innovative Approach to Urban Violence', *The Urban Age*, 1(4): 17

- *Hold regular open meetings between government officials and community members.*

Building participatory and inclusive solutions

Participatory governance means finding ways to have decisions made as close as possible to the people they affect. But local government seldom encourages inhabitants to contribute to the definition of needs, priorities and solutions. Even many NGOs fail to support participatory actions and processes, often because of conditions imposed by their funders, and they may come to be regarded as no more accountable and no less manipulative than local authorities. But some NGOs in urban areas of the South have developed excellent models of support for low-income communities and have helped to strengthen well organized community organizations and their federations – for instance, the Indian NGO, SPARC, working with the National Slum Dwellers Federation of India and *Mahila Milan* (a federation of women's collectives); and the South African NGO, People's Dialogue and its work with the South African Homeless People's Federation.[31] Local government would do well to learn from the successes of such fruitful partnerships.

One of the most notable experiments in encouraging true community participation in decision making has been the introduction of 'participatory budgeting' in many cities in Brazil. Through this approach, a proportion of the city's capital is allocated to investments which are prioritized within each neighbourhood, according to priorities established through community discussion.[32] The role of municipal authorities is simply to make the necessary information available, not to make the decisions. In Santo André, a city of 620,000 near São Paulo, 18 different districts hold meetings in which priorities for both neighbourhoods and the entire city are voted. Because of a decrease in industrial employment in recent years, the city has not been strong financially, and residents are included in discussion of ways to reduce expenses when necessary. This explicit willingness to include community members in spending decisions has generated a high level of attendance and involvement. One direct result of this democratization of investment has been the allocation of funds to public squares, street lighting, recreation areas and other forms of neighbourhood upgrading that have improved security and the quality of life for local residents.[33]

In his description of the successful participatory budgeting system in Porto Alegre, Navarro points out that the process has effectively trained hundreds of citizens to act as decision makers, taking into account not only the needs of the neighbourhoods they represent, but increasingly to recognize and act on the interests of the city as a whole. It has also generated stricter control of finances and a permanent level of pressure on governmental performance.[34]

Even when there are effective mechanisms to involve local residents, the issue of inclusion remains important. It is too easy to speak of 'the community' as though it were homogeneous, composed of people with equal needs and powers and similar goals and values. But most communities are complex, multi-faceted and often faction ridden, with important differences among individuals in income levels, access to

31 Bolnick, J (1996) 'uTshani Buyakhuluma (the Grass Speaks); Peoples' Dialogue and the South African Homeless Peoples' Federation, 1993–1996', Environment and Urbanization, 8(2): 153–170; and Patel, S (1996) *SPARC and its Work with the National Slum Dwellers Federation and Mahila Milan*, India, London: IIED

32 Boscio, R P (1997) 'Democratic Governance and Participation: A Tale of Two Cities', Paper presented at the GURI Conference on Governance in Action: Urban Initiatives in a Global Setting, Centre for Urban and Community Studies, University of Toronto, Toronto; Paixao Bretas, P R (1996) 'Participative Budgeting in Belo Horizonte: Democratization and Citizenship', *Environment and Urbanization*, 8(1 April)

33 Prefeitura Municipal de Santo André (1998) 'Integrated Strategies for Urban Poverty Reduction', Santo André, Office of the mayor

34 Navarro, Z (1998) 'Affirmative Democracy and Redistribution Development: the Case of Participatory Budgeting in Porto Alegre, Brasil (1989–1997)', Presentation at Seminar: Social Programs, Poverty and Citizen Participation, March 12–13, 1998, Cartagena, Colombia, Sponsored by the Inter-American Development Bank

including groups that are commonly excluded

resources and power, social support, loyalties and degree of self-interest. Some groups face more extreme difficulties because of discrimination.

It cannot be assumed that attention to the needs of 'the community' will actually address the needs of the most vulnerable. In fact, the opposite is likely to be true. Women and girls, for instance, may have the greatest interest in improved water provision because it affects their workload. Yet there are often strong social constraints on their capacity to make demands or to organize themselves. Local authorities must be aware of the complexity of community dynamics, and must find ways to promote the involvement of groups that might face discrimination or exclusion. They should make it clear that they favour working with community groups that are truly inclusive, or that represent the interests of commonly excluded groups. Programmes which specifically target these groups, such as UBSP in India, which was developed to favour poor women and children, can be critical.

There are also differences in the extent to which inhabitants are prepared to invest time in community initiatives. Renters and those living temporarily in a neighbourhood will generally have less interest than those who own housing. Adults without children will have less involvement in improving schools and day care centers. Households with the lowest and least stable incomes will have particular difficulty finding any time to contribute to community initiatives.

obstacles to participation

It may also be difficult to promote participatory solutions. When local residents' life experience has been largely with top-down decision-making, the promotion of democratic 'community governance' is seldom easy. When patron/client-oriented political structures are the norm, these also tend to undermine the possibility of inclusive community-oriented action. And for so many low-income neighbourhoods, a long history of political manipulation and unfulfilled promises from external agencies and institutions is not conducive to the kinds of community action that can help address the rights of children.[35] Establishing a truly participatory culture involves education, communication and real commitment.

- *Educate all groups, including women and children, in participatory democracy, conflict resolution and citizenship.*
- *Promote a participatory culture within communities by focusing support on those organizations which are democratic and inclusive.*
- *Establish with the community, mechanisms for the effective representation of the most vulnerable and excluded members.*

Practical support for community planning

When planning and decision making about local issues happen within the community, it is more likely that needs will be accurately assessed, that solutions will reflect local preferences, and that follow-up maintenance and management will be more willingly undertaken. It may be time-consuming and inefficient to involve community members in this way, but experience has shown it can be highly effective. On page 133 we discussed the planning process for a traffic calming project in Leicester,

[35] Hardoy, A, Hardoy, J E, Schusterman, R (1991) 'Building Community Organization: the History of a Squatter Settlement and its own Organizations in Buenos Aires', *Environment and Urbanization*, 3(2, October): 104–120

Britain. Subsequent evaluation demonstrated that resident involvement had saved the city both time and money. The process also built stronger community support for local government and public policy.[36]

problem identification and analysis

Purposeful planning must begin with identification of the issue, and a coalition of those individuals or groups most concerned. We have already discussed the importance of participatory problem identification and data collection as the first step in the assessment of any need. Even well-organized communities can use technical assistance in improving their participatory planning processes. Trained facilitators or planners (perhaps the community's liaison person), can help groups work together productively using a variety of methods. One method that has consistently been found helpful is the use of mapping, not only for collecting input from community members and experimenting with alternative solutions, but for presenting ideas in an accessible way to the community at large. Based on their common understanding of a situation, be it an assessment of water provision or the current use of space for recreation, a group can be encouraged to make a critical analysis of a problem and to discuss practical solutions. If this group process is undertaken with adequate information about available support, it is likely that community members will come up with feasible suggestions for improvement. In cases where there are different interests and viewpoints, groups may want to work separately to start with, to articulate their particular concerns. The way final decisions are made will depend on locally acceptable practice. Communities must be encouraged, however, to weigh the opinions of all groups. A representative committee can be assigned to prepare a synthesis of information and recommendations for presentation to the community as a whole. After open community discussion on the subject, it may be necessary to revise recommendations in order to achieve sufficient consensus on the issues.

reaching consensus

- *Train community organizers in techniques for promoting effective participatory planning (see resource list, p284).*

Supporting community-based management

There are some excellent examples of low-income communities developing the capacity to maintain and manage infrastructure and services. Among them are the Orangi sewer construction and management programme in Karachi;[37] the water supply system in El Mesquital, Guatemala City, managed by local residents;[38] the day care and child development centre in Barrio San Jorge in Buenos Aires.[39] Community-based organizations can have major roles in the planning, installation and management of infrastructure and services in many areas.[40]

Although low-income communities are likely to resent attempts by local authorities simply to transfer responsibility for maintenance and management, they may well respond positively to real partnerships through which authorities and community organizations work together to improve provision and maintenance. Community groups should be treated by local government with the same respect that would be given to a private company fulfilling similar functions. Wherever possible, these partnerships should generate income for community members. In Santos,

36 Adams, E and Ingham, S (1998) *Changing Places: Children's Participation in Environmental Planning*, London: The Children's Society
37 Hasan, A (1997) *Working with Government: The Story of the Orangi Pilot Project's Collaboration with State Agencies for Replicating its Low Cost Sanitation Programme*, Karachi: City Press
38 Espinosa and Lopez Rivera, 1994, op cit Note 18
39 Schusterman, R and Hardoy, A (1997) 'Reconstructing Social Capital in a Poor Urban Settlement: the Integrated Improvement Programme, Barrio San Jorge', *Environment and Urbanization*, 9(1): 91–119
40 Arévalo Torres, P (1997) 'May Hope be Realized: Huaycan Self-managing Urban Community in Lima', Environment and Urbanization, 9 (1, April): 59–79; and Turner, B (ed) (1988) *Building Community – A Third World Casebook from Habitat International Coalition*, London: Habitat International Coalition

Brazil, a long-term effort to upgrade an unplanned settlement in the marshy area of Dique da Vila Gilda involved the paid participation of community members in the installation and management of infrastructure. As of 1996, 200 people in the area were on the city payroll.[41]

In many countries in Africa during the 1980s and early 1990s, one response by governments lacking resources was establishing connections with urban community-based organizations which were linked to, if not integral to, political parties in one-party states.[42] Through these connections, self help and mass-mobilization became an important part of urban management. While these efforts might be viewed more as centrally directed local mobilization than as community participation, some of them contributed to better housing for low-income groups and improved basic service provision, within a context of very low incomes and weak and under-resourced local authorities.[43]

- *Establish real partnerships between municipal authorities and community organizations so that they can work together to improve provision and maintenance.*
- *Whenever possible put community members on the city payroll for managing local infrastructure.*

Involving children and youth in community action

Children can best learn to exercise their right to participation by being ensured a meaningful role in community action. Involvement in community projects and decisions can help children learn cooperative group skills, increase their sense of competence and confidence, and give them an awareness of the responsibilities of active citizenship. Earlier in this chapter we described some experiments involving children in city government bodies (see p259), and in Chapters 7 and 9, we have discussed a number of ways in which children can effectively be involved in local efforts for themselves and others.

- *See recommendations on pp145, 148, 150*

Places for community governance and the practice of citizenship

Community organizations need space for regular meetings which should ideally be neutral, non-exclusive and large enough to accomodate everyone. It is often through the control of space, buildings and other resources that power is retained in non-democratic forms of governance. If private or religious organizations are the sole providers of community space, the potential for democratic discussion may be affected by the biases of different power bases in the community. In Accra, Ghana, recent government reorganization has mandated the creation of local government units representing approximately 1,500 people at the community level. Elected representatives of these units will probably meet in the home courtyards of traditional chiefs within each neighbour-

[41] City of Santos (1996) 'Santos na Habitat II: Integrated Children's and Family Program', The City of Santos, SP, Brazil
[42] Lee Smith, D and Stren, R (1991) 'New Perspectives on African Urban Management', *Environment and Urbanization*, 3 (1): 23–36
[43] Jaglin, S (1994) 'Why Mobilize Town Dwellers: Joint Management in Ouagadougou, 1983–1990', *Environment and Urbanization*, 6 (2, October): 111–132

hood. While this solution would allow for a link between government and traditional leadership, there is a risk that it will not fulfill the goal of maximum inclusiveness.[44] Public primary schools should be an ideal location for meetings, since they are intended as a resource for the whole community. But there can be a number of practical drawbacks, as discussed on p166. When public buildings do not easily lend themselves to use by the wider community, it is important to find alternatives. Various creative solutions are possible. Within the South African Homeless People's Federation, when a savings and credit group finally acquire land on which they will construct their own homes, their first building is a modest meeting place where site plans, house designs and building schedules can be discussed and agreed upon, and from which the whole process can be managed.[45] In Barrio San Jorge in Argentina, when one of the households moved away, their shack was purchased by the community and converted into 'the house of the barrio', providing space not only for community management but also for training courses and other community activities.[46] Depending on the climate, meetings intended to include the entire community can be held outdoors, although this presents challenges for the amplification of sound, and for the effective presentation of graphic material.

a physical base for integrated community development

Shared community space has other important functions beyond that of providing a place for meeting and organizing. It can serve as an accessible base for community development workers, liaison officers, or the neighbourhood offices of local government agencies. When there is sufficient space to house a wide range of services and organizations in close proximity, the goal of integrated community provision is more easily realized, and the whole community can benefit from the resulting synergies (see pp55, 166).

- *Support community efforts to find or create places for meetings, planning, training and other community-based services and activities.*
- *Ensure that the space chosen for community use does not perpetuate discrimination and exclusion.*
- *Make publicly owned facilities such as schools and government offices available for community use.*

MONITORING, EVALUATION AND ENFORCEMENT

coordinating enforcement with support

No plan of action for meeting children's rights will be effective without follow-up to ensure that results are actually being achieved. Evaluation of individual agency efforts as well as the progress of the city as a whole should be an ongoing process, and part of more general data collection efforts. Municipal oversight is especially important where abuses most often occur. Enforcement of regulations should, wherever possible, be coordinated with the provision of municipal support and technical assistance, for instance in the monitoring of working conditions or child care provision (pp155, 197).

The CRC requires national governments to report to the international monitoring committee two years after ratification, and every five

[44] Bartlett and Hart, field trip 1997
[45] Bolnick, 1996, op cit Note 31
[46] Schusterman and Hardoy, 1997, op cit Note 39

years after that. This process ensures ongoing national self-examination on progress and difficulties in implementing children's rights. This self-assessment is also useful at the local level, although local reports should certainly be generated more frequently than every five years. Both government agencies and local structures for overseeing children's rights should maintain records of their efforts, progress and setbacks, and should be encouraged to make reports available to the public. The following checklist, loosely based on the committee's report format, covers the general areas that any local government should examine in assessing its own progress, and can be adapted and expanded to fit the particular situation. Similar checklists can also be developed for the self-evaluation of different agencies and institutions.

reporting on progress and setbacks

checklists for internal evaluation

- Have steps been taken towards developing and adopting a local plan of action for implementing children's rights?
- Have measures been taken to raise widespread awareness of the principles and provisions of the CRC – through workshops, publications, broadcasts on radio and television, within school curricula, and in parent education campaigns?
- Are all professionals, public officials and municipal staff who work with, and for, children educated in the principles of the Convention? Do their codes of conduct reflect the Convention?
- Have local codes and regulations been assessed to ensure compatibility with the standards of the Convention? Have changes been made to support compliance with the Convention?
- What steps have been taken to ensure coordination among government agencies in areas of action involving children's rights?
- What steps have been taken towards creating partnerships between local government and civil society to extend the capacity for responding to children's rights? What initiatives have been undertaken cooperatively?
- Has a government institution or independent body been established to promote and protect children's rights and to monitor their implementation?
- What progress has been made in gathering and analysing comprehensive, accurate, disaggregated data on children in the local area?
- What proportion of the local budget is devoted to social expenditures for children, including housing, health, welfare, education and play?
- How have the best interests of children been reflected in local policy making and decisions?
- What measures have been taken to reduce disparities between different groups of children and women in the provision of services? What protections exist for the most disadvantaged groups?
- Have appropriate standards in areas of safety, health, staffing and supervision been established for all public and private institutions, services and facilities that provide for children?
- What provision has been made for assessing and responding to the views of children in planning and decision making that directly affects them?

Evaluation of the performance of local government as a whole, and of individual agencies, institutions and organizations can be a valuable internal tool for reviewing policy, setting new goals and adjusting priorities. It is also important that the public be made regularly aware of the gains that have been achieved and the obstacles that remain. This can help to promote support for public policies, and to maintain a local culture that sees the achievement of children's rights as a high priority.

- *Require routine record keeping on activities relevant to children from all government agencies and institutions that come under government supervision.*
- *Require procedures for self-assessment within all these bodies, and reports to be made to local government, or to a local child rights oversight body.*
- *Prepare and disseminate to the public regular reports on progress and difficulties within the city in working towards the achievement of children's rights.*
- *Use the results of ongoing monitoring and evaluation to update the local plan of action on a regular basis.*

WORKING WITH OTHER MUNICIPALITIES TO AFFECT NATIONAL POLICY

Local city governments, as we have described in Chapter 13, too frequently lack the funds and powers to meet their ever-growing responsibilities. There are significant steps they can take to work more effectively with the resources they have available. But there is no question that part of their responsibility must be to advocate intensively at higher levels for increased capacity to solve their own problems. It is critical that they find ways to work together with other local governments at national, regional and international levels to strengthen their position. Just as all stakeholders at the local level have the right to participate in decision making and the management of resources, so should the right to be involved in bottom-up processes be extended to local governments. Effective alliances and networks of municipal leaders can work towards the following goals:

goals for municipal networks

- creating a common front for negotiating and lobbying with national governments and international organizations for funds and other assistance, and for recognition of local problems;
- creating entities that can be included at higher levels in discussions of policy and new legislation that affects local government;
- sharing good practices and technical knowledge with other municipalities, learning from them, and even undertaking common projects in order to make best use of existing skills and resources.

Over the last decade, impressive gains have been made worldwide in establishing and strengthening such alliances. This trend has been supported by the series of global conferences convened by the United Nations during the 1990s, which recognized the significant role of local authorities in furthering the social and environmental agenda, and which included them in discussion and negotiations. Some effective networks have grown out of these conferences. For instance, before the Habitat II Conference (also called the City Summit), local authorities banded together to establish The World Association of Cities and Local Authorities Co-ordination (WACLAC). This new umbrella association committed itself to taking an active role in promoting the well-being of children as the ultimate indicator of good governance; to promoting participatory policies rooted in active partnerships; to improving transparency and efficiency in management; and to strengthening direct cooperation between local authorities.[47] Other similar alliances are the International Union of Local Authorities (IULA) and Cités Unies.

new alliances

issue-based networks

Some of these networks have been organized around specific issues. A good example is the International Council for Local Environmental Initiatives, which put together a Local Agenda 21 handbook to assist in the development of local plans of action for the protection of the environment.[48] The Healthy Cities network is another well-known movement. Other networks are more regional in nature, focusing on concerns shared by cities in the same general area. In Brazil, for instance, the horizontal coordination of health programmes between municipalities has allowed for productive and optimal use of facilities.[49]

regional networks

Mayors Defenders of children

A municipal network that has been effective in promoting the implementation of children's rights is the Mayors Defenders of Children movement. This network is a partner and a component of the Child Friendly Cities Programme, a joint initiative of UNICEF and UNCHS (Habitat), which has worked towards strengthening partnerships at national and international levels, and promoting the development of child-friendly municipal plans of action. The Mayors Defenders of Children network embraces the various strategies of the Child Friendly Cities initiative, working to establish programmes that promote democratic participation of the most vulnerable children, youth and families in local level planning and management, and empower them in moving towards social equity. The Child Friendly Cities initiative also advocates for active collaboration between cities on specific initiatives.

In Senegal, for instance, 68 municipal representatives from around the country, led by the Mayors Defenders of Children movement, met in 1997 to develop indicators for monitoring compliance with the Convention, and to create a charter for children. In Tamil Nadu, India, 25 cities are actively engaged together through the coordination of their social sector departments and community groups in creating city plans that link the activities of the Urban Basic Services Programme with state goals for children.[50] Membership in this network has given mayors the opportunity not only to work closely with one another and learn from others' successes and failures, but has also given them access to the wide range of partnerships, information and assistance that can be made available through the Child Friendly Cities connection.

One promising outcome of the growing recognition of cities as active participants on the national and global stage is a new trend in lending and financing. The World Bank and regional lenders are now considering lending money directly to municipalities or groups of municipalities or

47 WACLAC (1996) 'World Assembly of Cities and Local Authorities Coordination (WACLAC) Final Declaration, 30–31 May 1996', United Nations Conference on Human Settlements (HABITAT II), Istanbul

48 ICLEI (1996) *Local Agenda 21 Planning Guide: An Introduction to Sustainable Development Planning*, The International Council for Local Environmental Initiatives

49 Dowbor, 1996, op cit Note 3

50 Information from Theresa Kilbane, Gender, Partnerships and Participation Section, UNICEF, 1998

other local government institutions, rather than always lending to central governments. The stated purpose is to avoid red tape and bottlenecks in the disbursement of funds. The opportunity to have direct access to capital markets could give local governments considerably more flexibility; but the success of this level of decentralization is, of course, dependent on their integrity, transparency and capacity for sound financial management. This decentralized lending approach presents the risk of further aggregating foreign loan payments to poor countries that are already experiencing difficulties servicing current financial obligations. It will be necessary for local authorities, NGOs and child rights advocates to monitor closely the real social impact of these new local financing schemes being promoted by international institutions.

For information on joining various networks for local authorities, see the resource list, p285.

- *Establish connections with other local governments in order to share information, skills and creative solutions.*
- *Work together to advocate with higher levels of government on shared concerns.*
- *Look into existing networks that can offer support in addressing relevant issues.*

PARTICIPATORY DEMOCRACY – THE BASIS FOR CHILDREN'S RIGHTS

superficial responses to rights

It is not unusual for children's rights to be responded to in a superficial, piecemeal way. It is possible, for instance, to provide free and compulsory schooling without really giving children a relevant, high quality education. It is possible to legislate against child labour and to enforce this legislation without paying attention to alternative means for survival. It is possible to give children a token presence in local government processes without ever allowing them to experience what it is to be truly involved and responsible citizens. Nor do improvements in children's lives necessarily depend on the kind of government that is in place. Even the most repressive and authoritarian societies are capable of ensuring registration at birth, of improving children's chances of survival, of providing safer streets and neighbourhoods.

rights come alive when people are involved

But in order for children's rights to become a truly integral part of a city's or a society's culture, it is essential that children, their families, their neighbours, their teachers, their government officials, all actively experience themselves as bearers of rights. This means more than having certain services or goods made available to them. It also means more than being informed about their rights, although that is a start. If it is nothing more than information, it will remain irrelevant to the reality of peoples' lives. The concept of rights can only become alive and meaningful when people actively grapple with solving the problems associated with acquiring those rights. This means not only receiving what they are legally entitled to, but acknowledging the responsibilities that accompany rights, and taking an active part in shaping their world. It means having the confidence and will to take problems into their own hands and to collaborate on making things

UNICEF/93 – 1048
Betty Press

better, not only for themselves but for those around them. It means not just waiting for schools to be built, but taking an interest in how those schools operate, having a say in what is taught, and helping to make sure that they are well maintained. It means joining together with neighbours to make communities safer and more supportive places, and making it clear to authorities what is needed to get the job done.

Local government, as we have seen, plays a vital role in allowing and encouraging people to involve themselves in this kind of participatory democracy. It can acknowledge and support community efforts; show community members opportunities they are not yet aware of; invite them into the decision making process; make the city's resources available to them; inspire, channel and coordinate their skills, creativity and commitment.

This kind of cooperation, interdependence and creative problem solving have characterized the best of human society for as long as it has existed. But these traits have been sadly undermined by the forces and pressures that have created an urban world and a global economy. Old supports have eroded; new ones have not yet reliably taken their place. In a world where there are the resources for all to live in dignity, increasing numbers live in sub-human conditions. The time has long since come to find new ways to tap into the best of human potential. Cities, for all their problems, offer an extraordinary opportunity for this kind of rich and vital exchange, and for the creation of a new culture of participation, creativity and mutual support.

There are undoubtedly many roads towards this vision, and many groups working hard to achieve it. This book has explored one approach – the essential contribution that hard-pressed local governments can make when they work with commitment to honour the rights of their youngest citizens.

Resources

CHAPTER 1

The Implementation Handbook for the Convention on the Rights of the Child

Hodgkin, R and Newell P, 1998, UNICEF, Geneva.
A practical tool for all those involved in the work of understanding and implementing the Convention's provisions, based on the developing interpretation of the Committee on the Rights of the Child
Item Code: NYHQ/O0578 ISBN: 92–806–3337–6 $45, less 50 per cent for UNICEF Field Offices
To order: UNICEF Publications Sales, Division of Communication, Room 943–1, 3 United Nations Plaza, New York, NY 10017, USA; Fax: 1 212 326 7375
Email: pubdoc@unicef.org (for enquiries only) Website: www.unicef.org (publications)

Institut International des Droits de l'Enfant

Provides information and training on children's rights and concerns; coordinates international seminars; facilitates contact between members and organizes exchanges. Scholarships granted for participation in IDE activities.
For information: c/o Institut universitaire Kurt Bösch, P.O. Box 4176, 1950 Sion 4, Switzerland. Tel: +41 27 203 7383; Fax +41 27 203 7384
E-mail: institut@ikb.vsnet.ch

Defence for Children International (DCI)

Coordinates legal defence teams, dossier on international standards related to children's rights, maintains documentation centre on children's rights issues, publishes newsletter on UN activities concerning the protection of children's rights. Website contains full text of all relevant international instruments.
For information contact: PO Box 88, CH–1211 Geneva 20, Switzerland Tel +41 22 7340558;
Fax +41 22 7401145
E-mail: dci-juv.justice@pingnet.ch Website: http://www.childhub.ch/ webpub/dcihome

CRIN (Child Rights Information Network)

A global network of children's rights organizations supporting the exchange of information on children and their rights.
For information on children's rights issues, or to join the network, contact Becky Purbrick, c/o Save the Children Fund, 17 Grove Lane, London SE5 8RD, UK
Tel + 44 171 703 5400; Fax +44 171 793 7630
E-mail: crin@pro-net.co.uk Website: http://www.crin.ch
From Spanish-speaking countries, contact Bruce Harris on bruce@casa-alianza.org

CHAPTER 2

Facts For Life

Adamson, P, 1993, P&LA, London for UNICEF, WHO, UNESCO, UNFPA
Basic health, nutrition, and child development information in plain language. Practical, low-cost approaches.
Available in English, Arabic, French, Portuguese, Spanish. National adaptations available in most UNICEF field offices $1 or free online www.unicef.org/ffl/
To order: www.unicef.org (publications) or UNICEF, Publications Sales, Division of Communication, Room 943–1, 3 United Nations Plaza, New York, NY 10017, USA, Fax: +1 212 326 7375
E-mail: pubdoc@unicef.org (enquiries only)

The Coordinator's Notebook

Consultative Group on Early Childhood Care and Development
A twice yearly journal on early childhood care and development. Linked to a networking process in which the 1,800 recipients of the notebook are asked to: 1) contribute 2) copy and distribute to others and 3) communicate directly with others in the network.
Some issues available in Spanish
Free in the South; otherwise $25 for 2 issues or $40 for 4 issues. Free on-line, GOTOBUTTON BM_@_ www.ecdgroup.com/cnonline.html
To order: The Consultative Group Secretariat, 6 The Lope, Haydenville, MA 01039 USA
Tel +1413 268 7272; Fax 268 7279
E-mail: info@ecdgroup.com

EPOCH-Worldwide (End Physical Punishment of Children)

International network of over 70 organizations. Publishes handbooks and materials on positive non-violent discipline; lobbies governments and organizations to encourage education and legal reform to end physical punishment; acts as an information network.
For information: Peter Newell, 77 Holloway Road, London N7 8JZ, UK
Tel +44 171 700 0627; Fax 700 1105
E-mail: epoch-worldwide@mcrl.poptel.org.uk

CHAPTER 3

From Want to Work: Job Creation for the Urban Poor

International Labour Office, 1993, ILO, Geneva
A practical guide to creating remunerative employment for urban populations through labour-intensive participatory methods in construction and public works.
ISBN: 92–2–109086–8 Free
To order: ILO Publications, Development Policies Department, ILO, CH 1211Geneva 22, Switzerland
E-mail: Pubvente@ilo.org

Urban Agriculture: Food, Jobs and Sustainable Cities

United Nations Development Programme, 1996, New York
Identifies the benefits of well-executed urban agriculture, and problems that can result from poor practices. Discusses methods for promoting urban agriculture.

Item code: E.96.III.B.4 ISBN: 92–1–126047–7 $19.95 USD, add five per cent for postage, with a $5 minimum.
Orders and enquiries for North America, Latin America, Asia, and Pacific Islands: UN Publications, Sales and Marketing Section, Room DC2–853, Dept. I004, New York, N.Y. 10017 USA.
Tel +1 212 963 8302; Fax 963 3489
For Europe, Africa, Middle East: UN Publications, Sales Office and Bookshop, CH–1211 Geneva 10, Switzerland. Tel: +41 22 917 2613

Environment and Urbanization

International Institute for Environment and Development, Human Settlements Programme, London
A twice yearly journal on urban and environmental issues mostly in Africa, Asia and Latin America. Each issue is based on a special theme and includes: 7–11 papers; a guide to the literature (in most issues); profiles of innovative Third World NGOs; papers on participatory tools and methods; summaries of new books, research reports and newsletters and how these can be obtained (including those in Spanish, French and Portuguese); information on current events and debates.
Free to NGOs and teaching institutions in Latin America, Asia (except Japan) and Africa. Half price for subscribers from Latin America, Asia (except Japan) and Africa and to students (xerox of current student card needed as proof). Municipal authorities that have difficulty obtaining foreign exchange can apply for a free subscription.
Otherwise: One year subscription: Institutions – £36; US$63; individuals – £22; US$37
For sample copy and further details: Human Settlements Programme, IIED, 3 Endsleigh Street, London WC1H ODD, UK. Tel +44 171 388 2117; Fax +44 171 388 2826
E-mail: humansiied@gn.apc.org Website: http://www.oneworld.org/iied/human.html

CHAPTER 4

Where Women have No Doctor: A Health Guide for Women

Burns, A, Lovich R, Maxwell, J, and Shapiro, K 1997, Hesperian Foundation, Berkeley, CA
Clearly written, more than 1,000 drawings; helps women identify obstacles to good health in their communities and shares ideas on how to overcome them.
Available in English and Spanish. Other editions in process: Shona, Cebuano, Filipino (Tagalog), Vietnamese, Khmer, Arabic, Haitian Creole, Hindi, Bengali, Teluga, Marathi, Chinese, Indonesian
ISBN: 0942364252 $20.00 ($10.00 for health workers in developing countries)
For information on ordering from The Hesperian Foundation, see p277

A Book for Midwives: A Manual for Traditional Birth Attendants and Community Midwives

Klein, S 1995, Hesperian Foundation, Berkeley, CA
Written in clear, simple language for people who live far from maternity centres or where it is difficult to get medical care.
Available in English, Spanish, Vietnamese, Bengali (pending).
ISBN: 0942364228 $22 (Ask for information about free copies or reduced prices in the developing world)
For information about ordering from The Hesperian Foundation, see p277

Safe Motherhood Initiative

A global alliance aimed at reducing deaths and illnesses among women and infants, especially in developing countries. Partners work together to raise awareness, set priorities, stimulate research, mobilize resources, provide technical assistance and share information.
For information contact: Local UNICEF country offices
or Family Care International, 588 Broadway, Suite 503, New York, NY 10012 USA
E-mail: info@safemotherhood.org Website: www.safemotherhood.org

Baby Friendly Hospital Initiative

Sponsored by the World Health Organization and UNICEF; a world-wide effort to improve breastfeeding rates. Based on the ten steps to successful breastfeeding, the initiative encourages hospitals to examine their practices, make the appropriate changes and then apply for recognition as a Baby Friendly Hospital.
For information contact: Health Officer at local UNICEF country offices or WHO.
The initiative also puts out a free monthly newsletter. For subscription: UNICEF, Division of Communication,
Attn: Chetana Hein, 3 UN Plaza 11–6F, New York, NY 10017 USA. Fax: +1 212 824 6465
E-mail: pubdoc@unicef.org
Back issues for 1996 available on-line at: gopher://gopher.unicef.org/11/.s496bfhi

CHAPTER 5

The Environment for Children: Understanding and Acting on the Environmental Hazards that Threaten Children and their Parents

Satterthwaite, D and others, 1996. Earthscan Publications, London.
A reference on the effects of environmental hazards on children's health and development, it also explains what can be done by communities, governments and aid workers to provide safe, healthy environments for children.
ISBN: 1 85383 326 6 £13.95 + postage and handling. For discount queries contact Andy Young at Earthscan
To order: Earthscan Publications Limited, 120 Pentonville Road, London N1 9JN, UK
Tel +44 171 278 0433, Fax 278 1142
E-mail: earthinfo@earthscan.co.uk

Improving Habitat for Children: A Handbook for Programme Decisions

Iyer, L and Goldenberg, D, 1997, Plan International
A brief manual for planning programmes focused on child-centred improvement of housing and related issues.
Free: Orders and enquiries: S Bowen, Plan International, Chobham House, Christchurch Way, Woking, Surrey GU2I IJG, UK. Tel +44 1483 733 240; Fax +44 1483 756 505

Disabled Village Children: A Guide for Community Health Workers, Rehabilitation Workers and Families.

Werner, D 1987, Hesperian Foundation, Palo Alto, CA
Practical suggestions for adapting the home and community environment, producing play equipment, and solving basic problems of care for children with disabilities. Although designed for village conditions, much of the manual is applicable to urban conditions.

Available in Arabic, Chinese, Dari, English(adapted for India), French, Hindi, Lao, Nepali, Oriya, Portugese, Russian, Spanish, Swahili, Vietnamese, Kannada. Some language versions are available from other publishers – contact Hesperian for details.
$22 + shipping and handling; countries at a subsidized price, or free of charge.
See Hesperian Foundation for information on ordering and enquiries.
See also Practical Approaches to Childhood Disability in Developing Countries, p278

Children's Rights and Participation in Residential Care

Willow, C, National Children's Bureau, London
A practical guide outlining the legal rights of young people in residential care, and providing useful suggestions about how staff and administrators can increase their participation in improving residential care services. Geared particularly towards conditions in the United Kingdom.
ISBN: 1–874579–92-X Members £10.00, Non Members £15.00
For orders and enquiries: National Children's Bureau, 8 Wakley Street, London EC1V 7QE, UK
Tel: +44 171 843 6028, Fax +44 171 278 9512
E-Mail: booksales@ncb.org.uk Website: www.ncb.org.uk/pubinfo.htm

CHAPTER 6

The Hesperian Foundation

Low-cost publications on health issues, developed with community-based groups and medical experts from many countries. Available in a number of languages, depending on the publication.
For information: The Hesperian Foundation, 1919 Addison St. #304, Berkeley, CA 94704, USA.
Tel+1 510 8454507; Fax+1510 845–0539 or 9141
E-mail: hesperianfdn@igc.apc.org Website: www.managingdesire.org/Hesperian

Child-to-Child Trust

An organization promoting the education of children on health (and other matters) through peer counseling and interaction. Through inexpensive booklets and activity sheets in over 15 languages, children learn simple measures appropriate to low-income communities for preventing accidents, promoting basic hygiene, responding to illness, etc. Resources include training materials for adults.
For information: Child-to-Child Trust, Institute of Education, 20 Bedford Way, London WC1H OAL, UK
Tel +44 0171 612 6648; Fax +44 0171 612 6645
Some Child-to-Child items are available only from TALC – for information see p280

Child-to-Child, A Resource Book Part 1 and Part 2

Hawes, H, Bailey, D, Bonati, G
Part 1 is a resource for those wanting to make the child-to-child approach part of their programs; sections on methodology, evaluation and running workshops, plus examples of action around the world. Part 2 consists of 35 activity sheets on topics including diarrhoea, malaria, sanitation, disability, immunisation, AIDS and many others. A useful section on how to use the streets to best effect.
£3 plus postage for Part 1; £4 plus postage for Part 2 For orders and enquiries: TALC (see p 280)

Heathlink Worldwide

An organization promoting appropriate, sustainable, cost-effective health policies and practices; focusing on practical aspects of primary health care and rehabilitation in developing countries, providing links between partners and opportunities worldwide, and creating publications for health and development workers. Includes the AIDS and Sexual Health Programme, which promotes broad understanding of HIV/AIDS and other sexual health issues in the context of developing countries; provides technical support to organizations and networks, runs an information service, and collaborates with partners on local and regional activities.
Publications are available in ten languages, and are free to individuals and organizations in developing countries
For information: Healthlink Worldwide, 29–35 Farringdon Road, London EC1M 3JB, UK
Fax +44 171 242 0041
E-mail: publications@healthlink.org.uk Website: www.healthnet.org.uk

Child Health Dialogue

Healthlink Worldwide (formerly AHRTAG)
A quarterly publication providing exchange of information about prevention and treatment of key childhood illnesses.
Available in 11 regional editions and an electronic edition.
Free in the developing world; otherwise £6 students; £12 other individuals; £24 institutions
Orders and enquiries: See above, Healthlink Worldwide

Practical Approaches to Childhood Disability in Developing Countries

Thorburn, M and Marfo, K, Global Age Publishing, Tampa, Florida
This book focuses on a variety of actions and programmes for meeting the needs of children with disabilities in developing countries: preventing the occurrence of impairment and disability; minimizing the impact of disability on the child's development and functioning; helping children with disabilities to develop optimally and adapt effectively to their environment; integrating disabled children successfully in the community, school, and workplace.
$25, $18 in developing countries, + shipping/handling.
To order: Global Age Publishing, 16057 Tampa Palms Blvd West#219,Tampa, Florida 33647, USA
Tel +1 813 991 4982, Fax +1 813 973 8166
See also Disabled Village Children, p276

CBR News (community-based rehabilitation)

Healthlink Worldwide (formerly AHRTAG)
The most widely circulated international newsletter on CBR. It covers successful community-based disability projects and developments in the international disabled people's rights movement and provides practical information about mobility aids and resources.
Published three times a year in English, French, Hindi, English Braille.
ISBN: 0963–5556 Free to individuals and organizations in developing countries. Otherwise: students £6/US$12 ; individuals £12/US$24; organizations £24/US$48
For orders and enquiries: see above, Healthlink Worldwide

Helping Children Cope with the Stresses of War

(useful also in other extreme situations)
Maksoud, M 1993, UNICEF
Based on methods and approaches tested extensively in war-torn Lebanon, a manual for helping children cope with the stresses of war and other forms of systematic violence. General guidelines on handling the

'problem behaviours' with which children of various ages respond to stresses are also presented. Ten specific problem behaviours ranging from bed-wetting to risk-taking are described, followed by practical advice on how parents and teachers can deal with them.
Item code: NYHQ/G0011 ISBN: 92–806–2087–8 $14.95
Orders and enquiries: UNICEF, Publications Sales, Division of Communication, Room 943–1, 3 United Nations Plaza, New York, NY 10017, USA. Fax +1 212 326 7375
Email: pubdoc@unicef.org (for enquiries only) www.unicef.org

CHAPTER 7

International Centre for the Prevention of Crime

Assists cities to reduce delinquency, violence and insecurity, harnessing best practices worldwide to solve local problems. Focuses on investing in youth and families, breaking the cycle of violence against women and children as well as promoting greater responsibility. Provides technical assistance, promotes public awareness, facilitates exchange of expertise.
For information: Irvin Waller, 507 Place d'armes no.2100, Montreal, Quebec, Canada H2Y 2W8
Tel +1 514 288 6731; Fax +1 514 288 8763
E-mail: cipc@web.net Website: www.crime-prevention-intl.org

Play for All Guidelines

Moore, Goltsman and Iacofano, 2nd Edition 1992, MIG Communications, Berkeley. CA
Comprehensive resource addressing the full range of play-related issues: safety and risk management, accessibility and integration, maintenance, and children's development.
Available in English and Japanese.
ISBN: 0944661173 $39.95 + postage. Orders and enquiries: MIG Communications, 800 Hearst Avenue, Berkeley, CA 94710, USA Tel +1 510 845 0953; Fax 845 8750

Getting in Touch with Play: Creating Play Environments for Children with Visual Impairments

Blakely, K, Lann, M, Hart, R 1991,Lighthouse Inc. New York
Offers design ideas supporting creative and satisfying play experiences for children who are blind or visually impaired.
$7.95 + $2 shipping, Order# P250
Orders and enquiries: The Lighthouse Inc., 36–20 Northern Blvd., Long Island City, NY 11101–1614
See also Practical Approaches to Childhood Disability in Developing Countries, p278 and Disabled Village Children, p276.

Children's Participation: The Theory and Practice of Involving Young Citizens in Community Development and Environmental Care

Hart, R, 1997, Earthscan Publications, London
Using detailed case studies from around the world, this book introduces the organizing principles, practical techniques and resources for involving young people in environmental projects in their own communities.
ISBN: 1 85383 322 3 22 £18.95 + postage and handling (For discount queries contact Andy Young at Earthscan)
To order: Earthscan Publications Limited, 120 Pentonville Road, London N1 9JN, UK
Tel +44 171 278 0433, Fax 278 1142
E-mail: earthinfo@earthscan.co.uk Website: www.earthscan.org

Changing Places: Young People's Participation in Environmental Planning

Adams, E, and Ingham, S 1998, The Children's Society, London
How professionals can enable young people to engage in the process of planning for change, both changing attitudes towards the environment and changing the environment itself. The book includes twenty detailed case studies from across the UK, illustrated with photographs, as well as practical advice on running projects.
ISBN: 1 899783 00 8 £9.95 + 10% postage & handling
Orders and enquiries: Publishing Department, The Children's Society, Edward Rudolf House, Margery Street, London WC1X 0JL. Tel +44 171 837 4299; Fax 837 0211
Website: www.the-childrens-society.org.uk/

We Are On the Radio (book plus tape)

Hanbury, C and McCrum, S
How to involve children in making radio programmes about health, environment and children's rights issues.
£6 in UK/Europe; £7 to rest of world, including postage and packing.
For orders and enquiries contact Child-to-Child Trust. See p277.

CHAPTER 8

Places and Spaces for Preschool and Primary (indoors)

Vergeront, J, 1987, NAEYC
Space design solutions for child care workers and administrators. Simply written, with drawings. Information organized by pattern (need category), situation, solution and suggestions.
Item#310 ISBN:0–935989–07–2 $2.50 Orders and enquiries: NAEYC, 1834 Connecticut Avenue, N.W., Washington, DC 20009–5786
Tel +1 202 232 8777

We can Play and Move: A Manual to Help Disabled Children Learn to Move by Playing with Others

Levitt, S 1987, (new edition 1999) Healthlink Worldwide, London
Shows play activities that can help a child with disabilities to improve and coordinate movement and balance. All activities described through numerous drawings.
ISBN: 0–9073020–13–9 Free to readers in the developing world; otherwise £6 including postage
Orders and enquiries: see Healthlink Worldwide p277. See also Chapter 2, 6, 7 resources.

CHAPTER 9

Teaching-aids At Low Cost (TALC)

An organization that produces a number of low-cost teaching aids and publications, including information on curriculum and design modifications for meeting the needs of children with a range of disabilities.
For information and publication list contact: TALC, PO Box 49, St. Albans, Herts AL1 4AX, United Kingdom
Tel +44 1727 853869; Fax +44 1727 846352

Health Promotion in Our Schools

Hawes, H (ed) Child-to-Child Trust
A resource book for health education and health promotion programmes that stress the involvement of children.
£3 plus postage. For orders and enquiries, see TALC, above.

It's Only Right: A Practical Guide for Learning about the Convention on the Rights of the Child

Fountain, S 1993, UNICEF, New York.
Activities for students 13 to 18; helps young people become familiar with the articles of the Convention, understand its relevance to their own lives, and make realistic plans for taking action on children's rights issues.
Available in English, Spanish, French.
Item Code: NYHQ/O0422 ISBN: 92–806–3056–3 $10.95
To order: UNICEF, Publications Sales, Room 943–1, 3 United Nations Plaza, New York, NY 10017, USA
Fax +1 212 326 7375, www.unicef.org (publications)
Email: pubdoc@unicef.org (for enquiries only)

Creative Conflict Resolution : More Than 200 Activities for Keeping Peace in the Classroom

Kreidler, W 1984, Scott, Foresman and Company, Glenview, Illinois.
A comprehensive guide to introducing peacemaking skills, including cooperation, communication, and awareness of stereotyping, with over 200 classroom activities for the primary grades.
ISBN: 0673156427 $13 from publisher, or $10.36 from www.amazon.com
To order: Educators for Social Responsibility, 23 Garden Street, Cambridge MA 02138 USA
Tel +1 617 492 1764, Fax +1 617 864 5164, Website: www.esrnational.org

Adventures in Peacemaking

Kreidler, W and Furlong, L 1995
This is an updated version of the book above, available from the same source for $22.

Discipline without Beating: A Challenge for Educators

Kuleana Centre for Children's Rights
Available in English and Swahili.
$2:00 US For information contact Kuleana, P.O. Box 27, Mwanza, Tanzania
Tel + 255 68 50911/50912; Fax+ 255 68 500486
E-mail: kuleana@tan2.healthnet.org

CHAPTER 10

What Works for Working Children

Boyden, J, Ling, B, and Myers, W 1998, Rädda Barnen and UNICEF
This book offers practical answers for those faced with developing policy and taking action that best serves the interests of working children.

ISBN: 91–88726–13–4, Code # 9066 250 Swedish Crowns, plus postage SEK 130 for one book. Unable to accept cheque or cash. Can accept Visa, Mastercard or Eurocard, or bank transfers to A/C 6102 200728598, Svenska Handelsbanken, SE–10670 Stockhom, Sweden. Add SE 15 service charge To order: Rädda Barnen, SE–107 88 Stockholm, Sweden. Fax +46 8 698 90 14

ECPAT (End Child Prostitution, Child Pornography and the Trafficking of Children for Sexual Purposes)

Helps local communities find strategies to protect children; works closely with NGOs, UNICEF, ILO and other groups; works with Interpol and local law enforcers to ensure that laws are implemented; monitors the activities of child traffickers and abusers; involves young people themselves in seeking solutions to commercial sexual exploitation; issues a quarterly newletter and a monthly bulletin of news clippings, and undertakes activities against the sexual abuse of children.
For information: ECPAT Information Centre, 328 Phyathai Road, Bangkok 10400, Thailand
Tel +66 2 2153388/6110972/6110973; Fax +66 2 2158272
E-mail: ecpatbkk@ksc15.th.com

Children's Participation in Action Research: a Training Course for Trainers

Dallape, F and Gilbert, C 1993 ENDA
A practical guide to conducting participatory research with working children and street children.
Free, except for postage. Orders and enquiries: ENDA –Zimbabwe, PO Box A113, Harare, Zimbabwe

Methods of Research with Street and Working Children: An Annotated Bibliography

http://www.rb.se/childwork

The Methodological Series of Booklets of the Regional Programme of Children in Especially Difficult Circumstances

These booklets offer useful guidance on the development of situation analyses for working children and on the evaluation of intervention programmes.
Available in Spanish and English. Orders and enquiries: UNICEF, Regional Office for Latin America and the Caribbean, PO Box 7555, Bogota, Colombia Fax + 571 2114071

DEP Newsletter

Development and Education Programme for Daughters and Community Centres
DEP is an organization devoted to providing high quality education as a measure to prevent girls from entering prostitution or other harmful forms of labour.
For information on their newsletter, write PO Box 10, Mae Sai, Chang Rai, 57130, Thailand

CHAPTER 11

Kuleana Centre for Children's Rights

NGO committed to the promotion of children's rights in Tanzania. Programmes include research, publications, awareness and training. Kuleana operates the largest street children's centre in Tanzania.
For information: Kuleana, P.O. Box 27, Mwanza, Tanzania Advocacy Center

Tel +255 68 50911/50912; Training Center +255 68 50486; Street Children's Center +255 68 50510
Fax + 255 68 42402
E-mail: kuleana@tan2.healthnet.org

Casa Alianza/Covenant House Latin America

Runs legal aid offices in Mexico, Guatamala and Honduras providing personal documentation for street children, prosecution of perpetrators of violence against street children; legal defense of child victims of rights abuses, awareness raising through the mass media. Provides support to organizations involved in the legal defense of street children, and responds to questions from the public.
For information: Bruce Harris, SJO 1039, PO Box 025216, Miami FL 33102–5216, USA
Tel (in Costa Rica) +506 253 5439; Fax (in Costa Rica): +506 224 5689
E-mail: bruce@casa-alianza.org
Website: http://www.casa-alianza.org

Street and Working Children: A Guide to Planning

Ennew, J 1994, Save the Children Development Manual 4
Practical guide to planning projects for street and working children; stresses working with children rather than for them; includes advice on assessing the local situation, organizing human resources, and coping with common problems.
ISBN: 1 870322 82 7
Save the Children Fund, 17 Grove Lane, London SE5 8RD, UK
Tel + 44 171 703 5400

For health information

See Child-to-Child, A Resource Book Part 1 and Part 2, Chapter 6 p277. See also p281

CHAPTER 12

International Association of Juvenile and Family Court Magistrates

Provides training for magistrates, judges and workers in the field of juvenile justice; carries out research in juvenile justice, family law and child protection. Provides information on research findings and on-going projects.
For information: Molenstraat 15, 4851 SG Ulvenhout, The Netherlands Tel and fax +31 76 561 2640

International Network on Juvenile Justice (INJJ)

Facilitates the exchange of information between partners; coordinates initiatives in the field of juvenile justice; maintains a documentation centre of items related to juvenile justice and a database on organizations active in the field. Over 60 partners on all continents.
For information: PO Box 88, CH–1211 Geneva 20, Switzerland
Tel +41–22–734–0558; Fax +41–22–740–1145
E-mail: dci-juv.justice@pingnet.ch

Casa Alianza/Covenant House Latin America

Provides legal defense and assistance to children under arrest, in pre-trial detention and in prison. Organizes training courses in areas such as the legal defense of street children.
For contact information: see above.

School-in-a-box

A joint initiative by UNESCO and UNICEF to provide education to children affected by war and emergency, also useful for children in detention. Sometimes referred to as a 'mobile classroom', the kits consist of class materials, teacher training and methodology to teach basic literacy and numeracy, grades 1–4. Intended as a temporary 6–12 month programme to prepare students for reintegration into formal, textbook-based, curriculum. Kits are assembled according to the unique needs of the targeted group of children and will vary in both content and materials. The two basic versions are the Teacher Education Programme (TEP) which generally includes slates, chalk, exercise books, lesson plans and other learning materials; and Edukit, which includes school supplies, teacher support materials, teacher in-service training, and community initiatives. Not simply supplies but 'approaches' for teaching.
Available in English, Somali, Kinyarwanda, Afar, Portugese, French, and others.
Costs are approximately $5–7 per child including supplies and teacher training
For information on TEPs: UNESCO-PEER, P.O. Box 30592, UN complex Gigiri, Nairobi, Kenya
For information on Edukits: Senior Education Advisor,UNICEF, 3 United Nations Plaza, Education Section TA26A, New York, NY 10017
Tel +1 212 824 6630, Fax 824 6481
E-mail: pbuckland@unicef.org

CHAPTER 14

Local Agenda 21 Planning Guide: An Introduction to Sustainable Development Planning

The International Council for Local Environmental Initiatives (ICLEI) 1996
Offers tested, practical advice on how local governments can adapt and implement the United Nations' Local Agenda 21 action plan for sustainable development and the related UN Habitat Agenda in their own communities. Includes information on partnerships, community-based issue analysis, action planning, implementation and monitoring, and evaluation and feedback; and uses figures, worksheets, case studies and appendices to help illustrate how different concepts and methods can be applied.
Available in English and Spanish.
$35 USD. Shipping Costs Per Copy: $8.00 USD (within US), $13.00 USD (overseas airmail)
To order: ICLEI World Secretariat, City Hall, East Tower, 8th Floor, Toronto, Ontario, Canada M5H 2N2
Tel +1 416 392 1462, Fax 392 1478
E-mail: iclei@iclei.org; Website: www.iclei.org/iclei/icleipub.htm

PLA Notes (Notes on Participatory Learning and Action)

International Institute for Environment and Development, Sustainable Agriculture Programme, London
Published three times a year, this journal serves as a clearing house for discussion on this rapidly developing field, and includes experiences from the field, methodological innovations and conceptual reflections.
Free to individuals and organizations in the South; otherwise £20/$30 per year or £37/$50 for 2 years
To order: Sust. Ag. Programme, IIED, 3 Endsleigh Street, London WC1H ODD
Tel +44 171 388 2117; Fax +44 171 388 2826
E-mail: sustag@iied.org

Visualisation in Participatory Programmes: A Manual for Facilitators and Trainers Involved in Participatory Group Events

UNICEF, 1993, Dhaka, Bangladesh
VIPP, or Visualisation in Participatory Programmes is a synthesis of methods for improving group interaction. A combination of approaches from Latin America, Europe and elsewhere, all of which emphasize

the importance of people's involvement.
Item code: NYHQ/V0489 ISBN: 92–806–3033–4 $16.95
To order: Information Section, UNICEF, P.O. Box 58, Dhaka 1000, Bangladesh Tel + 880 2 933 6701, Fax 2 933 5641

Creating Better Cities with Children and Youth: A Manual for Participation

D. Driskell and others, 1999, Growing Up In Cities, UNESCO.
A manual outlining the tested methods of the Growing Up in Cities Project, an international research project using action research with young people as a way of learning about and acting on their communities.
For information: UNESCO, MOST programme, 1 rue Miollis, 75732 Paris Fax 33 1 456857
E-mail: ssmost@unesco.org

ANDI

A Brazilian organization that promotes attention to children's rights within the media. For information, see their home page on the internet:
http://www2.uol.com.br/andi

International Union of Local Authorities (IULA)

Worldwide organization of local government helping to establish formal and regular contacts between associations of local government and between individual municipalities. Its aims include promoting local government as a cornerstone of democracy; strengthening local government and its institutions as instruments for socio-economic development; representing and defending the interests of local government at the national and international level; fostering improvement in the quality of local decision-making, administration, and service provision. Since the 1980s, IULA has undergone a process of decentralization and regionalization.
For information, contact IULA World Secretariat, PO Box 90646, 2509 LP The Hague, The Netherlands
Or Laan Copes van Cattenburch, 60 A 2585 GC, The Hague, The Netherlands
Tel: +31 70 306 6066, Fax: +31 70 350 0496,
E-mail: IULA@IULA-hq.nl
Website: www.cuapp.udel.edu/iula
For regional information: www.cuapp.udel.edu/iula/regions.htm
Information about other local government networks, including ICMA, ICLEI, IDCN, IULA; world.localgov.org/internlocal.htm

The Mayors Defenders of Children Network

UNICEF based initiative working towards strengthening partnerships at national and international levels, promoting the development of child-friendly municipal plans of action, and establishing programmes that promote democratic participation of the most vulnerable children, youth and families in local level planning and management.
For information, contact the Gender, Partnerships and Participation Section, Programme Division, 3 United Nations Plaza, TA 24A–80, New York, NY 10017.

Bibliography

Adams, E and S Ingham (1998) *Changing Places: Children's Participation in Environmental Planning*, London: The Children's Society

Agarwal, S, M Attah, N Apt, M Grieco, E A Kwakye and J Turner (1994) 'Bearing the weight: the kayayoo, Ghana's working girl child', Presented at the UNICEF Conference on the Girl Child, Ahmedebad, India

Aina, T A (1989) *Health, Habitat and Underdevelopment – with Special Reference to a Low Income Settlement in Metropolitan Lagos*, London, IIED

Alston, P (ed) (1994) *The Best Interests of the Child: Reconciling Culture and Human Rights*, Florence: UNICEF International Child Development Centre and Oxford: Clarendon Press

Altman, I (1975) *The Environment and Social Behavior: Privacy, Personal Space, Territory and Crowding*, Monterey CA: Brooks/Cole

Altman, I and M M Chemers (1983) *Culture and Environment*, New York: Cambridge University Press

American News Service (1997) 'Young dragons chase away nighttime fears in Dallas', *Doing Democracy*, (Winter 1997): 8

Anand, S and M Ravillion (1993) 'Human development in poor countries: on the role of private incomes and public services', *Journal of Economic Perspectives*, 7 (1 Winter): 133–150

Anzorena, J (1994) 'Grameen Bank – November 1993', *SELAVIP Newsletter, Journal of Low-Income Housing in Asia and the World*, April 1994

Anzorena, J, J Bolnick, S Boonyabancha, Y Cabannes, A Hardoy, A Hasan, C Levy and D Mitlin (1998) 'Reducing urban poverty: some lessons from experience', *Environment and Urbanization*, 10(1): 167–186

Appleyard, D and M Lintell (1972) 'The environmental quality of city streets: the residents' viewpoint', *Journal of the American Institute of Planners*, 38: 84–101

Aptekar, L and B Abebe (1997) 'Conflict in the neighborhood: Street and working children in the public space', *Childhood*, 4(4)

Arévalo Torres, P (1997) 'May hope be realized: Huaycan self-managing urban community in Lima', *Environment and Urbanization*, 9(1, April): 59–79

Arnold, C (1998) *Early Childhood – Building our Understanding and Moving Towards the Best of Both Worlds*, Redd Barna/Save the Children USA

Arrossi, S (1996) 'Inequality and health in Metropolitan Buenos Aires', *Environment and Urbanization*, 8(2): 43–70

Attahi, K, M Carr, R Stren (1992) *Metropolitan Planning and Management in the Developing World: Abidjan and Quito*, Nairobi: UNCHS (Habitat)

Badiwala, M (1998) 'Child labour in India: causes, governmental policies and the role of education', http://www.geocities.com/College Park/Library/9175/inquiry1.htm

Baizerman, M (1996) 'Youth work on the street: Community's moral compact with its young people', *Childhood*, 3(2): 157–167

Baker, R (1998) *Negotiating Identities: A Study of the Lives of Street Children in Nepal*, doctoral thesis, University of Durham

Balakrishnan, R (1994) 'The sociological context of girls' schooling: micro perspectives from the slums of Delhi', *Social Action*, 44 (July–September 1994)

Banaynal-Fernandez, T (1994) 'Fighting violence against women: the experience of the Lihok-Pilipina Foundation in Cebu', *Environment and Urbanization*, 6(2): 31–56

Barbarin, O and T de Wet (1997) 'Violence and emotional development in black townships of South Africa: an ecological approach', *Urban Childhood*, Trondheim, Norway

Barbosa, R, Y Cabannes, L Moraes (1997) 'Tenant today, posseiro tomorrow', *Environment and Urbanization*, 9(2): 17–41
Barker, R G and P V Gump (1964) *Big School, Small School: High School Size and Student Behavior*, Stanford, CA: Stanford University Press
Bartlett, S N (1997) 'Housing as a factor in the socialization of children: A critical review of the literature', *Merrill-Palmer Quarterly*, 43(2): 169–198
Bartlett, S N (1997) 'No place to play: implications for the interaction of parents and children', *Journal for Children and Poverty*, 3(1)
Bartlett, S N (1998) 'Does poor housing perpetuate poverty?', *Childhood*, 5(4): 403–421
Baumrind, D (1971) 'Current patterns of parental authority', *Developmental Psychology*, 4(Monograph 1): 1–103
Baumrind, D (1989) 'Rearing competent children' in W Damon (ed) *Child Development Today and Tomorrow*, San Francisco: Jossey Bass, 349–378
Beall, J (1996) *Urban Governance: Why Gender Matters*, Gender in Development Monograph Series, UNDP
Beers, H van (1996) 'A plea for a child-centred approach in research with street children', *Childhood*, 3(2): 195–201
Bibars, I (1998) 'Street children in Egypt: from the home to the street to inappropriate corrective institutions', *Environment and Urbanization*, 10(1): 201–216
Black, M (1993) 'Girls and girlhood: Time we were noticed', *New Internationalist*, (240): 4–7
Black, M (1993) 'Street children and working children', Innocenti Global Seminar Summary Report, 15–25 February 1993, Florence: UNICEF International Child Development Centre
Black, M (1996) *Children First: The Story of UNICEF, Past and Present*, Oxford: Oxford University Press
Black, M and C Smith (1997) 'Rights of institutionalized children', European Conference on the Rights of Institutionalized Children, Bucharest, Romania, UNICEF
Blanc, C S and contributors (1994) *Urban Children in Distress: Global Predicaments and Innovative Strategies*, Florence, Italy: UNICEF International Child Development Centre and London: Gordon and Breach
Blanchet, T (1996) *Lost Innocence, Stolen Childhoods*, Dhaka: The University Press
Blue, I (1996) 'Urban inequalities in mental health: the case of São Paulo, Brazil', *Environment and Urbanization*, 8(2): 91–99
Bolnick, J (1996) 'uTshani Buyakhuluma (the grass speaks); Peoples' Dialogue and the South African Homeless Peoples' Federation, 1993–1996', *Environment and Urbanization*, 8(2): 153–170
Bond, L S (1992) 'Street children and aids: Is postponement of sexual involvement a realistic alternative to the prevention of sexually transmitted diseases?', *Environment and Urbanization*, 4(1): 150–157
Boscio, R P (1997) 'Democratic governance and participation: A tale of two cities', Paper presented at the GURI Conference on Governance in Action: Urban Initiatives in a Global Setting, Centre for Urban and Community Studies, University of Toronto, Toronto
Bosnjak, V (1998) 'Child Labour: The Ten Commandments', Unpublished document, UNICEF, Brazil
Bowlby, J (1969) *Attachment and Loss Vol 1 Attachment*, New York: Basic Books
Boyden, J and P Holden (1991) *Children of the Cities*, London: Zed Books
Boyden, J, B Ling and W Myers (1998) *What Works for Working Children*, Stockholm: Radda Barnen and UNICEF
Bronfenbrenner, U (1989) 'Who Cares for Children', Presentation September 7, 1989, UNESCO, Paris
Bronfenbrenner, U and S J Ceci (1994) 'Nature-nurture reconceptualized in developmental perspective: a bioecological model', *Psychological Review*, 101(4): 568–586
Brown, W, S K Thurman and L F Pearl (1993) *Family-centered Early Intervention with Infants and Toddlers: Innovative Cross Disciplinary Approaches*, Baltimore: Paul H Brookes
Bryce-Heath, S B (1994) 'The project of learning from the inner-city youth perspective' in F A Villarruel and R M Lerner (eds) *Promoting Community Based Programs for Socialization and Learning*, San Francisco: Jossey Bass
Bureau of Young GRAPEs, (1996) *We're in Print: The Whole Story by Kids for Kids*, New York: City University of New York Graduate School
Burman, E (1994) *Deconstructing Developmental Psychology*, London: Routledge
Burman, E (1996) 'Local, global or globalized? Child development and international child rights legislation', *Childhood*, 3(1): 45–67
Cairncross, S (1990) 'Water supply and the urban poor' in J Hardoy, S Cairncross and D Satterthwaite (eds) *The Poor Die Young: Housing and Health in Third World Cities*, London: Earthscan

Cairncross, S (1992) 'Sanitation and watersupply: practical lessons from the decade', *Water and Sanitation Discussion Paper Series*, 9, Washington DC, World Bank
Cairncross, S and E A R Ouano (1990) *Surface Water Drainage in LowIncome Communities*, Geneva: WHO
Cameron, S (1998) *Making Peace with Children*, UNICEF Colombia
Cameron, S, N Kandula, J Leng and C Arnold (1998) *Urban Childcare in Bangladesh*, Save the Children USA
Cantwell, N (1998) 'Nothing more than justice', *Innocenti Digest: Juvenile Justice*, (3): 16–17
Carr, M (1992) 'Metropolitan planning and management in the Third World: a case study of Quito, Ecuador' in UNCHS (Habitat) (ed) *Metropolitan Planning and Management in the Developing World: Abidjan and Quito*, Nairobi: UNCHS, 83–137
Castillo Berthier, H (1993) 'Popular culture among Mexican teenagers', *The Urban Age*, 1(4): 14–15
Cayon, E (1998) *Selected References on Geographic Information System (GIS) and Urban Issues*, Ibadan, Nigeria: UNICEF Nigeria
Chawla, L (1992) 'Childhood place attachments' in I Altman and S Low (eds) *Place Attachment*, New York: Plenum
Chawla, L and R Hart (1988) 'The roots of environmental concern', *Proceedings of the 19th Conference of the Environmental Design Research Association*, EDRA, Washington DC,
Children's Defense Fund (1997) *The State of America's Children Yearbook 1997*, Washington DC: Children's Defense Fund
Connolly, M (1997) *The Health Matters for Street Children and Youth*, Newmarket UK: Global Gutter Press
Connolly, M and J Ennew (1996) 'Introduction: Children out of place', *Childhood*, 3(2): 131–147
Cooper Marcus, C and M Barnes (eds) (1999) *Healing Gardens: Therapeutic Landscapes in Healthcare Facilities*, New York: John Wiley and Sons
Cornia, G A, R Jolly and F Stewart (eds) (1987) *Adjustment with a Human Face*, Oxford: Oxford University Press
Cruz, L F (1994) 'NGO profile: Fundación Carvajal: The Carvajal Foundation', *Environment and Urbanization*, 6(2): 175–182
Cussianovich Villaran, A (1997) *Some Premises for Reflection and Social Practices with Working Children and Adolescents*, Rädda Barnen
Dall, F P (1995) 'Children's right to education' in J R Himes (ed) *Implementing the Convention on the Rights of the Child*, The Hague: Martinus Nijhoff
Dallape, F (1987) *An Experience with Street Children*, Nairobi, Kenya: Undugu Society
Dallape, F and C Gilbert (1994) *Children's Participation in Action Research*, Harare, Zimbabwe: ENDA
Dasen, P R and G Jahoda (1986) 'Cross-cultural human development', *International Journal of Behavioural Development*, 9: 413–416
Davey and Lightbody (1987, 5th edition (revised by D Stevenson)) *The Control of Disease in the Tropics: A Handbook for Physicians and Other Workers in Tropical and International Community Health*, London: H K Lewis & Co
Davey, K (1992) 'The structure and functions of urban government: the institutional framework of urban management', Birmingham, Development Administration Group, University of Birmingham
de la Barra, X (1996) 'Impact of urbanization on employment and social equity', Presentation at World Resources Institute
de la Barra, X (1998) 'Poverty: the main cause of ill health in urban children', *Health, Education and Behavior*, 25(1): 45–49
De Zoysa, I, M Rea, J Martines (1991) 'Why promote breastfeeding in diarrhoeal disease control programmes?', *Health Policy Planning*, 6: 371–379
Denn, P and G J Ebrahim (1986) *Practical Care of Sick Children: A Manual for Use in Small Tropical Hospitals*, London: Macmillan
Dennis, F and D Castleton (1991) 'Women's mobilization in human settlements case study: The Guarari Housing Project, Costa Rica', in S Sontheimer (ed) *Women and the Environment: A Reader*, London: Earthscan, 147–162
Development and Education Programme (1996) 'The development of youth participation: an experience of the Development and Education Programme for Daughters and Communities', in National Council for Child and Youth Development (ed) *Youth Participation in Thailand*, Bangkok: National Council for Child and Youth Development
Dillinger, W (1993) 'Decentralization and its implications for urban service delivery', Washington DC, World Bank

Dizon, A M and S Quijano (1997) 'Impact of eviction on children', Report for Urban Poor Associates, Asian Coalition for Housing Rights (ACHR) and United Nations Economic and Social Commission for Asia and the Pacific (UN-ESCA)
Dow, U (1998) 'Birth registration: the "first" right' in UNICEF (ed) Progress of Nations 1998, New York: UNICEF
Dowbor, L (1986) *Aspectos Economicos da Educacaõ*, Saõ Paulo: A'tica Ed
Dowbor, L (1996) 'Urban children in distress', *Development*, 1: 81–84
Dowbor, L (1997) 'Municipal information system:practical guidelines', http://ppbr.com/ld
Dowbor, L (1998) 'Decentralization and governance', *Latin American Perspectives*, 25(98): 28–44
Ebrahim, G J (1985) *Social and Community Paediatrics in Developing Countries: Caring for the Rural and Urban Poor*, Houndmills, Basingstoke, Hampshire: Macmillan
EDev News (1993) *Education for Development Bulletin*, 4(1) March 1993)
Ekblad, S (1995) 'Helping children cope with urban environment stresses in developing countries' in T Harpham and I Blue (eds) *Urbanization and Mental Health in Developing Countries*, Aldershot: Avebury, 103–123
Ekblad, S and others (1991) 'Stressors, Chinese City Dwellings and Quality of Life', Stockholm, Swedish Council for Building Research
El Baz, S (1996) *Children in Difficult Circumstances: A Study of Institutions and Inmates*, UNICEF
Engle, P L, P Menon, J L Garrett and A Slack (1997) 'Urbanization and caregiving: a framework for analysis and examples from southern and eastern Africa', *Environment and Urbanization*, 9(2): 253–271
Ennew, J (1994) *Street and Working Children: A Guide to Planning*, London: Save the Children UK
Erikson, E H (1950/ 1963) *Childhood and Society*, New York: W W Norton and Company
Espinosa, L and O A Lopez Rivera (1994) 'UNICEF's Urban Basic Services Programme in illegal settlements in Guatamala City', *Environment and Urbanization*, 6(2): 9–31
Espinosa, M F (1997) 'Working children in Ecuador mobilize for change', *Social Justic: Special Issue on Children and the Environment*, 24(3): 64–70
Evans, G W and S Cohen (1987) 'Environmental stress' in D Stokols and I Altman (eds) *Handbook of Environmental Psychology*, New York: Wiley
Evans, G W, S J Lepore, B R Shejwal and M N Palsane (1998) 'Chronic residential crowding and children's well-being: an ecological perspective', *Child Development*, in press
fabrizio@enda.sn (1998) 'Two Good News for Organised Working Children of the Third World', edited and distributed by HURINet (the Human Rights Information Network) 1998
Felson, L (1997) 'Youth in action', *Doing Democracy*, Winter 1997
Feuerstein, M-T (1997) *Poverty and Health: Reaping a Richer Harvest*, London: Macmillan
Friedman, S A (1998) *Girls at Work*, New York: UNICEF
Frones, I (1993) 'Changing childhood', *Childhood*, 1(1)
Fyfe, A (1989) *Child Labour*, Cambridge, UK: Blackwell and Cambridge MA, USA: Polity Press
Garbarino, J (1992) *Children and Families in the Social Environment*, New York: Aldine de Gruyter
Garbarino, J (1998) 'Stress in children', *Child and Adolescent Psychiatric Clinics of America*, 7(1)
Garbarino, J and C Bedard (1996) 'Spiritual challenges to children facing violent trauma', *Childhood*, 3(4): 467–479
Gaye, M and F Diallo (1997) 'Community participation in the management of the urban environment in Rufisque (Senegal)', *Environment and Urbanization*, 7(2): 91–119
Gilada, I S (1997) 'Child prostitution: a blot on humanity', Indian Health Organization presentation at the Urban Childhood conference, Trondheim, Norway, 9–12 June 1997
Giri, K (1995) 'Safe motherhood strategies in the developing countries' in H M Wallace, K Giri and C V Serrano (eds) *Health Care of Women and Children in Developing Countries*, Oakland CA: Third Party Publishing Company
Glauser, B (1990) 'Street children: deconstructing a construct' in A James and A Prout (eds) *Constructing and Reconstructing Childhood*, London: Falmer Press
Glowacki, F, M Marcus, G Mennetrier, C T Mennetrier and C Vourc'h (1996) *Urban Security Practices*, Paris: European Forum for Urban Security
Godin, L (1987) 'Preparation des projets urbains d'amenagement', Washington DC: World Bank
Goonesekere, S (1992) *Women's Rights and Children's Rights: The United Nations Conventions as Compatible and Complementary International Treaties*, Florence, Italy: UNICEF International Child Development Centre
Goonesekere, S (1994) 'National policies on children's rights and international norms' in S Asquith and M Hill (eds) *Justice for Children*, Dordrecht: Martinus Nijhoff

Government of West Bengal, (1995) 'Calcutta Plan of Action for Children', Calcutta, Institute of Local Government and Urban Studies (ILGUS), Department of Municipal Affairs, Government of Bengal and Calcutta Municipal Corporation

Guerrero, R (1993) 'Cali's innovative approach to urban violence', *The Urban Age*, 1(4): 17

Halfani, M (1997) 'Civic associational development and public sector reforms in Tanzania: disjuncture in transforming urban governance', Paper presented at the GURI Conference on Governance in Action: Urban Initiatives in a Global Setting, Centre for Urban and Community Studies, University of Toronto, Toronto

Hall, E T (1966) *The Hidden Dimension*, New York: Doubleday

Hammarberg, T (1992) 'Making Reality of the Rights of the Child' in E Verhellen (ed) *Rights of the Child Lectures – Part 2*, Ghent: Children's Rights Centre

Hardoy, A, J E Hardoy and R Schusterman (1991) 'Building community organization: the history of a squatter settlement and its own organizations in Buenos Aires', *Environment and Urbanization*, 3(2, October): 104–120

Hardoy, J E, S Cairncross and D Satterthwaite (eds) (1990) *The Poor Die Young*, London: Earthscan

Hardoy, J E, D Mitlin and D Satterthwaite (1992) *Environmental Problems in Third World Cities*, London: Earthscan

Hardoy, J E and D Satterthwaite (1989) *Squatter Citizen*, London: Earthscan

Hart, R (1984) 'The changing city of childhood: implications for play and learning', City College Workshop Center, New York

Hart, R (1997) *Children's Participation: The Theory and Practice of Involving Young Citizens in Community Development and Environmental Care*, London: Earthscan/UNICEF

Hart, R, C Dauite, S Iltus, D Kritt, M Rome and K Sabo (1997) 'Developmental Theory and Children's Participation in Community Organizations', *Social Justice*, 24(3): 33–63

Hart, R H, M A Belsey and E Tarimo (1990) *Integrating maternal and child health services with primary health care*, Geneva: World Health Organization

Hassan, A (1997) 'School dropouts and the myth of child labour in India', Presentation at Urban Childhood conference, 9–12 June, 1997, Trondheim, Norway

Hassan, A (1997) *Working with Government: The Story of the Orangi Pilot Project's Collaboration with State Agencies for Replicating its Low Cost Sanitation Programme*, Karachi: City Press

Haughton, G and C Hunter (1994) *Sustainable Cities*, Regional Policy and Development Series 7: Jessica Kingsley Publishers

Hecht, R (1995) 'Urban health: an emerging priority for the World Bank' in T Harpham and M Tanner (eds) *Urban Health in Developing Countries: Progress and Prospects*, London: Earthscan, 121–141

Herscovitch, L (1997) 'Moving child and family programmes to scale in Thailand', UNICEF

Hill, B (1996) 'Safe places for youth: programming, strategy and examples as identified through interviews with participants of the World Youth Forum of the UN system', UNICEF

Hillman, M (1995) *One False Move: A Study of Children's Independent Mobility*, London: Policy Studies Institute

Himes, J R (1995) *Implementing the Convention on the Rights of the Child: Resource Mobilization in Low-Income Countries*, The Hague : Martinus Nijhoff/UNICEF

Himes, J R, V Colbert de Arboleda and E Garcia Mendez (1994) *Child Labour and Basic Education in Latin America and the Caribbean*, Florence: UNICEF International Child Development Centre

Hodgkin, R and P Newell (1996) *Effective Government Structures for Children*, London: Gulbenkian Foundation

Hodgkin, R and P Newell (1998) *Implementation Handbook for the Convention on the Rights of the Child*, New York: UNICEF

Holland, T (1998) 'Human rights education for street and working children: principles and practice', *Human Rights Quarterly*, 20: 173–193

http://news.bbc.co.uk/hi/english/world/s/w_asia/newsis_78000/78953.stm (1998, April)

Hutchby, I and J M Ellis (1998) *Children and Social Competence: Arenas of Action*, London: Falmer Press

Iberia, A (1993) 'Report on a Visit to Cecil Province: Increased Participation of Mothers in Daughters' Education', UNICEF, Burkina Faso: UNICEF

ICLEI (1996) *Local Agenda 21 Planning Guide: An Introduction to Sustainable Development Planning*, The International Council for Local Environmental Initiatives

ILO (1996) *Child Labour Surveys: Results of Methodological Experiments in Four Countries 1992–93*, Geneva: International Labour Office

ILO (1996) *Child Labour: Targeting the Intolerable*, Geneva: International Labour Office
Iltus, S (1994) 'Parental ideologies in the home safety management of one to four year old children', doctoral thesis, Environmental Psychology Program, New York, The Graduate School and University Center of the City University of New York
International Federation of Red Cross and Red Crescent Societies (1998) *World Disasters Report 1998*, Oxford: Oxford University Press
Islam, S (1997) 'Carrots, not sticks', *Far Eastern Economic Review*, March 27, 1997
Iyer, L and D A Goldenberg (1996) *We Live Here Too! Moving Toward Child-Centred Habitat Programmes*, PLAN International: South Asia Regional Office
Jaglin, S (1994) 'Why mobilize town dwellers: joint management in Ouagadougou, 1983–1990', *Environment and Urbanization*, 6(2, October): 111–132
James, A and A Prout (eds) (1990) *Constructing and Reconstructing Childhood: Contemporary Issues in the Sociological Study of Childhood*, London: Falmer Press
Johnson, V, J Hill and E Ivan Smith (1995) *Listening to Smaller Voices: Children in an Environment of Change*, Chard, Somerset UK: Actionaid
Kagitçibasi, C (1996) *Family and Human Development Across Cultures*, Mahwah, NJ: Lawrence Erlbaum
Kaplan, S and R Kaplan (eds) (1982) *Humanscape: Environments for People*, Ann Arbor MI: Ulrich's Books
Kenning, M, A Merchant and A Tompkins (1991) 'Research on the effects of witnessing parental battering: clinical and legal policy implications' in M Steinman (ed) *Woman Battering: Policy Responses*, Cincinnati OH: Anderson
Kibel, M A and L A Wagstaff (eds) (1995) *Child Health for All: A Manual for Southern Africa*, Capetown, New York: Oxford University Press
Korten, D C (1996) 'Civic engagement in creating future cities', *Environment and Urbanization*, 8(1): 35–51
Kuo, F E, W C Sullivan, R L Coley and L Brunson (1998) 'Fertile ground for community: inner city neighborhood common space', *American Journal of Community Psychology*, in press
La Florida Municipality (1994) *Qué Hacer en Vez de... Material de Apoyo para la Crianza de Nuestros Hijos: Proyecto de Capacitacion de Padres para el Desarrollo Infantil*, Municipalidad de la Florida and UNICEF, Chile
Lajoie, R (1998) 'Shelter from the storm', *Amnesty Action*, Summer 1998: 6–8
Landers, C (1989) *Early Childhood Development: Summary Report*, Florence: UNICEF International Child Development Centre
Landers, C (1989) 'A theoretical basis for investing in early child development: review of current concepts', Innocenti Global Seminar on Early Child Development, Florence, UNICEF International Child Development Centre
Lansdowne, G (1997) 'Ombudswork for children', *Innocenti Digest*, (3)
LeBlanc, L J (1995) *The Convention on the Rights of the Child: United Nations Lawmaking on Human Rights*, Lincoln: University of Nebraska Press
Lee Smith, D and A Schlyter (1991) 'Women, environment and urbanization: editor's introduction', *Environment and Urbanization*, 3(2): 3–6
Lee Smith, D and R Stren (1991) 'New perspectives on African urban management', *Environment and Urbanization*, 3(1): 23–36
Lee, Y S (1996) Discussion of institutionalization in Korea at IAPS (International Association for People-Environment Studies) conference, Stockholm, Sweden
Levitt, M J and M Minden (1995) 'The role of traditional birth attendants in safe motherhood' in *Health Care of Women and Children in Developing Countries*, Oakland CA: Third Party Publishing Company
Lloyd, C B and N Duffy (1995) 'Families in transition' in J Bruce, C B Lloyd and A Leonard (eds) *Families in Focus: New Perspectives on Mothers, Fathers, and Children*, New York: The Population Council
Lorenz, N and P Garner (1995) 'Organizing and managing urban health services' in T Harpham and M Tanner (eds) *Urban Health in Developing Countries: Progress and Prospects*, London: Earthscan, 48–63
Löw, U (1998) 'A world of violence: the daily battles of Nairobi's street children', *UNCHS Habitat Debate*, 4(1): 20–21

Lungo, M (1997) 'Governance, urban development plans and sustainability in Central American cities', Paper presented at the GURI Conference on Governance in Action: Urban Initiatives in a Global Setting
MacPherson, S (1987) *Five Hundred Million Children: Poverty and Child Welfare in the Third World*, New York: St Martin's Press
Mahila Milan-NSDF-SPARC (1998) 'Taking children's toilet needs seriously at Viyamshala Gymkhana', *Citywatch: India, 6:20*
Mara, D and S Cairncross (1990) *Guidelines for the Safe Use of Wastewater and Excreta in Agriculture and Aquaculture*, Geneva: WHO
Marcus, M (1995) *Faces of Justice and Poverty in the City*, Paris: European Forum for Urban Security
Marcus, R and C Harper (1996) 'Small hands: children in the working world', Working Paper 16: Save the Children UK
Mathur, O P (1997) 'Fiscal innovations and urban governance', Paper presented at the GURI Conference on Governance in Action: Urban Initiatives in a Global Setting, Centre for Urban and Community Studies, University of Toronto, Toronto
McGranahan, G, J Songsore, et al (1996) 'Sustainability, poverty and urban environmental transitions' in C Pugh (ed) *Sustainability, the Environment and Urbanization*, London: Earthscan, 103–134
McLoyd, V C (1990) 'The impact of economic hardship on black families and children: psychological distress, parenting, and socioemotional development', *Child Development*, 61: 311–346
Mehrotra, S and R Jolly (1997) *Development with a Human Face*, Oxford: Clarendon Press
Mehta, M (1993) *Convergence in UBSP: An Exploratory Study of Nasik and Aligarh*: UNICEF
Menary, S (1990) *Play Without Frontiers: A Policy Document on Community Relations in Children's Play*, Belfast: Playboard
Millar, S (1997) 'Youth crime cut by victim contact', *The Guardian*, London, 7
Misra, H (1990) 'Housing and health problems in three squatter settlements in Allahabad, India' in , J E Hardoy, S Cairncross and D Satterthwaite (eds) *The Poor Die Young: Housing and Health in Third World Cities*, London: Earthscan
Missair, A (1994) 'Construction technology in developing countries' in J W Wescott and R M Henak (eds) *Construction in Technology Education*, Columbus, Ohio: Macmillan/McGraw Hill, 298
Missair, A (1998) 'The illicit sale of pharmaceuticals in Africa: "the dangerous solution"', Unpublished research
Moll, K (1991) 'Working with disabled people in Bangalore, South India', CBR News,(9)
Moore, R (1985) *Childhood's Domain: Play and Place in Childhood Development*, London: Croom Helm
Moore, R C and H H Wong (1997) *Natural Learning: The Life History of an Environmental Schoolyard*, Berkeley, CA: MIG Communications
Morley, D and H Lovel (1986) *My Name is Today: An Illustrated Discussion of Child Health, Society and Poverty in Less Developed Countries*, London: Macmillan
Moser, C O N (1993) 'Domestic violence and its economic causes', *The Urban Age*, 1(4): 13
Moser, C O N (1996) *Confronting Crisis: A Summary of Household Responses to Poverty and Vulnerability in Four Poor Urban Communities*, Washington DC: The World Bank
Moser, C O N, A J Herbert and R E Makonnen (1993) 'Urban poverty in the context of structural adjustment; recent evidence and policy responses', TWU Discussion Paper 4, Washington DC, Urban Development Division, World Bank
Myers, R (1992) *The Twelve who Survive: Strengthening Programmes of Early Childhood Development in the Third World*, London: Routledge
Myers, R G (1997) 'Removing roadblocks to success: transitions and linkages between home, preschool, and primary school', *Coordinators' Notebook: An International Resource for Early Child Development*, (21, 1997): 1–19
Narasimhan, S (1993) 'The unwanted sex', *The New Internationalist*, (240)
Navarro, Z (1998) 'Affirmative democracy and redistribution development: the case of participatory budgeting in Porto Alegre, Brazil (1989–1997)', Presentation at Seminar: Social Programs, Poverty and Citizen Participation, March 12–13, 1998, Cartagena, Colombia, sponsored by the Inter-American Development Bank
Needleman, H L, A Schell, D Bellinger, A Leviton and E N Allred (1991) 'The long-term effects of exposure to low doses of lead in childhood: an eleven year follow up report', *New England Journal of Medicine*, 322(2): 83–88
Newell, P (1995) 'Respecting children's right to physical integrity' in B Franklin (ed) *The Handbook of Children's Rights: Comparative Policy and Practice*, London and New York: Routledge, 215–226

Newell, P (1997) 'Children and violence', *Innocenti Digest* 2, Florence: UNICEF International Child Development Centre

Newman, O (1972) *Defensible Space*, New York: Macmillan

Newson, J and E Newson (1970) *Four Years Old in an Urban Community (2nd edition)*, New York: Penguin Books

Nieuwenhuys, O (1994) *Children's Lifeworlds: Gender, Welfare and Labour in the Developing World*, London and New York: Routledge

Nieuwenhuys, O (1997) 'Spaces for the children of the urban poor: experiences with participatory action research (PAR)', *Environment and Urbanization*, 9(1): 233–249

Ochola, L (1996) 'The Undugu Society Approach in Dealing with Children at Risk to Abuse and Neglect' in E Verhellen (ed) *Monitoring Children's Rights*, The Hague and Boston: Nijhoff

O'Connell, H (1994) *Women and the Family*, London and New Jersey: Zed Books

ODA (1996) 'Computers in urban spatial planning', *ODA Urbanization*, (2): 7–8

Ogbu, J (1981) 'Origins of human competence: a cultural-ecological perspective', *Child Development*, 52: 413–429

Ogbuagu, S C (1994) 'Facilitating the empowerment of African children for the defence of their rights' in T O Pearce and T Falola (eds) *Child Health in Nigeria: The Impact of Depressed Economy*, Aldershot, UK: Avebury

OPP (1995) 'Orangi Pilot Project', *Environment and Urbanization*, 7(2): 227–236

Osofsky, J D and E Fenichel (eds) (1994) *Caring for Infants and Toddlers in Violent Environments: Hurt, Healing, and Hope*, Arlington, Virginia: Zero to Three/ National Center for Clinical Infant Programs

Pacheco, M (1992) 'Recycling in Bogota: developing a culture for urban sustainability', *Environment and Urbanization*, 4(2): 74–79

PAHO (1996) 'Healthy people, healthy spaces', Report of the Director, Pan American Health Organization

Paixao Bretas, P R (1996) 'Participative budgeting in Belo Horizonte: democratization and citizenship', *Environment and Urbanization*, 8(1 April)

Pappu, K (1997) 'Elimination of child labour and its impact on families', Presentation at Urban Childhood Conference, 9–12 June 1997, Trondheim, Norway

Parry-Jones, W L (1991) 'Mental health and development of children and adolescents in cities' in W Parry-Jones and N Queloz (eds) *Mental Health and Deviance in Inner Cities*, Geneva: WHO/ UNICRI/University of Naples, 13–19

Parry-Jones, W L and N Queloz (eds) (1991) *Mental Health and Deviance in Inner Cities*, Geneva: WHO/ UNICRI/University of Naples

Patel, S (1996) *SPARC and its Work with the National Slum Dwellers Federation and Mahila Milan, India*, London: IIED

Paul, D (1995) 'Child labour in context', World Vision, Research and Policy Unit

Pelletier, D L, E A Frongillo and J P Habicht (1993) 'Epidemiological evidence for a potentiating effect of malnutrition on child mortality', *American Journal of Public Health*, 1993(83)

Penne Firme, T (1994) 'Meeting at-risk children where they get together' in S Asquith and M Hall (eds) *Justice for Children*, Dordrecht: Marinus Nijhoff

Peterman, P J (1981) 'Parenting and environmental considerations', *American Journal of Orthopsychiatry*, 5(2): 351–355

Piot, P (1997) 'Fighting AIDS together' in UNICEF (ed) *Progress of Nations*, New York: UNICEF

Porio, E, L Moselina and A Swift (1994) 'Philippines: urban communities and their fight for survival' in C S Blanc (ed) *Urban Children in Distress: Global Predicaments and Innovative Strategies*, Florence, Italy: UNICEF International Child Development Centre and London:Gordon and Breach

Pradhan, G (1993) 'Child delinquencies and children in adult prisons in Nepal', *Voice of Child Workers: Newsletter of Child Workers in Nepal Concerned Centre*, (17 and 18)

Prefeitura Municipal de Santo André (1998) *Integrated Strategies for Urban Poverty Reduction*, Santo André, Office of the Mayor

Pryer, J (1993) 'The impact of adult ill-health on household income and nutrition in Khulna, Bangladesh', *Environment and Urbanization*, 5(2): 35–50

Queloz, N (1991) 'Urban process and its role in strengthening social disadvantages, inequalities and exclusion' in W Parry-Jones and N Queloz (eds) *Mental Health and Deviance in Inner Cities*, Geneva: WHO/ UNICRI/University of Naples, 31–36

Rajani, R (1997) 'Street children hijack the urban childhood agenda', Presentation at Urban Childhood Conference, June 1997, Trondheim, Norway

Ramirez, R (1996) *Local Governance Models: Decentralization and Urban Poverty Eradication*, London: Development Planning Unit, University College London

Rialp, V (1993) *Children and Hazardous Work in the Philippines*, Geneva: ILO

Richman, N (1996) 'Principles of help for children involved in organised violence', Working Paper 13, Save the Children UK

Rispel, L, J Doherty, F Makiwane and N Webb (1996) 'Developing a plan for primary health care facilities in Soweto, South Africa, Part 1: Guiding principles and methods', *Health Policy and Planning*, 11(4): 385–393

Rizzini, I, I Rizzini, M Munhoz and L Galeano (1992) *Childhood and Urban Poverty in Brazil: Street and Working Children and their Families*, Florence, Italy: UNICEF

Robson, B (1989) 'Premature obituaries: change and adaptation in great cities' in R Lawton (ed) *The Rise and Fall of Great Cities*, London and New York: Belhaven Press, 45–54

Rossi-Espagnet, A, G B Goldstein and I Tabibzadeh (1991) 'Urbanization and health in developing countries: a challenge for the health of all', *World Health Statistical Quarterly*, 44(4): 186–244

Sabo, K and S Iltus (1998) 'What do young people around the world think about prevention programmes?', UNDCP

Safe Motherhood Initiative (1998) *Safe Motherhood Fact Sheets*, New York: Family Care International

Santos, City of (1996) 'Santos na Habitat II: Integrated Children's and Family Program', The City of Santos, SP, Brazil

Satterthwaite, D (1997) *The Scale and Nature of International Donor Assistance to Housing, Basic Services and Other Human Settlements Related Projects*, Helsinki: WIDER

Satterthwaite, D (1997) 'Urban poverty: reconsidering its scale and nature', *IDS Bulletin*, 28(2): 9–23

Satterthwaite, D (1998) 'Can UN conferences promote poverty reduction? a review of the Habitat II documents in relation to their consideration of poverty and the priority they give to poverty reduction', *Occasional Paper Series*, Washington DC: Woodrow Wilson International Center for Scholars

Satterthwaite, D, R Hart, C Levy, D Mitlin, D Ross, J Smit, C Stephens (1996) *The Environment for Children*, London: Earthscan

Scheper-Hughes, N (1989) 'Culture, scarcity and maternal thinking: mother love and child death in north east Brazil' in Scheper-Hughes, N (ed) *Child Survival: Anthropological Perspectives on the Treatment and Maltreatment of Children*, Dordrecht: Reidel

Scheper-Hughes, N (1992) *Death Without Weeping: The Violence of Everyday Life in Brazil*, Berkeley: University of California Press

Schusterman, R and A Hardoy (1997) 'Reconstructing social capital in a poor urban settlement: the Integrated Improvement Programme, Barrio San Jorge', *Environment and Urbanization*, 9(1): 91–119

Sen, A (1995) *Mortality as an Indicator of Economic Success and Failure*, Florence: UNICEF International Child Development Centre

Sharp, C (1984) 'Environmental design and child maltreatment' in D Duerk and D Campbell (eds) *Environmental Design Research Association 15*

Sida (1997) 'Seeking more effective and sustainable support to improving housing and living conditions for low income households in urban areas: Sida's initiatives in Costa Rica, Chile and Nicaragua', *Environment and Urbanization*, 9(2): 213–231

Singh, K (1996) 'The impact of seventy fourth constitutional amendment of urban management' in K Singh and F Steinberg (eds) *Urban India in Crisis*, New Delhi: New Age International Ltd, 423–435

Sinnatamby, G (1990) 'Low cost sanitation' in J Hardoy, S Cairncross and D Satterthwaite (eds) *The Poor Die Young: Housing and Health in Third World Cities*, London: Earthscan

Smith, J B and J A Fortney (1996) 'Birth kits: an assessment', UNICEF Report, New York: UNICEF

Spitz, R A (1945) 'Hospitalism: an inquiry into the genesis of psychiatric conditions in early childhood', *Psychoanalytic Study of the Child*, 1: 53–74

Stalker, P (1996) *Child Labour in Bangladesh: A Summary of Recent Investigations*, New York: UNICEF

Stein, A (1996) *Decentralization and Urban Poverty Reduction in Nicaragua: The Experience of the Local Development Programme (PRODEL)*, London: IIED

Stephens, C (1996) 'Healthy cities or unhealthy islands? The health and social implications of urban inequality', *Environment and Urbanization*, 8(2): 9–30

Stephens, C, A Akerman, S Avle, P Borlina Maia, P Campanario, B Doe and D Tetteh (1997) 'Urban equity and urban health: using existing data to understand inequalities in health and environment in Accra, Ghana and São Paulo, Brazil', *Environment and Urbanization*, 9(1, April): 181–203

Stewart, F (1995) *Adjustment and Poverty: Options and Choices*, London: Routledge
Street Kids International (1995) *Participatory Methods: Community-based Programs*, Toronto, Canada: Street Kids International
Swift, A (1993) 'A passage out of hell', *New Internationalist*, (240): 13
Swilling, M (1997) 'My soul I can see: the limits of governing African cities in a context of globalization and complexity', Paper presented at the GURI Conference on Governance in Action: Urban Initiatives in a Global Setting, Centre for Urban and Community Studies, University of Toronto, Toronto
Szilagyi, J (1997) 'Some specialties of the Hungarian Child Law', Urban Childhood Conference, 9–12 June 1997, Trondheim, Norway
Tacoli, C (1998) 'Beyond the rural urban divide', *Environment and Urbanization*, 10(1): 3–4
Tagoe, G T (1985) *Children and Adolescents and Video Films and Discotheques: A Study of the Jamestown and Mamprobi Areas of Accra*, thesis, University of Science and Technology, Kumasi Faculty of Social Sciences
Tattum, D P and D A Lane (eds) (1988) *Bullying in Schools*, Stoke-on-Trent, UK: Trentham Books
Therborn, G (1996) 'Child politics: dimensions and perspectives', *Childhood*, 3(1): 29–44
Titman, W (1994) *Special Places, Special People: The Hidden Curriculum of Schoolgrounds*, Godalming, Surrey: World Wide Fund for Nature
Tobin, J J, D Y H Wu and D H Davidson (1989) *Preschool in Three Cultures: Japan, China, and the United States*, New Haven: Yale University Press
Tobler, N S (1997) 'Meta-analysis of adolescent drug prevention programs: results of the 1993 meta analysis', *NIDP Research Monograph*, US Department of Health and Human Services
Together Foundation 'Best practices: Building communities of opportunity', www.together.org
Tolfree, D (1995) 'Residential care for children and alternative approaches to care in developing countries', Working Paper 11, Save the Children UK
Transgrud, R (1997) 'Adolescent sexual and reproductive health in eastern and southern Africa: building experience', *paper prepared for USAID/REDSO*
Trevathan, W R and J J McKenna (1994) 'Evolutionary environments of birth and infancy: insights to apply to contemporary life', *Children's Environments*, 11(2): 88–105
Turner, B (ed) (1988) *Building Community – A Third World Case Book from Habitat International Coalition*, London: Habitat International Coalition
UNCHS (1996) *An Urbanizing World: Global Report on Human Settlements 1996*, New York: Oxford University Press
UNDP (1992) *Human Development Report 1992*, New York: Oxford University Press
UNDP (1994) *Human Development Report 1994*, New York: Oxford University Press
UNDP (1994) 'Report of the International Colloquium of Mayors on Social Development', 18–19 August, 1994, New York, UNDP
UNDP (1995) *Living Arrangements of Women and their Children in Developing Countries*, Department for Economic and Social Information and Policy Analysis, Population Division, United Nations
UNDP (1996) *Human Development Report 1996*, New York: Oxford University Press
UNDP (1997) *Human Development Report 1997*, New York: Oxford University Press
UNEP (1988) *Young Action for the Future*, Nairobi: UNEP
UNICEF (1979) *Urban Examples for Basic Services Development in Cities: The Infant and the Young Child – A Focus for Assistance and a Stimulus for Family Improvement*,
UNICEF (1990) *The Invisible Child: A Look at the Urban Child in Delhi*, Delhi: UNICEF Middle North India Office
UNICEF (1991) 'Guatemala Urban Basic Services', Guatamala, UNICEF
UNICEF (1994) *The Urban Poor and Household Food Security*,
UNICEF (ed) (1996) *The Progress of Nations 1996*, New York: UNICEF
UNICEF (ed) (1997) *The Progress of Nations 1997*, New York: UNICEF
UNICEF (1997) 'Relationships between Education and Child labour', Background Paper for International Conference on Child Labour, Oslo, 27–30 October 1997
UNICEF (1997) 'Social Mobilization and Child Labour', Background Paper for International Conference on Child Labour, Oslo, 27–30 October 1997
UNICEF (1997) *The State of the World's Children 1997*, New York: Oxford University Press
UNICEF (1997) 'Strategies for Eliminating Child Labour: Prevention, Removal and Rehabilitation' Background Paper for International Conference on Child Labour, Oslo, 27–30 October 1997
UNICEF (1998) *Girls at Work*, New York: UNICEF

UNICEF (1998) ' Juvenile justice', *Innocenti Digest* 3, Florence: UNICEF International Child Development Centre
UNICEF (ed) (1998) *The Progress of Nations 1998*, New York: UNICEF
UNICEF (1998) *The State of the World's Children 1998*, New York: Oxford University Press
UNICEF and UNEP (1990) *Children and the Environment*, UNICEF/UNEP
United Nations (1991) *The World's Women: Trends and Statistics 1970–1990*, New York: United Nations
US Department of Health and Human Services (1996) *Child and Adolescent Emergency Department Visit Handbook*, Washington DC: US Department of Health and Human Services
Valsiner, J (1987) *Culture and the Development of Children's Action*, New York: Wiley
Valsiner, J (ed) (1988) *Child Development Within Culturally Structured Environments*, Norwood, New Jersey: Ablex
Valsiner, J (1989) *Human Development and Culture; The Social Nature of Personality and its Study*, Lexington, Massachusetts: Lexington Books
van der Linden, J (1997) 'On popular participation in a culture of patronage: patrons and grassroots organizations in a sites and services project', *Environment and Urbanization*, 9(1): 81–90
Vanderschueren, F (1996) 'From violence to justice and security in cities', *Environment and Urbanization*, 8(1): 93–112
Vanderschueren, F (1998) 'Towards safer cities', *Habitat Update*, 4(1): 1–6
Vanderschueren, F, E Wegelin and K Wekwete (1996) *Policy Programme Options for Urban Poverty Reduction*, Washington DC: The World Bank/Urban Management Programme
Verhellen, E (1994) *Convention on the Rights of the Child: Background, Motivation, Strategies, Main Themes*, Leuven – Kessel-Lo, Belgium: Garant
Wachs, T D and O Camli (1991) 'Do ecological or individual characteristics mediate the influence of the physical environment upon maternal behavior?', *Journal of Environmental Psychology*, 11: 249–264
WACLAC (1996) World Assembly of Cities and Local Authorities Coordination (WACLAC) Final Declaration, 30–31 May 1996, United Nations Conference on Human Settlements (HABITAT II), Istanbul
Ward, C (1978) *The Child and the City*, London: Architectural Press
Wegelin-Schuringa, M and T Kodo (1997) 'Tenancy and sanitation provision in informal settlements in Nairobi: revisiting the public latrine option', *Environment and Urbanization*, 9(2): 181–190
Weil, N (1996) 'In teen courts young people set their peers straight', *Doing Democracy*, Winter 1996
Werner, D (1987) *Disabled Village Children: A Guide for Community Health Workers, Rehabilitation Workers, and Families*, Palo Alto CA: The Hesperian Foundation
Werner, E E and R S Smith (1992) *Overcoming the Odds: High Risk Children from Birth to Adulthood*, Ithaca NY: Cornell University Press
Whiting, B B and C P Edwards (1988) *Children of Different Worlds: The Formation of Social Behavior*, Cambridge MA: Harvard University Press
Whiting, B B and J W M Whiting (1975) *Children of Six Cultures: A Psychocultural Analysis*, Cambridge, MA: Harvard University Press
WHO (1991) *Environmental Health in Urban Development*, Geneva: World Health Organization
WHO (1994) *Home-based Maternal Records: Guidelines for Development, Adaptation and Evaluation*, Geneva: World Health Organization
WHO (1995) *The World Health Report 1995: Bridging the Gaps*, Geneva: World Health Organization
WHO (1996) *Creating Healthy Cities in the Twenty-First Century*, Geneva: WHO
WHO (1996) 'Lead and Health', One of a special series of reports for local authorities, Copenhagen, WHO Regional Office for Europe
Winchester, L, T Cáreces and A Rodriguez (1997) 'Urban governance from the citizen's perspective: the defence of a barrio in the city of Santiago: the case of Bellavista', Paper presented at the GURI Conference on Governance in Action: Urban Initiatives in a Global Setting, Centre for Urban and Community Studies, University of Toronto, Toronto
Winterbottom, D (1998) 'Casitas, gardens of reclamation: the creation of cultural/social spaces in the barrios of New York City', 29th Annual Conference of the Environmental Design Research Association, St Louis, USA
Wohlwill, J and H Heft (1987) 'The physical environment and the development of the child' in D Stokols and I Altman (eds) *Handbook of Environmental Psychology*, New York: Wiley
Wohlwill, J and W van Vliet (1985) *Habitats for Children: The Impacts of Density*, Hillsdale NJ: Lawrence Erlbaum

Women Legislators in Action (1998) 3(2): 7
Woodhead, M (1998) *Children's Perspectives on their Working Lives: A Participatory Study in Bangladesh, Ethiopia, the Philippines, Guatemala,Nicaragua and El Salvador*, Stockholm: Radda Barnen
Woodward, D (1992) *Debt, Adjustment and Poverty in Developing Countries: Volume 1: National and International Dimensions of Debt and Adjustment in Developing Countries*, London: Pinter Publishers with Save the Children
Woodward, D (1992) *Debt, Adjustment and Poverty in Developing Countries: Volume 2: The Impact of Debt and Adjustment at the Household Level in Developing Countries*, London: Pinter Publishers with Save the Children
World Bank (1988) *World Development Report 1988*, New York: Oxford University Press
World Bank (1993) *World Development Report 1993: Investing in Health*, Washington DC: Oxford University Press
World Commission on Environment and Development (1987) *Our Common Future*, Oxford: Oxford University Press
Youth Vision Jeunesse (1998) , Youth Vision Jeunesse Drug Abuse Prevention Forum, April 14–18, 1998, Banff, Alberta, sponsored by UN International Drug Control Programme (UNDCP)
Zeitlin, M F and E D Babatunde (1995) 'The Yoruba family: kinship, socialization, and child development' in M F Zeitlin, R Megawangi, E M Kramer, N Colletta, E D Babatunde and D Garman (eds) *Strengthening the Family: Implications for International Development*, Tokyo, New York, Paris: United Nations University Press
Zeitlin, M F, R Megawangi, E Kramer, N Colletta, E D Babatunde and D Garman (1995) *Strengthening the Family: Implications for International Development*, Tokyo, New York, Paris: United Nations University Press

Index